BRiAn conte

CAMBRIDGE TEXTS IN THE
HISTORY OF PHILOSOPHY

FRIEDRICH NIETZSCHE
The Anti-Christ, Ecce Homo, Twilight of the Idols

CAMBRIDGE TEXTS IN THE
HISTORY OF PHILOSOPHY

Series editors

KARL AMERIKS

Professor of Philosophy at the University of Notre Dame

DESMOND M. CLARKE

Professor of Philosophy at University College Cork

The main objective of Cambridge Texts in the History of Philosophy is to expand the range, variety and quality of texts in the history of philosophy which are available in English. The series includes texts by familiar names (such as Descartes and Kant) and also by less well-known authors. Wherever possible, texts are published in complete and unabridged form, and translations are specially commissioned for the series. Each volume contains a critical introduction together with a guide to further reading and any necessary glossaries and textual apparatus. The volumes are designed for student use at undergraduate and postgraduate level and will be of interest not only to students of philosophy, but also to a wider audience of readers in the history of science, the history of theology and the history of ideas.

For a list of titles published in the series, please see end of book.

FRIEDRICH NIETZSCHE

The Anti-Christ, Ecce Homo, Twilight of the Idols, and Other Writings

EDITED BY

AARON RIDLEY

University of Southampton

JUDITH NORMAN

Trinity University, Texas

TRANSLATED BY

JUDITH NORMAN

CAMBRIDGE
UNIVERSITY PRESS

CAMBRIDGE UNIVERSITY PRESS

Cambridge, New York, Melbourne, Madrid, Cape Town, Singapore, São Paulo

Cambridge University Press

The Edinburgh Building, Cambridge CB2 2RU, UK

Published in the United States of America by Cambridge University Press, New York

www.cambridge.org

Information on this title: www.cambridge.org/9780521016889

First published 2005

Printed in the United Kingdom at the University Press, Cambridge

A catalogue record for this book is available from the British Library

ISBN-13 978-0-521-81659-5 hardback
ISBN-10 0-521-81659-9 hardback
ISBN-13 978-0-521-01688-9 paperback
ISBN-10 0-521-01688-6 paperback

Contents

Introduction

In Turin, on 3 January 1889, Nietzsche suffered an irrevocable mental collapse. By the time of his death, in 1900, he had become wholly physically incapacitated as well.[1] It seems probable that the cause was syphilis. It is apparently common for syphilitics to experience a period of uplift, a remarkable sense of well-being, in the months preceding the final collapse. Certainly this was so in Nietzsche's case. In the year before his breakdown his letters are increasingly touched with euphoria. His health, extremely poor for well over a decade, seems to him to be on the mend: 'I have just looked at myself in a mirror – I have never before appeared as I do now: in exemplary good spirits, well-nourished, and looking ten years younger than I ought to';[2] 'my health, like the weather, appears every day with irrepressible brightness and gaiety'.[3] He feels more equal than he has ever felt to the most demanding of intellectual tasks: 'it is my great *harvest-time*. Everything comes easily to me, everything I try succeeds, notwithstanding that no one has yet had such great matters in hand as I have';[4] 'the heaviest tasks, for which no man has yet been sufficiently strong, come easily'.[5] His estimate of himself and of his abilities acquires a megalomanic tinge: 'in two months I shall be the first name on earth'; 'What is remarkable here in Turin is the fascination I exercise on people . . . every face changes; women gaze after me in the street';[6]

---

[1] For a sensitive account of Nietzsche's decline, see R. J. Hollingdale, *Nietzsche: The Man and his Philosophy* (Cambridge: Cambridge University Press, 1999). The letters cited in nn. 2–7 are taken from Hollingdale. See also Lesley Chamberlain, *Nietzsche in Turin* (London: Quartet, 1996).

[2] To Peter Gast, 30 October 1888.   [3] To Carl Fuchs, 18 December 1888.

[4] To Franz Overbeck, 18 October 1888.   [5] To his mother, 21 December 1888.

[6] To Franz Overbeck, 25 December 1888.

'there are no longer any accidents in my life'.[7] And these remarks – and there are many like them – inevitably raise a preliminary question. Are the philosophical works that Nietzsche produced in this final year, the works collected here in this volume, the products of an already-deranged mind?

Nietzsche's sanity

The 1888 texts are certainly very diverse. One – *Twilight of the Idols* – proceeds in a distilled version of Nietzsche's established aphoristic manner. Two – *The Anti-Christ* and *The Case of Wagner* – are sustained polemics, directed, respectively, against institutionalized Christianity and Richard Wagner's music dramas. One – *Ecce Homo* – is a strange sort of autobiography. And the remaining work – *Nietzsche contra Wagner* – is an anthology of aphorisms culled, sometimes with minor alterations, from Nietzsche's other books.[8] But variety is hardly a sign of madness.

It used to be common to say that 1888 marked a falling-off of Nietzsche's creativity as a thinker, and to link this to a decline in his mental capacities. So, for example, *Twilight of the Idols* was often said to be little more than a noisy résumé of some of his more strongly held opinions. And there is a measure of truth in this. It is true that comparatively few of the ideas that Nietzsche committed to paper in that book had not been expressed by him before. But this is entirely to overlook the kind of expression that they receive there. *Twilight* represents a pinnacle of aphoristic economy and wit, an example of Nietzsche's mature style at its very best. And this is hard to square with the suspicion of mental decline.

I think that this conclusion is now generally accepted, certainly as far as *Twilight* is concerned. Elsewhere matters may be less clear-cut. *The Case of Wagner*, for instance, has been very widely ignored, presumably for two main reasons. First, not many Nietzsche scholars regard Nietzsche's attitude towards Wagner as the most interesting thing about him; and second, he'd been going on about Wagner in broadly similar terms for years, as the passages assembled in *Nietzsche contra Wagner* attest.[9]

---

[7] To August Strindberg, 7 December 1888.

[8] There is in fact a sixth work from 1888, *Dionysian Dithyrambs*, not included here. This is a collection of poems whose absence is not to be regretted.

[9] Indeed, this was probably the point of *Nietzsche contra Wagner*. *The Case of Wagner*, when it was published, went down badly. Wagner had died in 1883, and the book was taken as a rather graceless posthumous attack on him by an erstwhile devotee. *Nietzsche contra Wagner* demonstrated that Nietzsche had been being nasty about Wagner since at least 1878.

But – again – this latter fact is no mark of mental decline. *The Case of Wagner* is an exhilarating read, fully the equal of *Twilight* in the pithiness of its delivery, and if anything even funnier. And although it is true that much of what he says there he had said before, it would be a mistake to imagine that he says nothing new. *The Case of Wagner* would repay more attention than it has received.

The question mark looms largest over the remaining two works, *The Anti-Christ* and *Ecce Homo*. *The Anti-Christ* is Nietzsche's longest sustained discussion of a single topic since the mid 1870s, when he wrote the four *Untimely Meditations*. In tone it is quite unlike *Twilight* (with which it is often compared). Where *Twilight* is graceful, light, and even effervescent in its intensity, *The Anti-Christ* strikes one as over-emphatic and rather tiring. Nietzsche really *hates* Christianity, and he makes the reader feel it. He hectors; he insists. But it is surely the degree of his antipathy that has got the better of him here, rather than any diminution of his powers. He is sharp and incisive throughout; and much of his material – which is like a concrete, historically more rooted version of themes treated in *On the Genealogy of Morality* – is distinctive and new. *The Anti-Christ* should be read, I think, as the work of someone who finds Christianity genuinely maddening, not as the work of someone who is already mad.

Ecce Homo, Nietzsche's autobiography, is the hardest case of all. Even R. J. Hollingdale, Nietzsche's excellent and sympathetic biographer, has problems with this book. While he praises it as 'undoubtedly one of the most beautiful in German', and remarks that many 'passages are a *non plus ultra* of richness combined with economy',[10] he also picks out a current in the book that strikes him as insane. 'Where Nietzsche leaves philosophy and writes about himself', says Hollingdale, 'his sense of his own quality passes the bounds of reasonableness and lands in absurdity . . . Nietzsche quietly attributes to himself impossible abilities.'[11] What Hollingdale hears in the passages that bother him he takes to be symptomatic of Nietzsche's impending mental collapse: euphoria, megalomania.

He may be right about this: I don't know. Nor does it seem tremendously important to know. Incipient insanity may take the form of hyperbole, and what is exaggerated may be true, or interesting, even when pitched at a level that can seem deranged. And I think that there are good reasons to conclude that this is so with *Ecce Homo*. Precisely the kinds of passage

---

[10] Hollingdale, *Nietzsche*, p. 216.   [11] *Ibid.*, pp. 199–200.

that Hollingdale singles out as early signs of madness strike me as helpful dramatizations of a distinctive strand in Nietzsche's later philosophy, a strand having to do with freedom and self-realization – with what, in the subtitle to *Ecce Homo*, he calls becoming 'what you are'. Indeed, I propose to build the bulk of this introduction around just this aspect of Nietzsche's thought.

Overall, then, there would seem to be little reason to worry about the sanity of these final writings. It is true that Nietzsche's letters at this period reveal a state of mind that is almost certainly to be explained by the progress of his illness. But it appears that in his work he retained a focus and a kind of mastery over his material that insulated it from the effects of his condition. As Hollingdale puts it, 'The philosopher has not lost his grip on his material, he has tightened it . . . There is no intellectual degeneration: the mind is as sharp as ever.'[12] And, unlike Hollingdale, I am inclined to think that this verdict is as good as safe for the last works in their entirety – not just for those parts of them that Hollingdale identifies as 'philosophy'.

Becoming who you are

Nietzsche had first begun to take the idea of becoming 'who you are' seriously some years earlier. An aphorism in the 1882 edition of *The Gay Science* reads: '*What does your conscience say?* – "You shall become who you are"' (*GS* 270); and Nietzsche expands on the thought in a later section called '*Long live physics!*' It is important, he says, not to take the deliverances of conscience at face value, as if their source somehow guaranteed their truth: 'Your judgement "this is right" has a pre-history in your instincts, likes, dislikes, experiences and lack of experiences'; indeed, 'that you take this or that judgement for the voice of conscience . . . may be due to the fact that you have never thought much about yourself and have simply accepted blindly that what you had been *told* ever since your childhood was right' (*GS* 335).

What is needed to rectify this '*faith*', he claims, is 'an intellectual conscience', a 'conscience behind your "conscience"' (*GS* 335) – a determination, precisely, to think about yourself, 'to scrutinize [your]

---

[12] *Ibid.*, pp. 199, 216.

experiences as severely as a scientific experiment – hour after hour, day after day' (*GS* 319). By these means we can

> *become who we are* – human beings who are new, unique . . . who give themselves laws, who create themselves! To that end we must become the best students and discoverers of everything lawful and necessary in the world: we must become *physicists* in order become creators in this sense . . . So, long live physics! And even more so that which *compels* us to turn to physics – our honesty! (*GS* 335)

Thus, it is our 'intellectual conscience', our 'honesty', that both says 'You shall become who you are' and also makes becoming who you are possible.

At one level, Nietzsche's thought here is straightforward. One becomes who one is by getting to know oneself, and by getting to know the conditions under which one operates ('everything lawful and necessary in the world'). One ceases, on the one hand, idly to accept falsehoods about oneself – for instance, that one has an infallible organ of judgment, one's 'conscience', whose deliverances are somehow independent of one's 'instincts, likes, dislikes, experiences' etc. – and one ceases, on the other hand, to accept falsehoods about the world – for instance, that it is governed by 'providential reason and goodness' (*GS* 277), or that it is somehow organized with human purposes in mind, or indeed with any purpose at all.[13] At this level, then, one becomes who one is by honestly acknowledging, first, that one is essentially just an animal, rather than a creature with supernatural capacities, and second, that the world in which one has one's being, in which one must act and try to make sense of oneself, is a world without God. We necessarily misunderstand ourselves, Nietzsche holds, if we fail to acknowledge either kind of truth.

But we are more than *merely* animals. Unlike the other animals, we also have a 'second nature',[14] a nature produced by culture. And it is this that is expressed through our practices, including those practices in which various misunderstandings of ourselves are encoded. An animal without a 'second nature' could no more mistake itself for a transmitter of the 'voice of conscience', or for an inhabitant of a divinely ordered world, than it could enter into a contract, form a friendship, or go to war. Our 'second nature' is what makes us 'interesting', as Nietzsche later has it,[15] and the 'experiences' that are rooted there are pre-eminently among those to be

---

[13] See, e.g., *GS* 109.   [14] See, e.g., *Daybreak* (*D*) 38.
[15] See, e.g., *On the Genealogy of Morality* (*GM*) 1.6.

subjected to the 'intellectual conscience'. In order to 'become who we are', then, we must be honest with ourselves not merely as pieces of nature, as animals in an undesigned world, but as pieces of 'second nature', as animals whose character and circumstances are significantly constituted by culture.

There are many ways in which we can misunderstand ourselves. We can, as it were, be factually wrong about some matter concerning nature or second nature. Or we can adopt, perhaps unconsciously, a perspective on such matters that systematically occludes or distorts them. Nietzsche is particularly interested in misunderstandings of this latter kind – in habits of thought that have the effect of making whole dimensions of ourselves and of our worldly circumstances obscure to us. The most famous example, of course, is the perspective that Nietzsche diagnoses under the label 'morality'. But that is a diagnosis that advances along several fronts: here, I will focus on just one of these, and attempt to indicate how Nietzsche understands the relation – obscured, he holds, by 'morality' – between our becoming our own 'creators' and our being the 'discoverers of everything lawful and necessary in the world'.

Two well-known passages from *The Gay Science* are helpful here. In one, Nietzsche speaks of the 'great and rare art' of giving '"style" to one's character':

> It is practised by those who survey all the strengths and weaknesses of their nature and then fit them into an artistic plan . . . Here a large mass of second nature has been added; there a piece of original nature has been removed – both times through long practice and daily work at it. Here the ugly that could not be removed is concealed; there it has been reinterpreted and made sublime. (*GS* 290)

Four points are worth making about this passage. First, what Nietzsche is here describing is a form of self-creation, that is, a version of becoming who you are; second, this form of self-creation depends upon self-understanding, upon surveying one's nature and identifying the strengths and weaknesses in it; third, weaknesses or uglinesses are sometimes removable; and fourth, irremovable uglinesses are to be concealed if they cannot be 'reinterpreted' and transformed. The first two points connect this passage directly to our discussion so far: becoming who you are depends upon the exercise of the intellectual conscience. And the remaining two points provide the connection to the second passage:

> I want to learn more and more to see as beautiful what is necessary in things; then I shall be one of those who make things beautiful. *Amor fati*: let that be my love henceforth! (*GS* 276)

The connection comes to this: becoming who you are requires that you distinguish between what is and what is not necessary in things, including yourself (a job for the intellectual conscience). What is not necessary, and is weak or ugly, should be removed. What *is* necessary should, if weak or ugly, either be concealed ('*Looking away* shall be my only negation' (*GS* 276)) or else 'reinterpreted', so that one learns to see it as beautiful, as a strength.

A distinctive conception of the relation between self-creation and necessity – whether in nature, second nature, or circumstance – is implicit in these passages, and it is this that Nietzsche regards as obscured by the perspective of 'morality'. He develops the point explicitly in *Beyond Good and Evil* (1886). 'Morality', he claims, trades on an impossible notion of freedom. It encourages 'the desire to bear the entire and ultimate responsibility for one's actions oneself, and to absolve God, the world, ancestors, chance and society'. It encourages, that is, a quite peculiar conception of autonomy, according to which we are properly self-governing and properly responsible for our actions only to the extent that what we do is the product of '"freedom of the will" in the superlative metaphysical sense', a freedom that is supposedly operative independently of our nature, our second nature, or our circumstances. But this, observes Nietzsche, 'is the best self-contradiction that has been conceived so far'; it involves the desire 'to pull oneself up into existence by the hair, out of the swamps of nothingness'. And – crucially – it encourages us to perceive in every necessity 'something of constraint, need, compulsion to obey, pressure and unfreedom' (*BGE* 21).

The truth, Nietzsche holds, is quite otherwise. As the self-stylization and the *amor fati* passages make clear, he treats necessities of various kinds as material to be exploited and, where possible, affirmed. Indeed, he treats them as *conditions* of effective action, rather than as impediments to it, and hence as integral to the possibility of freedom, rather than as limits upon it:

one should recall the compulsion under which every language so far has achieved strength and freedom – the metrical compulsion of rhyme and rhythm. How much trouble the poets and orators . . . have taken . . . 'submitting abjectly to capricious laws', as anarchists say, feeling 'free' . . . But the curious fact is that all there is or has been on earth of freedom, subtlety . . . and masterly sureness . . . in thought itself . . . in the arts just as in ethics, has developed only owing to the 'tyranny of such capricious laws'; and in all seriousness, the probability is . . . that this is 'nature' and 'natural' – and *not* that *laisser aller*. (*BGE* 188)

So Nietzsche offers a picture of freedom that roots it explicitly in the 'tyranny' of 'capricious laws', which is to say, in the necessities that constitute our second nature.

Only someone who acknowledges the rules of language has the capacity – the freedom – to communicate in it. Only someone who acknowledges the laws of chess has the freedom to castle his king, say. Only someone who acknowledges the norms and courtesies of conversation has the freedom to engage in one. And so on, for any human practice at all. To resent such 'necessities' as a threat to one's '"responsibility"', to one's 'belief in' *oneself*, to one's 'personal right to [one's *own*] merits at any price' would be, quite simply, to render oneself impotent (*BGE* 21). Yet it is precisely such a resentment that 'morality', with its fantasy of freedom in the 'superlative metaphysical sense', expresses. Nietzsche's point, then, is that if we are to understand ourselves as actors in the world as it is, we have to acknowledge that certain necessities are integral to our agency, to our 'freedom' and 'responsibility'.[16] And this is a form of self-understanding – a finding of the intellectual conscience – that the peculiar perspective of 'morality' necessarily occludes; which is one of the reasons why it stands in the way of our becoming who we are.

When Nietzsche says, therefore, that we must become 'discoverers of everything lawful and necessary in the world' if we are to become 'creators' of ourselves, part of what he means is that we must determine *which* of the circumstances of our existence really are necessities. Some of these circumstances, for instance, 'morality', may appear to be or may present themselves as being necessities,[17] when in fact they are only contingent

---

[16] Cf. *TI*, 'Skirmishes', 38.
[17] Morality 'says stubbornly and inexorably: "I am morality itself, and nothing besides is morality"' (*BGE* 202).

sources of self-misunderstanding: such circumstances are uglinesses or weaknesses, and they should be removed. Other of our circumstances really are necessities. And, of these, some will be ineluctably ugly, and will have to be concealed or looked away from.[18] The remainder, however, are to be understood – perhaps *via* 'reinterpretation' – as conditions of the possibility of agency, of freedom. And it is through the acknowledgement and affirmation of these that the discovery, development, and – perhaps – the perfection of one's capacities is to be realized. To the extent that those capacities *are* realized, one has succeeded in becoming who one is.

It is not surprising that Nietzsche should link this process to art and creativity. Artistry is law-like, in the sense that it is possible to go wrong, to make mistakes. Yet the laws against which these mistakes offend often declare themselves only in the moment at which they are breached, indeed *in* the breaching of them. And this is why getting something *right* feels like – is – getting what one was after all along, even when one could not have said in advance precisely what that was. In this way, successful artistry is also a form of self-discovery – it is the discovery, in the lawfulness of one's actions, of the innermost character of one's intentions:

> Every artist knows how far from any feeling of letting himself go his most 'natural' state is – the free ordering, placing . . . giving form in the moment of 'inspiration' – and how strictly and subtly he obeys thousandfold laws precisely then, laws that precisely on account of their hardness and determination defy all formulation through concepts (*BGE* 188)

– and this, in turn, is a large part of the reason why Nietzsche so consistently connects self-creation to having one's *own* laws. In becoming who we are, he says, we become 'human beings who are new, unique, incomparable, who give themselves laws, who create themselves!' (*GS* 335); self-stylists 'enjoy their finest gaiety . . . in being bound by but also perfected under a law of their own' (*GS* 290); 'the "individual" appears, obliged to give himself laws and to develop his own arts and wiles for self-preservation, self-enhancement, self-redemption' (*BGE* 262).

So artistry represents a limit case of Nietzsche's understanding of agency. Like every kind of agency, artistry is possible only for those who acknowledge necessity as a condition of, rather than as a limit upon, their

---

[18] Cf. *BGE* 39.

freedom to act. We misunderstand ourselves if we misunderstand this. But in artistry we also perpetually discover ourselves, as our actions express those 'thousandfold' unformulable laws which are, Nietzsche suggests, most truly our own. We become most fully who we are, as he puts it at one point, when we become the 'poets of our lives' (*GS* 299).

Nietzsche on Nietzsche

This gives some of the background required to understand *Ecce Homo*, much of which is devoted to explaining – or perhaps to dramatizing – how Nietzsche has become who he is. But Nietzsche does not merely present his life as a work of art; he presents it as a fully achieved work of art, one that exhibits 'masterly sureness' throughout – that shows at every point his '*sureness of instinct* in practice' (*EH*, 'Wise', 6).

It is important to bear this latter point in mind, if the text is to stay in its proper focus. It can appear, for instance, that Nietzsche's conception of *amor fati* must have changed since 1882. In *The Gay Science*, as we have seen, *amor fati* involves learning 'to see as beautiful what is necessary in things' (*GS* 276), which leaves it open just how much *is* necessary in things (an indeterminacy that is vital if self-stylization, for instance, is to remain intelligible). In *Ecce Homo*, by apparent contrast, we read this: 'My formula for human greatness is *amor fati*: that you do not want anything to be different, not forwards, not backwards, not for all eternity. Not just to tolerate necessity . . . but to *love* it' (*EH*, 'Clever', 10), which may suggest that Nietzsche now regards *everything* as necessary.

But this is misleading. His claim, rather, is that a great human being is one who has learned to see as beautiful every circumstance of his life, has learned to treat every fact about himself and his world as necessary conditions of his freedom to act and to create himself under laws of his own. And *this* achievement may well require that quite a lot that is true of him now has only become true of him because of (unnecessary) things in his life that he has changed – for instance, that he has cast off certain weaknesses or uglinesses that masqueraded as necessities: examples that Nietzsche gives in his own case include ridding himself of the conviction that he is just 'like everyone else', of 'a forgetting of distance' between himself and others, an '"idealism"' (*EH*, 'Clever', 2). Or perhaps the great human being has altered one set of circumstances in his life so as to accommodate another, as Nietzsche reports himself as having altered his diet and his environs in order to accommodate his physiology (*EH*, 'Clever', 1, 2). Nor does this mean that he must necessarily have cause to regret the *status quo ante*, to want things 'to be different . . . backwards'. For he may well understand it as a condition of his having arrived where he is now that he had to overcome things as they were before: 'he uses mishaps to his advantage', Nietzsche says; 'what does not kill him makes him stronger' (*EH*, 'Wise', 2).

The best way to construe *amor fati* throughout Nietzsche's work, then, is as an ethical injunction concerning one's attitude towards the world, rather than as a (disguised) metaphysical thesis about how much of the world is necessary. Indeed, the only difference between 1882 and 1888 is that whereas in *The Gay Science* the presentation had been aspirational ('I want to learn more and more . . .'), in *Ecce Homo* the learning-process is presented as complete. He now (he claims) affirms *all* of his worldly circumstances: '*How could I not be grateful to my whole life?*' (*EH*, 'On this perfect day'[19]); and, in this limiting case, he achieves 'masterly sureness' in every aspect of his existence – he has '*learned*', as Nietzsche elsewhere puts it, '*to love*' himself (*GS* 334).[20]

These points bring out another strong continuity between the work of the earlier and the later 1880s, a kind of naturalized theodicy that Nietzsche first airs in the section of *The Gay Science* that immediately follows the *amor fati* passage:

> *Personal providence* – There is a certain high point in life: once we have reached that, we are, for all our freedom, once more in the greatest danger of spiritual unfreedom . . . For it is only now that the idea of a personal providence confronts us . . . now that we can see how palpably always everything that happens to us turns out for the best . . . Whatever it is, bad weather or good, the loss of a friend, sickness . . . it proves to be something that 'must not be missing'; it has a profound significance and use precisely for *us*. (*GS* 277)

The 'high point', clearly enough, is attained when one has learned to affirm all of one's worldly circumstances, when one's *amor fati* is complete; and the 'danger of spiritual unfreedom' is posed by the temptation to believe that there must, as an explanation for this, be 'some petty deity who is full of care and personally knows every little hair on our head', a supernatural

---

[19] Inscription placed between the Preface and the first chapter.
[20] *GS* 334 provides an essential hinge between the notions of *amor fati* and of becoming who one is.

source of 'providential reason and goodness' in our lives (*GS* 277). The danger, in other words, is that one will start to misunderstand oneself (to become who one isn't) by believing that it is a condition of one's freedom that there be a God who ensures that all is for the best in this, the best of all possible worlds.

The truth, of course, in Nietzsche's view, is that the condition of our freedom is not a benevolent God, but nature, second nature, and our attitude to these. If we are 'strong enough', he says, then 'everything *has to* turn out best' for us (*EH*, 'Wise', 2), for which the credit should be given, not to anything supernatural, but to 'our own practical and theoretical skill in interpreting and arranging events' (*GS* 277). As an example, Nietzsche describes how his illness has had 'a profound significance and use precisely for' *him*: sickness can

> be an energetic *stimulus* to life . . . This is, in fact, how that long period of illness looks to me *now*: I discovered life anew . . . myself included, I tasted all good and even small things in ways that other people cannot easily do . . . [Indeed,] the years of my lowest vitality were the ones when I *stopped* being a pessimist. (*EH*, 'Wise', 2)

Nietzsche's illness has turned out to be for the best, to be one of those things that '"must not be missing"'.

So if a traditional, more or less Leibnizian, theodicy seeks to show that every apparent evil is a necessary part of God's benevolent grand plan, Nietzsche's naturalized version of it urges us to find a perspective on our circumstances from which even the most grim-seeming of them can be regarded as indispensable *to us*. In place of Leibniz's ambition to redeem the whole world from a God's-eye point of view, that is, Nietzsche's hope is that individual lives might be redeemed from the point of view of those who live them, from a first-person perspective.[21]

This dimension of Nietzsche's thought is largely backward-looking. One is to look back and interpret one's past as having been for the best; but one is to do so from a present whose character – whose rightness – is partly to be constituted by one's success in this very enterprise. Of course, one's past might need a good deal of interpretation in order to bring this

---

[21] Nietzsche does occasionally seem tempted by supra-mundane world-redemption, especially when he starts talking about 'eternal recurrence'. But eternal recurrence is different from *amor fati*, and it is the strand of his thought that stems from the latter that concerns us here.

off. It is not as if one had been all along the deliberate architect of one's life – indeed, one must *not* be such an architect:

> you [must] not have the slightest idea *what* you are. If you look at it this way, even life's *mistakes* have their own meaning and value . . . [Here, *know thyself*] is the recipe for decline . . . *misunderstanding* yourself, belittling, narrowing yourself, making yourself mediocre . . . the threat that instinct will 'understand itself' too early. – In the mean time, the organizing, governing 'idea' keeps growing deep inside . . . it slowly leads *back* from out of the side roads and wrong turns, it gets the *individual* qualities and virtues ready [which] will prove indispensable as means to the whole . . . Viewed in this light, my life is just fantastic [– the product of] the lengthy, secret work and artistry of my instinct. (*EH*, 'Clever', 9)

To have turned out well, from this point of view, is to be able to interpret one's development as the unconscious unfolding of one's latent potential, as the gradual, invisible piecing-together of a coherent self. And the 'happiness' of such a development lies, as Nietzsche puts it, 'in its fatefulness' (*EH*, 'Wise', 1).

In *Ecce Homo*, then, Nietzsche presents his life as a species of artistry, in several senses. First, his life as it is now is one that he can affirm in all of its circumstances; he has learned to treat everything about himself and his world as necessary to his freedom to act and to create himself under his own laws. Second, he has interpreted his history in such a way that everything in it is 'for the best', so that his past unfolds like a work of art. And third, he attributes that unfolding to the 'artistry' of his 'instinct', since much that contributed to its course was not (and perhaps could not have been) consciously chosen. In each of these senses, Nietzsche portrays himself as the poet of his life, and hence as one who has become who he is.

Nietzsche's integrity

In the final sections of this introduction I turn to two of the circumstances of Nietzsche's life that make it most distinctively *his* – namely Christianity and Wagner. But before that, it might be worth asking what – in the light of the foregoing – we should make of *Ecce Homo*. I suggested at the outset that the book is not in any interesting or important way the product of insanity. But it may now seem as if the truth is if anything worse than that – that *Ecce Homo* is actually no more than a self-help manual, of a sort that endorses a peculiarly self-serving variety of positive thinking. It may seem, too, as if the demands of the 'intellectual conscience', upon which I have laid a good deal of weight, have disappeared without trace. One is, it appears, opportunistically to reinterpret one's past in a way that makes it seem providential. And one is to take seriously the thought – the fantasy, surely – that one might regard one's life as a work of art, and oneself as its moment-by-moment creator.

The first thing to say is that Nietzsche remains fully committed at this period to the value of honesty and the intellectual conscience. Sections 50–6 of *The Anti-Christ* contain one of the longest discussions of 'the service of truth' (*AC* 50) in any of Nietzsche's works, and he summarizes that discussion in *Ecce Homo*: 'How much truth can a spirit *tolerate*, how much truth is it willing to *risk*? This increasingly became the real measure of value for me . . . [E]very step forward in knowledge comes from *courage*, from harshness towards yourself' (*EH*, Preface, 3). These are not the words of a witting fantasist, or of one bent on falsifying his past. Moreover, the positions – such as 'morality' – against which Nietzsche most consistently ranges himself in *Ecce Homo*, and which he labels 'idealism', he regards as 'errors' and as the products of 'cowardice' (*EH*, Preface, 3).

But Nietzsche's objection to 'idealism' is not merely that it falsifies the world – by pretending that there is a God, for example, or by pretending that freedom in 'the superlative metaphysical sense' is possible. It is also that 'idealism' devalues the world, by according the highest value to its own inventions, at the world's expense and out of resentment against it – out of a 'deadly hostility to life' (*EH*, 'Destiny', 8). And this means that Nietzsche's own project also has two dimensions. One is to diagnose the errors of 'idealism'; the other is to suggest how life and the world might still have value for us once we have refused to resort to supernatural or metaphysical remedies. The thoughts canvassed in the previous section are an important part of Nietzsche's attempt to engage with the second of these issues. They are, in effect, an exploration of the intuition, first expressed in 1882, that 'As an aesthetic phenomenon existence is still *bearable* for us' (*GS* 107).

It is true that nothing could correspond to living one's life, from moment to moment, as if it were a work of art. So in this sense, Nietzsche's self-presentation does have an air of fantasy about it. But two points are worth making. The first is that, as I have argued, Nietzsche understands artistry as a limit case of agency in general, a limit at which one is, as it were, perfectly intelligible to oneself. And while it is surely true that that limit is not occupiable indefinitely, it is at least visitable from time to time; and it seems plausible to say that one is better off, by and large, for being closer to it than otherwise. And if this is right, it is hard to see why one might not try to imagine, as Nietzsche does, what it would be like if, *per impossible*, one could occupy that limit for the whole of the time – if only as a way of dramatizing a regulative ideal. The other point is that the expression of *Ecce Homo* is, as I said earlier, often hyperbolic. In part, of course, this is just to say that it is exaggerated, and to that extent the present point is the same as the first. But hyperbole is also a means of self-deflation, a form of deliberate over-statement that is meant to be seen through, if not at once, then at least pretty quickly. And from this point of view, it is not implausible to read Nietzsche as debunking his aesthetic ideal, as admitting that it is not fully realizable, at the same time as he dramatizes its realization.

So one shouldn't worry about the essential honesty of *Ecce Homo*, I think. Nor is it very troubling to think that it might be taken as a self-help manual, as a promoter of positive thinking. Positive thinking is surely better than the reverse; and, if Nietzsche is right that supernatural or metaphysical remedies are hard to do without, it seems entirely reasonable to suppose that, in their absence, some self-help might be needed. Nor, finally, do the charges of self-servingness and opportunism seem well directed. Nietzsche is explicitly out to serve the self; he says so repeatedly. And we can pointfully be charged with opportunism only when there are alternatives available to us. Confronted with some grim fact about our past, we can of course try to forget it; indeed, Nietzsche speaks warmly and often about the value of forgetting.[22] But if that is not possible, it is scarcely opportunistic to try to see it instead as something that '"must not be missing"', that has 'a profound significance and use precisely for *us*'. To refuse to recuperate what we can out of life is to turn our backs on it. And that, according to Nietzsche, is exactly what 'idealists' do.

---

[22] See, e.g., *EH*, 'Wise', 2.

Nietzsche on Christianity

Nietzsche does tell at least one clear lie in *Ecce Homo*, and it is this: 'I only attack things where there is no question of personal differences, where there has not been a history of bad experiences . . . I have the right to wage war on Christianity because I have never been put out or harmed by it' (*EH*, 'Wise', 7). Most of Nietzsche's readers will find this assertion hard to square with the temperature of his rhetoric whenever Christianity is in his sights; and readers of the *Genealogy*, in particular, will find the following claim equally unbelievable: '"God", "immortality of the soul", "redemption", "beyond", are simply ideas that I have not paid any attention to or devoted any time to' (*EH*, 'Clever', 1).

The truth is that Nietzsche's relation to Christianity and to Christian concepts is both personal and intense. On the one hand, he regards Christianity as a calamity, as the worst sort of life-slandering 'idealism', existing only 'to *devalue* nature' (*AC* 38). On the other hand, faith in God had given life meaning, and once 'God is dead' (*GS* 125) we are cast adrift in a world whose emptiness Nietzsche feels acutely. So if Nietzsche attacks Christianity, frequently and vehemently, he is also keenly aware that victory must come at a price: the 'uncovering' of Christianity, he says, is 'an event without equal, a real catastrophe. Anyone who knows about this . . . splits the history of humanity into two parts. Some live *before* him, some live *after* him' (*EH*, 'Destiny', 8).

If *Ecce Homo* is, at least in part, an effort to see how one might live 'after him', *The Anti-Christ* is Nietzsche's most sustained attempt to ensure that the history of mankind is, indeed, split in two. At the heart of the book lies a contrast between the figure of Christ and institutionalized Christianity, a contrast that Nietzsche pursues energetically, and across several different dimensions, but always to the detriment of Christianity. His crispest *précis* of the contrast is this: 'A new way of life, *not* a new faith' (*AC* 33). And his claim, in a nutshell, is that the church (pre-eminently St Paul) has systematically perverted and distorted Christ's real significance – which lay in *how* he lived his life – by turning his example into the set of beliefs, doctrines, and dogmas that we know as 'Christianity'.

It is worth distinguishing between two aspects of Nietzsche's critique. One is concerned with the form of Christianity (i.e. with the fact that it consists of doctrines and dogmas), and the other is concerned with its content (i.e. with what those doctrines and dogmas actually are). I will treat these aspects in turn, and try to indicate how each connects to issues touched on earlier.

Nietzsche's objection under the first head is essentially Aristotelian. We might hope to do what an exemplary figure does by learning some rules, by acquiring a set of beliefs about what is required and what is prohibited. But no such rules or beliefs can, by themselves, enable us to do what the exemplary figure does *as* he does it.[23] We cannot move, that is, from a 'way of life' to a set of requirements or prohibitions that is equivalent to it: something goes missing. And what goes missing, in effect, is the relation between who we are and what we do.[24] Christianity, as Nietzsche construes it, takes that relation to be externally mediated – by a learnable rule or prescription that is specifiable independently of the relevant 'way of life'. In the exemplary figure, by contrast, that relation is altogether internal: he does as he does because it is his nature to do so (whether that nature be original or second). The exemplar expresses and discloses himself in his actions. He is, in short, one of those whose 'most "natural" state' is to obey a 'thousandfold laws . . . that precisely on account of their hardness and determination defy all formulation through concepts' (*BGE* 188).

In seeking to extract a set of beliefs or rules from the life of Christ, then, Christianity has failed to treat Christ as an exemplar, and so has falsified the significance that his 'way of life' has. As Nietzsche puts it, Christ's faith 'does not prove itself with miracles, rewards, or promises . . . at every moment it is its own miracle, its own reward, its own proof . . . This faith does not formulate itself either – it *lives*, it resists formulas' (*AC* 32); indeed, it

> projects itself into a new *practice*, the genuinely evangelical practice. Christians are not characterized by their 'faith': Christians . . . are characterized by a *different* way of acting . . . The life of the redeemer was nothing other than *this* practice, – even his death was nothing else . . . He no longer needed formulas . . . or even prayer. He . . . knew how the *practice* of life is the only thing that can make you feel 'divine', 'blessed' . . . 'Atonement' and 'praying for forgiveness' are *not* the way to God: *only the evangelical practice* leads to God, in fact it *is* 'God'. (*AC* 33)

[23] See Aristotle, *Nicomachean Ethics*, Book II, chapter 4.
[24] Nietzsche had long been interested in the ethical role of exemplars, as the third of the *Untimely Meditations*, 'Schopenhauer as Educator' (1874), attests.

'The "kingdom of God" is not', therefore, 'something that you wait for; it does not have a yesterday or a day after tomorrow . . . it is an experience of the heart; it is everywhere and it is nowhere' (*AC* 34). And it is this that is shown in the life of Christ.

Yet it is also this, precisely this, that goes missing when Christianity, as Nietzsche construes it, translates Christ's practice into a set of 'formulas'. Indeed, 'the history of Christianity . . . is the story of [a] progressively cruder misunderstanding', as a new way of life is obscured more and more by 'doctrines and rites' (*AC* 37). And the effect of this is that Christ's '*glad tidings*', that 'any distance between God and man', is 'abolished' (*AC* 33), is turned upside down. In place of a practice, which '*is* God', the church erects 'formulas' which mediate between man and God, and so hold them apart. '[Y]ou will not find a greater example of *world-historical irony*' than 'that humanity knelt down before the opposite of the origin, the meaning . . . of the evangel, the fact that in the concept of "church", humanity canonized the very thing the "bearer of glad tidings" felt to be *beneath* him, *behind* him' (*AC* 36).

For present purposes it doesn't greatly matter whether Nietzsche is right about Christ or the church. What matters is the point about the *form* of Christianity (or at any rate of Nietzsche's version of it), the fact that it replaces practices with 'formulas'. For this, in Nietzsche's view, is to promote a distorted picture of a person's relation to his own actions. It is to privilege those cases in which one puts a statable policy into effect over those in which one's policy is disclosed in getting one's actions right. It is to privilege conformity *in abstracto* over self-discovery *in concreto*. And that is why Nietzsche claims that 'for two thousand years' Christianity has been 'just a psychological self-misunderstanding' (*AC* 39); and why he claims elsewhere that to root one's entire ethics in impersonal, codified prescriptions is 'not yet [to have] taken five steps toward self-knowledge' (*GS* 335). His point, in other words, is that the form of Christianity impedes the kind of understanding of oneself that is integral to 'becoming who one is' – indeed, that it renders the very possibility of doing that invisible.

The second aspect of Nietzsche's critique concerns the content of Christianity, what its 'formulas' actually are. These are derived, obviously enough, from Christ's 'way of life'; and this way of life Nietzsche regards as 'necessary' (*AC* 39) for the 'psychological type of the redeemer' (*AC* 29).

This type has two defining traits, of which the second is essentially an elaboration of the first:

> *The instinct of hatred for reality*: the consequence of an extreme over-sensitivity and capacity for suffering that does not want to be 'touched' at all because it feels every contact too acutely.
> *The instinctive exclusion of all aversion, all hostility* . . . the consequence of an extreme over-sensitivity and capacity for suffering that perceives every reluctance . . . as . . . an unbearable *pain* . . . and only experiences bliss . . . when it stops resisting everyone and anything, including evil, – love as the only, the *final* possibility for life. (*AC* 30)

And so in Christ's life, according to Nietzsche, these traits are exemplified: 'The polar opposite of struggle . . . has become instinct here . . . blessedness in peace . . . in an *inability* to be an enemy.' His nature is expressed 'as a flight into the "unimaginable", into the "inconceivable" . . . as a being-at-home in a world that has broken off contact with every type of reality, a world that has become completely "internal", a "true" world, an "eternal" world . . . "The kingdom of God is *in each of you*"' (*AC* 29).

The practice of Christ's life is entirely proper to him. He becomes who he is through his way of life, freely creating himself under a law of his own.[25] But such a life is not for everyone. And when Christianity lays hold of it, with its determination to '*vulgarize*' it into a set of formulas (*AC* 37), the result is calamitous.

> From now on, a number of different things started seeping into the type of the redeemer: the doctrines of judgment and return . . . the doctrine of the *resurrection*; and at this point the whole idea of 'blessedness', the solitary reality of the evangel, vanishes with a wave of the hand – and all for the sake of a state *after* death! . . . And in one fell swoop, the evangel becomes the most contemptible of all unfulfillable promises, the *outrageous* doctrine of personal immortality. (*AC* 41)

And when, by these means, 'the emphasis of life is put on the "beyond" rather than on life itself – when it is put *on nothingness* . . . the emphasis has been completely removed from life' as such (*AC* 43).

---

[25] I return to this claim in the following section.

An important dimension, then, of Nietzsche's critique is that Christianity, as an integral part of its '*disvaluing*' of life, encourages precisely the sorts of views about the self (as immortal) and the world (as a divinely ordered prelude to the 'Beyond') that guarantee self-obscurity. So the content of Christianity, he claims, no less than its form, stands squarely in the way of becoming 'who you are'.

'Have I been understood? – *Dionysus versus the crucified*': that is the famous final slogan of *Ecce Homo* (*EH*, 'Destiny', 9). And a rich slogan it is, too. Nietzsche is insistent that one's opponents should be worthy of one – 'an attack is proof of good will . . . I do something or someone honour, I confer distinction on it when I associate my name with it: for or against' (*EH*, 'Wise', 7). And '*the crucified*' passes muster. As one who has become who he is, Christ earns Nietzsche's respect, even if the psychological type that he represents is not remotely to Nietzsche's taste. And as the saviour concocted by Christianity, he is the most momentous foe imaginable: in *his* name, the world has been stripped of all value, and the possibility of human freedom has been removed from view.

Nietzsche on decadence

Christ is a 'decadent', Nietzsche claims (*AC* 31); and he says the same of himself. Indeed, he attributes the fact that 'I have a subtler sense of smell for the signs of ascent and decline than anyone has ever had' to a 'double birth, from the highest and lowest rungs on the ladder of life . . . simultaneously decadent and *beginning*'. It is this, he claims, that allows him to look 'from the optic of sickness towards *healthier* concepts' and, conversely, 'to look down from the fullness and self-assurance of the *rich* life into the secret work of the instinct of decadence . . . if I became the master of anything, it was this' (*EH*, 'Wise', 1).

'Decadence' is a tricky concept to handle, however. We should begin by noting that Nietzsche, as his own case attests, does not regard decadence as incompatible with becoming who one is: decadence can be an ingredient in self-creation. Decadence is not, therefore, equivalent to the kinds of 'idealism' that he attacks in *Ecce Homo*, even if, in the event, 'idealism' may be one of its most frequent effects. The fact that Nietzsche uses the term 'decadence' indiscriminately to refer to both cause *and* effect often tends to obscure this. But we must keep them apart, and understand decadence as a necessary, but not as a sufficient, condition of 'idealism'.

Construed thus, decadence is a form of suffering from life, of suffering from being oneself. As one component of a psyche, it can be something which, if it 'does not kill' one, makes one 'stronger'; it can be one of those 'qualities' which 'will prove indispensable as means to the whole', an element subordinated to an 'organizing . . . "idea"' which produces a totality whose 'incredible multiplicity . . . is nonetheless the converse of chaos'. And this, according to Nietzsche, is how his own decadence is to be understood, as having been woven by the 'secret work and artistry' of his 'instinct' into that greater whole which is 'what he is' (*EH*, 'Clever', 9). Where no such 'secret work and artistry' is present, on the other hand, one is apt to be driven to 'idealism' – to be driven by one's suffering to falsify and devalue the world.

Twilight of the Idols is devoted to the uncovering and diagnosis of decadence, both as cause (suffering) and as effect ('idealism'). It also, via the person of Socrates, offers a case study in how one *ceases* to be who one is. Nietzsche portrays Socrates as the product of decay. Standing behind him is an idealized Greek noble – vibrant, healthy, in tune with himself and his instincts, an artist of his life to his finger-tips – and it is this figure whose decay Socrates represents. '[D]egeneration was quietly gaining ground everywhere', Nietzsche says: 'old Athens was coming to an end . . . Everywhere, instincts were in anarchy' (*TI*, 'Socrates', 9). In place of a more or less unconscious regulation of the instincts, chaos threatened; the 'organizing "idea"' of the Athenian soul was loosening its grip; and people began to suffer from themselves and from life as if it were a sickness (*TI*, 'Socrates', 1). The Athenians became decadent.

But in Socrates there appeared to be a cure at hand. He became 'master of *himself*'. Although he was only 'an extreme case' of the general crisis, he nevertheless held out the prospect that 'a stronger *counter-tyrant*' might be opposed to the tyranny of the instincts (*TI*, 'Socrates', 9). And this tyrant was to be dialectic – '*reason*':

> Rationality was seen as the *saviour*, neither Socrates nor his 'patients' had any choice about being rational . . . it was their *last* resort. [T]hey had only one option: be destroyed or – be *absurdly rational* . . . [Socrates established] a permanent state of *daylight* against all dark desires – the daylight of reason. You have to be clever, clear, and bright at any cost: any concession to the instincts . . . leads *downwards*. (*TI*, 'Socrates', 10)

So Socrates became an 'idealist'. He accorded absolute value to a hyper-trophied version of one human capacity, rationality, invented a realm of the Forms that would answer to it, and then used it as a rod with which to beat and denigrate the rest of human nature and the world. And this, although it may well have addressed the 'anarchy' of the instincts, also confirmed him in the view that life is to be suffered as a sickness. What appeared as 'salvation', that is, turned out to be 'only another expression [i.e. effect] of decadence' (*TI*, 'Socrates', 11).

Three things are worth highlighting here. First, 'anarchy' of the instincts is already sufficient for someone to cease to be (or not yet to have become) who he is; no 'organizing "idea"' is present; and this explains Nietzsche's remark that 'our modern concept of "freedom"' – that is, '*laisser aller*', letting go – is 'a symptom of *decadence*', is another 'proof of the degeneration of the instincts' (*TI*, 'Skirmishes', 41). Second, the counter-tyranny – the 'idealism' – that Socrates proposes as a cure for 'anarchy' serves further to obscure oneself to oneself: 'instinctively to choose what is harmful to *yourself*' [that is, for the self who one is to become], 'to be *tempted* by "disinterested" motives, this is practically the formula for decadence [as effect, as 'idealism']' (*TI*, 'Skirmishes', 35). And third, and the foregoing notwithstanding, 'anarchy' of the instincts is not a necessary feature of decadence. Such 'anarchy' was present in the Greeks' case, perhaps – was what *they* suffered from; and for them it might have been true that 'To *have* to fight the instincts' was 'the formula for decadence [as cause]' (*TI*, 'Socrates', 11). But decadence can be rooted in other sources than this.

In Nietzsche's own case, he tells us, it was rooted largely in his ill-ness. 'Anarchy' threatened, no doubt, and he suffered from himself; but thanks to the 'organizing "idea"' that was secretly germinating within him, he succeeded in becoming who he was anyway. And the case of Christ makes the point still more clearly. Christ is a decadent. Yet in his case there simply aren't enough instincts in play to allow for an anar-chic free-for-all between them; there is no multiplicity in him (*AC* 31). Rather, Christ's decadence, as Nietzsche diagnoses it, is expressed directly in a single instinct, in a no-holds-barred '*hatred of reality*'. He is, in this sense, decadence incarnate; his life just *is* a suffering from life. And this is why he is no 'idealist'. He has no other resources to draw upon: he stands

outside . . . all natural science, all experience of the world, all knowledge . . . he never had any reason to negate 'the world', the . . .
concept of 'world' never occurred to him . . . *Negation* is out of the
question for him. – Dialectic is missing as well, there is no conception that . . . a 'truth' could be grounded in reasons (– *his* proofs are
inner 'lights'.). (*AC* 32)

And so he inhabits 'a merely "inner" world, a "real" world, an "eternal"
world'; and he becomes who he is there by becoming, in effect, no one at
all, by sublimating himself into a pure symbol of love.

Nietzsche on Wagner

Decadence is not a univocal phenomenon, then. One can suffer from
being oneself in many different ways and to many different effects.
And this should arm one against thinking that Nietzsche's late writings
about Wagner, in which he presents Wagner as the modern decadent *par
excellence*, are likely to be especially one-dimensional. Indeed, it should
alert one to the strong possibility that in this case, where Nietzsche's
claim to be personally unembroiled is even less plausible than in the case
of Christianity, his judgment may go awry.

Nietzsche is not unaware of this potential worry, and in *Ecce Homo*
he seeks to disarm it directly: 'I need to express my gratitude', he says,
'for what was by far the friendliest and most profound' relationship of
my life, that with Richard Wagner (*EH*, 'Clever', 5). 'I know better than
anyone what tremendous things Wagner could do . . . and being what I am,
strong enough to take advantage of the most questionable and dangerous
things and become even stronger in the process, I name Wagner as the
greatest benefactor of my life' (*EH*, 'Clever', 6). So Wagner is one of those
things in Nietzsche's biography that 'must not be missing': he is one of
the conditions of Nietzsche's having become who he is.

Indeed, Nietzsche makes a stronger claim than this. He suggests in
The Case of Wagner that, as a decadent, Wagner is indispensable, not
merely for Nietzsche, but for every philosopher. 'Modernity speaks its
most *intimate* language in Wagner: it does not hide its good or its evil . . .
And vice versa: if you are clear about . . . Wagner, you have just about
summed up the *value* of modernity' (*CW*, Preface). So for a philosopher

interested in modernity – and hence, Nietzsche insists, in decadence – Wagner is a '*lucky case*' (*CW*, Epilogue). But he is also complex, multi-faceted, and wide-ranging; and Nietzsche's treatment of him reflects that. His objections are legion, but are also closely interconnected. And this makes it more or less impossible to give a convincing *précis*. So instead, I focus here on three aspects of Nietzsche's critique that link directly to the discussion so far, and hope that something of the general flavour will emerge through that. The issues that I focus on are style, 'idealism', and who Wagner *is*.

We have already seen that 'style' matters to Nietzsche. It is, after all, what one has to give to one's character if one is to create oneself under a law of one's own. And Nietzsche's model of style – which is drawn, obviously, from art – is a conventional one: style is a higher 'lawfulness' (*CW* 8), he says, marked by the fact that 'life' dwells 'in the totality', with the parts being related to one another in an 'organic' way (*CW* 7); it is marked by '*necessity*' but gives 'the impression of freedom' (*CW* 9); it has its own sort of 'logic' (*CW* 2). It is, in short, precisely what one gets when an 'organizing "idea"' is at work. And style, according to Nietzsche, is what Wagner lacks: indeed, Wagner has 'no stylistic facility whatsoever' (*CW* 7).

In part, Nietzsche's objection arises from his dislike of so-called 'end-less melody', which '*wants* to break up all evenness of tempo', with the result that the listener finds himself 'Swimming, floating – no longer walking, dancing': there is a 'complete degeneration of the feeling for rhythm, *chaos* in place of rhythm . . .' (*Nietzsche contra Wagner* (*NCW*), 'Wagner as a Danger', 1). But chaos, to Nietzsche's ear, is endemic to Wagner's music: there is 'an anarchy of the atom, disintegration of the will'; '[p]aralysis everywhere, exhaustion . . . *or* hostility and chaos: both becoming increasingly obvious the higher you climb in the forms of orga-nization. The whole does not live at all any more.' Wagner 'forges little unities', 'animates them', and 'makes them visible. But this drains him of strength: the rest is no good.' 'Wagner is admirable . . . only in his inventiveness with the very small'; he is 'our greatest *miniaturist* in music' (*CW* 7).

In the light of the huge scale of Wagner's works, it is perhaps unsurpris-ing that Nietzsche should enjoy the charge of 'miniaturism'; he returns to it repeatedly. Wagner specializes, he says, in some very small and microscopic features of the soul, the scales of its amphibious nature, as it were –, yes, he is *master* at the very small. But he doesn't *want* to be! His *character* likes great walls and bold frescos much better! . . . It escapes him that his *spirit* has a different taste and disposition . . . [H]idden from himself, he paints his real masterpieces, which are all very short, often only a bar long. (*NCW*, 'Where I Admire')

But it is not just the (alleged) 'decline in organizing energy', 'the abuse of traditional methods without any ability to *justify* this abuse', the 'counterfeit in duplicating great forms' (*CW*, Second Postscript), or the 'miniaturism' that attracts Nietzsche's fire. It is the *content* of Wagner's 'small units', the fact that each one of them has been drawn from the 'drained cup' of 'human happiness', where 'the most bitter and repulsive drops have merged . . . with the sweetest ones' (*NCW*, 'Where I Admire'). Wagner's states are uniformly pathological; and strung together in a way that is at once *'brutal'*, *'artificial'*, and *'innocent'*, they result, not in a style, but in something closer to a nervous condition: Wagner, says Nietzsche, *'est une névrose* [neurosis]' (*CW* 5).

What Nietzsche construes as Wagner's incapacity for style, then, is the absence of an 'organizing "idea"' in his works, which is, in turn, symptomatic of a nervous and 'physiological degeneration (a form of hysteria, to be precise)' (*CW* 7). 'Wagner's art is sick', Nietzsche says (*CW* 5). It is a sign of 'declining life' (*CW*, Epilogue), of life that lacks the energy for itself – indeed, that suffers of itself. It is, in a word, decadent.

This connects directly to the second aspect of Nietzsche's critique, the one concerning 'idealism'. Wagner's audience, like him, are decadents, and so hunger for something that will call them 'back to life' (*CW* 5), for something 'sublime', 'profound', 'overwhelming' (*CW* 6). They 'do not even *want* to be clear about themselves' (*EH*, 'Wagner', 3); instead, they want 'presentiments'. And Wagner obliges – 'Chaos' induces 'presentiments' (*CW* 6) – and turns his listeners into 'moon-cal[ves]' – into '"idealist[s]"' (*CW*, Postscript). But 'It was not *music* that Wagner conquered them with, it was the "Idea": – the fact that his art . . . plays hide-and-seek under a hundred symbols' (*CW* 10). Indeed, claims Nietzsche, Wagner's elusiveness is a major source of his power to corrupt:

He has an affinity for everything equivocal . . . everything that in
general persuades the uncertain without letting them know *what*
they are being persuaded of. Wagner is a seducer in the grand style.
There is nothing tired . . . life-threatening, or world-denying in
matters of spirit that his art fails secretly to defend . . . He flatters
every nihilistic . . . instinct and disguises it in music, he flatters every
aspect of Christianity . . . Just open your ears: everything that has
ever grown on the soil of *impoverished* life, the whole counterfeit
of transcendence and the beyond, has its most sublime advocate in
Wagner's art. (*CW*, Postscript)

And – to Nietzsche's ears, at least – Wagner's relation to 'idealism' reaches
its most intimate pitch in his final work, *Parsifal*. 'Did *hatred of life* gain
control over him?', Nietzsche asks: 'Because Parsifal is a work of malice,
of vindictiveness, a secret poisoning of the presuppositions of life, a *bad*
work. – The preaching of chastity remains an incitement to perversion: I
despise anyone who does not regard Parsifal as an attempt to assassinate
ethics' (*NCW*, 'Wagner as Apostle of Chastity', 3).

So Wagner is a decadent; he lacks style, an 'organizing "idea"'; his art
stands in perilously close relations to 'idealism'. But who *is* he? *What* is he?
Nietzsche canvasses several possibilities: 'Is Wagner even a person?', he
asks; 'Isn't he really just a sickness?' (*CW* 5). Is he 'a dramatist'? No: 'He
loved the word "drama": that is all' (*CW* 9). Is he even 'a musician'? Perhaps; but 'he [is] something *more*: an incomparable histrion', an 'excellent
actor' – that is 'who this Wagner is' (*CW* 8).

To be an 'actor', in Nietzsche's sense, is to want 'effects, nothing but
effects' (*CW* 8).[26] And his claim in Wagner's case can be taken at two
levels. First, Wagner is an actor with respect to his art: he produces the
effect of art, but not its substance. He counterfeits style; he mimics drama;
his characters are forgeries. 'Wagner's music is never true', Nietzsche
says (*CW* 8). But second, and perhaps more importantly, Wagner is an
actor with respect to life. He is made for the modern age: 'in declining
cultures . . . genuineness becomes superfluous . . . a liability. Only actors
arouse *large* amounts of enthusiasm. – This ushers in the *golden age* for
actors' (*CW* 11). In a robust culture, the instincts are in good shape; people
can be seen to have 'turned out well' (*CW*, Epilogue), to have become
masters and creators of themselves. In a declining culture, by contrast,

---

[26] Cf. *GS* 361.

where the 'instinct is weakened' (*CW* 5), the resources required for self-creation are largely absent. And hence the importance, the timeliness, of the actor. With him, one gets the *effect* of personality, at least – even if the substance is entirely lacking.

'Is it any wonder', Nietzsche asks, 'that falseness has become flesh and even genius in precisely our age? That *Wagner* "dwelled among us"?' (*CW*, Epilogue). And he pursues the issue of Wagner's falseness into his 'idealism'. He imagines Wagner addressing his fellow composers:

> *Let us be idealists!* – This is . . . certainly the wisest thing we can do. In order to raise people up, we need to be elevated ourselves. Let us wander over the clouds, haranguing the infinite, surrounding ourselves with great symbols! . . . 'How could anyone who improves us not be good himself?' This is how humanity has always reasoned. So let us improve humanity! – that will make us good. (*CW* 6)

Wagner's 'idealism' is thus presented as a policy – as a policy that he adopts, like an actor, exclusively for the sake of 'effects'. And in the face of this, Nietzsche suddenly becomes rather warm about Christianity:

> The need for *redemption*, the embodiment of all Christian needs . . . is the most honest expression of decadence, it affirms decadence in the most convinced, most painful way . . . The Christian wants to *escape* from himself. *Le moi est toujours haïssable* [The 'I' is always hateful]. (*CW*, Epilogue)

So there is at least some honesty in the Christian's 'idealism'. In Wagner's, by contrast, Nietzsche sees nothing but mendaciousness – the absence of an intellectual conscience – all the way down.

One might summarize the aspects of Nietzsche's critique that I have discussed in the following way: Wagner lacked style, an 'organizing "idea"'; he was a decadent, he suffered from himself; therefore he was drawn to 'ideals' that slander the world; but, since there was, strictly speaking, no one who he *was* (no 'organizing "idea"'), he became an actor; and he became an actor *even* in his 'idealism'. And this, in Nietzsche's view, is decadence taken to the limit – the polar opposite of the conditions required for self-creation, for becoming who one is.

Nietzsche is quite wrong about Wagner, it seems to me – as perhaps he is too about Christ and Socrates, although that is a different matter. Certainly there is a temptation to read his writings on Wagner as a (mostly) unwitting self-portrait – and to wonder why Wagner mightn't have redeemed himself, *à la* Nietzsche, through his own version of *Ecce Homo*.[27] But these are questions for another occasion. Here, I have tried only to show how the idea of becoming 'who one is' runs through all of Nietzsche's final works, and to show how it rounds off a line of thought that characterizes his maturity as a whole. And if the effect of that, at certain levels, is to make it quite hard to regret that Nietzsche had to stop writing when he did, then perhaps that is no more than another – indeed, the ultimate – sign of his *'sureness of instinct* in practice'.[28]

Aaron Ridley

[27] Wagner's *Mein Leben* doesn't quite count as that.
[28] For comments on earlier versions of this introduction, I am grateful to Chris Janaway and Alex Neill. My principal debt, however, is to David Owen. The main ideas expressed here are uniformly the product of our conversations over the years, as is the general conception of Nietzsche's philosophy which underlies those ideas.

Chronology

1844   Born in Röcken, a small village in the Prussian province of
Saxony, on 15 October.

1846   Birth of his sister Elisabeth.

1848   Birth of his brother Joseph.

1849   His father, a Lutheran minister, dies at age thirty-six of
'softening of the brain'.

1850   Brother dies; family moves to Naumburg to live with father's
mother and her sisters.

1858   Begins studies at Schulpforta, Germany's most famous school
for education in the classics.

1864   Graduates from Schulpforta with a thesis in Latin on the Greek
poet Theognis; enters the University of Bonn as a theology
student.

1865   Transfers from Bonn, following the classical philologist Friedrich
Ritschl to Leipzig, where he registers as a philology student;
reads Schopenhauer's *The World as Will and Representation*.

1866   Reads Friedrich Lange's *History of Materialism*.

1868   Meets Richard Wagner.

1869   On Ritschl's recommendation is appointed professor of classical
philology at Basle at the age of twenty-four before completing his
doctorate (which is then conferred without a dissertation);
begins frequent visits to the Wagner residence at Tribschen.

1870   Serves as a medical orderly in the Franco-Prussian war; contracts
a serious illness and so serves only two months. Writes 'The
Dionysiac World View'.

1872 Publishes his first book, *The Birth of Tragedy*; its dedicatory
      preface to Richard Wagner claims for art the role of 'the highest
      task and truly metaphysical activity of this life'; devastating
      reviews follow.
1873 Publishes 'David Strauss, the Confessor and the Writer', the first
      of his *Untimely Meditations*; begins taking books on natural
      science out of the Basle library, whereas he had previously
      confined himself largely to books on philological matters. Writes
      'On Truth and Lying in a Non-Moral Sense'.
1874 Publishes two more *Meditations*, 'The Uses and Disadvantages of
      History for Life' and 'Schopenhauer as Educator'.
1876 Publishes the fourth *Meditation*, 'Richard Wagner in Bayreuth',
      which already bears subtle signs of his movement away from
      Wagner.
1878 Publishes *Human, All Too Human* (dedicated to the memory of
      Voltaire); it praises science over art as the mark of high culture
      and thus marks a decisive turn away from Wagner.
1879 Terrible health problems force him to resign his chair at Basle
      (with a small pension); publishes 'Assorted Opinions and
      Maxims', the first part of Vol. II of *Human, All Too Human*;
      begins living alone in Swiss and Italian boarding-houses.
1880 Publishes 'The Wanderer and his Shadow', which becomes the
      second part of Vol. II of *Human, All Too Human*.
1881 Publishes *Daybreak*.
1882 Publishes *Idylls of Messina* (eight poems) in a monthly magazine;
      publishes *The Gay Science*; friendship with Paul Rée and Lou
      Andreas-Salomé ends badly, leaving Nietzsche devastated.
1883 Publishes the first two parts of *Thus Spoke Zarathustra*; learns of
      Wagner's death just after mailing the first part to the publisher.
1884 Publishes the third part of *Thus Spoke Zarathustra*.
1885 Publishes the fourth part of *Zarathustra* for private circulation
      only.
1886 Publishes *Beyond Good and Evil*; writes prefaces for new editions
      of *The Birth of Tragedy*, *Human, All Too Human*, Vols. I and II,
      and *Daybreak*.
1887 Publishes expanded edition of *The Gay Science* with a new
      preface, a fifth part, and an appendix of poems; publishes *Hymn*

to *Life*, a musical work for chorus and orchestra; publishes *On the Genealogy of Morality*.

1888   Publishes *The Case of Wagner*, composes a collection of poems, *Dionysian Dithyrambs*, and four short books: *Twilight of the Idols, The Anti-Christ, Ecce Homo*, and *Nietzsche contra Wagner*.

1889   Collapses physically and mentally in Turin on 3 January; writes a few lucid notes but never recovers sanity; is briefly institutionalized; spends remainder of his life as an invalid, living with his mother and then his sister, who also gains control of his literary estate.

1900   Dies in Weimar on 25 August.

Further reading

While the secondary literature on Nietzsche is enormous, and grows by the week, that devoted specifically to Nietzsche's last works is comparatively sparse. The main reason for this, one must suppose, is that in his last works Nietzsche was largely concerned to draw out and to develop themes that were already prominent in his earlier writings, a fact that has led the majority of commentators to treat his final thoughts on those themes as addenda to discussions whose real meat is elsewhere. And there is quite a lot to be said for this way of establishing the priorities. Indeed, the reader new to Nietzsche might wish to step back still further, and begin with an overview of the general intellectual climate in which Nietzsche's thought developed. If so, there is nowhere better or more helpful to go than to Robin Small's *Nietzsche in Context* (Aldershot: Ashgate, 2001), a book that might usefully be complemented by Adrian Del Caro's *Nietzsche contra Nietzsche: Creativity and the Anti-Romantic* (Baton Rouge: Louisiana State University Press, 1997). Or the reader might prefer to approach the late Nietzsche by way of his life, in which case R. J. Hollingdale's biography, *Nietzsche: The Man and his Philosophy* (Cambridge: Cambridge University Press, 1999), is the natural first port of call, with Lesley Chamberlain's *Nietzsche in Turin* (London: Quartet, 1996) an excellent supplement that focuses on Nietzsche's final productive year. Among the more obviously philosophical books to accord weight to Nietzsche's late thoughts, even if only as addenda, three stand out: Alexander Nehamas's *Nietzsche: Life as Literature* (Cambridge, Mass.: Harvard University Press, 1985), Maudemarie Clark's *Nietzsche on Truth and Philosophy* (Cambridge: Cambridge University Press, 1990), and Henry Staten's *Nietzsche's Voice* (Ithaca: Cornell University Press, 1990), all of which show deftly how abiding preoccupations of Nietzsche's receive their final treatments.

Nietzsche's last works are more than addenda, however, and the secondary literature expressly devoted to them, although not abundant, is not inconsequential either. Valuable essays on *The Anti-Christ* include Gary Shapiro, 'The Writing on the Wall: *The Antichrist* and the Semiotics of History', in K. Higgins and R. Solomon, eds., *Reading Nietzsche* (Oxford: Oxford University Press, 1988). *Ecce Homo* is well discussed in, for example, Daniel Conway, 'Nietzsche's Doppelganger: Affirmation and Resentment in *Ecce Homo*', in K. Ansell Pearson, ed., *The Fate of the New Nietzsche* (Avebury: Brookfield, 1993). And *Twilight of the Idols* has perhaps been best served of all. Conway's *Nietzsche's Dangerous Game: Philosophy in the Twilight of the Idols* (Cambridge: Cambridge University Press, 1997) is the most nuanced treatment available of the later Nietzsche's complex relationship to the phenomenon of decadence, while Tracy B. Strong's introductory essay to the Hackett translation of *Twilight* (Indianapolis: Hackett, 1997) is the best piece yet written on Nietzsche's mature philosophy of music. Both of these are profitably to be read alongside chapter 5 of Julian Young's generally admirable *Nietzsche's Philosophy of Art* (Cambridge: Cambridge University Press, 1992). Nietzsche's Wagner writings, by contrast, have been neglected, although one might regard Thomas Mann, *Pro and Contra Wagner* (London: Faber, 1985), as valuable extensions to them. The most rewarding recourse, however, is to Michael Tanner's 'The Total Work of Art', in P. Burbidge and R. Sutton, eds., *The Wagner Companion* (London: Faber, 1979), which is not only the richest essay on Wagner to be found, but is also, read rightly, the most sustained existing critique of Nietzsche's critique of Wagner – a critique that is conducted, moreover, in a thoroughly Nietzschean spirit.

Note on the texts and translation

At a number of points in the text, passages are quoted from the following translations:

Beyond Good and Evil, ed. Rolf-Peter Horstmann and Judith Norman, trans. Judith Norman (Cambridge University Press, 2002)

The Gay Science, ed. Bernard Williams, trans. Josefine Nauckhoff (Cambridge University Press, 2001)

The Genealogy of Morality, ed. Keith Ansell Pearson, trans. Carol Diethe (Cambridge University Press, 1994)

Human, All Too Human, trans. R. J. Hollingdale with an introduction by Richard Schacht (Cambridge University Press, 1996)

The translation follows the German text as printed in the critical edition of Nietzsche's works edited by G. Colli and M. Montinari (Berlin: de Gruyter, 1967–), vol. VI.

The Anti-Christ
A Curse on Christianity

PREFACE

This book belongs to the very few. Perhaps none of them are even alive yet. Maybe they are the ones who will understand my *Zarathustra*. There are ears to hear some people – but how could I ever think there were ears to hear me? – My day won't come until the day after tomorrow. Some people are born posthumously.

The conditions required to understand me, and which in turn *require* me to be understood, – I know them only too well. When it comes to spiritual matters, you need to be honest to the point of hardness just to be able to tolerate my seriousness, my passion. You need to be used to living on mountains – to seeing the miserable, ephemeral little gossip of politics and national self-interest *beneath* you. You need to have become indifferent, you need never to ask whether truth does any good, whether it will be our undoing . . . The sort of predilection strength has for questions that require more courage than anyone possesses today; a courage for the *forbidden*; a predestination for the labyrinth. An experience from out of seven solitudes. New ears for new music. New eyes for the most distant things. A new conscience for truths that have kept silent until now. *And* the will to the economy of the great style: holding together its strength, its *enthusiasm* . . . Respect for yourself; love for yourself; an unconditional freedom over yourself . . .

Well then! These are my only readers, my true readers, my predestined readers: and who cares about the *rest of them*? The rest are just humanity. You need to be far above humanity in strength, in *elevation* of soul, – in contempt . . .

Friedrich Nietzsche

I

– Let us look ourselves in the face. We are Hyperboreans,[1] – we are well aware how far off the beaten track we live. 'Neither by land nor by sea will you find the way to the Hyperboreans': Pindar had already known this about us. Beyond the North, beyond ice, beyond death – *our* lives, *our* happiness . . . We have discovered happiness, we know the way, we have

---

[1] Hyperborea is a land of plenty in Greek mythology.

found the way out of the labyrinth of whole millennia. Who *else* has found this? – Maybe the modern man? 'I don't know where I am; I am everything that doesn't know where it is' – sighs the modern man . . . *This* modernity made us ill – this indolent peace, this cowardly compromise, the whole virtuous filth of the modern yes and no. This tolerance and *largeur* of the heart that 'forgives' everything because it 'understands' everything is *sirocco* for us. Better to live on the ice than among modern virtues and other south winds! . . . We were brave enough, we did not spare ourselves or other people: but for a long time we did not know *what to do* with our courage. We became miserable, people called us fatalists. *Our* fate – that *was* abundance, tension, a damming up of forces. We thirsted for lightning and action, we stayed as far away as possible from the happiness of weaklings, from 'resignation' . . . There was a storm in our air, the nature that we *are* grew dark – *because we had no path*. Formula for our happiness: a yes, a no, a straight line, a *goal* . . .

2

What is good? – Everything that enhances people's feeling of power, will to power, power itself.

What is bad? – Everything stemming from weakness.

What is happiness? – The feeling that power is *growing*, that some resistance has been overcome.

Not contentedness, but more power; *not* peace, but war; *not* virtue, but prowess (virtue in the style of the Renaissance, *virtù*, moraline-free virtue).

The weak and the failures should perish: first principle of *our* love of humanity. And they should be helped to do this.

What is more harmful than any vice? – Active pity for all failures and weakness – Christianity . . .

3

The problem I am posing is not what should replace humanity in the order of being (– the human is an *endpoint* –): but instead what type of human should be *bred*, should be *willed* as having greater value, as being more deserving of life, as being more certain of a future.

This more valuable type has appeared often enough already: but only as a stroke of luck, as an exception, never as *willed*. In fact *he* was precisely what people feared most; so far, he has been practically the *paradigm* of the terrible; – and out of terror, the opposite type was willed, bred, *achieved*: the domestic animal, the herd animal, the sick animal: man, – the Christian . . .

4

Humanity does *not* represent a development for the better, does not represent something stronger or higher the way people these days think it does. 'Progress' is just a modern idea, which is to say a false idea. Today's European is still worth considerably less than the Renaissance European; development is *not* linked to elevation, increase, or strengthening in any necessary way.

In another sense, there is a continuous series of individual successes in the most varied places on earth and from the most varied cultures; here, a *higher type* does in fact present itself, a type of overman in relation to humanity in general. Successes like this, real strokes of luck, were always possible and perhaps will always be possible. And whole generations, families, or peoples can sometimes constitute this sort of bull's eye, *right on the mark*.

5

You should not beautify Christianity or try to dress it up: it has waged a *war to the death* against this *higher* type of person, it has banned all the basic instincts of this type, it has distilled 'evil' and 'the Evil One' out of these instincts – the strong human being as reprehensible, as 'depraved'. Christianity has taken the side of everything weak, base, failed, it has made an ideal out of whatever *contradicts* the preservation instincts of a strong life; it has corrupted the reason of even the most spiritual natures by teaching people to see the highest spiritual values as sinful, as deceptive, as *temptations*. The most pitiful example – the corruption of Pascal, who believed that his reason was corrupted by original sin when the only thing corrupting it was Christianity itself! –

6

A painful, terrible spectacle is playing itself out in front of me: I lifted the curtain to reveal the *corruption* of humanity. This word, coming from my mouth, is absolved of one suspicion at least: the suspicion that it implies some moral indictment of human beings. It is – I want to keep stressing this – *moraline-free*: and this to the extent that I see the most corruption precisely where people have made the most concerted effort to achieve 'virtue', to attain 'godliness'. I understand corruption (as I am sure you have guessed by now) in the sense of decadence: my claim is that all the values in which humanity has collected its highest desiderata are *values of decadence*.

I call an animal, a species, an individual corrupt when it loses its instincts, when it chooses, when it *prefers* things that will harm it. A history of the 'higher feelings', the 'ideals of humanity' – and I might have to tell this history – would amount to an explanation of *why* human beings are so corrupt.

I consider life itself to be an instinct for growth, for endurance, for the accumulation of force, for *power*: when there is no will to power, there is decline. My claim is that *none* of humanity's highest values have had this will, – that *nihilistic* values, values of decline, have taken control under the aegis of the holiest names.

7

Christianity is called the religion of *pity*. – Pity is the opposite of the tonic affects that heighten the energy of vital feelings: pity has a depressive effect. You lose strength when you pity. And pity further intensifies and multiplies the loss of strength which in itself brings suffering to life.[2] Pity makes suffering into something infectious; sometimes it can even cause a total loss of life and of vital energy wildly disproportionate to the magnitude of the cause (– the case of the death of the Nazarene). That is the first point to be made; but there is a more significant one. The mortal dangers of pity will be much more apparent if you measure pity according to the value of the reactions it tends to produce. By and large, pity runs counter to the law of development, which is the law of *selection*. Pity preserves things that are ripe for decline, it defends things that have been disowned and condemned by life, and it gives a depressive and questionable character to life itself by keeping alive an abundance of failures of every type. People have dared to call pity a virtue

---

[2] Nietzsche is playing with the similarities between the terms 'pity' (*Mitleid*) and 'suffering' (*Leiden*).

(– in every *noble* morality it is considered a weakness –); people have gone even further, making it into *the* virtue, the foundation and source of all virtues, – but of course you always have to keep in mind that this was the perspective of a nihilistic philosophy that inscribed the *negation of life* on its shield. Schopenhauer was right here: pity negates life, it makes life *worthy of negation*, – pity is the *practice* of nihilism. Once more: this depressive and contagious instinct runs counter to the instincts that preserve and enhance the value of life: by *multiplying* misery just as much as by *conserving* everything miserable, pity is one of the main tools used to increase decadence – pity wins people over to *nothingness*! . . . You do not say 'nothingness': instead you say 'the beyond'; or 'God'; or 'the *true* life'; or nirvana, salvation, blessedness . . . This innocent rhetoric from the realm of religious-moral idiosyncrasy suddenly appears *much less innocent* when you see precisely *which* tendencies are wrapped up inside these sublime words: tendencies *hostile to life*. Schopenhauer was hostile to life: which is *why* he considered pity a virtue . . . Aristotle famously saw pity as a dangerous pathology that should be purged from the system every once in a while: he thought of tragedy as a purgative. In fact, the instincts of life should lead people to try to find a remedy for the sort of pathological and dangerous accumulation of pity you see in the case of Schopenhauer (and, unfortunately, in the case of our whole literary and artistic decadence from St Petersburg to Paris, from Tolstoy to Wagner), to prick it and make it *burst* . . . In the middle of our unhealthy modernity, nothing is less healthy than Christian pity. To be the doctor *here*, to be merciless *here*, to guide the blade *here* – this is for *us* to do, this is *our* love for humanity, this is what makes *us* philosophers, we Hyperboreans! – – –

8

We need to say *whom* we feel opposed to – theologians and everything with theologian blood in its veins – the whole of our philosophy . . . You need to have seen this disaster from up close – even better, you need to have experienced it, you need almost to have been destroyed by it – to see that it is no joke (– the *real* joke, as far as I am concerned, is when our esteemed natural scientists and physiologists claim to be 'free thinkers', – they do not have any passion for these things, they do not *suffer* from them[3] –).

---

[3] Nietzsche is playing with the similarities between the terms 'suffering' (*Leiden*) and 'passion' (*Leidenschaft*).

The contamination extends much further than people think: I find the theologian-instinct of arrogance cropping up wherever people consider themselves 'idealists', – wherever people think that their pedigree gives them the right to contemplate Reality and gaze out into the distance . . . The idealist, like the priest, holds all the great concepts in his hand (– and not just his hand); he plays them with a sort of good-natured disdain for 'understanding', the 'senses', 'honour', 'the good life', 'science'; he thinks that these sorts of things are *beneath* him, like so many pernicious, seductive forces over which 'spirit' hovers in its pure 'for-itself'-ness: – as if humility, chastity, poverty (in a word: *holiness*) have not done life unspeakably more harm than any vices or horrors ever have . . . Pure spirit is a pure lie . . . As long as the priest is considered a *higher* type of person – this *professional* negater, slanderer, poisoner of life – there will not be an answer to the question: What *is* truth? Truth has already been turned on its head when someone who consciously champions nothingness and negation passes for the representative of 'truth' . . .

9

I wage war on this theologian instinct: I have found traces of it everywhere. Anyone with theologian blood in his veins will approach things with a warped and deceitful attitude. This gives rise to a pathos that calls itself *faith*: turning a blind eye to yourself for once and for all, so you do not have to stomach the sight of incurable mendacity. This universally faulty optic is made into a morality, a virtue, a holiness, seeing-*wrong* is given a *good* conscience, – *other* types of optic are not allowed to have value any more now that this one has been sanctified with names like 'God', 'redemption', and 'eternity'. I have unearthed the theologian instinct everywhere: it is the most widespread and genuinely *subterranean* form of deceit on earth. Anything a theologian thinks is true *must* be false: this is practically a criterion of truth. His most basic instinct of self-preservation does not allow any scrap of reality to be honoured or even expressed. Wherever the influence of theologians is felt, *value judgments* are turned on their heads and the concepts of 'true' and 'false' are necessarily inverted: whatever hurts life the most is called 'true', and whatever improves, increases, affirms, justifies life or makes it triumph is called 'false' . . . When theologians use the 'conscience' of princes (*or* peoples –) to reach out for *power*, let us be very clear about *what* is really taking place: the will to an end, the *nihilistic* will willing power . . .

10

Germans understand me immediately when I say that philosophy has been corrupted by theologian blood. The Protestant minister is the grandfather of German philosophy, Protestantism itself is its *peccatum originale.*[4] Definition of Protestantism: the partial paralysis of Christianity – *and* of reason . . . You only need to say 'Tübingen seminary'[5] to understand just *what* German philosophy really is – an underhanded theology . . . The Swabians are the best liars in Germany, they lie with perfect innocence . . . Why did the world of German scholars, three-quarters of whom are pastors' and teachers' sons, go into such fits of delight at the appearance of *Kant* –, why were Germans so convinced (you can still find echoes of this conviction) that Kant marked a change for the *better*? The theologian instinct of the German scholar had guessed just *what* was possible again . . . A hidden path to the old ideal lay open; the concept of a '*true* world', the concept of morality as the *essence* of the world (– the two most vicious errors in existence!) were once again (thanks to an exceedingly canny scepticism), if not provable, then at least no longer *refutable* . . . Reason, the *right* of reason, does not extent that far . . . Reality was made into 'mere appearance'; a complete lie called 'the world of being' was made into a reality . . . Kant's success is just a theologian success: Kant, like Luther, like Leibniz, was one more drag on an already precarious German sense of integrity – –

11

One more word against Kant as a *moralist*. A virtue needs to be our *own* invention, our *own* most personal need and self-defence: in any other sense, a virtue is just dangerous. Whatever is not a condition for life *harms* it: a virtue that comes exclusively from a feeling of respect for the concept of 'virtue', as Kant would have it, is harmful. 'Virtue', 'duty', 'goodness in itself', goodness that has been stamped with the character

---

[4] Original sin.
[5] The seminary where both Hegel and Schelling received their secondary-school education.

of the impersonal and universally valid – these are fantasies and mani-
festations of decline, of the final exhaustion of life, of the Königsberg[6]
Chinesianity. The most basic laws of preservation and growth require the
opposite: that everyone should invent his *own* virtues, his *own* categorical
imperatives. A people is destroyed when it confuses its *own* duty with
the concept of duty in general. Nothing ruins us more profoundly or
inwardly than 'impersonal' duty, or any sacrifice in front of the Moloch of
abstraction. – To think that people did not sense the *mortal danger* posed
by Kant's categorical imperative! . . . The theologian instinct was the
only thing that came to its defence! – When the instinct of life compels
us to act, pleasure proves that the act is *right*: and this nihilist with the
intestines of a Christian dogmatist saw pleasure as an *objection* . . . What
could be more destructive than working, thinking, feeling, without any
inner need, any deeply personal choice, any *pleasure*? as an automaton
of 'duty'? It is almost the *recipe* for decadence, even for idiocy . . . Kant
became an idiot. – And this was a contemporary of *Goethe*! This disaster
of a spider passed for the *German* philosopher, – and still does! . . . I am
careful not to say what I think about the Germans . . . Wasn't it Kant
who saw the French Revolution as the transition from the inorganic to
the *organic* form of the state? Didn't he ask himself whether there was an
event that could be explained *only* by a moral predisposition in humanity,
thus *proving* once and for all the 'human tendency to goodness'? Kant's
answer: 'this is the Revolution'. The instinct that is wrong about everything, anti-nature as instinct, German decadence as philosophy – *this is
Kant!* –

12

I will make an exception for a couple of the sceptics, the decent types
in the history of philosophy; but the rest of them have no conception of
the basic demands of intellectual integrity. They all act like little females,
these admiring fans, these prodigies, – they think that 'beautiful feelings'
constitute an argument, that a 'heaving bosom' is God's bellows, that conviction is a *criterion* of truth. In the end, Kant even tried, with 'German'
innocence, to take this form of corruption, this lack of intellectual conscience, and render it scientific under the concept of 'practical reason': he

---

[6] Kant lived in Königsberg.

invented a special form of reason so that people would not have to worry about it when morality, when the sublime command 'thou shalt', is heard. If you stop and think that among almost all peoples the philosopher is just a further development of the priestly type, then this legacy of the priests, the art of *falling for your own forgeries*, will not seem particularly surprising. If you have a holy task like improving, saving, or redeeming mankind, if you carry God in your bosom and serve as the mouthpiece for imperatives issuing from the beyond, then this sort of a mission already puts you outside any merely rational assessment, – you are sanctified by a task like this, you are a type belonging to a higher order of things! . . . Why should a priest care about *science*? He is above all that! – and so far, priests have been in *control*! They have *determined* the concepts 'true' and 'untrue'! . . .

13

Let us not underestimate the fact that *we ourselves*, we free spirits, already constitute a 'revaluation of all values', a *living* declaration of war on and victory over all old concepts of 'true' and 'untrue'. The most valuable insights are the last to be discovered; but *methods* are the most valuable insights. *All* the methods, *all* the presuppositions of our present scientific spirit have been regarded with the greatest contempt for thousands of years, they barred certain people from the company of 'decent' men, – these people were considered 'enemies of God', despisers of the truth, or 'possessed'. As scientific characters, they were Chandala . . .[7] We have had the whole pathos of humanity against us – its idea of what truth *should* be, of what serving the truth *should* entail: so far, every 'thou shalt' has been directed *against* us . . . Our objectives, our practices, our silent, cautious, distrustful nature – all of this seemed totally unworthy and despicable. – In the end, and in all fairness, people should ask themselves whether it was not really an aesthetic taste that kept humanity in the dark for so long: people demanded a *picturesque* effect from the truth, they demanded that the knower make a striking impression on their senses. Our *modesty* is what offended their taste for the longest time . . . And didn't they know it, these strutting turkey-cocks of God – –

---

7 Untouchables.

14

We have changed our minds. We have become more modest in every way. We have stopped deriving humanity from 'spirit', from 'divinity', we have stuck human beings back among the animals. We see them as the strongest animals because they are the most cunning: one consequence of this is their spirituality. On the other hand, we are also opposed to a certain vanity that re-emerges here too, acting as if human beings were the great hidden goal of animal evolution. Humans are in no way the crown of creation, all beings occupy the same level of perfection . . . And even this is saying too much: comparatively speaking, humans are the biggest failures, the sickliest animals who have strayed the most dangerously far from their instincts – but of course and in spite of everything, the most *interesting* animals as well! – As far as animals are concerned, it was Descartes who, with admirable boldness, first ventured the idea that they could be seen as *machina*: the whole of physiology has been working to prove this claim. We are even logically consistent enough not to exclude humans, as Descartes did: to the extent that human beings are understood at all these days, they are understood as machines. People were once endowed with 'free will' as their dowry from a higher order of things: today we have taken even their will away, in the sense that we do not see it as a faculty any more. The old word 'will' only serves to describe a result, a type of individual reaction that necessarily follows from a quantity of partly contradictory, partly harmonious stimuli: – the will does not 'affect' anything, does not 'move' anything any more . . . People used to see consciousness, 'spirit', as proof that humanity is descended from something higher, that humanity is divine; people were advised to become *perfect* by acting like turtles and pulling their senses inside themselves, cutting off contact with worldly things and shedding their mortal shrouds: after this, the essential element would remain, the 'pure spirit'. We are more sensible about all this too: we see the development of consciousness, 'spirit', as a symptom of precisely the relative *imperfection* of the organism, as an experimenting, a groping, a mistaking, as an exertion that is sapping an unnecessarily large amount of strength away from the nervous system, – we deny that anything can be made perfect as long as it is still being made conscious. 'Pure spirit' is a pure stupidity: when we discount the nervous system and the senses, the 'mortal shroud', *we miscount* – nothing more! . . .

15

In Christianity, morality and religion are both completely out of touch with reality. Completely imaginary *causes* ('God', 'soul', 'I', 'spirit', 'free will' – or even an 'unfree' one); completely imaginary *effects* ('sin', 'redemption', 'grace', 'punishment', 'forgiveness of sins'). Contact between imaginary *entities* ('God', 'spirits', 'souls'); an imaginary *natural* science (anthropocentric; total absence of any concept of natural cause); an imaginary *psychology* (complete failure to understand oneself, interpretations of pleasant or unpleasant general sensations – for instance, the states of *nervus sympathicus* – using the sign language of religious-moral idiosyncrasy, – 'repentance', 'the pangs of conscience', 'temptation by the devil', 'the presence of God'); an imaginary *teleology* ('the kingdom of God', 'the Last Judgment', 'eternal life'). – This entirely *fictitious world* can be distinguished from the world of dreams (to the detriment of the former) in that dreams *reflect* reality while Christianity falsifies, devalues, and negates reality. Once the concept of 'nature' had been invented as a counter to the idea of 'God', 'natural' had to mean 'reprehensible', – that whole fictitious world is rooted in a *hatred* of the natural (– of reality! –), it is the expression of a profound sense of unease concerning reality . . . *But this explains everything.* Who are the only people motivated to *lie their way out of* reality? People who *suffer* from it. But to suffer from reality means that you are a piece of reality that has *gone wrong* . . . The preponderance of feelings of displeasure over feelings of pleasure is the *cause* of that fictitious morality and religion: but a preponderance like this provides the *formula* for decadence . . .

16

A critique of the *Christian idea of God* will necessarily lead to the same conclusion. – A people that still believes in itself will still have its own god. In the figure of this god, a people will worship the conditions that have brought it to the fore, its virtues, – it projects the pleasure it takes in itself, its feeling of power, into a being that it can thank for all of this. Whoever has wealth will want to give; a proud people needs a god to *sacrifice* to . . . On this supposition, religion is a form of gratitude. People are grateful for themselves: and this is why they need a god. – This sort of god has to be able to help and to harm, has to be able to be a friend and an enemy, – people admire him as good but also as bad. The *anti-natural* castration of a god into a god of pure goodness would hold no attraction at all. Evil gods are just as necessary as the good ones: after all, people do not exactly owe their own existence to tolerance and love of humanity . . . Why bother with a god who does not know about anger, revenge, envy, scorn, cunning, violence? who might not even know the exquisite *ardeurs*[8] of victory and destruction? Nobody would understand a god like this: what would be the point of having him for a god? – Of course: when a people is destroyed, when it feels that its belief in the future, its hope for freedom, is irretrievably fading away, when it becomes conscious of subjugation as its first principle of utility and conscious of the virtues of the subjugated as the conditions of its preservation, then its god will *necessarily* change as well. He will become modest and full of fear, he will cringe in corners and recommend 'peace of soul', forbearance, an end to hatred, and 'love' of friends and enemies. He will constantly moralize, he will creep into the crevices of every private virtue, he will be a god for one and all, a private and cosmopolitan god . . . He used to represent a people, the strength of a people, all the aggression and thirst for power in the soul of a people: now he is just the good god . . . In the end, gods have no other choice: *either* they are the will to power – in which case they will still be the gods of a people – *or* they are powerless in the face of power – and then they will necessarily become *good* . . .

17

Whenever the will to power falls off in any way, there will also be physiological decline, decadence. And when the most masculine virtues and drives have been chopped off the god of decadence, he will necessarily turn into a god of the physiologically retrograde, the weak. They do not call themselves weak, they call themselves 'the good' . . . There is no great mystery as to when, historically, the dualistic fiction of good and evil gods becomes possible. With the same instincts they use to reduce their god to 'goodness in itself', the subjugated scratch out the good qualities from their conquerors' god. They take revenge by *demonizing* their masters' god. – The *good* God as well as the devil: both are rotten fruits of decadence. – How can anyone still defer to the naïveté of Christian

---

[8] Ardours.

theologians these days when they decree that the development of the idea of God from the 'God of Israel', the god of a people, to the Christian God, the epitome of all goodness, counts as *progress?* – But even Renan does this. As if Renan had the right to naïveté! The opposite is what strikes the eye. When the presuppositions of *ascending* life, when everything strong, brave, domineering, and proud is eliminated from the idea of God, when he sinks little by little into the symbol of a staff for the weary, a life-preserver for the drowning, when he turns into the God of the poor, the sinners, the sickly, when the predicates of 'saviour' and 'redeemer' are the only ones *left*, the only divine predicates: what does this sort of transformation tell us? this sort of *diminution* in the divine? – Of course: this will increase the size of 'the kingdom of God'. God used to have only his people, his 'chosen' people. But then he took up travelling, just as his people did, and after that he did not sit still until he was finally at home everywhere, the great cosmopolitan, – until he had 'the great numbers' and half the earth on his side. Nonetheless, the God of the 'great numbers', the democrat among gods, did not become a proud, heathen god: he stayed Jewish, he was still the cranny God, the God of all dark nooks and corners, of unhealthy districts the world over! . . . His empire is as it ever was, an empire of the underworld, a hospital, a basement-kingdom, a ghetto-kingdom . . . And he himself, so pale, so weak, so decadent . . . Even the palest of the pale would still get the upper hand over him, our dear Messrs Metaphysician, the conceptual albinos. They spun around him for so long that in the end he was hypnotized by their movement and became a spider, a *metaphysicus* himself. Then he spun the world from out of himself again, – *sub specie Spinozae*[9] –, then he transfigured himself into something increasingly thin and pale, became 'Ideal', became 'pure spirit', became '*absolutum*', became 'thing-in-itself' . . . *The decline of a god*: God became the 'thing-in-itself' . . .

18

The Christian idea of God – God as a god of the sick, God as spider, God as spirit – is one of the most corrupt conceptions of God the world has ever seen; this may even represent a new low in the declining development of the types of god. God having degenerated into a *contradiction of life* instead

---

[9] From the standpoint of Spinoza.

of its transfiguration and eternal *yes*! God as declared aversion to life, to nature, to the will to life! God as the formula for every slander against 'the here and now', for every lie about the 'beyond'! God as the deification of nothingness, the canonization of the will to nothingness! . . .

19

The fact that the stronger races of northern Europe failed to reject the Christian God does not say very much for their skill in religion, not to mention their taste. They really *should* have been able to cope with this sort of diseased and decrepit monster of decadence. But they were damned for their failure: they brought sickness, age, and contradiction into all of their instincts, – they have not *created* any more gods since then. Almost two thousand years and not one new god! And all the while, this pathetic God of Christian monotono-theism instead, acting as if it had any right to exist, like an *ultimatum* and *maximum* of god-creating energy, of the human *creator spiritus*! this hybrid creature of ruin, made from nullity, concept, and contradiction, who sanctions all the instincts of decadence, all the cowardices and exhaustions of the soul! – –

20

I do not want my condemnation of Christianity to lead me to be unfair to a related and – measured by the number of adherents – even more prevalent religion, *Buddhism*. The two belong together as nihilistic religions – they are religions of decadence –, but there are the most striking differences between them. Critics of Christianity owe scholars of India an enormous debt of gratitude for the fact that these two can now be *compared*. – Buddhism is a hundred times more realistic than Christianity, – its body has inherited the art of posing problems in a cool and objective manner, it came *after* a philosophical movement that lasted hundreds of years, the idea of 'God' had already been abandoned before Buddhism arrived. Buddhism is the only really *positivistic* religion in history; even in its epistemology (a strict phenomenalism –) it has stopped saying 'war against *sin*' and instead, giving reality its dues, says 'war against *suffering*'. In sharp contrast to Christianity, it has left the self-deception of moral concepts behind, – it stands, as I put it, *beyond* good and evil. – It is based on *two* physiological facts that it always keeps in mind: *first*, an excessively acute sensitivity that is expressed as a refined susceptibility to pain, and *second*, having lived all too long with concepts and logical procedures, an over-spiritualization that has had the effect of promoting the 'impersonal' instincts at the expense of the personal ones (– at least a few of my readers, 'objective' types like me, will know both these states from their own experience). These physiological conditions give rise to *depression*. The Buddha took hygienic measures against this, including: living out in the open, the wandering life, moderation and a careful diet; caution as far as liquor is concerned; caution when it comes to all affects that create bile or raise the blood temperature; no *worrying* about either yourself or other people. He insists on ideas that produce either calm or amusement – he comes up with methods for phasing out all the others. He sees goodness and kindness as healthy. *Prayer* is out of the question, as is *asceticism*; there is no categorical imperative, no *compulsion* in any form, not even within the monastic community (– which you can always leave –). All of these would be means of exacerbating that already excessive sensitivity. This is why he does not try to rout out heterodoxy; there is nothing his teachings resist more than feelings of revenge, aversion, *ressentiment* (– 'enmity will not bring an end to enmity': the moving refrain of all Buddhism . . .). And rightly so: these are precisely the affects that would be disastrously *unhealthy* with respect to the primary, dietetic objective. The Buddha detects a spiritual fatigue that manifests itself in an all-too-great 'objectivity' (which is to say an individual's diminished sense of self-interest, loss of a centre of gravity, loss of 'egoism'), he combats this by leading even the most spiritual interests directly back to the *person*. In the Buddha's teachings, egoism is a duty: the 'one thing needed', the 'how do *you* get rid of suffering', regulates and restricts the entire spiritual diet (– we might remember a certain Athenian who also waged war on pure 'science', which is to say Socrates, who raised personal egoism to an ethic, even in the realm of problems).

21

Buddhism presupposes a very mild climate, extremely gentle and liberal customs, the complete *absence* of militarism, and the existence of higher, even scholarly classes to give focus to the movement. The highest goals are cheerfulness, quiet, and an absence of desire, and these goals are *achieved*.

Buddhism is not a religion where people only aspire to perfection: perfection is the norm. –

In Christianity, the instincts of the subjugated and oppressed come to the fore: the lowest classes are the ones who look to it for salvation. Casuistry of sin, self-critique, and inquisitions of conscience are sources of *employment*, cures for boredom; affects inspired by a *great power* called God are continuously cultivated (through prayer); the highest is considered unachievable, a gift, 'grace'. There is no sense of a public presence; the hide-away, the unlit room is Christian. The body is an object of hatred, hygiene is rejected as sensuousness; the church defends itself even against cleanliness (– the first Christian edict following the expulsion of the Moors was the closure of the public baths – there were some 270 in Córdoba alone). There is a distinctively Christian sense of cruelty towards yourself and others; hatred of heterodoxy; the will to persecute. Dismal and upsetting thoughts have pride of place; the most highly prized states, described with the highest names, are epileptoid; diet is constructed to promote morbid appearances and over-stimulate the nerves. It is Christian to harbour a deadly hatred of the masters of the earth, the 'nobles' – while maintaining a hidden, secret edge of competition (– they can have the 'body', we *only* want the 'soul' . . .). It is Christian to hate *spirit*, to hate pride, courage, freedom, libertinism of the spirit; it is Christian to hate the *senses*, to hate enjoyment of the senses, to hate joy in general . . .

22

When this Christianity abandoned its first soil, the lowest classes, the *underworld* of the ancient world – when it went looking for power among the barbarian peoples, it stopped presupposing people who were *exhausted* and began presupposing people who were self-lacerated and inwardly feral, – strong but failed human beings. They were dissatisfied with themselves, they suffered from themselves – *not* because of an excessive sensitivity and susceptibility to pain as with Buddhism, but quite the reverse, because of an overpowering desire to *cause* pain, to vent their inner tension in hostile thoughts and action. To conquer barbarians, Christianity needed *barbaric* ideas and values like the sacrifice of the firstborn, the drinking of blood in Communion, the contempt for spirit and culture, torture of all types, sensuous and non-sensuous, the great pomp of the cult. Buddhism is a religion for *mature* people, for kindly, gentle races that have become excessively spiritual and are too sensitive to pain (– Europe is nowhere near this stage): it leads these races back to peace and cheerfulness, to a spiritual diet, to a certain physical fortification. Christianity wants to rule over *beasts of prey*; its method is to make them *sick*, – weakening is the Christian recipe for *domestication*, for 'civilization'. Buddhism is a religion for the end and exhaustion of civilization, while Christianity has not even managed to locate civilization yet – it might lay the foundation for it, though.

23

To say it again, Buddhism is a hundred times colder, truer, more objective. It no longer needs to make its suffering, its susceptibility to pain *respectable* by interpreting it as a sin, – it just says what it thinks: 'I suffer.' But to barbarians there is nothing respectable about suffering: they need an interpretation before they can admit to themselves *that* they suffer (their instincts would sooner have them deny the pain and suffer in silence). The word 'devil' was a real boon to them: they had an overpowering and terrible enemy, – there is no shame in suffering from an enemy like this. –

There are a couple of oriental subtleties at the bottom of Christianity. Above all, Christianity knows that it is a matter of complete indifference whether or not something is true, but it is of supreme importance that people have faith in its truth. Truth and the *faith* that something is true: these sets of interests belong to entirely different, almost opposite worlds – you get to them by fundamentally different paths. In the East, knowing this is almost the *defining characteristic* of a wise man: the Brahmins[10] understand this, Plato understands this, and so does every student of esoteric wisdom. For instance, you do *not* need to presuppose that people *are* sinful in order to understand the *happiness* caused by faith in redemption from sin – you just need to presuppose that people *feel* sinful. But if *faith* is needed above all else, then reason, knowledge, and inquiry have to be discredited: the path to truth becomes the *forbidden* path. – Strong *hope* is a much greater stimulus to life than any piece of individual happiness that actually falls our way. Suffering people need to be sustained by a hope that cannot be refuted by any reality, – that is not *removed* by any fulfilment: hope for a beyond. (Precisely because of this capacity to string unhappy

---

[10] The highest Hindu caste.

people along, the Greeks considered hope to be the evil of evils, the truly *insidious* evil: it was left behind in the box of evils.) – For *love* to be possible, God has to be a person; for the lowest instincts to be involved, God has to be young. A beautiful saint is put up front to excite the ardour of females, and men are given a Mary. This on the presupposition that Christianity wants to rule on ground where Aphrodite or Adonis cults have already determined the *concept* of a cult. The requirement of *chastity* strengthens the vehemence and inward character of the religious instinct – it raises the temperature of the cult, makes the cult more soulful and fanatical. – Love is the state in which people are most prone to see things the way they are *not*. The force of illusion reaches a high point here, and so do the forces that sweeten and *transfigure*. People in love will tolerate more than they usually do, they will put up with anything. A religion had to be invented where people could love: it gets them through the worst in life – they stop noticing the bad aspects completely. – So much for the three Christian virtues: faith, love, and hope. I call them the three Christian *shrewd-nesses*. – Buddhism is too mature, too positivist to be shrewd like this. –

24

I will only touch on the problem of the *origin* of Christianity. The *first* proposition for solving this problem is: Christianity can only be under-stood on the soil where it grew, – it is *not* a counter-movement to the Jewish instinct, it is its natural consequence, a further conclusion drawn by its terrifying logic. In the formula of the redeemer, 'salvation comes from the Jews.' – The *second* proposition is: the psychological type of the Galilean is still recognizable, but it had to assume a completely degenerate form (simultaneously mutilated and full of alien features –) before it came to be used as a *redeemer* of humanity. –

The Jews are the most remarkable people in world history; when faced with the question of being or non-being, they showed an absolutely uncanny awareness and chose being *at any price*: this price was the radical *falsification* of all of nature, all naturalness, all reality, the entirety of the inner world as well as the outer. They defined themselves in *opposition* to all the conditions under which peoples so far had been able to live, had been *allowed* to live, they created from themselves a counter-concept to *natural* conditions, – they took religion, cults, morality, history, and psychology, and twisted them around, one after the other, to the point where they were in irreversible *contradiction to their natural values*. We come across the same phenomenon once again and in immeasurably greater proportions, but nonetheless only as a copy: – the Christian church, unlike the 'holy people', cannot lay claim to originality. This is precisely why the Jews are the *most disastrous* people in world history: they have left such a falsified humanity in their wake that even today Christians can think of themselves as anti-Jewish without understanding that they are the *ultimate conclusion of Judaism*.

In my *Genealogy of Morality* I introduced a psychology of the opposing concepts of *noble* morality and *ressentiment* morality; the latter originating *out of a no* to the former: but this is the Judaeo-Christian morality through and through. The instinct of *ressentiment* said no to everything on earth that represented the *ascending* movement of life: success, power, beauty, self-affirmation; but it could do this only by becoming ingenious and inventing *another* world, a world that viewed *affirmation of life* as evil, as intrinsically reprehensible. Looked at psychologically, Jews are the people with the toughest life force; when transplanted into impossible conditions they took sides with all the instincts of decadence, and they did this freely and out of the most profoundly shrewd sense of self-preservation – *not* because they were dominated by these instincts, but rather because they sensed that these instincts had a power that could be used to prevail *against* 'the world'. The Jews are the opposite of decadents: they had to *act* like decadents to the point of illusion, they knew, with a *non plus ultra* of theatrical genius, how to put themselves at the forefront of all movements of decadence (– like the Christianity of *Paul* –) so they could make these movements into something stronger than any *yes-saying* defenders of life. For the type of person who wields power inside Judaism and Christianity, a *priestly* type, decadence is only a *means*: this type of person has a life-interest in making humanity *sick* and twisting the concepts 'good' and 'evil', 'true' and 'false' to the point where they endanger life and slander the world. –

25

The history of Israel is invaluable because it is typical of all histories where natural values are *denatured*: I will point to five relevant facts here.

Originally, particularly in the time of the kings, Israel had a *correct*, which is to say natural, relation to all things. Its Yahweh expressed a consciousness of power, Israel's joy in itself and hope for itself: Yahweh allowed people to expect victory and salvation, he allowed people to trust that nature would provide what they needed – above all, rain. Yahweh is the god of Israel and *consequently* the god of justice: the logic of every people that wields power with a good conscience. Festival cults express these two sides of a people's self-affirmation: they are grateful for the magnificent destiny that elevated them to their present position, they are grateful for the yearly cycle and all the luck they have had in agriculture and breeding cattle. – This state of things remained the ideal for quite a while, even when it was being brought to a tragic end: anarchy from the inside, Assyrians from the outside. But the people kept their supreme desire alive: that vision of a king who is both good soldier and strict judge: above all, that typical prophet (which is to say critic and satirist of the moment), Isaiah. – But all hopes were left unfulfilled. The old god *could* not do the things he used to do. He should have been let go. What happened? His concept was *altered*, – his concept was *denatured*: this was the price for retaining it. – Yahweh, the god of 'justice', – *not* one with Israel or the expression of a people's self-esteem any more: now just a god, under certain conditions . . . His concept becomes a tool in the hands of priestly agitators who now interpret all happiness as a reward, all unhappiness as a punishment for disobeying God, for 'sins': that most deceitful of all modes of interpretation, the supposed 'moral world order', which turns the natural concepts of 'cause' and 'effect' on their heads once and for all. After people use the concepts of reward and punishment to banish natural causality from the world, they need an *anti-natural* causality: all the rest of un-nature now follows. A God who *demands* – in place of a God who helps and gives advice and is basically a term for any lucky inspiration of courage or self-confidence . . . Morality, not the expression of the conditions of a people's life and growth any more, not its most basic instinct of life any more, but instead something abstract, an opponent of life, – morality as the thorough deterioration of the imagination, as the 'evil eye' for all things. *What* is Jewish morality, *what* is Christian morality? Chance robbed of its innocence; happiness polluted by the concept of 'sin'; well-being as danger, as 'temptation'; physiological ailments poisoned with the worm of conscience . . .

26

The concept of God falsified; the concept of morality falsified: – the Jewish priesthood did not stop at that. The whole *history* of Israel proved useless: get rid of it! – These priests performed a miracle of falsification and we have large portions of the Bible to prove it: in an unparalleled act of scorn for tradition and historical reality, they translated the history of their own people *into religion*, which is to say they made it into an idiotic salvation mechanism of guilt before Yahweh and punishment, of piety to Yahweh and reward. This is the most disgraceful act of historical falsification that has ever taken place, and we would find it much more upsetting if we were not already dulled to the demand for justice *in historicis* by thousands of years of *ecclesiastical* interpretations of history. And philosophers supported the church: the *lie* of 'the moral world order' runs through the entire development of philosophy, even modern philosophy. And what does 'moral world order' mean? That there is a will of God – once and for all – relating to what human beings do and do not do; that the value of a people, of an individual, can be measured by how much or how little each one obeys the will of God; that the will of God is *dominant* in the destiny of a people, an individual, which is to say it punishes and rewards depending on the degree of obedience. The *reality* behind this pitiful lie is: a parasitical type of person who thrives at the expense of all healthy developments of life – the *priest* –, abuses the name of God: he gives the name 'kingdom of God' to a state of affairs where the priests determine the value of things; he gives the name 'will of God' to the means used to reach or maintain this state; he coldly and cynically measures peoples, ages, and individuals according to whether they promote or oppose the domination of the priests. Just look how they operate: in the hands of the Jewish priests, the *great* age in Israel's history was turned into an age of decline; the exile, the long period of hardship, was transformed into an eternal *punishment* for the great age – an age when priests had no significance . . . The priests took the powerful, *very free* characters from Israel's history and refashioned them into miserable cowards and fools, or alternatively into 'godless infidels', depending on what was needed at the time; the priests simplified the psychology of every great event into the idiotic formula 'obedience *or* disobedience to God'. – Advancing to the next stage: the 'will of God', which is to say: the conditions for maintaining power in the hands of the priests, needs to be *divulged*, – this calls for a 'revelation'. In simple terms: an enormous literary falsification is needed, a 'holy scripture' is discovered, – it is published with all due hieratic pomp, with days of repentance and shrieks of lamentation for the long period of 'sin'. The 'will of God' had been firmly fixed for a long time: the whole trouble was that people had distanced themselves from the 'holy scripture' . . . The 'will of God' had already been revealed to Moses . . . What happened? In strict and pedantic formulas, the priests had stipulated once and for all *what they wanted*, 'what the will of God is', specified right down to the large- and small-scale taxes that are their due (– and don't forget the tastiest bits of meat: the priest likes his steak) . . . From now on, everything in life will be arranged so that the priest is *everywhere indispensable*; the holy parasite will show up at all the natural occasions of life, at birth, marriage, illness, death, not to mention sacrifice ('meals'), and *denature* them all: in his words, 'sanctify' them . . . Because there is one thing you need to understand: the parasitism of the priests (or the 'moral world order') takes every natural custom, every natural institution (state, judicial order, marriage, care for the sick and the poor), everything required by the instinct of life, in short, everything *intrinsically* valuable, and renders it fundamentally worthless, of *negative* value: these things now require some extra sanction, – a power is needed *to lend value to things*, to negate what is natural about them and in so doing *create* value . . . The priest devalues nature, he *desecrates* it: this is the price of his existence. – Disobedience to God, which is to say to the priest, to 'the law', now acquires the name 'sin'; the means of 'reconciling yourself with God' are, as expected, the means of guaranteeing an even more fundamental subjugation to the priests: the priest is the only one who can 'redeem' . . . Viewed psychologically, 'sins' are indispensable in every society organized by priests. They are the real levers of power, the priest *lives* on sin, he needs 'sinning' to happen . . . Highest proposition: 'God forgives those who do penance' – in plain language: *those who subordinate themselves to the priest. –*

27

Christianity grew up on this sort of *false* soil, where every nature, every natural value, every *reality* ran counter to the deepest instincts of the ruling class; accordingly, Christianity assumed the form of a deadly hostility to reality, a hostility unsurpassed to this day. The 'holy people' had kept only the priestly values, priestly words for things; with terrifyingly logical consistency, they had detached themselves from all other powers on earth, considering them 'unholy', 'worldly', 'sinful'; now this people produced a final formula for their instinct, one that was logical to the point of self-annihilation: as *Christianity*, they negated the final form of reality, the 'holy people', the 'chosen people', *Jewish* reality itself. It is a first-rate case: the small, rebel movement christened with the name of Jesus of Nazareth is the Jewish instinct *once again*, – in other words, the priestly instinct that could no longer tolerate priests for its reality, the invention of an existence that is even more *threadbare*, of a worldview that is even more *unreal* than what is dictated by the organization of a church. Christianity *negates* the church . . .

This rebellion that Jesus has been understood or *misunderstood* to have caused – I cannot imagine what it was directed *against* if not the Jewish church (using the word 'church' in precisely the sense we understand it today). It was a rebellion against the 'good and the just', against the 'saints of Israel', against the social hierarchy – *not* against its corruption, but rather against caste, privilege, order, formula; it was a *refusal to believe* in 'higher men', a *no* said to everything priestly or theologian-like. But the hierarchy that was put into question (however briefly) was the house on stilts that had allowed the Jewish people to survive in the middle of the 'water', it was the *last* hard-won chance for survival, the residuum of their independent political existence: an attack on this was an attack on the deepest instinct, on the most stubborn will to life that had ever existed in any people on earth. This holy anarchist who called out to the lowly people, the outcasts and the 'sinners', the *Chandala* within Judaism, telling them to protest against the dominant order – with a speech that (if the Gospels are to be trusted) would get you banished to Siberia even today – this holy anarchist was a political criminal, to the extent that political criminals were possible in an *absurdly apolitical* society. This is what brought him to the cross: the proof is written on the cross. He died for his *own* guilt, – no matter how many times people say it, there is simply no evidence that he died for anyone else's guilt.

28

It is a completely different question whether this sort of opposition was what he had in mind, – or whether he was just *seen* as representing this opposition. And this brings me to the problem of the *psychology of the redeemer*. – I have to admit, there are not many books I have found as difficult as the Gospels. My difficulties are different from those demonstrated by the scholarly curiosity of the German spirit in one of its most unforgettable triumphs. The days are long gone when, like every young scholar, I took great pleasure in the work of the inimitable Strauss, read at the shrewd and plodding pace of a refined philologist. I was twenty then: now I am too serious for this. What do I care about the contradictions in the 'tradition'? And besides, how can anyone call saints' legends a 'tradition'! The stories of the saints are the most ambiguous pieces of literature in existence: to apply scientific method to them *in the absence of any other records* seems to me like a project that is doomed from the start – just scholars wasting time . . .

29

What I *do* care about is the psychological type of the redeemer. After all, the Gospels *might* actually provide information on this point, in spite of themselves, however garbled or crammed with alien features it might be: just as the psychology of Francis of Assisi can be found in his legends, in spite of *themselves*. *Not* the truth about what he did, what he said, how he really died: but rather the question: Can we even conceive of his type any more? Has it been 'passed down'? – The attempts that I have seen to read the Gospels even as the *history* of a 'soul' are proofs to me of a hateful sort of psychological thoughtlessness. Mr Renan, this buffoon *in psychologicis*, imported the most *inappropriate* concepts imaginable into his explanation of Jesus' type: the concept of *genius* and that of *hero* ('*héros*'). But if anything is unevangelical, it is the concept of a hero. The polar opposite of struggle, of any feeling of doing-battle, has become instinct here: an incapacity for resistance has become morality here ('resist not evil', the most profound saying of the Gospels, the key to their meaning in a certain sense), blessedness in peace, in gentleness, in an *inability* to be an enemy. What are the 'glad tidings'? That the true life, the eternal life has been found – it is not just a promise, it exists, it is in *each of you*: as a life of love, as a love without exceptions or rejections, without distance. Everyone is a child of God – Jesus did not claim any special privileges – as a child of God, everyone is equal to everyone else . . . And to make Jesus into a *hero*! – Even this word 'genius': what a misunderstanding it is! Our whole notion, our cultural notion of 'spirit' made absolutely no sense in the world where Jesus lived. The rigorous language of physiology would use a different word here: the word 'idiot'. We are familiar with a condition where the *sense of touch* is pathologically over-sensitive and recoils from all contact, from grasping any solid objects. Just follow this sort of physiological *habitus*[11] to its ultimate consequences – as an instinct of hatred for *every* reality, as a flight into the 'unimaginable', into the 'inconceivable', as an aversion to every formula, to every concept of space and time, to everything solid, to every custom, institution, church, as a being-at-home in a world that has broken off contact with every type of reality, a world that has become completely 'internal', a 'true' world, an 'eternal' world . . . 'The kingdom of God is *in each of you*' . . .

30

The instinct of hatred for reality: the consequence of an extreme over-sensitivity and capacity for suffering that does not want to be 'touched' at all because it feels every contact too acutely.

The instinctive exclusion of all aversion, all hostility, all boundaries and distances in feelings: the consequence of an extreme over-sensitivity and capacity for suffering that perceives every reluctance, every needing-to-be-reluctant as itself an unbearable *pain* (which is to say *harmful, proscribed* by the instinct of self-preservation) and only experiences bliss (pleasure) when it stops resisting everyone and anything, including evil, – love as the only, the *final* possibility for life . . .

These are the two *physiological realities* on which, out of which, the doctrine of redemption has grown. I call it a subsequent and refined development of hedonism on a thoroughly morbid foundation. Its closest relation is Epicureanism, paganism's doctrine of redemption, although Epicureanism has a strong dose of Greek vitality and nerves. Epicurus is a *typical* decadent: I was the first to recognize this. – The fear of pain, even of infinitesimal amounts of pain – this could end up *only* as a *religion of love* . . .

31

I have already given away the answer to my problem. It presupposes that the type of the redeemer has been preserved for us only in a distorted form.

---

[11] Condition.

This distortion is in itself very plausible: there are many reasons why a type like this could not have stayed pure, whole, or free of embellishments. The environment where this strange figure moved must have left its traces on him; but even more, the type would have been marked by the history, the *destiny* of the first Christian community, and retroactively enhanced with features that can only be understood as emerging from war and intended as propaganda. The strange, sick world that the Gospels introduce to us – a world like a Russian novel, where the dregs of society, nerve cases, and 'childlike' idiocy all seem to converge – this world, in any case, would have *coarsened* the type; the first disciples in particular: when faced with a being awash in symbols and incomprehensibilities, they had to translate it into their own crudeness in order to make head or tail of it, – the type did not *exist* for them until they had reduced it to familiar forms . . . The prophet, the Messiah, the future judge, the teacher of morality, the miracle worker, John the Baptist – all so many opportunities for mistaking the type . . . Finally, we should not underestimate the *proprium*[12] of all great (which is to say all sectarian) worship: it effaces the initial, often embarrassingly foreign, features and idiosyncrasies from the object of worship – *it does not even see them.* It is a pity that there was no Dostoevsky living near this most interesting decadent, I mean someone with an eye for the distinctive charm that this sort of mixture of sublimity, sickness, and childishness has to offer. A final aspect to be noted: being decadent, the type *could* in fact have been peculiarly diverse and contradictory: this possibility cannot be completely ruled out. Nonetheless, everything speaks against this: the tradition would have had to be strangely faithful and objective if this were the case: and we have evidence to the contrary. Meanwhile, there is a gaping contradiction between, on the one hand, the preacher from the mountain, sea, and meadows, who appeared like a Buddha on soil that was not very Indian, and, on the other hand, that fanatic of aggression, the mortal enemy of theologians and priests, snidely celebrated by Renan as *'le grand maître en ironie'*.[13] For my part, I have no doubt that the turbulent state of Christian propaganda infused the type of the master with ample quantities of bile (and even *esprit*): everyone knows how sectarians won't think twice before turning their masters into their own *apologetics*. When the first congregation needed a judging, quarrelsome, wrathful, malicious, nit-picking theologian to use *against* theologians, they *created* a 'God' to

---

[12] Characteristic.   [13] 'The great master of irony'.

28

fit these requirements: just as they did not hesitate to put words into his mouth, those totally unevangelical words that they could not do without, 'Second Coming', 'Last Judgment', every type of temporal expectation and promise. –

32

It bears repeating that I am against introducing the fanatic into the type of the redeemer: Renan's term *impérieux* nullifies the type all by itself. The 'glad tidings' are just that the contradiction is gone; the kingdom of heaven belongs to the *children*; the faith expressed here is not a hard-won faith, – it is here, it has been from the start, it is, as it were, an infantilism that has receded into spirituality. Physiologists, at least, are familiar with cases where delayed puberty is the result of an organism's degeneration. – A faith like this does not get angry, does not lay blame, does not defend itself: it does not brandish 'the sword', – it does not have the slightest suspicion that it might ever separate things from each other. It does not prove itself with miracles, rewards, or promises, certainly not 'through scriptures': at every moment it is its own miracle, its own reward, its own proof, its own 'kingdom of God'. This faith does not formulate itself either – it *lives*, it resists formulas. Of course, accidents of environment, language, and context will dictate a determinate sphere of concepts: the first form of Christianity dealt *only* with Jewish-Semitic concepts (– the eating and drinking at the Last Supper is one such concept, one that was badly misused by the church, which misused everything Jewish). But you should guard against seeing this as more than a sign language, a semiology, an opportunity for allegories, an excuse for parables. For this anti-realist, speech is made possible precisely by *not* taking words literally. Among Indians he would have used the Sankhyam[14] concepts, among Chinese the concepts of Lao-tse[15] – and never known the difference. – Jesus could be called a 'free spirit', using the phrase somewhat loosely – he does not care for solid things: the word *kills*, everything solid *kills*. The concept, the *experience* of 'life' as only he knew it, repelled every type of word, formula, law, faith, or dogma. He spoke only about what was inside him most deeply: 'life' or 'truth' or 'light' are his words for the innermost, – he saw everything else, the whole of reality, the whole of nature, language

---

[14] Sankhya is a Hindu system of philosophy.   [15] I.e. Taoist concepts.

itself, as having value only as a sign, a parable. – It is very important to be clear about this, however great the temptation of Christian (and, I should say, *ecclesiastical*) prejudice really is: this sort of symbolism *par excellence* is positioned outside all religion, all cult concepts, all history, all natural science, all experience of the world, all knowledge, all politics, all psychology, all books, all art – his 'knowing' is just *pure stupidity* concerning the fact *that* things like this exist. He does not know anything about *culture*, even in passing, he does not need to struggle against it, – he does not negate it . . . The same is true about the *state*, about the whole civic order and society, about *work*, about war – he never had any reason to negate 'the world', the ecclesiastical concept of 'world' never occurred to him . . . *Negation* is out of the question for him. – Dialectic is missing as well, there is no conception that a belief, a 'truth', could be grounded in reasons (– *his* proofs are inner 'lights', inner feelings of pleasure and self-affirmations, pure 'proofs of strength' –). A doctrine like this *cannot* contradict, it has no idea that there are, that there *could* be any other doctrines, it has no idea how even to form the thought of an opposing judgment . . . If it comes across an opposing judgment, it will feel deeply sympathetic and grieve over this 'blindness' – since it sees the 'light' – but it would not offer any objections . . .

33

The concepts of guilt and punishment are completely missing from the psychology of the 'evangel'; so is the concept of reward. 'Sin', any distance between God and man: these are abolished, – *this is what the 'glad tidings' are all about*. Blessedness is not a promise, it has no strings attached: it is the *only* reality – everything else is just a symbol used to speak about it . . .

This state projects itself into a new *practice*, the genuinely evangelical practice. Christians are not characterized by their 'faith': Christians act, they are characterized by a *different* way of acting. By the fact that they do not offer any resistance, in their words or in their heart, to people who are evil to them. By the fact that they do not make any distinction between foreigners and natives, between Jews and non-Jews ('the neighbour' is really the co-religionist, the Jew). By the fact that they do not get angry at anyone or belittle anyone. By the fact that they do not let themselves be seen in or involved with ('sworn in' to) courts of law. By the fact that they would not get a divorce under any circumstances, even when the wife has been proven unfaithful. – All of this is fundamentally a single proposition, all of this is the result of a single instinct –

The life of the redeemer was nothing other than *this* practice, – even his death was nothing else . . . He no longer needed formulas, rites for interacting with God – or even prayer. He had settled his accounts with the whole Jewish doctrine of atonement and reconciliation; he knew how the *practice* of life is the only thing that can make you feel 'divine', 'blessed', 'evangelic', like a 'child of God' at all times. 'Atonement' and 'praying for forgiveness' are *not* the way to God: *only the evangelical practice* leads to God, in fact it *is* 'God' – What the evangel *did away with* was the Judaism of the concepts of 'sin', 'forgiveness of sin', 'faith', 'redemption through faith' – the whole Jewish *church doctrine* was rejected in the 'glad tidings'.

The profound instinct for how we must *live* to feel as if we are 'in heaven', to feel as if we are 'eternal', given that we do not feel *remotely* as if we are 'in heaven' when we behave in any other way: this, and this alone, is the psychological reality of 'redemption'. – A new way of life, *not* a new faith . . .

34

If I understand anything about this great symbolist, it is that he accepted only *inner* realities as realities, as 'truths', – that he considered everything else, everything natural, temporal, spatial, historical to be just a sign, an excuse for a parable. The concept 'son of man' is not some concrete person belonging to history, someone individual or unique, but rather an 'eternal' facticity, a psychological symbol that has been redeemed from the concept of time. The same holds true again and in the highest sense for the *God* of this typical symbolist, for the 'kingdom of God', for the 'kingdom of heaven', and for the filial relation to God. Nothing is less Christian than the *ecclesiastical crudity* of God as a *person*, of a 'kingdom of God' that is *yet to come*, a 'kingdom of heaven' in the *beyond*, a 'son of God' as the *second person* in the Trinity. This is all (if you will excuse the expression) one big *fist* in the eye[16] (and what an eye it is!) of the evangel; a *world-historical cynicism* in the derision of symbols . . . But it

---

[16] The German phrase 'fist in the eye' means a misfit, two things that do not go together well.

is obvious – although probably not to everyone – what the signs 'father' and 'son' suggest: the word 'son' expresses the *entrance* into a feeling of the total transfiguration of all things (blessedness), and the word 'father' expresses *this feeling itself*, the feeling of eternity, of perfection. – I am ashamed to think what the church has made out of this symbolism: hasn't it stuck an Amphitryon story[17] on the threshold to the Christian 'faith'? And a dogma of 'immaculate conception' into the bargain? . . . *But this just maculates the conception – –*

The 'kingdom of heaven' is a state of the heart – not something lying 'above the earth' or coming 'after death'. The whole idea of a natural death is *missing* from the evangel: death is not a bridge, not a transition, it is absent because it belongs to an entirely different, merely apparent world that is useful only as a symbol. The 'hour of death' is *not* a Christian concept – 'hours', time, and the physical life with its crises just do not exist for the teacher of the 'glad tidings' . . . The 'kingdom of God' is not something that you wait for; it does not have a yesterday or a day after tomorrow, it will not arrive in a 'thousand years' – it is an experience of the heart; it is everywhere and it is nowhere . . .

35

This bearer of 'glad tidings' died the way he lived, the way he *taught* – *not* 'to redeem humanity', but instead to demonstrate how people need to live. His bequest to humanity was a *practice*: his behaviour towards the judges, towards the henchmen, the way he acted in the face of his accusers and every type of slander and derision, – his conduct on the *cross*. He does not offer any resistance, he does not defend his rights, he does not make a single move to avert the worst, what is more, *he invites it* . . . And he begs, he suffers, he loves *with* those, *in* those people who did him evil . . . The whole evangel is contained in the words to the *thieves* on the cross. 'That was a truly *divine* man, a "child of God"', said the thief. 'If this is how you feel', the redeemer replied, *'then you are in paradise*, then you too are a child of God . . .' *Not* to defend yourself, *not* to get angry, *not* to lay blame . . . But not to resist evil either, – to *love* it . . .

---

[17] Amphitryon is a character in Greek myth whose virgin bride is seduced by Zeus.

36

– We alone, we spirits *who have become free*, have the requisite presuppositions for understanding what nineteen centuries have misunderstood, – the honesty that has become instinct and passion, that wages war on the 'holy lie' above all other lies . . . People have been unspeakably far removed from our affectionate and cautious neutrality, from that discipline of spirit needed to figure out such strange, such delicate matters: with unabashed selfishness, people have always wanted only what was best for *themselves*, people have constructed the *church* out of the opposite of the evangel . . .

Anyone looking for signs that an ironic divinity is keeping his finger in the great game of the world will find them in the *enormous question mark* called Christianity. The fact that humanity knelt down before the opposite of the origin, the meaning, the *right* of the evangel, the fact that in the concept of 'church', humanity canonized the very thing the 'bearer of glad tidings' felt to be *beneath* him, *behind* him – you will not find a greater example of *world-historical irony* – –

37

– Our age is proud of its historical sense: so how could it convince itself of this piece of nonsense, that Christianity began with this *crude fable of a miracle worker and redeemer*, – and that everything spiritual and symbolic developed only later on? To the contrary: the history of Christianity – starting, in fact, with the death on the cross – is the story of the progressively cruder misunderstanding of an *original* symbolism. Every time Christianity expanded to greater and cruder masses of people whose presuppositions were increasingly remote from the presupposition under which it arose, it became increasingly necessary *to vulgarize Christianity and make it barbaric*, – Christianity soaked up doctrines and rites from all the *subterranean* cults of the *imperium Romanum* and bits of nonsense from all kinds of sick reason. Christianity's faith was fated to become as sick, base, and vulgar as the sick, base, and vulgar needs it catered to. *Sick barbarism* itself finally achieved power in the church, – the church, this form of deadly hostility to everything honest, to every *height* of the soul, to every discipline of spirit, to everything kind and candid in humanity. – Christian values – *noble* values: we alone, we spirits *who have become free*, have restored this opposition, the greatest opposition of values there is! – –

38

I won't hold back a sigh at this point. There are days when I am haunted by a feeling that is blacker than the blackest melancholy – a *contempt for humanity*. And just to remove any doubts about *what* I despise, *who* I despise: people these days, the people I have been fated to call my contemporaries. People these days – I feel suffocated by their filthy breath . . . Like all researchers I have a lot of tolerance for the past, which is to say I exercise *generous* self-restraint: I go through the madhouse worlds of whole millennia, whether they are called 'Christianity', 'Christian faith', or the 'Christian church' with a sort of bleak caution, – I am careful not to hold humanity responsible for its mental illnesses. But my feelings suddenly change and erupt as soon as I come to more recent times, to *our* times. Our age *knows better* . . . What used to be just sickness is indecency today, – it is indecent to be a Christian these days. *And this is where my disgust begins.* – I look around: there are no words left for what used to be called 'truth', we cannot stand to hear priests even mention the word 'truth' any more. These days anyone with even the most modest claim to honesty *has* to know that every sentence pronounced by a theologian, a priest, a pope, is not only wrong, it is a *lie*, – and he is not free to lie out of 'innocence' or 'ignorance' any more. The priest knows as well as anyone that there is no 'God' any more, that there is no such thing as 'sin', or the 'redeemer', – that 'free will' and the 'moral world order' are *lies*: – the seriousness, the profound self-overcoming of spirit does not *allow* people *not* to know this any more . . . *All* church concepts are known for what they are, the most malicious counterfeits that exist to *devalue* nature and natural values; the priests themselves are known for what they are, the most dangerous type of parasite, the true poisonous spiders of life . . . We know, our *consciences* are conscious of it these days –, just what value those uncanny inventions of the priests and the church have, *how they were used* to reduce humanity to such a state of self-desecration that the sight of it fills you with disgust – the concepts 'beyond', 'Last Judgment', 'immortality of the soul', the 'soul' itself; these are instruments of torture, these are systems of cruelty that enable the priests to gain control, maintain control . . . Everyone knows this: *and yet everything goes on as before*. Where are the remnants of self-respect or any sense of decency when even our statesmen, who are generally very impartial and thoroughly anti-Christian in practice, still call themselves Christian and take communion? . . . A young prince at the head of his regiments, whose magnificence is an expression of the selfishness and self-importance of his people, – he calls himself Christian without a *hint* of shame! . . . So *who* exactly does Christianity negate? What does it consider 'worldly'? The fact that people are soldiers, judges, patriots; that they defend themselves; that they defend their honour; that they do what is best for themselves; that they are *proud* . . . Every practice at every moment, every instinct, every value judgment that people *act* on is anti-Christian these days: what *miscarriages of duplicity* modern people are, that in spite of all this they are *not ashamed* to call themselves Christians! – – –

39

– I will come back, I will tell the *true* history of Christianity. – Even the word 'Christianity' is a misunderstanding –, there was really only one Christian, and he died on the cross. The 'evangel' *died* on the cross. What was called 'evangel' after that was the opposite of what *he* had lived: a '*bad* tidings', a *dysangel*. It is false to the point of absurdity to think that Christians are characterized by their 'beliefs', like a belief in salvation through Christ: only the *practice* of Christianity is really Christian, *living* like the man who died on the cross . . . A life like this is *still* possible today, for *certain* people it is even necessary: true, original Christianity will always be possible . . . *Not* a believing but a doing, above all a *not*-doing-much, a different *being* . . . States of consciousness, any sort of belief, such as taking something to be true, are (as every psychologist knows) trivial matters of fifth-rate importance compared to the value of the instincts: to put it more rigorously, the whole idea of spiritual causation is false. To reduce Christianity, to reduce being Christian to a set of claims taken to be true, to a simple phenomenalism of consciousness, is to negate Christianity. *In fact, there have never been any Christians.* 'Christians', the people who have been called Christian for two thousand years, are just a psychological self-misunderstanding. Examined more closely and in *spite* of all 'belief', they have been governed *only* by instincts,– and *what instincts they are!* – In every age (with Luther, for instance), 'belief' has just been a cloak, a cover, a *curtain* behind which the instincts play their game –, a shrewd *blindness* about the dominance of *certain* instincts . . . 'Faith' – I have already called this the characteristic *shrewdness* of Christianity, – people have always talked about 'faith', they have always *acted* from instinct . . .

In the world of Christian representations, nothing that happens has any bearing on reality: on the contrary, we have recognized the instinct of hatred *against* every reality as the driving, the only driving element, at the root of Christianity. What follows from this? That even *in psychologicis*, this is a radical error, which is to say it is the *substance*, which is to say it determines the essence. Throw out a *single* idea, put a single reality in its place – and the whole of Christianity would fade into nothing! – Seen from above, this strangest fact of all, a religion that has not only been determined by errors but has been creative to the point of genius *only* with those errors that damage and poison life and the heart – this religion is a *spectacle for the gods*, – for those deities, for example, who are also philosophers and who I met in those famous dialogues on Naxos.[18] As soon as they (– and we!) get over any initial feelings of *disgust*, they become grateful for the spectacle of the Christian: perhaps the miserable little star called 'earth' merits a divine glance, divine regard, only because of *this* curiosity . . . Let us not underestimate the Christian: the Christian, false *to the point of innocence*, is far above the apes, – with respect to Christians, a certain well-known theory of descent becomes a mere politeness . . .

40

– The disastrous fate of the evangel was sealed with his death, – it hung on the 'cross' . . . It took this death, this unexpected, ignominious death, it took the cross, which was generally reserved for the rabble, – it took this horrible paradox to bring the disciples face to face with the true riddle: '*Who was that? What was that?*' – The feeling of shock and profound offence, the suspicion that a death like this might *refute* their case, the terrible question mark 'Why this, of all things?' – this situation is only too easy to understand. Everything really *needed* to be necessary, sensible, rational, supremely rational here; a disciple's love is not left to chance. Cracks only began to appear at this point: '*Who* killed him? *Who* was his natural enemy?' – these questions jumped out like a bolt of lightning. Answer: the Jewish *rulers*, their upper class. At this point, people started to feel as if they were in revolt *against* the order, they started to understand Jesus as having been *in revolt against the order*. Before this, his image had

---

[18] These dialogues are by Nietzsche himself, and were still unpublished when he wrote *The Anti-Christ*.

not had any belligerent, no-saying, no-doing features at all; in fact, he was the opposite of all this. The small congregation had evidently *failed* to understand the main point, the exemplary character of dying in this way, the freedom, the superiority *over* every feeling of *ressentiment*: – a sign of how little they understood about him in general! Jesus could not have wanted anything more from his death itself than publicly to give his doctrine its strongest test, to *prove* it . . . But his disciples were far from being able to *forgive* this death, – which would have been evangelical in the highest sense; or even more, from *offering themselves up* for a similar death in the sweet and gentle calm of the heart . . . *Revenge* resurfaced, the most *un*evangelical feeling of all. It was impossible for this death to be the end of the matter: 'retaliation' was needed, 'judgment' (– and really, what could be less evangelical than 'retaliation', 'punishment', 'passing judgment'!). Once again, the popular expectation of a messiah came to the fore; it was considered a historical moment: the 'kingdom of God' will come to judge its enemies . . . But this is a misunderstanding of everything: the 'kingdom of God' as a closing ceremony, as a promise! The evangel was precisely the existence, the fulfilment, the *actuality* of this 'kingdom'. A death like this *was* this very 'kingdom of God' . . . Only at this point did people take all the contempt and bitterness against the Pharisees and theologians and put it into the master's type, – and in doing so, *make* him into a Pharisee and theologian! On the other hand, the frenzied adoration of these unhinged souls could not tolerate Jesus' evangelical teaching that everybody has an equal right to be a child of God; their revenge was to *elevate* Jesus in an extravagant manner, distancing him from themselves: just as the Jews once took revenge on their enemies by separating off their God and raising him up into the heights. The one God and the one son of God: both are products of *ressentiment* . . .

41

– And from now on there is the ridiculous problem of 'how *could* God have let this happen!' The unbalanced reason of the small community found a horribly absurd answer: God gave his son to forgive sins, as a *sacrifice*. This brought the evangel to an end in one fell swoop. The *guilt sacrifice*, and in fact in its most revolting, barbaric form, the sacrifice of the *innocent* for the sins of the *guilty*! What gruesome paganism! – In fact, Jesus had done away with the very idea of 'guilt', – he denied that there was any gap between God and man, he *lived* this unity of God as man as *his* 'glad tidings' . . . And *not* as his privilege! – From now on, a number of different things started seeping into the type of the redeemer: the doctrines of judgment and return, the doctrine of death as a sacrifice, and the doctrine of the *resurrection*; and at this point the whole idea of 'blessedness', the solitary reality of the evangel, vanishes with a wave of the hand – and all for the sake of a state *after* death! . . . With the rabbinical impudence that characterizes everything about him, Paul put this interpretation, this *perversion* of an interpretation into a logical form: '*if* Christ did not rise from the dead, then our faith is in vain'. – And in one fell swoop, the evangel becomes the most contemptible of all unfulfillable promises, the *outrageous* doctrine of personal immortality . . . Paul himself still taught it as a *reward*! . . .

42

You can see just *what* came to an end with the death on the cross: a new, a completely original attempt at a Buddhistic peace movement, at an actual *happiness on earth, not* just a promissory one. And this – as I have already pointed out – is the fundamental difference between the two religions of decadence: Buddhism does not promise, it delivers, Christianity promises everything and *delivers nothing*. – On the heels of the 'glad tidings' came *the very worst ones of all*: Paul's. Paul epitomizes a type that is the antithesis of the 'bringer of glad tidings', the genius in hatred, in the vision of hatred, in the merciless logic of hatred. And *how much* this dysangelist sacrificed to hatred! Above all, the redeemer: he nailed him to his *own* cross. The life, example, teachings, death, meaning, and rights of the whole evangel – nothing was left after this hatred-inspired counterfeiter realized what he and he alone could use. *Not* reality, *not* the historical truth! . . . And once again, the Jew's priestly instinct perpetrated the same enormous crime against history, – he simply crossed out Christianity's yesterday, its day before yesterday, *he invented for himself a history of the first Christianity.* Even more, he falsified the history of Israel once again, to make it look like the prehistory of his *own* actions: all the prophets have talked about *his* 'redeemer' . . . Later, the church even falsified the history of human-ity into the prehistory of Christianity . . . The type of the redeemer, the doctrine, the practice, the death, the meaning of his death, even the after-math of his death – nothing was left untouched, nothing was left bearing any resemblance to reality. Paul simply shifted the emphasis of this whole being, putting it *behind* this being, – into the *lie* of Jesus' 'resurrection'. Basically, he had no use whatsoever for the life of the redeemer, – he needed the death on the cross *and* something else besides . . . To take this Paul (whose homeland was the centre of the Stoic enlightenment) at his word when he takes a hallucination and dresses it up as a *proof* that the redeemer *still* lives, or even to accept that he *had* this hallucination in the first place, would be a true *niaiserie*[19] on the part of a psychologist: Paul wanted the end, and *consequently* he wanted the means to it as well . . . What he did not believe himself was believed by the idiots he threw *his* doctrines to. – What *he* needed was *power*; with Paul, the priests wanted to return to power, – he could only use ideas, doctrines, symbols that would tyrannize the masses and form the herds. – *What* was the only thing that Mohammed would later borrow from Christianity? Paul's invention, his method of priestly tyranny, of forming the herds, the belief in immortality – *which is to say the doctrine of the 'judgment'* . . .

43

When the emphasis of life is put on the 'beyond' rather than on life itself – when it is put *on nothingness* –, then the emphasis has been completely removed from life. The enormous lie of personal immortality destroys all reason, everything natural in the instincts, – everything beneficial and life-enhancing in the instincts, everything that guarantees the future, now arouses mistrust. To live *in this way*, so that there is no *point* to life any more, *this* now becomes the 'meaning' of life . . . What is the point of public spirit, of being grateful for your lineage or for your ancestors, what is the point of working together, of confidence, of working towards any sort of common goal or even keeping one in mind? . . . These are all so many 'temptations', so many diversions from the 'proper path' – '*one thing* is necessary' . . . That as immortal souls, everyone is on the same level as everyone else, that in the commonality of all beings, the 'salvation' of *each* individual lays claim to an eternal significance, that the small-minded and the half-mad can think well of themselves, that the laws of nature are constantly *broken* for their sake – you cannot heap enough contempt on this, every type of selfishness increasing *shamelessly* to the point of

---

[19] Gullibility.

infinity. And yet Christianity owes its *victory* to *this* miserable flattery of personal vanity, – it is precisely the failures, the rebellion-prone, the badly developed, all the rejects and dejects of humanity, that Christianity has won over by these means. 'Salvation of the soul' – in plain language: 'the world revolves around *me*' . . . The poisonous doctrine '*equal* rights for everyone' – Christianity disseminated this the most thoroughly; from out of the most secret corners of its bad instincts, Christianity has waged a deadly war on every feeling of respect and distance between people, which is to say the *presupposition* of every elevation, of every growth of culture, – it has used the *ressentiment* of the masses as its *main weapon* against *us*, against everything on earth that is noble, joyful, magnanimous, against our happiness on earth . . . Granting 'immortality' to every Tom, Dick, and Harry has been the most enormous and most vicious attempt to assassinate *noble* humanity. – *And* let us not underestimate the disaster that Christianity has brought even into politics! Nobody is courageous enough for special privileges these days, for the rights of the masters, for feelings of self-respect and respect among equals – for *a pathos of distance* . . .[20] Our politics is *sick* from this lack of courage! – The aristocraticism of mind has been undermined at its depths by the lie of the equality of souls; and when the belief in the 'privileges of the majority' creates (and it *will create*) revolutions, do not doubt for a minute that it is Christianity, that it is *Christian* value judgments these revolutions are translating into blood and crimes! Christianity is a rebellion of everything that crawls on the ground against everything that has *height*: the evangel of the 'lowly' *makes* things lower . . .

44

– The Gospels are invaluable testimony to the already inescapable corruption *within* the first congregation. With the logical cynicism of a rabbi, Paul would later complete a process of decline that had already begun with the death of the redeemer. – You cannot read these Gospels carefully enough; every word is problematic. I have to confess – and please do not think badly of me for saying so – but this is what makes them a first-rate pleasure for a psychologist, – they are the *opposite* of naïve corruption, they are refinement *par excellence*, they are psychological corruption raised to

[20] The 'pathos of distance' was an important concept for Nietzsche: see, e.g., *BGE* 257 and *GM* I.2.

an art. The Gospels stand on their own. The Bible in general is without equal. We are among Jews: the *first* thing to note, so as not to lose the thread completely. The pretence at 'holiness' is conducted with a talent bordering on genius (no book or person has ever come close), this counterfeiting of words and gestures as an *art form* is not some one-off, accidental talent, some exception of nature. It is part of the *race*. As the art of the holy lie, Christianity brings to perfection the whole of Judaism, a Jewish preparatory exercise and technique developed over many hundreds of years with the greatest seriousness. The Christian, this *ultima ratio* of lies, is the Jew once again – or even *three* times again . . . – The fundamental will to use only those ideas, symbols, and attitudes that have been proven by the practice of the priests, the instinctual rejection of any *other* practice, any *other* perspective on what is valuable or useful – that is not only tradition, it is *endowment*: only as endowment would it act like nature. The whole of humanity, even the best minds of the best ages – (with a single exception, someone who is perhaps just inhuman –) have allowed themselves to be deceived. The Gospels were read as the *book of innocence* . . .: which is no small indication of the ultimate artistry with which this piece of drama has been played out. – Of course: if we were to *see* all these bizarre fools and artificial saints even in passing, there would be an end to it, – and precisely because *I* cannot read a single word without seeing gestures, *I am putting an end to it* . . . I cannot stand a certain way they have of rolling their eyes upwards. – Luckily, the vast majority of people treat books only as *literature* – – Do not be fooled: they say 'judge not!' but then they send to hell everything that gets in their way. By letting God be the judge, they themselves are the judge: by exalting God, they exalt themselves; by *demanding* the very virtues that they themselves have – more, that they *need* to have to stay on top –, they give themselves the exalted appearance of struggling for virtue, of fighting to master the virtues. 'We live, we die, we sacrifice ourselves *for goodness*' (– the 'truth', 'the light', the 'kingdom of God'): in point of fact, they are just doing what they cannot fail to do. They act like sycophants, sit in corners, and live shadowy lives in the shadows, and then they make this their *duty*: as a duty, their lives seem humble, and this humility is one more proof of piety . . . Oh, this humble, chaste, charitable type of duplicity! 'Virtue itself is our witness' . . . You can read these Gospels as books that use *morality* as a technique for seduction: morality gets taken over by these petty people, – they know all about morality! – Morality is the best way of *leading people around by the*

41

nose! – The truth of the matter is that the highly conscious *conceit of being chosen* is putting on airs of modesty here: people firmly put *themselves*, the 'congregation', the 'fair and the good' on one side, the side of 'truth' – and everything else, 'the world', on the other . . . *This* was the most disastrous type of megalomania the world has ever seen: petty, misshapen liars and idiots started claiming the ideas of 'God', 'truth', 'light', 'spirit', 'love', 'wisdom', 'life' for themselves, as synonyms for themselves, in order to define themselves over and against the 'world', superlative little Jews, ready for any type of madhouse, took values and twisted them around to their *own* liking, as if only the Christian were the meaning, the salt, the measure, as well as the *ultimate tribunal* on everything else . . . The whole disaster was made possible only by the fact that a related, a racially related, type of megalomania already existed in the world, the *Jewish* type: as soon as the gap between Jew and Judaeo-Christian appeared, the latter had no choice except to use the same methods of self-preservation dictated by the Jewish instinct *against* the Jews themselves, while the Jews had only ever used them against *non*-Jews. The Christian is just a Jew with less rigorous beliefs.

45

– I will give a couple of samples of what these petty people fill their heads with, what they have put *into their master's mouth*: professions of 'beautiful souls'. –[21]

'And whosoever shall not receive you, nor hear you, when ye depart thence, shake off the dust under your feet for a testimony against them. Verily I say unto you, It shall be more tolerable for Sodom and Gomorrha in the day of judgment, than for that city' (Mark 6:11) – How *evangelical*! . . .

'And whosoever shall offend one of these little ones that believe in me, it is better for him that a millstone were hanged about his neck, and he were cast into the sea' (Mark 9:42) – How *evangelical*! . . .

'And if thine eye offend thee, pluck it out: it is better for thee to enter into the kingdom of God with one eye, than having two eyes to be cast into hell fire: Where the worm dieth not, and the fire is not quenched' (Mark 9:47) – And it is not really the eye they are talking about . . .

[21] Translations taken from the King James Bible.

'Verily I say unto you, That there be some of them that stand here, which shall not taste of death, till they have seen the kingdom of God come with power' (Mark 9:1) – *Well lied*, lion . . .

'Whosoever will come after me, let him deny himself, and take up his cross, and follow me. *For –*' (*A psychologist's note*. Christian morality refutes itself whenever it says '*for*': its 'reasons' refute, – that is what makes it Christian). Mark 8:34. –

'Judge not, *that* ye be not judged. With what measure ye mete, it shall be measured to *you* again' (Matt. 7:1) – What a concept of justice, of a 'just' judge! . . .

'For if ye love them which love you, *what reward have ye?* do not even the publicans the same? And if ye salute your brethren only, *what do ye more than others?* do not even the publicans so?' (Matt. 5:46) – Principle of 'Christian love': in the end it wants to be *paid* well . . .

'But if *ye* forgive not men their trespasses, neither will your Father forgive your trespasses' (Matt. 6:15) – Very compromising for the above-mentioned 'Father' . . .

'But seek ye first the kingdom of God, and his righteousness; and all these things shall be added unto you' (Matt. 6:33). All these things: namely food, clothing, all the basic needs of life. An *error*, to put it modestly . . . Immediately afterwards, God appears as a tailor, at least in certain circumstances . . . [22]

'Rejoice ye in that day, and leap for joy: *for*, behold, your reward is great in heaven: for in the like manner did their fathers unto the prophets' (Luke 6:23) *Shameless* rubbish! They are even comparing themselves with the prophets . . .

'Know ye not that ye are the temple of God, and that the Spirit of God dwelleth in you? If any man defile the temple of God, *him shall God destroy*; for the temple of God is holy, *which temple ye are*' (Paul, I Cor. 3: 16) – You cannot hate this sort of thing enough.

'Do ye not know that the saints shall judge the world? and if the world shall be judged by you, are ye unworthy to judge the smallest matters?' (Paul, I Cor. 6:2). Unfortunately, these are not just the words of a mad-man . . . This *appalling fraud* actually goes on to say: 'Know ye not that we shall judge angels? how much more things that pertain to this life!' . . .

---

[22] Matt. 6:28–30.

'Hath not God made foolish the wisdom of this world? For after that in the wisdom of God the world by wisdom knew not God, it pleased God by the foolishness of preaching to save them that believe. Not many wise men after the flesh, not many mighty, not many noble, are called: But *God hath chosen* the foolish things of the world to confound the wise; and God hath chosen the weak things of the world to confound the things which are mighty; And base things of the world, and things which are despised, hath God chosen, yea, and things which are not, to bring to nought things that are: That no flesh should glory in his presence' (Paul, I Cor. 1:20) – Read the first section of my *Genealogy of Morality* if you want to *see* this as a first-rate testimony to the psychology of every Chandala morality: here for the first time, the contrast is made clear between a *noble* morality and a Chandala morality born of *ressentiment* and impotent revenge. Paul was the greatest of all apostles of revenge . . .

46

– *What follows from this?* That you should put on gloves before taking up the New Testament. The presence of so much uncleanliness almost forces you to. We would not want to associate with the 'first Christians' any more than with Polish Jews: not that you would even need to raise any objections . . . Neither of them smells good. – I have looked in vain through the New Testament for a single likeable feature; there is nothing free, kind, candid, or honest about it. Humane qualities have not even begun to appear, – the instinct of *cleanliness* is missing . . . There are only *bad* instincts in the New Testament, there is not even the courage for these bad instincts. Everything is cowardice, everything is closed-eyes and self-deceit. Any book looks clean after you have read the New Testament: to give an example, right after reading Paul, I happily read that most charming, high-spirited satirist, Petronius; you can say about him what Domenico Boccaccio said about Cesare Borgia to the Duke of Parma: '*è tutto festo*'[23] – immortally healthy, immortally cheerful and well constituted . . . These little fools go wrong just where it matters most. They attack, but everything becomes *excellent* when it is attacked by them. *Nobody* is defiled by being attacked by a 'first Christian' . . . On the contrary: it is an honour to have the 'first Christians' against you.

[23] Probably: 'all is festive'.

You cannot read the New Testament without feeling a certain affection for what it abuses, – not to mention the 'wisdom of this world', which an insolent windbag tries to confound 'through foolish preaching' – although to no effect . . . But with enemies like this, even the Pharisees and the scribes look good: they must have done something right to inspire such indecent hatred. Hypocrisy – what an objection, coming from the 'first Christians'! – In the end, they were people of *privilege*: this was enough, the Chandala hatred did not need any other reason. The 'first Christians' – and, I am afraid, also the 'last Christians' *who, perhaps, I will live to see –* rebel against all privilege from out of their most basic instincts, – they live, they keep fighting for '*equal* rights' . . . Looked at more closely, they have no choice. If someone wants to be 'chosen by God' – or a 'temple of God', or a 'judge of angels' –, then any *other* principle of selection, like one according to honesty, according to spirit, according to masculinity and pride, according to beauty and freedom of the heart, is simply 'worldly', – *evil in itself* . . . Moral: every word coming from the mouth of a 'first Christian' is a lie, everything he does is an instinctive falsehood, – all of his values, all of his goals are harmful, but *who* he hates, *what* he hates, *these have value* . . . The Christian, the Christian priest in particular, is a *criterion of value* – – Do I still need to say that in the whole of the New Testament there is only *one* honourable figure? Pilate, the Roman governor. To take Jewish affairs seriously – he could not convince himself to do this. One Jew more or less – what does it matter? . . . The noble scorn of a Roman when faced with an unashamed mangling of the word 'truth' gave the New Testament its only statement *of any value*, – its critique, even its *annihilation*: 'What is truth!' . . .

47

– The fact that we have not rediscovered God, either in history or in nature or behind nature: this is not what separates *us*. Rather, we are separated by the fact that we view the thing worshipped as God as pathetic, absurd, and harmful, not as 'divine'; the fact that we do not treat it as a simple error but as a *crime against life* . . . We deny that God is God . . . If someone were to *prove* this Christian God to us, we would believe in him even less. – In a word: *deus, qualem Paulus creavit, dei negatio.*[24] – A

[24] God, as created by Paul, is a negation of God.

religion like Christianity, which is completely out of touch with reality, which immediately falls apart if any concession is made to reality, would of course be mortally opposed to the 'wisdom of this world', which is to say *science*, – it will approve of anything that can poison, slander, or *discredit* discipline of spirit, integrity or spiritual rigour of conscience, or noble assurance and freedom of the spirit. The imperative of 'faith' is a *veto* on science, – *in praxi*, the lie at any cost . . . Paul *understood* that lying – that 'belief' was necessary; later, the church understood Paul. – The 'God' that Paul invented for himself, a God who 'confounds all worldly wisdom' (to be exact, the two great rivals of all superstition, philology and medicine) is in truth just Paul's firm *decision* to do it himself: to call his own will 'God', torah,[25] that is Jewish to the core. Paul *wants* to confound all 'wisdom of the world': his enemies are the *good* philologists and doctors from the Alexandrian schools –, he wages war on them. In fact, you cannot be a philologist or doctor without being *anti-Christian*[26] at the same time. This is because philologists look *behind* the 'holy books', and doctors see *behind* the physiological depravity of the typical Christian. The doctor says 'incurable', the philologist says 'fraud' . . .

48

– Have people really understood the famous story at the beginning of the Bible, – how God was scared stiff of *science*? . . . People have not understood this. This priestly book *par excellence* begins, as is only fitting, with the priest's enormous inner difficulty: *he* has one great danger, *consequently* 'God' has one great danger. –

The old God, wholly 'spirit', wholly high-priest, wholly perfection, takes a stroll in his garden: but he is bored. Even gods cannot escape boredom.[27] What does he do? He invents human beings, – the human is entertaining . . . But look, even the human is bored. God has boundless compassion for the only problem in any paradise: soon he creates other animals too. God's *first* mistake: the human was not amused by the other animals, – he ruled over them, he did not even want to be an 'animal'. – So God created woman. And this really did put an end to boredom, – but it put an end to other things as well! The woman was God's *second*

---

[25] The law.   [26] The word Nietzsche uses is *Anti-Christ* – the title of this essay.
[27] Adapted from a line in Schiller's *Maid of Orleans*.

mistake. – 'The woman is by nature a serpent, Heva' – every priest knows this; 'woman brings *all* troubles into the world' – every priest knows this too. '*Consequently* she brings *science* as well' . . . It was woman who taught people to eat from the tree of knowledge. – What had happened? The old God was scared stiff. People had turned out to be his *biggest* mistake, he had created a rival for himself, science makes you *godlike*, – it is all over for priests and gods when people become scientific! – *Moral*: science is the taboo of all taboos, – it is the only thing forbidden. Science is the *first* sin, the seed of all sins, the *original* sin. *Only this is morality.* – 'Thou shalt *not* know': – everything else follows from this. – God's big scare did not stop him from being shrewd. How do you *defend* yourself from science? That was his main problem for a long time. Answer: get people out of paradise! Happiness, idleness give rise to thinking, – all thoughts are bad thoughts . . . People *should* not think. – And the 'priest-in-itself' invents troubles, death, the moral dangers of pregnancy, every type of misery, age, hardship, and above all *illness*, – these are just tools in the struggle against science! Troubles *prevent* people from thinking . . . And nonetheless! Horrible! The edifice of knowledge piles up, storming heaven, bringing twilight to the gods, – what can be done! – The old God invents *war*, he separates peoples, he causes people to destroy each other (– priests have always needed war . . .). War – among other things, a huge source of disruption for science! – Unbelievable! Knowledge, *emancipation from the priests*, keeps growing in spite of war. – And the old God makes a final decision: 'people have become scientific, – *there's nothing left to do except drown them!*' . . .

49

– You understood me. The beginning of the Bible contains the *whole* psychology of the priest. – The priest can only imagine one great danger: and that is science – the healthy concepts of cause and effect. But science generally only flourishes in favourable conditions, – you need a *surplus* of time and spirit in order to 'know' . . . '*Consequently*, people need to be made unhappy', – that was always the logic of priests. – You can already guess *what* would enter the world, given this logic: – '*sin*' . . . The concepts of guilt and punishment, the whole 'moral world order' is invented *against* science, – *against* priests losing their hold on people . . . People should *not* look to the outside, they should look within; and being learners, they should *not* be too clever or careful at looking into things, they should not look at anything at all: they should *suffer* . . . And they should suffer so that they are always in need of a priest. – Get rid of doctors! *People need a saviour.* – The concepts of guilt and punishment, including the doctrines of 'mercy', 'redemption', and 'forgiveness', (*lies* through and through, without any grounding in psychological reality) are invented to destroy people's *senses of causation*: they are assassination attempts on the concepts of cause and effect! – And *not* using fists, or knifes, or honesty in love and in hate! But instead coming from the lowest, most cowardly, crafty instincts! A *priestly* assassination! A *parasite's* assassination! A vampirism of pale, subterranean bloodsuckers! . . . When the natural consequences of an action are not 'natural' any more but instead are attributed to spectral, superstitious concepts, to 'God', to 'spirit', to the 'soul', as exclusively 'moral' consequences, as reward, punishment, warning, as a lesson, then the presuppositions of knowledge have been destroyed, – *and this is the greatest crime against humanity.* – Once more: sin, this supreme form of human self-desecration, was invented to block science, to block culture, to block every elevation and ennoblement of humanity; the priests *rule* through the invention of sin. –

50

– At this point, I won't let myself go without providing a psychology of 'faith', of 'the faithful', for the benefit of the 'faithful' themselves, which is only fitting. These days there might still be no shortage of people who are unaware of the extent to which 'faith' is *indecent – or* a mark of decadence, of a broken will to life –, but people will certainly be aware of this tomorrow. My voice reaches even the hard of hearing. – It seems, if I have not misheard, that Christians have a sort of criterion for truth called 'the proof of strength'. 'Faith makes blessed: *therefore* it is true.' – We should begin by pointing out that this blessedness has not been proven, only *promised*: blessedness is conditional on 'faith' – you *will* become blessed *because* you have faith . . . But whether this *really* takes place, given that the priest's promises involve a 'beyond' which is inaccessible to verification – how can *that* be proven? – So the would-be 'proof of strength' is itself basically just another article of faith that the result promised by faith will come to pass. In short: 'I have faith that faith makes blessed; – *consequently* it is true.' – But this brings us to the end.

This 'consequently' would be the *absurdum* itself as criterion of truth. – But let us suppose, just to be accommodating, that blessedness has been *proven* through faith – *not* just desired, *not* just promised from out of the somewhat dubious mouth of a priest: in this case, would blessedness, – or, to put it technically, *pleasure* – ever be a proof of truth? This is so far from being the case that it is practically a counter-proof, but in any event there is the greatest suspicion against 'truth' when pleasurable sensations are invoked to answer the question 'What is true?' The proof of 'pleasure' is a proof of 'pleasure', – nothing more; how in the world could it ever be established that *true* judgments are more enjoyable than false ones, and are necessarily followed by pleasant sensations according to some pre-established harmony? – The experience of all rigorous, of all profoundly constituted spirits teaches *the opposite*. We have had to wring the truth out of ourselves every step of the way, we have had to give up almost everything that our heart, our love, our trust in life relied on. It requires greatness of soul: the service of truth is the hardest service. – So what does it mean to be *honest* in spiritual matters? That you are strict with your heart, that you look down on 'beautiful feelings', that you make your conscience from every yes and no! – – – Faith makes blessed: *consequently* it lies . . .

51

That faith can make blessed under certain circumstances, that blessed-ness does not make a fixed idea into a *true* one, that faith does not move mountains but *sets mountains down* where there aren't any: a quick walk through an *insane asylum* is enough to demonstrate all this. *Not* to a priest, of course: because he will instinctively deny that sickness is sickness, that an insane asylum is an insane asylum. Christianity *needs* sickness, more or less as Greece needed a surplus of health, – *making* things sick is the real intention behind the church's whole system of salvation procedures. And the church itself – doesn't it have the Catholic insane asylum as its the ultimate ideal? – The earth as one big insane asylum? – The sort of religious people the church *wants* are typical decadents; every age in which a religious crisis gains control over a people is characterized by neurological epidemics; the 'inner world' of religious people looks just like the 'inner world' of victims of exhaustion or over-excitement; the 'highest' conditions that Christianity held up to humanity as the value of all values are forms of epilepsy, – the only people the church has declared holy have been lunatics *or* enormous frauds *in majorem dei honorem*[28] . . . I once let myself characterize the entire Christian training[29] in atonement and repentance (which is best studied in England these days) as a methodically produced *folie circulaire*[30] on already prepared (which is to say: thoroughly morbid) soil. Nobody is free to become Christian: nobody gets 'converted' to Christianity, – you have to be sick enough for it . . . We who are different, who have the *courage* for health *and* also for contempt, imagine how much *we* can despise a religion that teaches a misunderstanding of the body! that does not want to escape from the superstition of the soul! that makes a 'merit' out of poor nutrition! that fights health as a type of enemy, devil, temptation! that talks itself into believing that people can carry around a 'perfect soul' in a cadaverous body, a belief that would require a new idea of 'perfection', a pale, sickly, idiotic-fanatic state called 'holiness', – holiness, itself just the set of symptoms of an impoverished, enervated, incurably corrupted body! . . . The Christian movement, being a European movement, was from the very start a whole movement of rejected and dejected elements of every type: – they want to gain power through Christianity. They do *not* express the decline of a race, they are an aggregate of decadent forms from everywhere, who look for each other and huddle together. It was *not* (as is commonly believed) the corruption of antiquity itself, of the nobles of antiquity that made Christianity possible: we cannot be harsh enough in opposing the scholarly idiocy that continues to maintain these ideas even today. At the point when Christianity was spreading among the sick, corrupt, Chandala classes throughout the whole *imperium*, the *counter-type*, the nobility, had assumed its most beautiful and mature form. The great numbers gained control; the democratism of the Christian instinct had *won* . . . Christianity was not 'national', not the function of race, – it appealed to all the types that had been disinherited by life, it had its allies everywhere. Christianity is based on the rancour of the sick, the instinct *against* the healthy, *against* health. Everything well-constituted, proud, high-spirited, beauty above all, hurt their ears and eyes. This reminds me again of the invaluable words of Paul. 'The *weak* things of the world, the *foolish* things of the world, the *base* things of the world, and the things that are *despised*, hath God chosen': *this* was

---

[28] To the greater honour of God.
[29] Nietzsche uses the English world 'training'.   [30] Manic depression.

the formula; decadence was victorious *in hoc signo*.[31] – *God on the cross* – have people still not grasped the gruesome ulterior motive behind this symbol? – Everything that suffers, everything nailed to the cross is divine . . . We are all nailed to the cross, consequently *we* are divine . . . We are the only ones who are divine . . . Christianity won, and with this, a *nobler* sensibility was destroyed, – Christianity has been the worst thing to happen to humanity so far. – –

52

Christianity is also opposed to everything that is *spiritually* well constituted, – only a sick reason can be used as Christian reason, Christianity sides with everything idiotic, it puts a curse on 'spirit', on the *superbia*[32] of healthy spirit. Since sickness belongs to the essence of Christianity, the typical Christian state of 'faith' *has* to be a form of sickness, the church *has* to condemn all straight, honest, scientific paths to knowledge as *forbidden* paths. Doubt is already a sin . . . The priest's total lack of psychological cleanliness – his eyes give it away – is a *consequence* of decadence, – if you observe hysterical females or children with rickets, you will see how regularly an instinctive falseness, a pleasure in lying for the sake of lying, and an inability to look or walk straight are expressions of decadence. 'Faith' means not *wanting* to know the truth. The pietist, the priest of both sexes, is false *because* he is sick: his instinct *demands* that truth be denied at every point. 'Whatever makes things sick is *good*; whatever comes from fullness, from over-fullness, from power is *evil*': this is how the faithful see things. *Not being free not to lie* – I can pick out someone who is predestined for theology in this way. – Another mark of a theologian is his *incapacity for philology*. Philology should be understood here in a very general sense, as the art of reading well, – to be able to read facts *without* falsifying them through interpretations, *without* letting the desire to understand make you lose caution, patience, subtlety. Philology as *ephexis*[33] in interpretation: whether it concerns books, newspaper articles, destinies, or facts about the weather, – not to mention 'salvation of the soul' . . . The way a theologian, whether in Berlin or Rome, interprets a 'verse of Scripture' or an event (a military victory by his fatherland, for instance) in the higher light of the Psalms of David is *brazen* enough to drive a philologist crazy.

[31] In this sign.   [32] Pride.   [33] Suspension of judgment.

And what is he supposed to do when pietists and other Swabian cows take their everyday, humdrum, miserable little lives and, using the 'hand of God', fashion them into miracles of 'grace', 'Providence', or the 'experience of salvation'! The slightest effort of spirit, not to mention *decency*, would have to convince these interpreters of the complete childishness and unworthiness of this sort of abuse of divine manual dexterity. It would take only the tiniest bit of piety to see that a God who cures our cold at just the right moment or who tells us to climb into the coach just when it starts to rain is so absurd that we would have to get rid of him even if he *did* exist. God as a domestic, as a mailman, as an almanac maker, – basically, a term for all the most stupid coincidences . . . 'Divine Providence', a belief held by about a third of all people in 'educated Germany', would be the strongest conceivable objection to God. And at any rate, it is an objection to Germans! . . .

53

– The idea that *martyrs* prove anything about the truth of a matter is so far from being true that I would like to deny that martyrs have ever had anything to do with the truth. A martyr throws his truth claims in the world's face in a tone that shows so little intellectual integrity and expresses such a *stupor* in the face of the question of truth that you never have to refute a martyr. Truth is not something that one person might have and another not: at best, peasants or their apostles like Luther might think about truth this way. You can be sure that modesty, *moderation* in this matter increases in proportion to the degree of conscientiousness in spiritual things. To have *knowledge* about five things and gently refuse to know anything *else* . . . 'Truth', as every prophet, every sectarian, every free spirit, every socialist, every churchman understands the word, is a thorough-going proof that the process of self-overcoming and the discipline of spirit needed to find some small, ever so small bit of the truth, has not even begun. – The deaths of the martyrs, by the way, were enormous pieces of historical bad luck: they were *seductive* . . . The conclusion reached by all idiots, including females and folk peoples, that there must be something to a cause that someone has died for (or even, as with the first Christianity, a cause that produces a longing for death of epidemic proportions), – this conclusion has defied any and all analysis, spirit of analysis, or caution. Martyrs *harm* the truth . . . Even today, it only takes the crudeness of a persecution to give the most indifferent sectarianism an *honourable* name. – What? Does the value of something change when someone gives up their life for it? – A mistake that has become honourable is a mistake that has one more seductive charm: do you think, my dear theologians, that we would give you cause to martyr yourselves for your lies? – You refute a matter by putting it respectfully on ice, – this is how you refute theologians too . . . The world-historical stupidity of all persecutors has been just this, that they gave the cause they were fighting against an honourable appearance –, they gave it the gift of the fascination of martyrdom . . . Even today, females still kneel down in front of a mistake because they are told that somebody died on the cross for it. *So is the cross an argument?* – – But only one commentator has said what has needed to be said for centuries about all of these things, – *Zarathustra*.

They wrote signs of blood on the path where they walked, and their foolishness taught that truth is proved with blood.

But blood is the worst witness for truth; blood poisons the purest teaching until it becomes a delusion and a hatred of the heart.

And if somebody goes through fire for his teaching, – what does that prove? It is more when your own teaching comes from your own fire.[34]

54

Make no mistake about it: great spirits are sceptics. Zarathustra is a sceptic. The vigour, the *freedom* that comes from the strength and super-strength of spirit *proves* itself through scepticism. Where basic issues about value or lack of value are concerned, people with convictions do not come into consideration. Convictions are prisons. These people do not see far enough, they do not see *beneath* themselves: but if you are going to talk about value and lack of value, you need to see five hundred convictions *beneath* you, – *behind* you . . . A spirit who wills greatness and also wills the means to it is necessarily a sceptic. The freedom from every sort of conviction, being *able* to see freely, is *part* of strength . . . His whole intellect is devoted to the great passion, the foundation and the power of its being, more enlightened, more despotic than he is himself; it gives him assurance; it gives him the courage even for unholy means; it *allows* him

---

[34] *Thus Spoke Zarathustra* (*Z*), Part III, 'Of the Priests'.

convictions under certain circumstances. Conviction as a *means*: there are many things that can be achieved only by means of a conviction. Great passion uses convictions and uses them up, it does not subordinate itself to them, – it knows its own sovereignty. – Conversely: the need for faith, for some unconditional yes or no, Carlylism if you will excuse the expression, is a need of the *weak*. Men of faith, the 'faithful' of every type, are necessarily dependent people, – the sort of people who cannot posit *themselves* as a goal, who are utterly incapable of positing goals from out of themselves. The 'man of faith' does not belong to *himself*, he can only be a means, he needs to be *used up*, he needs someone to use him up. He instinctively holds a morality of self-abnegation in the greatest honour; everything urges him to adopt it, his shrewdness, experience, vanity. Every type of faith is an expression of self-abnegation, of self-alienation . . . Just think how the vast majority of people need some regulative guideline as an external principle of bondage or mooring, how compulsion, *slavery* in a higher sense, is the only and ultimate condition for the thriving of the weak-willed person, particularly the female: this is how conviction, 'faith', should be understood as well. It gives the man of convictions a backbone. *Not* to see many things, *not* to be free on a single point, to be partisan through and through, to have a strict and necessary optic in all values – these are the only conditions under which this type of a person can even arise. But this makes him the opposite, the *antagonist* of the truthful person, – of truth . . . A faithful person is not free to have any sort of conscience for the question 'true' or 'untrue': honesty on *this* point would be his immediate downfall. People with convictions have pathologically conditioned optics, which makes them into fanatics – Savonarola, Luther, Rousseau, Robespierre, Saint-Simon, – the antithesis of strong spirits who have become *free*. But the grand poses struck by these *sick* spirits, these conceptual epileptics, can affect the great masses, – fanatics are picturesque, humanity would rather see gestures than listen to *reasons* . . .

55

– One more step into the psychology of conviction, of 'faith'. A long time ago I posed the problem of whether convictions are not more dangerous enemies of truth than lies (*Human, All Too Human*, §483). Now I would like to ask the decisive question: Are lies and convictions even opposed? – The whole world believes that they are; but what doesn't the whole world believe! – Every conviction has its history, its pre-formations, its ventures and its mistakes: it *becomes* a conviction after *not* being one for a long time, after *barely* being one for even longer. What? Could lies be among these embryonic forms of convictions too? – Sometimes all you need is a change of characters: what were lies for the father are convictions for the son. – I call lies *not* wanting to see what you see, not wanting to see it the *way* you do: it makes no difference whether the lies take place in front of witnesses. The most common lie is the one you tell yourself; lying to other people is a relatively exceptional case. – Now, this *not* wanting to see what you see, this not wanting to see the *way* you do, is almost the first condition for being *partisan* in any sense of the term: the partisan will necessarily turn into a liar. German historical scholarship, for instance, is convinced that Rome was a despotism, that the inhabitants of Germania brought the spirit of freedom into the world: what is the difference between this sort of conviction and a lie? Is it any wonder that all partisans, even German historians, instinctively go around with great moral words in their mouths, – that morality almost owes its *continued existence* to its indispensability among partisans of every type? – 'This is *our* conviction: we profess it to the world, we will live and die for it, – respect anyone with convictions!' – I have even heard this sort of thing coming from anti-Semites. On the contrary, my dear sir! An anti-Semite does not become one bit more respectable by lying as a matter of principle . . . Priests have more subtlety in these matters, they have a good understanding of why someone might object to the idea of a conviction, which is to say a lie that is principled *because* it serves an end; accordingly, these priests adopted the prudent Jewish measure of inserting the idea of 'God', 'God's will', 'God's revelation' at this point. Even Kant was on the same path with his categorical imperative: his reason became *practical* here. – There are some questions that people are *not* entitled to decide the truth of; all the ultimate questions, all the ultimate problems of value are beyond human reason . . . To grasp the boundaries of reason – now, *that* is real philosophy . . . Why did God reveal himself to humanity? Would God have done something superfluous? People *cannot* figure out what is good and evil on their own, that is why God taught them his will . . . Moral: priests do *not* lie, – there is simply no room for lying about 'truth' or 'untruth' in the sorts of issues priests talk about. This is because you cannot lie unless you can decide *what* is true. And this is impossible for human beings to do; which means that the priest is only a mouthpiece of God. – This sort of priestly syllogism is not at all exclusive to Judaism and Christianity: the right to lie and the *shrewdness* of 'revelation' belong to the priestly type, the priests of decadence as well as the pagan priests (– a pagan is anyone who says yes to life, who sees 'god' as the word for the great yes to all things). – The 'law', the 'will of God', the 'holy book', 'inspiration' – All these are just words for the conditions under which priests come to power and maintain their power, – these concepts can be found at the bottom of all priestly organizations, all structures of priestly or philosophical-priestly control. The 'holy lie' – this is common to Confucius, the law book of Manu, Mohammed, and the Christian church: and it is not absent from Plato either. 'The truth is there': wherever you hear this, it means that the *priest is lying* . . .

56

– In the end, it comes down to the *purpose* the lie is supposed to serve. The fact that 'holy' purposes are lacking in Christianity is *my* objection to its means. Only *bad* purposes: poison, slander, negation of life, hatred of the body, the degradation and self-violation of humans through the concept of sin, – *consequently* its means are bad as well. – I get the opposite feeling when I read the law book of *Manu*, an incomparably spiritual and superior work; it would be a sin against *spirit* even to mention its name in the same breath as that of the Bible. You see it immediately: there is a genuine philosophy behind it, *in* it, not just a foul-smelling *Judain* of rabbinism and superstition, – it has something for even the most discriminating psychologist to chew on. And do not forget the central point, the fundamental difference between it and every type of Bible: it lets the *noble* classes, the philosophers and the warriors, stand above the crowd; noble values everywhere, a feeling of perfection, saying yes to life, a triumphant sense of well-being both for its own sake and for the sake of life, – the *sun* shines over the entire book. – All the things that Christianity treated with its unfathomable meanness, procreation, for instance, woman, marriage, are treated here with seriousness, with respect, with love and trust. How can you really put a book into the hands of children and women when it contains that mean-spirited passage: 'to avoid fornication, let every man have his own wife and let every woman have her own husband: it is better to marry than to burn'?[35] And

[35] I Cor. 6:2, 9.

can anyone really be Christian, as long as the idea of *immaculata concep-tio* christianizes, which is to say *dirties*, the human origin? . . . I do not know any book that says as many kind and delicate things to females as the law book of Manu; these old men and saints have a way of minding their manners in front of women that has perhaps never been surpassed. 'The mouth of a woman', it says at one point, 'the breasts of a girl, the prayer of a child, the smoke of a sacrifice are always pure.' Another pas-sage: 'there is absolutely nothing more pure than the light of the sun, the shadow of a cow, air, water, fire, and the breath of a girl'. A final passage – perhaps a holy lie too –: 'all bodily orifices above the navel are pure, all the ones below are impure. Only in girls is the whole body pure.'

57

If you measure the *Christian goal* against the goal of the law book of Manu – if you examine these starkly antithetical goals under a strong light – you will catch the *unholiness* of the means Christians use *in flagrante*. The critic of Christianity cannot help but make Christianity look *despicable*. – A law book like that of Manu comes about in the same way as every good book of law: it summarizes the experience, shrewdness, and experiments in morality of many centuries, it draws a conclusion, nothing more. This sort of codification presupposes an insight into the following fact: the way that a slowly and expensively acquired truth becomes author-itative is fundamentally different from the way that this truth would be proven. A book of law never describes the uses, the reasons, and the casu-istry in the prehistory of a law: this would make it lose its imperative tone, the 'thou shalt', the presupposition for being obeyed. This is precisely where the problem is. – At a certain point in the development of a peo-ple, its most circumspect (which is to say far-sighted and hind-sighted) class declares that the experience according to which life should be con-ducted – that is, *can* be conducted –, is over. Its goal is to harvest the richest and most perfect crop possible from the ages of experiment and *bad* experience. Accordingly, what now needs to be prevented at all cost is any further experimentation, the continuation of values in a fluid state, scrutiny, selection, and criticism of values *in infinitum*. A double wall is set up against this: first: *revelation*, the claim that the reasoning behind the law does *not* have a mortal provenance, has *not* been slowly and painstakingly looked for and discovered, but instead had a divine origin, arriving whole, complete, without history, a gift, a miracle, simply communicated . . . And second: *tradition*, which is to say the claim that the law existed from time immemorial, that it is irreverent to cast doubt on it, a crime against the ancestors. The authority of the law is grounded in the theses: God *gave* it, the ancestors *lived* by it. – The higher reasoning behind a procedure like this involves the intention to push back consciousness gradually – to identify some life as the proper one (which is to say one that has been *proven* through immense and highly filtered experiences) and to prevent people from becoming conscious of it: to achieve a perfect automatism of the instinct, – this is the presupposition of every type of mastery, of every type of perfection in the art of life. To prepare a book of law in the style of Manu means to give a people the right to become master one day, to become perfect, – to aspire to the highest art of life. *To this end, it must be made unconscious*: this is the goal of every holy lie. – *Caste-order*, the most supreme, domineering law, is just the sanction of a *natural order*, natural lawfulness *par excellence* – chance and 'modern ideas' have no sway over it. In every healthy society, three mutually conditioning physiological types separate out and gravitate in different directions, each one having its own hygiene, its own area of work, its own feelings of perfection and field of mastery. Nature, *not* Manu, separates out predominantly spiritual people from people characterized by muscular and temperamental strength from a third group of people who are not distinguished in either way, the mediocre, – the latter being the great number, the first being the exceptions. The highest caste – which I call *the few* –, being the perfect caste, also has the privilege of the few: this includes representing happiness, beauty, goodness on earth. Only the most spiritual human beings are allowed to be beautiful: only among them is goodness not a weakness. *Pulchrum est paucorum hominum*:[36] goodness is a privilege. On the other hand, nothing can be tolerated less in this type than ugly manners or a pessimistic look, an eye that *makes things ugly* –, or even an indignation over the way of the world. Indignation is the privilege of the Chandala; pessimism too. '*The world is perfect*' – this is how the instinct of the most spiritual people speaks, the yes-saying instinct: 'imperfection, every type of being that is *beneath* us, distance, the pathos of distance, even the Chandala belongs to

[36] Beauty is for the few.

this perfection'. The most spiritual people, being the *strongest*, find their happiness where other people would find their downfall: in labyrinths, in harshness towards themselves and towards others, in trials; they take pleasure in self-overcoming: asceticism is their nature, requirement, instinct. They see difficult tasks as a privilege, they *relax* by playing with burdens that would crush other people . . . Knowledge – a form of asceticism. – They are the most admirable type of people: which does not prevent them from being the most cheerful, the kindest. They do not rule because they want to, but rather because they *exist*, they are not free to be second. – The ones who are second: these are the custodians of the law, the guardians of order and security, these are the noble warriors, this is above all the *king*, as the highest formula of the warrior, judge, and preserver of the law. The ones who are second are the executives of the most spiritual people; they are closest to them, belong to them, and take over everything *crude* in the work of ruling – they are their attendants, their right hand, their best pupils. – In all of this, to say it again, there is nothing arbitrary, nothing 'contrived'; anything *different* is contrived, – contrived to put nature to shame . . . Caste-order, *order of rank*, is just a formula for the supreme law of life itself, splitting off into three types is necessary for the preservation of society, to make the higher and highest types possible, – *unequal* rights are the condition for any rights at all. – A right is a privilege. Everyone finds his privilege in his own type of being. Let us not underestimate the privileges of the *mediocre*. Life becomes increasingly difficult the *higher* up you go, – it gets colder, there are more responsibilities. A high culture is a pyramid: it needs a broad base, its first presupposition is a strongly and healthily consolidated mediocrity. Crafts, trade, farming, *science*, most of art – in a word, *employment* can only really function on the basis of a mediocrity of ability and desire: this sort of thing would be out of place among exceptional people, the associated instinct would contradict both aristocratism and anarchism. To be a public utility, a wheel, a function – you need to be destined for this by nature: it is *not* society but rather the type of *happiness* that the vast majority of people cannot rise above that make them intelligent machines. For the mediocre, mediocrity is a happiness; mastery of one thing, specialization as a natural instinct. It would be completely unworthy of a more profound spirit to have any objection to mediocrity as such. Mediocrity is needed *before* there can be exceptions: it is the condition for a high culture. When an exceptional person treats a mediocre one more delicately than he treats himself and his equals, this is not just courtesy of the heart,[37] – it is his *duty* . . . Who do I hate most among the rabble today? The socialist rabble, the Chandala-apostles who undermine workers' instincts and pleasures, their feelings of modesty about their little existences, – who make them jealous, who teach them revenge . . . Injustice is never a matter of unequal rights, it is a matter of claiming '*equal*' rights . . . What is *bad*? But I have already said it: everything that comes from weakness, from jealousy, from *revenge*. – The anarchist and the Christian are descended from the same lineage . . .

58

In fact, it makes a difference *why* you are lying: whether you are lying in order to sustain or to *destroy*. *Christians* are perfectly identical with *anarchists*: their only goal, their only instinct is to destroy. Just look at history: it proves this proposition with gruesome clarity. We just learned about a form of religious legislation whose goal was to 'eternalize' the supreme condition for a *thriving* life, a great organization of society; Christianity, by contrast, saw its mission as bringing this sort of an organization to an end *because it led to a thriving life*. In this society, the returns of reason from the long ages of experiment and uncertainty *should* have been invested for the greatest long-term advantage, and the greatest, richest, most perfect crop possible should have been harvested: but quite the opposite happened here, the harvest was *poisoned* overnight . . . What stood as *aere perennius*,[38] the *imperium Romanum*, the most magnificent form of organization ever to be achieved under difficult conditions, compared to which everything before or after has just been patched together, botched and dilettantish, – those holy anarchists made a 'piety' out of destroying 'the world', *which is to say* the *imperium Romanum*, until every stone was overturned, – until even the Germans and other thugs could rule over it . . . The Christian and the anarchist: both are decadents, neither one can do anything except dissolve, poison, lay waste, *bleed dry*, both have instincts of *mortal hatred* against everything that stands, that stands tall, that has endurance, that promises life a future . . . Christianity was the vampire of the *imperium Romanum*, – overnight, it obliterated the Romans' tremendous deed of

---

[37] A line from Goethe's novel *Elective Affinities*. [38] More enduring than bronze.

laying the ground for a great culture *that had time.* – You still don't understand? The *imperium Romanum* that we know, that we are coming to know better through the history of the Roman provinces, this most remarkable artwork in the great style was a beginning, its design was calculated to *prove* itself over the millennia, –, nothing like it has been built to this day, nobody has even dreamed of building on this scale, *sub specie aeterni!*[39] – This organization was stable enough to hold up under bad emperors: the accident of personalities cannot make any difference with things like this, – *first* principle of all great architecture. But it was not stable enough to withstand the *most corrupt* type of corruption, to withstand *Christians* . . . This secretive worm that crept up to every individual under the cover of night, fog, and ambiguity and sucked the seriousness for *true* things, the instinct for *reality* in general right out of every individual, this cowardly, feminine, saccharine group gradually alienated the 'souls' from that tremendous structure, – those valuable, those masculine-noble natures that saw Rome's business as their own business, their own seriousness, their own *pride.* The priggish creeping around, the conventicle secrecy, dismal ideas like hell, like the sacrifice of the innocent, like the *unio mystica*[40] in the drinking of blood, above all the slowly fanned flames of revenge, of Chandala revenge – *that* is what gained control over Rome, the same type of religion that Epicurus had already waged war against in its pre-existent form. You should read Lucretius to see *what* Epicurus had fought, *not* paganism but 'Christianity', I mean the corruption of the soul through the ideas of guilt, punishment, and immortality. – He fought the *subterranean* cults, the whole of latent Christianity, – at that time, to deny immortality was nothing less than *salvation.* – And Epicurus would have won, every respectable spirit in the Roman empire was an Epicurean: *but then Paul came into the picture* . . . Paul, Chandala hatred of Rome, against 'the world', become flesh, become genius; the Jew, the *wandering* Jew *par excellence* . . . What he guessed was how you can use the small, sectarian Christian movement outside Judaism to kindle a 'world fire', how you can use the symbol of 'God on the cross' to take everything lying below, everything filled with secret rebellion, the whole inheritance of anarchistic activities in the empire, and unite them into an incredible power. 'Salvation comes from the Jews.' – Christianity as a formula for surpassing – *and* summing up – every type of subterranean cult, that of Osiris, of the

[39] From the standpoint of eternity.   [40] Mystical union.

great mother,[41] of Mithras, for instance: Paul's genius consists of this insight. His instinct in this was so certain that he took the ideas people found fascinating in Chandala religions and, with ruthless violence to the truth, put them into the mouth (and not just the mouth) of his invention, the 'saviour', – he *made* him into something that even a Mithras priest could understand . . . This was his Damascene moment: he understood that he *needed* the belief in immortality to devalue 'the world', that the idea of 'hell' could still gain control over Rome, – that the 'beyond' could be used to *kill life* . . . Nihilist and Christian: this rhymes,[42] it does more than just rhyme . . .

59

The entire work of the ancient world *in vain*: I do not have words to express my feelings at something so enormous. – And given that the work was preparatory, just laying the foundations with granite self-consciousness for a work that would take millennia, the entire *meaning* of the ancient world has been in vain! . . . What was the point of the Greeks? What was the point of the Romans? – All the presuppositions for a scholarly culture, all the scientific *methods* were already there, the great, incomparable art of reading well had already been established – this presupposition for the tradition of culture, for the unity of science; natural science was on the very best path, together with mathematics and mechanics, – the *factual sense*, the last and most valuable of all the senses had schools and traditions that were already centuries old! Do you understand? Everything *essential* had been found so that work could be started: – the methods, it should be said ten times over, *are* the essential thing, as well as the most difficult thing, as well as the thing that can be blocked by habit and laziness for a very long time. What we have won back today with unspeakable self-overcoming (since we all still have bad instincts, Christian instincts in our bodies), a free view of reality, a cautious hand, the patience and the seriousness for the smallest things, all the *integrity* of knowledge – this had already existed! for more than two thousand years! *And*, on top of this, a good, a refined sense of tact and taste! *Not* as some sort of dressage of the brain! *Not* as a 'German' education with the manners of a thug! But

---

[41] Presumably a reference to Cybele, the pagan Earth Goddess.
[42] It does rhyme in German: *Nihilist* and *Christ*.

as body, as gesture, as instinct, – in a word: as reality . . . *All of this in vain!* Turned overnight into just a memory! – Greeks! Romans! The nobility of the instincts and of taste, methodical research, genius in organization and administration, the belief, the *will* to a future for humanity, the great yes to all things made visible as the *imperium Romanum*, made visible to all the senses, the great style no longer just as art, but turned into reality, truth, *life* . . . – And not buried overnight by some natural event! Not trampled by Germans and other clodhoppers! But instead defiled by sly, secretive, invisible, anaemic vampires! Not defeated, – just sucked dry! . . . The hidden need for revenge, petty jealousy come to *power*! Everything miserable, suffering from itself, plagued by bad feelings, the whole *ghetto world* of the soul risen *to the top* in a single stroke! – – Just read any Christian agitator, Saint Augustine, for example, and you will realize, you will *smell* the sort of unclean people this brought to the top. You would be lying to yourself if you thought that the leaders of the Christian movement were lacking in intelligence: – oh, they are shrewd, shrewd to the point of holiness, these dear Mr Church Fathers! What they lack is something entirely different. Nature neglected them, – it forgot to give them a modest dowry of respectable, decent, *cleanly* instincts . . . Just between us, they are not even men . . . Islam is a thousand times right in despising Christianity: Islam presupposes men . . .

60

Christianity cheated us out of the fruits of ancient culture, and later it cheated us a second time out of the fruits of *Islamic* culture. The wonderful cultural world of Moorish Spain, which is fundamentally more closely related to *us* and speaks more clearly to our senses and tastes than Rome or Greece, was *trampled down* (I won't discuss the sort of feet that did this), and why? because this culture owed its origin to noble, to masculine instincts, because it said yes to life, albeit with the rare and refined preciousness of Moorish life! . . . The crusaders later fought something that they should by all rights have prostrated themselves in front of, – a culture that makes even our nineteenth century seem very poor, very 'late'. – Of course, they wanted loot: the Orient was rich . . . Let us be fair! The crusades – a higher piracy, nothing else! – The German aristocracy, which was basically a Viking aristocracy, was in its element here: the church knew all too well how to *get* German aristocrats . . . The German aristocracy was always the 'Swiss Guard' of the church, always in the service of all the church's bad instincts, – but *well paid* . . . And the church waged moral combat on everything noble on earth, precisely with the help of German swords, German blood and bravery! A number of painful questions arise at this point. The German aristocracy is almost entirely *absent* from the history of higher culture: you can guess why . . . Christianity, alcohol – the two *great* means of corruption . . . In itself, there really should not be any choice between Islam and Christianity, any more than between Arabs and Jews. The decision is given, nobody is free to have any choice here. Either you *are* a Chandala or you are *not* . . . 'War to the death against Rome! Peace, friendship with Islam': this is what that great free spirit felt, this is how he *acted*, the genius among German emperors, Friedrich II. What? Does a German need to be a genius, a free spirit, in order to have *decent* feelings? – I do not understand how a German could ever have *Christian* feelings . . .

61

Here we need to stir up a memory that is a hundred times more embarrassing for the Germans. The Germans have robbed Europe of the last great cultural harvest that it still could have brought home, – the *Renaissance*. Do people finally understand, do they *want* to understand *what* the Renaissance was? The *revaluation of all Christian values*, an attempt using all means, all instincts, all genius, to allow the *opposite* values, *noble* values to triumph . . . So far, there has only been this one great war, so far, there has not been any question more decisive that that of the Renaissance, – *my* question is its question –: there has also never been a form of *attack* where the whole front was led more fundamentally, directly, and strenuously against the centre! Attacking at the decisive spot, at the seat of Christianity itself, putting *noble* values on the throne, I mean into the instincts, *inside* the most basic needs and desires of the people sitting there . . . I have a vision of a *possibility*, one that has a perfect, super-terrestrial magic and multi-coloured charm: – it seems to shimmer with all the tremors of refined beauty, it seems that an art is at work in it, so divine, so diabolically divine that you will look in vain through millennia for a second possibility like this; I see a spectacle so ingenious and at the same time so wonderfully paradoxical that it would have given all the Olympic gods cause for immortal laughter – *Cesare Borgia as Pope* . . . Do you understand me? . . . Well then, *that* would have been the victory that I am the only one demanding these days –: with this, Christianity was *abolished*! – What happened? A German monk, Luther, came to Rome. This monk, whose body had all the vindictive instincts of a wounded priest, flew into a rage in Rome *against* the Renaissance . . . Instead of feeling the most profound gratitude at the scale of what had taken place, the fact that Christianity had been overcome at its *source* –, his hatred only saw how it could feed itself on this spectacle. Religious people only think about themselves. – Luther saw the *corruption* of the papacy when precisely the opposite was palpable: the old corruption, the *peccatum originale*,[43] Christianity, was *not* sitting on the papal seat any more! But rather, life! Rather, the triumph of life! The great yes to all high, beautiful, daring things! . . . And Luther *re-established the church*: he attacked it . . . The Renaissance – a meaning-less event, a great *In Vain!* – Oh, these Germans, what they have cost us! In vain – that was always the *work* of the Germans. – The Reformation; Leibniz; Kant and what people call 'German philosophy'; the Wars of Liberation; the *Reich* – in each case, an 'in vain' for something that was already there, for something *irretrievable* . . . I confess it, these Germans are *my* enemies: I despise them for every type of uncleanliness in concepts and values, every type of *cowardice* in the face of every honest yes and no. For the better part of a millennium they have brought everything they have touched into chaos and confusion, they have on their conscience all the half-hearted (three-eighths-hearted!) measures that Europe is sick from, – they also have on their conscience the most unclean type of Christianity, that there is, the most incurable, the most irrefutable, Protestantism . . . If we do not get rid of Christianity, it will be the fault of the *Germans* . . .

62

– Now I have come to the end and I pronounce my judgment. I *condemn* Christianity, I indict the Christian church on the most terrible charges an accuser has ever had in his mouth. I consider it the greatest corruption conceivable, it had the will to the last possible corruption. The Christian church has not left anything untouched by its corruption, it has made an un-value out of every value, a lie out of every truth, a malice of the soul out of every piece of integrity. And people still dare to tell me about its

43 Original sin.

'humanitarian' blessings! The idea of *abolishing* any distress ran counter to the church's deepest sense of its own advantage, – it lived on distress, it *created* distress in order to eternalize *itself* . . . The worm of sin, for instance: the church was the first to enrich humanity with *this* bit of distress! – The 'equality of souls before God', this falseness, this *pretext* for the rancour of everything low-minded, this explosive concept which finally became a revolution, a modern idea, and the principle of the decline of the whole social order – is *Christian* dynamite . . . The 'humanitarian' blessings of Christianity! To breed a self-contradiction out of *humanitas*, an art of self-violation, a will to lie at any cost, a disgust, a hatred of all good and honest instincts! – Those would be the blessings of Christianity as far as I am concerned! – Parasitism as the church's *only* practice; drinking all the blood, all the love, all the hope out of life with its ideals of anaemia and 'sanctity'; the beyond as the will to negate every reality; the cross as the mark of the most subterranean conspiracy that ever existed, – against health, beauty, against anything well constituted, against courage, spirit, *goodness* of the soul, *against life itself* . . .

I want to write this eternal indictment of Christianity on every wall, wherever there are walls, – I have letters that can make even blind people see . . . I call Christianity the one great curse, the one great innermost corruption, the one great instinct of revenge that does not consider any method to be poisonous, secret, subterranean, *petty* enough, – I call it the one immortal blot on humanity . . .

And time is counted from the *dies nefastus*[44] when this catastrophe began, – from the *first* day of Christianity! – *Why not count from its last day instead? – From today?* – Revaluation of all values! . . .

Law against Christianity

Given on the Day of Salvation, on the first day of the year one (– 30 September 1888, according to the false calculation of time)

War to the death against vice: the vice is Christianity

First proposition. – Every type of anti-nature is a vice. The priest is the most vicious type of person: he *teaches* anti-nature. Priests are not to be reasoned with, they are to be locked up.

[44] Unlucky day.

Second proposition. – Any participation in church services is an attack on public morality. One should be harsher with Protestants than with Catholics, harsher with liberal Protestants than with orthodox ones. The criminality of being Christian increases with your proximity to science. The criminal of criminals is consequently the *philosopher*.

Third proposition. – The execrable location where Christianity brooded over its basilisk eggs should be razed to the ground and, being the *depraved* spot on earth, it should be the horror of all posterity. Poisonous snakes should be bred on top of it.

Fourth proposition. – The preacher of chastity is a public incitement to anti-nature. Contempt for sexuality, making it unclean with the concept of 'uncleanliness', these are the real sins against the holy spirit of life.

Fifth proposition. – Eating at the same table as a priest ostracizes: you are excommunicated from honest society. The priest is *our* Chandala, – he should be ostracized, starved, driven into every type of desert.

Sixth proposition. – The 'holy' history should be called by the name it deserves, the accursed history; the words 'God', 'saviour', 'redeemer', 'saint' should be used as terms of abuse, to signify criminals.

Seventh proposition. – The rest follows from this.

The Anti-Christ

Ecce Homo
How to Become What you Are

PREFACE

1

In the expectation that soon I will have to confront humanity with the most difficult demand it has ever faced, it seems imperative for me to say *who I am*. People really should know this: since I have not left myself 'without testimony'. But the discrepancy between the greatness of my task and the *smallness* of my contemporaries is apparent from the fact that people have not listened or even looked at me. I am living off my own credit, perhaps it is just a prejudice that I am living at all? . . . I only need to speak with some 'educated' person who happens to be in Upper Engadine[1] for the summer to convince myself that I am *not* alive . . . Under these circumstances it is a duty (albeit one that my habits and especially the pride of my instincts rebel against at a basic level) to say: *Listen to me! I am the one who I am! Above all, do not mistake me for anyone else!*

2

For instance, I am absolutely not some evil spirit or monster of morality, – if anything, I am the opposite of the type of person who has been traditionally admired as virtuous. Just between us, this seems to be a point of pride for me. I am a disciple of the philosopher Dionysus; I would rather be a satyr than a saint. But just read this essay. Perhaps I have succeeded, perhaps the whole purpose of this essay was to articulate this opposition in a cheerful and philanthropic way. The last thing *I* would promise would be to 'improve' humanity. I won't be setting up any new idols; let the old ones learn what it means to have feet of clay. *Knocking over idols* (my word for 'ideals') – that is more my style. You rob reality of its meaning, value, and truthfulness to the extent that you *make up* an ideal world . . . The 'true world' and the 'world of appearances' – in plain language, the *made-up* world and reality . . . So far, the *lie* of the ideal has been the curse on reality, it has made humanity false and hypocritical down to its deepest instincts – to the point of worshipping values that are the *reverse* of those that might begin to guarantee it prosperity, a future, a high *right* to a future.

---

[1] An Alpine valley where Nietzsche often spent the summer.

3

– Anyone who knows how to breathe the air of my writings will know that it is the air of high places, a *strong* air. You need to be made for it or you will catch a cold. The ice is close by, the solitude is tremendous – but how peacefully everything lies in the light! How freely you can breathe! How many things you feel to be *beneath* you! – Philosophy as I have understood it and lived it so far is a life lived freely in ice and high mountains – visiting all the strange and questionable aspects of existence, everything banned by morality so far. My long experience from these wanderings in the *forbidden* has taught me to see the reasons why people have been moralizing and idealizing very differently than might be desired: the *hidden* history of the philosophers, the psychology of its greatest names came to light for me. – How much truth can a spirit *tolerate*, how much truth is it willing to *risk*? This increasingly became the real measure of value for me. Error (– the belief in the ideal –) is not blindness, error is *cowardice* . . . Every achievement, every step forward in knowledge, comes from *courage*, from harshness towards yourself, from cleanliness with respect to yourself . . . I do not refute ideals, I just put on gloves when I have to deal with them . . . *Nitimur in vetitum*[2]: my philosophy will triumph under this sign, because it is precisely the truth that has been absolutely forbidden so far. –

4

– My *Zarathustra* has a special place for me in my writings. With it, I have given humanity the greatest gift it has ever received. This book, with a voice that spans millennia, is not only the most elevated book there is, the book that truly captures the atmosphere of high places – the whole fact of humanity lies incredibly far *beneath* it –, it is also the most *profound* thing to be born out of the innermost richness of the truth, and any bucket sent down to it will emerge from this inexhaustible fountain filled with gold and goodness. It is not a 'prophet' speaking here, not one of those awful amalgams of sickness and will to power known as founders of religions. Above all, you need to *listen* properly to the tone coming from this mouth, the halcyon tone, so as not to be miserably unfair to the meaning of its

[2] We strive for the forbidden.

wisdom. 'It is the stillest words that bring on the storm, the thoughts that come on doves' feet are the ones that guide the world –'[3]

> The figs fall from the trees, they are sweet and good: and in falling they lose their red skin. I am a north wind to ripe figs.
>
> So, these teachings fall like figs, my friends: now drink their juice and their sweet flesh! Autumn is around us and pure sky and after-noon –[4]

These are not the words of some fanatic, nothing is being 'preached' here, nobody is demanding that you *believe*: drop after drop, word after word falls from an infinite fullness of light and depth of happiness, – the tempo of this speech is tender and slow. Things like this only reach the most select; it is a privilege without equal to be able to listen to them; nobody is free to have ears for Zarathustra . . . Doesn't all this mean that Zarathustra is a *seducer*? . . . But what were his own words when he returned to his solitude for the first time? The exact opposite of what a 'wise man', 'saint', 'world redeemer', or other decadent would say in this situation . . . He does not just talk differently, he *is* different . . .

> I will go by myself, my disciples! You go as well, and alone! This is what I want.
>
> Leave me now and guard yourselves against Zarathustra! Even better: be ashamed of him! Perhaps he has deceived you.
>
> The man of knowledge does not just need to love his enemies, he needs to be able to hate his friends as well.
>
> You repay a teacher badly by remaining a pupil. And why don't you want to pluck at my wreath?
>
> You admire me: but what if your admiration *subsides* someday? Be careful not to be killed by a statue!
>
> You say you believe in Zarathustra? But who cares about Zarathustra! You are my believers, but who cares about believers!
>
> You have not looked for yourselves yet: and you found me. That is what all believers are like; that is why belief means so little.
>
> Now I call upon you to lose me and find yourselves; and *only after you have all denied me* will I want to return to you . . .[5]
>
> Friedrich Nietzsche

---

[3] *Z*, Part II, 'The Stillest Hour'.
[4] *Z*, Part II, 'On the Blissful Islands'.   [5] *Z*, Part I, 'Of the Bestowing Virtue', 3.

CONTENTS

On this perfect day, when everything is ripe and the grapes are not the only things that are turning brown, I have just seen my life bathed in sunshine: I looked backwards, I looked out, I have never seen so many things that were so good, all at the same time. It is not for nothing that I buried my forty-fourth year today, I had *the right* to bury it, – all its living qualities have been rescued, they are immortal. The *Revaluation of All Values*,[6] the *Dionysian Dithyrambs*, and, for recuperation, the *Twilight of the Idols* – all gifts of this year, of the last three months, in fact! *How could I not be grateful to my whole life?* And so I will tell myself the story of my life.

WHY I AM SO WISE

I

The happiness of my existence, perhaps its uniqueness, lies in its fatefulness; to give it the form of a riddle: as my father I am already dead and as

---

[6] *The Anti-Christ.*

my mother I am still alive and growing old. This double birth, from the highest and lowest rungs on the ladder of life, as it were, simultaneously decadent and *beginning* – this, if anything, explains that neutrality, that freedom from partisanship in relation to the overall problems of life, that is, perhaps, my distinction. I have a subtler sense of smell for the signs of ascent and decline than anyone has ever had, I am their teacher *par excellence*, – I know both of them, I am both of them. – My father died when he was thirty-six years old: he was frail, kind, and morbid, like a creature who was not long for this world, – more a kind memory of life than life itself. My life went downhill the same year as his: at the age of thirty-six I hit the low point in my vitality, I kept on living, but without being able to see three steps ahead of me. At that time – it was 1879 – I resigned from my post as professor in Basle, survived the summer in St Moritz *like* a shadow, and then survived the following winter in Naumburg, the least sunny of my life, *as* a shadow. This was my low point: *The Wanderer and his Shadow* came out of this. No doubt I was very good with shadows at that point . . . The following winter, the first I spent in Genoa, *Daybreak* emerged from that sweetening and spiritualization that is almost always the result of an extreme lack of blood and muscle. The perfect lightness and cheerfulness, even the exuberance of spirit that is reflected in this work, was accompanied not only by the deepest physiological weakness, but by an excess of painful feelings as well. In the middle of the tortures that go with an uninterrupted three-day headache together with exhausting bouts of vomiting, – I had a dialectician's clarity *par excellence* and could think with cold-blooded lucidity about things that, in healthier conditions, I was not enough of a mountain climber, not refined, not *cold* enough for. My readers might know the extent to which I see dialectics as a symptom of decadence, in the most famous case of all, for instance: the case of Socrates. – All pathological intellectual disturbances, even that half-stunned condition that follows a fever, have been completely alien to me to this day, and I have had to learn about their nature and frequency through study. My blood flows slowly. Nobody has ever detected a fever in me. A doctor who treated me for a long time as a neurological patient finally said: 'No! The problem is not your nerves, I am the one who is nervous.' Any sort of local degeneration simply cannot be proven; there is no organic cause for stomach pain, however profound the weakness of my gastric system may be as the result of a state of complete exhaustion. Even the eye-aches that sometimes come dangerously close to blindness are just the effect, not the cause: so that with every increase in vital energy, my visual acuity increases as well. – A long, all-too-long succession of years meant recuperation for me, – it also unfortunately meant relapse, decay, the period of a type of decadence. After all this do I need to add that I am *experienced* in questions of decadence? I know it inside and out. Even that filigree art of grasping and comprehending in general, that finger for nuances, that psychology of 'looking around the corner', and the other specialities of mine, I only learned then, they were genuine gifts of that time when I refined everything, observation itself as well as all the organs of observation. To be able to look out from the optic of sickness towards *healthier* concepts and values, and again the other way around, to look down from the fullness and self-assurance of the *rich* life into the secret work of the instinct of decadence – that was my longest training, my genuine experience, if I became the master of anything, it was this. I have a hand for switching *perspectives*: the first reason why a 'revaluation of values' is even possible, perhaps for me alone. –

2

Granting that I am a decadent, I am the opposite as well. My proof for this is, among other things, that I have always instinctively chosen the *correct* remedy for bad states; while complete decadents always choose the means that hurt themselves. As *summa summarum*[7] I was healthy; as a niche, as a speciality, I was decadent. That power absolutely to isolate and detach myself from my usual concerns, the compulsion not to allow myself to be cared for, waited on, *doctored* – this shows that I had a perfect, instinctive certainty for *what* was needed above all. I took myself in hand, I made myself healthy again: this is possible – as any physiologist will admit – *as long as you are basically healthy*. Something with a typically morbid nature cannot become healthy, much less make itself healthy; on the other hand, for something that is typically healthy, sickness can actually be an energetic *stimulus* to life, to being more alive. This is, in fact, how that long period of illness looks to me *now*: I discovered life anew, as it were, myself included, I tasted all good and even small things in ways that other people cannot easily do, – I created my philosophy from out of my will to health, to *life* . . . So you should pay careful attention: the

---

[7] Taken all-in-all.

years of my lowest vitality were the ones when I *stopped* being a pessimist: the instinct for self-restoration *prohibited* any philosophy of poverty or discouragement . . . And basically, how do you know that someone has *turned out well*! By the fact that a well-turned-out person does our senses good: by the fact that he is cut from wood that is simultaneously hard, gentle, and fragrant. He only has a taste for what agrees with him; his enjoyment, his desires stop at the boundary of what is agreeable to him. He works out how to repair damages, he uses mishaps to his advantage; what does not kill him makes him stronger. He instinctively gathers *his* totality from everything he sees, hears, experiences: he is a principle of selection, he lets many things fall by the wayside. He is always in his *own* company, whether dealing with books, people, or landscapes: he honours by *choosing*, by *permitting*, by *trusting*. He reacts slowly to all types of stimuli, with that slowness that has been bred in him by a long caution and a wilful pride, – he scrutinizes whatever stimulus comes near him, he would not go to meet it. He does not believe in 'bad luck' or 'guilt': he comes to terms with himself and with others, he knows how to *forget*, – he is strong enough that everything *has to* turn out best for him. – Well then, I am the *opposite* of a decadent: because I have just described *myself*.

3

I consider it a great privilege to have had a father like this: the farmers he preached to – because he was a minister in his final years, after living for a while in the court of Altenburg – said that this is what an angel must look like. – And this is where I come to the question of race. I am a pure-blooded Polish nobleman without a single drop of bad blood, certainly not German blood. When I look for my diametric opposite, an immeasurably shabby instinct, I always think of my mother and sister, – it would blaspheme my divinity to think that I am related to this sort of *canaille*.[8] The way my mother and sister treat me to this very day is a source of unspeakable horror: a real time bomb is at work here, which can tell with unerring certainty the exact moment I can be hurt – in my highest moments, . . . because at that point I do not have the strength to resist poison worms . . . Physiological contiguity makes this sort of *disharmonia*

---

[8] Riff-raff.

praestabilita[9] possible . . . But I will admit that the greatest objection to 'eternal return', my truly *abysmal* thought, is always my mother and sister. – But I am a huge atavism, even as a Pole. You would need to go back centuries to find instincts as pure as mine in this noblest race on earth. I have a sovereign feeling of distinction over and against everything called *noblesse* these days, – I would not allow the young German emperor the honour of driving my coach. There is only one case where I acknowledge my equal – I confess it with profound gratitude. Frau Cosima Wagner is by far the most noble nature; and so as not to say too little, I will say that Richard Wagner was by far the man most closely related to me . . . Everything else is silence . . . All prevailing ideas about degrees of relationship are unsurpassable pieces of physiological absurdity. The Pope deals in these absurdities even today. People are *least* related to their parents: it would be the most extreme sign of vulgarity to be related to your parents. Higher natures have their origins infinitely further back; collecting, economizing, accumulating has gone on longest for their sake. *Great* individuals are the oldest: I do not understand it, but Julius Caesar could be my father – *or* Alexander, that Dionysus incarnate . . . As I am writing this, the postman is bringing me a head of Dionysus . . .

4

I have never understood the art of setting people against me, even when it seemed like a worthwhile thing to do – I have my incomparable father to thank for this too. However un-Christian it might seem, I have never even taken sides against myself. You can examine my life from whatever angle you choose, you won't find a trace (except in one case) of anyone ever having a bad will towards me, – although you might find too many traces of *good* will . . . My experiences with other people are all, without exception, to their credit – even people everyone has bad experiences with; I tame every bear, I make clowns modest. During the seven years I taught Greek to the senior class of the Basle *Pädagogium*, I never had to punish anybody; the laziest students worked hard for me. I am always able to deal with accidents; I have to be unprepared in order to be in control of myself. Let the instrument be what it may, let it be as out of tune as only the instrument 'humanity' can be – I would have to be sick if

---

[9] Pre-established disharmony.

I could not get something worth hearing out of it. And how often have I heard the 'instruments' themselves tell me that they have never sounded like *this* before . . . Most nicely, perhaps, from Heinrich von Stein, who died so unpardonably young; he once came to Sils-Maria for three days, after carefully asking permission, and explained to everyone that he was *not* there to see the Engadine. This exceptional man who waded into the Wagnerian morass (– and into the Dühring morass as well!) with the impetuous naïveté of a Prussian *junker* – during these three days, it was as if he had been transformed by the stormy winds of freedom into someone who has suddenly been raised to *his* height and given wings. I always said to him that the air is good up here, as everyone finds out, and that it is not for nothing that we are 6,000 feet above Bayreuth,[10] – but he did not want to believe me . . . If in spite of this I have been wronged a number of times in large and small ways, it was not because of 'the will', and certainly not because of any *evil* will: I would have more reason to complain – as I have just suggested – about the good will that has wreaked no small amount of havoc in my life. My experiences give me a right to be generally mistrustful of so-called 'selfless' drives, the whole phenomenon of 'neighbour love' that is always ready with a helpful word and a helping hand. I think of it as an inherent weakness, as a case of being unable to defend yourself against stimuli, – *pity* is only a virtue for decadents. My problem with people who pity is that they easily lose any sense of shame or respect, or any sensitivity for distances, that pity quickly begins to smell of the mob and is almost indistinguishable from bad manners, – that in certain circumstances, pitying hands can really interfere destructively in a great destiny, in the isolation of the wounded, in the *privilege* of heavy debt. I consider the overcoming of pity a *noble* virtue: I have written about the case of 'Zarathustra's temptation', where he hears a loud cry for help and pity tries to assault him, tries to lure him away from *himself*, like a final sin.[11] To stay in control, to keep the *height* of your task free from the many lower and short-sighted impulses that are at work in supposedly selfless actions, this is the test, the final test, perhaps, that a Zarathustra has to pass – his real *proof* of strength . . .

[10] Wagner built the *Festspielhaus* in Bayreuth for the performance of his music dramas. It opened in 1876.
[11] *Z*, Part IV, 'The Cry of Distress'.

5

There is another respect in which I am just my father once again, and, as it were, a continuation of his life after his all-too-early death. Like everyone else who has never lived among equals and who has as little access to the idea of 'retaliation' as to the idea of 'equal rights', I do not allow myself to take steps or precautions, – or, as is proper, defensive or 'justificatory' measures – in cases where I find myself the target of some piece of stupidity, small or *very large*. My type of retaliation consists of following up the stupidity as quickly as possible with something clever: and this might make up for it. Metaphorically: I get over a *bitter* episode by sending a pot of jam . . . You just need to do me some wrong, I will 'retaliate', you can be sure of that: I quickly find some opportunity to thank the 'wrong-doer' (occasionally even for the wrong) – or to *ask* him for something, which can be friendlier than giving him something . . . It also seems to me that the rudest word, the rudest letter, is more good-natured, more honest, than silence. People who are silent are almost always lacking in subtlety and courtesy of the heart; silence is an objection, swallowing things down will always lead to a bad character, – it ruins your stomach too. Silent people are always dyspeptic. – You see that I do not want to underestimate the value of rudeness, it is by far the most *humane* way of contradicting somebody, and, given the modern tendency to coddle and overprotect, it is one of our primary virtues. – If you are rich enough for it, it is even good luck to be wronged. A god who descends to earth should *only* do wrong, – it is not divine to take the punishment upon yourself – it is divine to take on the *guilt*.

6

Freedom from *ressentiment*, lucidity about *ressentiment* – who knows how much I ultimately have to thank my long sickness for these as well! The problem is not exactly a simple one: you need to have experienced it out of strength and out of weakness. If there are any drawbacks to being sick and weak, it is that these states wear down the true instinct for healing, which is the human instinct for *weapons and war*. You do not know how to get rid of anything, you do not know how to get over anything, you do not know how to push anything back, – everything hurts. People and things become obtrusive, events cut too deep, memory is a festering wound. Sickness is itself a kind of *ressentiment*. – The sick person has only one great remedy for this – I call it *Russian fatalism*, the fatalism without revolt that you find when a military campaign becomes too difficult and the Russian soldier finally lies down in the snow. Not taking anything else on or in, – not reacting at all any more . . . The excellent reasoning behind this fatalism, which is not always just courage in the face of death, but can preserve life under the most dangerous circumstances, is that it reduces the metabolism, slows it down, a type of will to hibernation. Taking this logic a few steps further, you have the fakir who sleeps for weeks in a grave . . . Since any sort of reaction wears you out too quickly, you do not react at all: this is the reasoning. And nothing burns you up more quickly than the affects of *ressentiment*. Annoyance, abnormal vulnerability, inability to take revenge, the desire, the thirst for revenge, every type of poisoning – these are definitely the most harmful ways for exhausted people to react: they inevitably lead to a rapid consumption of nervous energy and a pathological increase in harmful excretions, of bile into the stomach, for instance. *Ressentiment* should be what is forbidden most rigorously for people who are sick – it is *their* great evil: and unfortunately their most natural tendency as well. – This was understood very well by that profound psychologist, the Buddha. His 'religion', which could be better described as a *hygiene* (so as not to confuse it with anything as pathetic as Christianity) – the effectiveness of this religion depends on conquering *ressentiment*: to free the soul of *this* – the first step to recovery. 'Enmity will not bring an end to enmity, friendship brings an end to enmity': this is how the Buddha's teaching begins – this is *not* the voice of morality, this is the voice of physiology. – Born from weakness, *ressentiment* is most harmful to the weak themselves, – wherever a rich nature is presupposed, an *overflowing* feeling, a feeling of maintaining control over *ressentiment*, is almost the proof of richness. Anyone who knows how seriously my philosophy has taken up the fight against lingering and vengeful feelings, right up into the doctrine of 'free will' – the fight against Christianity is just one instance of this – anyone aware of this will understand why I am calling attention to my own behaviour, my *sureness of instinct* in practice. When I was a decadent I *prohibited* these feelings as being harmful to me; as soon as my life became rich and proud enough again, I prohibited these feelings as being *beneath* me. I showed signs of that 'Russian fatalism' I mentioned by sticking doggedly (for years, even) to almost intolerable situations, places, lodgings, company, just because they happened to come my way, – this was better than changing them, than *thinking* that they could be changed – than rebelling against them . . . At that time, I took mortal offence at any attempt to disturb me in this fatalism, to snap me out of it: – which would in fact have been mortally dangerous as well. – To accept yourself as a fate, not to want to 'change' yourself – in situations like this, that is *reason par excellence*.

7

War is another matter. I am warlike by nature. I have an instinct for attack. To be *able* to be an enemy, to be an enemy, perhaps that presupposes a strong nature, in any case it is a part of every strong nature. Strong natures need resistance, that is why they *look* for resistance: an *aggressive* pathos is an essential component of strength in the same way that lingering feelings of revenge are an essential component of weakness. Females are vengeful, for instance: this is a constituent part of their weakness, just like their sensitivity to the needs of others. – One way of *measuring* the strength of an attacker is by looking at the sort of opponents he needs; you can always tell when something is growing because it will go looking for powerful adversaries – or problems: since a warlike philosopher will challenge problems to single combat. The task is *not* to conquer all obstacles in general but instead to conquer the ones where you can apply your whole strength, suppleness, and skill with weapons, – to conquer opponents that are your *equals* . . . Equality among enemies – first presupposition of an *honest* duel. You *cannot* wage war against things you hold in contempt; and there *is* no war to be waged against things you can order around, things you see as *beneath* you. – My practice of war can be summed up in four propositions. First: I only attack a winner, – in some cases, I wait until it has won. Second: I only attack where I will not have any allies, where I am all alone, – where I am only compromising myself . . . I have never taken a step in public that did not compromise me: that is *my* criterion for acting right. Third: I never attack people, – I treat people as if they were high-intensity magnifying glasses that can illuminate a general, though insidious and barely noticeable, predicament. This is how I attacked David Strauss or, more precisely, the *success* of an old and decrepit book in German 'culture', – I caught this culture in the act . . .[12]

---

[12] In the first of the *Untimely Meditations*.

And this is also how I attacked Wagner or, more precisely, the falseness, the half-couth instincts of our 'culture' that mistakes subtlety for richness and maturity for greatness. Fourth: I only attack things where there is no question of personal differences, where there has not been a history of bad experiences. On the contrary, for me an attack is proof of good will or even gratitude under some circumstances. I do something or someone honour, I confer distinction on it when I associate my name with it: for or against – this is not important to me. I have the right to wage war on Christianity because I have never been put out or harmed by it, – the most serious Christians have always been well disposed towards me. I myself, a *de rigueur* opponent of Christianity, will certainly not hold individuals to blame for the disaster of millennia. –

8

Do I dare hint at another feature of my character that has caused no end of difficulties in my dealings with people? The sensitivity of my instinct for cleanliness is perfectly uncanny, and I can physiologically perceive the presence or – what am I saying? – the very centre, the 'intestines', of every soul – I can *smell* it . . . This sensitivity gives me psychological antennae to feel and get hold of every secret: I notice the abundant, *hidden* dirt at the bottom of so many characters (the result of bad blood, perhaps, but whitewashed by education) almost as soon as I come into contact with it. If my eyes do not deceive me, the characters who offend my sense of cleanliness are also, for their part, aware of the guardedness of my disgust: it does not make them smell any better . . . This has always been my habit – extreme purity with respect to myself is the condition for my existence, I find uncleanliness deadly –, I constantly swim, bathe, and ripple around in water, in any sort of perfectly transparent and lustrous element. This presents no minor test of patience when I have to deal with people; my humanity does *not* consist in sympathizing with people as they are, but instead in *putting up with* the fact that I sympathize with them . . . My humanity is a constant self-overcoming. – But I need *solitude*, by which I mean recovery, a return to myself, the breath of a free, light, playful air . . . The whole of my *Zarathustra* is a dithyramb to solitude, or, if you have understood me, to *purity* . . . Luckily not to *pure stupidity*. – Anyone with an eye for colour will call it diamond. – *Disgust* with people, with 'the dregs' of humanity, has always been my greatest danger... Do you want to hear how Zarathustra discusses *redemption* from disgust?

> What really happened to me? How did I redeem myself from disgust? Who rejuvenated my eyes? How did I fly to the heights where the dregs of humanity do not sit by the fountain any more?
>
> Is it my disgust itself that gave me wings and the ability to divine water? Truly, I needed to fly to the highest heights in order to find the fount of pleasure again! –
>
> Oh, I found it, my brothers! Here in the highest of heights the fount of pleasure gushes out for me! And there is a life that the dregs of humanity do not drink!
>
> You flow towards me almost too forcefully, source of pleasure! And you often empty the cup by wanting to fill it.
>
> And I still need to learn to approach you more modestly: my heart flows towards you all too forcefully:
>
> – my summer is burned on my heart, short, hot, melancholy, over-blissful: how my summer heart longs for your coolness!
>
> Gone is the hesitant sorrow of my spring! Gone are the snowflakes of my June-time malice! In the summer I became whole, I became a summer noon, –
>
> – a summer in the highest heights with cold fountains and blissful silence: oh come, my friends, so that the silence might be even more blissful!
>
> Because this is *our* height and our home: we live in places too high and steep for the unclean and their thirsts.
>
> Cast only your clean eyes on the fount of my pleasure, my friends! How could that make it muddy? It will laugh back at you with *its* cleanliness.
>
> We build our nest on the tree called 'future'; eagles will bring meals in their beaks to us solitary ones!
>
> Truly, no meals that the unclean can eat as well! They would think that they were feeding on fire and they would burn their mouths.
>
> Truly, we do not keep a home ready for the filthy! Their bodies and their spirits would think of our happiness as caverns of ice!
>
> And we want to live above them like strong winds; neighbours of eagles, neighbours of the snow, neighbours of the sun: this is the life of strong winds.
>
> And like a wind I still want to blow among them one day and with my spirit take away the breath of their spirit: my future wills that it be so.

Truly, Zarathustra is a strong wind to everyone low: and he gives
this advice to his enemies and to everything that spits and spews:
take care not to spit *into* the wind! . . .[13]

WHY I AM SO CLEVER

I

– Why do I know a few *more* things? In general, why am I so clever? I
have never thought about questions that do not amount to anything, –
I have not wasted myself on that. – For example, I do not have any
experience with genuine *religious* difficulties. I have never paid attention
to how 'sinful' I might be. Similarly, I have no reliable criterion for what
a sting of conscience is: given what is *said* about it, a sting of conscience
does not seem very respectable to me . . . I would not want to leave an
act in the lurch *after the fact*; as a matter of principle I would rather separate the bad outcome, the *consequences*, from questions of value. When
the outcome is bad, it is far too easy to lose an *accurate* view of what you
have done; a sting of conscience seems like a sort of '*evil* eye' to me. To
honour something that has gone wrong all the more *because* it has gone
wrong – that is more in keeping with my morals. – 'God', 'immortality
of the soul', 'redemption', 'beyond', are simply ideas that I have not paid
any attention to or devoted any time to, even as a child, – perhaps I was
never childish enough for them? – I have no sense of atheism as a result,
and even less as an event: for me it is an instinct. I have too much curiosity,
too many doubts and high spirits to be happy with a ridiculously crude
answer. God is a ridiculously crude answer, an *undelicatesse* against us
thinkers –, basically even a ridiculously crude *ban* on us: thou shalt not
think! . . . Another question interests me in a much different way: the
question of *nutrition*; the 'salvation of humanity' is much more dependent on this question than on any theological oddity. We can formulate it
in rough and ready terms: 'what do you *yourself* eat in order to achieve
the maximum of strength, of *virtù* in the style of the Renaissance, of
moraline-free virtue?' – My experiences here are as bad as can be; I am
amazed that I heard this question so late, that I learned 'reason' so late
from these experiences. Only the complete worthlessness of our German

---

[13] *Z*, Part ii, 'Of the Rabble'.

education – its 'idealism' – makes it somewhat explicable to me why I was backward to the point of holiness about this issue in particular. The first thing this 'education' teaches you is to lose sight of *reality* and chase after completely problematic, so-called 'ideal' goals, a 'classical education', for instance: – as if it were not a lost cause to combine 'classical' and 'German' in a single concept! What is more, it is actually quite funny, – just think of a 'classically educated' Leipziger! – In fact, I always ate *badly* until I was fairly old, – in moral terms, 'impersonally', 'selflessly', 'altruistically', for the sake of cooks and other fellow Christians. For instance, between Leipzig cuisine and my first studies of Schopenhauer (1865), I effected a very serious denial of my 'will to life'. How to ruin your stomach for the sake of inadequate nutrition – the aforementioned cuisine seemed like the perfect solution to this problem. (It is said that 1866 changed all this –.[14]) But German cooking in general – what *doesn't* it have on its conscience! Soup *before* the meal (sixteenth-century Venetian cookbooks still refer to this as *alla tedesca*[15]); overcooked meats, vegetables cooked with fat and flour; the degeneration of starchy foods into paperweights! Just add to this the almost brutal post-prandial drinking habits of the ancient, but by no means only the *ancient*, Germans, and you will also understand the origin of *German spirit* – from depressive intestines . . . German spirit is indigestion, it is never through with anything. – But my own instincts are profoundly opposed to the *English* diet too, which in comparison with the German and even the French is a type of 'return to nature', namely to cannibalism; it seems to me that it gives spirit *heavy* feet – the feet of an Englishwoman . . . The best cuisine is from *Piedmont*. Alcoholic drinks are bad for me; one glass of wine or beer in the course of a day is more than enough to turn my life into a 'veil of tears', – my antipodes are in Munich. Since I was a little late in understanding this, I really *experienced* it from the time I was a child. When I was a boy, I thought that drinking wine, like smoking tobacco, started off as just a *vanitas* of young men and became a bad habit later on. Perhaps the Naumburg wine is partly to blame for this *harsh* judgment.[16] I would need to be a Christian to think of wine as a *stimulant*, which is to say I would need to believe something I find absurd. Strangely enough, given my extreme susceptibility to small doses of strongly diluted alcohol, I am practically a sailor when it comes

---

[14] In 1866, the Prussians marched into Saxony, of which Leipzig is the second city.
[15] In the German manner.   [16] Nietzsche grew up in Naumberg.

to *strong* doses. Even as a boy this was a particular point of courage for me. Writing and then copying out a long Latin essay in a single night, with an ambition in my pen to imitate Sallust, my model of rigour and conciseness, and pouring the strongest-calibre grog over my Latin – this was in no way at odds with my physiology when I was a student at the venerable Schulpforta, or perhaps with that of Sallust – however at odds it might have been with the venerable Schulpforta . . . Later, of course, towards the middle of my life, I became more and more strongly *opposed* to those 'spiritual' beverages: experience has made me an opponent of vegetarianism, and, like Richard Wagner who converted me, I cannot recommend seriously enough that all *spiritual* natures give up alcohol entirely. *Water* is enough . . . I prefer places where there are opportunities all around you to drink out of running fountains (Nice, Turin, Sils); a small glass accompanies me like a dog. *In vino veritas*;[17] it seems that here too, my idea of 'truth' is at odds with the rest of the world: – as far as I am concerned, spirit hovers over the *water* . . . Another couple of pointers from my morality. A hearty meal is easier to digest than one that is too small. The first presupposition of a good digestion is that the stomach as a whole becomes active. You need to be *aware* of the size of your stomach. For the same reasons, I would not recommend those protracted meals I call interrupted sacrificial feasts, those at the *table d'hôte*. – No snacking, no coffee: coffee darkens things. *Tea* is only good in the morning. Small quantities, but strong; tea is very bad for you and will make you sick all day if it is even a little too weak. Everyone has their own standards here, sometimes between the narrowest and most delicate boundaries. In a very *agaçante*[18] climate you should not start with tea: you should start an hour earlier with a cup of thick, oil-free cocoa. – *Sit* as little as possible; do not believe any idea that was not conceived while moving around outside, – with your muscles in a celebratory mode as well. All prejudices come from the intestines. – Sitting down – I have said it before – is a true *sin* against the Holy Spirit. –

2

The question of nutrition is most closely related to the questions of *location* and *climate*. Nobody is free to live everywhere; and someone with

---

[17] In wine there is truth.   [18] Provocative.

great tasks that require all his energy has particularly limited options here. The influence of climate on *metabolism*, inhibiting it or speeding it up, is so significant that a bad choice of location or climate can not only alienate someone from his task, but can keep him from it altogether: he never comes face to face with it. His animal vigour never reaches the point where freedom overflows into the most spiritual things and gives rise to the realization: I am the only one who can do *this* . . . If it becomes a bad habit, the smallest intestinal inertia is more than enough to turn a genius into something mediocre, something 'German'; the German climate is itself enough to discourage strong and even heroically disposed intestines. Metabolic tempo is in a precise relation to the agility or paralysis of the spirit's *feet*; in fact, 'spirit' itself is just a type of metabolism. Just list the places where there are and have been brilliant people, where wit, refinement, and malice were components of happiness, where genius has, almost necessarily, felt itself at home: they all have superbly dry air. Paris, Provence, Florence, Jerusalem, Athens – these names prove something: dry air and clear skies are *conditions* for genius, which is to say its conditions include a rapid metabolism and the possibility of a constant supply of large, even enormous, amounts of energy. I am thinking of a case where an outstanding spirit, one predisposed to be free, turned into a narrow, withdrawn, sour-tempered killjoy of a specialist just because he did not have any instinctive sensitivity for climate. This might ultimately have happened to me too if sickness had not forced me to be rational, to think hard about reason in reality. Now that I have had considerable experience in charting the effects of climatic and meteorological factors, using myself as a very subtle and reliable instrument, and checking how I am physiologically affected by a change in humidity even during a short trip, say from Turin to Milan, – I am horrified by the *hair-raising* fact that until ten years ago (when I began to be in mortal danger), I spent my life exclusively in places that are inappropriate and downright *forbidden* for me. Naumburg, Schulpforta, Thuringia in general, Leipzig, Basle – all disastrous locations, given my physiology. If I do not have any happy memories from my childhood and youth, it would be silly to blame so-called 'moral' factors, – like the indisputable dearth of *adequate* company: because this dearth is just as much the case today as it ever was, but it does not stop me from being cheerful and brave. No, ignorance *in physiologicis* – damned 'idealism' – has been the real catastrophe of my life, something completely stupid and unnecessary, with no redeeming features whatsoever, with nothing to make up for it or counterbalance it. I can explain all my mistakes as results of this 'idealism'; it is responsible for all the times I have really strayed away from my instincts, for all my 'modesties' that led me away from the *task* of my life, for instance, the fact that I became a philologist – why not a doctor at least, or something else a little more eye-catching? When I was in Basle, my whole spiritual diet, including how I scheduled my time, was a completely senseless abuse of extraordinary energies without any sort of supply system for replenishing this expenditure, without even thinking about consumption and replacement. There was no evidence of any subtler form of self-concern, no *care* on the part of a domineering instinct, I thought I was like everyone else, it was a form of 'selflessness', a forgetting of distance, – something I can never forgive myself for. When I was close to my end, *because* I was close to my end, I became thoughtful about this fundamental unreason of my life – 'idealism'. *Sickness* was what restored me to reason. –

3

The choice of nutrition; the choice of climate and location; – the third thing that you should not get wrong at any cost is the choice of your *mode of recuperation*. Here too, the boundaries of the permissible (which is to say the *useful*) are increasingly narrow, according to the extent to which a spirit is *sui generis*. In my case, *reading* as a whole is a way of recuperating: accordingly, it is one of the things that lets me detach from myself and walk among foreign disciplines and souls, – who I do not take seriously any more. Reading recuperates me even from my *own* seriousness. When I am hard at work, you will not find me with books: I try not to be around anyone who is talking or even thinking. And that is what reading would certainly mean . . . Have you ever really noticed that chance and any sort of external stimulus have too violent an effect, 'strike' too deeply at the profound tension of the spirit? This is the tension that the spirit and basically the whole organism is condemned to by pregnancy. You need to steer clear of chance, of external stimuli as much as possible. In spiritual pregnancy a certain cleverness of instincts directs you to wall yourself in; would I let an *alien* thought secretly scale this wall? – And that is what reading would certainly mean . . . A period of recuperation follows a period of work and fruitfulness: come to me, you pleasant books, you brilliant books, you books that I have shunned! – Will they be German books? I have to go back

half a year to catch myself with a book in my hand. What was it again? –
An excellent study by Victor Brochard, *Les Sceptiques Grecs*, that puts
my *Laertiana* to good use as well.[19] The sceptics were the only *respectable*
types among the philosophical tribes, tribes that generally talk out of both
sides of their mouths (they would talk out of five sides if they could)! . . .
Otherwise, I almost always take refuge in the same books, a small number
all told, books that have been *proven* to me. Perhaps it is not my way to
read much or many things: reading rooms make me sick. It is also not
my way to love much or many things. Caution, even hostility towards
new books, is more in line with my instincts than 'tolerance', '*largeur du
cœur*',[20] or any other form of 'neighbour love' . . . I basically keep coming
back to a small number of old Frenchmen: I only believe in French culture
and I consider everything else that gets called 'culture' in Europe to be
a misunderstanding; I won't even mention German culture . . . The few
cases of higher culture that I have found in Germany were all of French
extraction, above all Frau Cosima Wagner, by far the leading voice that
I have heard in questions of taste . . . I do not read Pascal, I *love* him as
Christianity's most instructive victim, massacred slowly, first physically
then psychologically, the whole logic of this most horrible form of inhuman cruelty; perhaps I have something of Montaigne's mischief in my
spirit, who knows? Perhaps in my body too; the fact that my artistic taste
defends names like Molière, Corneille, and Racine, not without anger,
over and against a wild genius like Shakespeare: this ultimately does not
stop me from finding the very latest Frenchmen to be charming company. I cannot imagine another century in history where you could cobble
together such a list of inquisitive and, at the same time, delicate psychologists as you can with contemporary Paris: I will tentatively (because their
number is not small) name Messieurs Paul Bourget, Pierre Loti, Gyp,
Meilhac, Anatole France, Jules Lemaître, or, to draw attention to someone
from a strong race, a real Latin who I particularly like, Guy de Maupassant. Just between us, I prefer *this* generation even to its great teachers,
who were all spoiled by German philosophy: Mr Taine, for instance,
was spoiled by Hegel, who is behind Taine's misunderstanding of great
men and ages. Wherever Germany extends, it *spoils* culture. Only war
'redeemed' spirit in France . . . Stendhal, one of the best accidents in my
life – because all the epochal events of my life came to me by chance and

---

[19] Nietzsche's studies of Diogenes Laertius, published in the late 1860s.   [20] Greatness of heart.

not through anybody's recommendation – is completely invaluable, with his anticipatory psychologist's eye and his grasp of the facts, a grasp that reminds you of that greatest facticity of all (*ex ungue Napoleonem*[21]–); and finally, not least of all as an *honest* atheist, a rare species in France and one that you almost never come across, – with all due respect to Prosper Mérimée . . . Perhaps I am jealous of Stendhal myself? He beat me to the best atheism joke, just the sort of thing that I would say: 'God's only excuse is that he doesn't exist' . . . I myself said somewhere: what has been the greatest objection to existence so far? *God* . . .

4

Heinrich Heine has provided me with the highest concept of the lyric poet. I have not found music this sweet and passionate in any other realm of history. Heine has that divine malice which is an indispensable part of perfection, as far as I am concerned, – I measure the value of people, of races, by how difficult it is for them to divorce a god from a satyr. – And how he handles his German! It will be said someday that Heine and I were by far the premier artists of the German language – immeasurably removed from anything that mere Germans have made out of it. – I must be closely related to Byron's *Manfred*: I have found all these abysses in myself, – I was ready for this work when I was thirteen. I do not have a single word, just a glare, for anyone who dares to pronounce the word 'Faust' in the presence of Manfred. Germans are *incapable* of any concept of greatness: Schumann is proof of this. I once composed a counter-overture to *Manfred* because I was so angry at this saccharine Saxon – Hans von Bülow said that he had never seen anything like it on paper before: that it was the rape of Euterpe.[22] – When I look for the highest formula for *Shakespeare*, the only thing I can find is the fact that he conceived the type of Caesar. You cannot guess at this sort of thing, – either you are it or you are not. Great poets create *only* from their own reality – to the point where they cannot stand their work any more afterwards . . . Whenever I glance through my *Zarathustra*, I walk around the room for half an hour, sobbing uncontrollably. – Shakespeare is the most poignant reading I know: how much suffering does it take for somebody to need to play the clown! – Have people *understood* Hamlet? It is not doubt, it is

---

[21] From the claw, you can tell that it is Napoleon.   [22] Euterpe is the muse of music.

certainty that drives people mad . . . But you need to be deep, an abyss, a philosopher, to feel this way . . . We are all *afraid* of the truth . . . And just to confess, I have an instinctive certainty that Lord Bacon was the author, the self-torturer of animals who is behind this uncanniest type of literature: what do *I* care about the pathetic drivel of American idiots and asses? But the strength for the most powerful reality of vision is not just compatible with the most powerful strength for action, for monstrosities of actions, for crimes – *it even presupposes it* . . . We do not know nearly enough about Lord Bacon, the first realist in every great sense of the term, to know *what* he did, *what* he wanted, *what* he experienced in himself . . . And damn it, my dear Mr Critic! If I had published my *Zarathustra* under a different name, 'Richard Wagner', for instance, the collective acuity of two hundred years would not have been enough to guess that the author of *Human, All Too Human* was the visionary of *Zarathustra* . . .

5

As long as I am talking about the recuperations in my life, I need to express my gratitude for what was by far the friendliest and most profound recuperation of my life. Without a doubt, this has been my intimate association with Richard Wagner. None of my other personal relationships amounts to much; but I would not give up my Tribschen[23] days for anything, days of trust, of cheerfulness, of sublime chance – of *profound* moments . . . I do not know what other people's experience of Wagner has been: no clouds ever darkened our skies. – And this takes me back to France, – I do not have any reasons, just a contemptuous scowl, for Wagnerians *et hoc genus omne*[24] who think that they are honouring Wagner by saying how similar he is to *themselves* . . . Being what I am, with my deepest instincts foreign to anything German, so that even the proximity of a German slows down my digestion, my first contact with Wagner was also the first time in my life I was really able to breathe freely: I saw him, I worshipped him as a *foreign country*, as the opposite of – a living protest against – all 'German virtues'. – Those of us who were children during the quagmire of the fifties are necessarily pessimistic about the concept 'German'; we cannot help being revolutionaries, – we won't accept a state of affairs where some *idiot* is in charge. I couldn't care less if he changes his

---

[23] Wagner's home in Switzerland.   [24] And all that crowd.

stripes, puts on scarlet, and wears a hussar's uniform . . . Well then! Wagner was a revolutionary – he ran away from the Germans . . . . As an *artist*, Paris is your only home in Europe; the *délicatesse* in all five artistic senses that Wagner's art presupposes, the finger for nuances, the psychological morbidity, you only find these in Paris. There is nowhere else that people have such passion for questions of form, such seriousness about the *mise en scène*[25] – it is the Parisian seriousness *par excellence*. Germans have no idea what enormous ambition lives in the soul of a Parisian artist. Germans are good-natured – Wagner was not remotely good-natured . . . but I have already described in sufficient detail (*Beyond Good and Evil*, 256) where Wagner belongs, who his next of kin really are: they are the late French Romantics, that high-flying, upwards-raging type of artist like Delacroix, like Berlioz, with a *fond*[26] of sickness, of fundamental incurability, all of them fanatics of *expression*, virtuosos through and through . . . Who was the first *intelligent* follower of Wagner? Charles Baudelaire, who was also the first to understand Delacroix, that typical decadent in whom a whole generation of artists recognized themselves – he might also have been the last . . . What have I never forgiven Wagner for? That he *condescended* to the Germans, – that he became *reichsdeutsch*[27] . . . Wherever Germany extends it *spoils* culture. –

6

All things considered, my youth would have been intolerable without Wagner's music. Because I was *condemned* to Germans. You need hashish to get rid of an unbearable pressure. Well then, I needed Wagner. Wagner is the antidote *par excellence* for all things German, – poison, this I won't deny . . . From the moment there was a piano score for *Tristan* – my complements, Herr von Bülow! – I was a Wagnerian. I thought that Wagner's older works were beneath me – too common, too 'German' . . . But I have never found a work as dangerously fascinating, with as weird and sweet an infinity, as *Tristan*, – I have looked through all the arts in vain. Everything strange and alien about Leonardo da Vinci is demystified with the first tones of *Tristan*. This work is without a doubt Wagner's *non plus ultra*; he recuperates from it with *Meistersinger* and the *Ring*. Becoming healthier – this is a *regress* for someone like Wagner . . . I think that it is a

[25] Staging.   [26] Core.   [27] Faithful to the *Reich*, the German empire.

supreme piece of luck to have lived at the right time and specifically among Germans so as to be *ripe* for this work: my psychologist's curiosity goes this far. The world is an impoverished place for anyone who was never sick enough for this 'hellish voluptuousness': it is permissible, it is almost imperative, to reach for mystical formulas at this point. – I think that I know better than anyone what tremendous things Wagner could do, the fifty worlds of foreign delights that only he had wings to reach; and being what I am, strong enough to take advantage of the most questionable and dangerous things and become even stronger in the process, I name Wagner as the greatest benefactor of my life. We are related by virtue of having suffered more deeply (from each other too) than people of this century are able to suffer, and this fact will unite our names forever; and just as it is certain that Wagner is a simple misunderstanding among Germans, it is equally certain that I am and will always be a misunderstanding as well. – To *start* with, you would need two hundred years of psychological and artistic discipline, my dear Teutons! . . . And you cannot make up for that. –

7

– I will say another word for the choicest of ears: what *I* really want from music. That it be cheerful and profound, like an afternoon in October. That it be distinctive, exuberant, and tender, a sweet little female, full of grace and dirty tricks . . . I will never admit that a German *could* know what music is. The people called 'German musicians', the greatest above all, are *foreigners*, Slavs, Croats, Italians, Dutch – or Jews; or else Germans of a strong race, *extinct* Germans like Heinrich Schütz, Bach, and Handel. I myself am still enough of a Pole to give up all other music for the sake of Chopin: there are three reasons why I will make an exception for Wagner's *Siegfried Idyll*, perhaps also for Liszt, who excels all other musicians when it comes to the noble accents of his orchestration; finally, everything that has grown up beyond the Alps – *on this side* . . . I wouldn't know how to do without Rossini, or even less without *my* southernness in music, the music of my Venetian maestro, Pietro Gasti.[28] And when I say 'beyond the Alps', I really am only saying Venice. When I look for another word for music, I only ever find the word 'Venice'. I cannot tell any difference

---

[28] Nietzsche's friend Peter Gast.

between tears and music, I know the happiness of not being able to think
of the *South* without a shudder of apprehension.

> I lately stood on the bridge
> in the dark of the night.
> A song came from out of the distance:
> pouring away in golden drops
> over the trembling space.
> Gondolas, lights, music –
> it swam drunkenly away into the twilight . . .
>
> My soul, a stringed instrument,
> Secretly sang a barcarole,
> Moved by invisible forces
> Trembling with bright bliss.
> – Did anyone hear? . . .

8

Each of these choices – of nutrition, of location and climate, and of recuperation – is governed by an instinct for self-preservation that is most
clearly expressed as an instinct for *self-defence*. Not seeing much, not
hearing much, not letting many things come close – this is a first principle
of cleverness and the first proof that you are not just a piece of chance
but rather a necessity. The usual word for this instinct of self-defence is
taste. Its imperative not only demands that you say no where yes would be
an act of 'selflessness', it also demands that you *say no as little as possible*.
To separate yourself, to detach yourself from people who will be needing
their 'no' again and again. The reason for this is that expenditures in the
service of defence, however small they might be, will lead to an extraordinary and totally superfluous impoverishment as soon as they turn into
a rule or a habit. Our *large* expenditures are the small ones that take place
most frequently. Warding things off, not letting them come to you, these
are expenditures – make no mistake about it –, energy *wasted* on negative
goals. In the constant need to ward things off, you can become so weak
that you are unable to protect yourself any more. – Suppose I were to walk
out of my house and, instead of quiet, aristocratic Turin, I found myself
in a small German town: my instincts would have to put up a barrier in
order to push back everything assaulting it from this flat and cowardly
world. Or suppose I found myself in a large German city, one of those

built-up vices where nothing grows, where everything both good and bad needs to be trucked in. Wouldn't this turn me into a *hedgehog*? – But it is a waste to have spines, a double luxury even, if it is possible to have *open* hands instead . . . Another clever idea and principle of self-defence is to *react as infrequently as possible* and avoid situations and conditions where you would be condemned to unhook your 'freedom', as it were, your initiative, and turn into a simple reagent. A parable would be how you interact with books. Scholars who spend basically all their time 'poring over' books – a modest estimate for a philologist would be 200 a day – ultimately become completely unable to think for themselves. When they are not poring over books, they are not thinking. When they think, they are *responding* to some stimulus (– a thought they have read about). In the end, all they do is react. Scholars spend all their energy saying yes and no, criticizing what other people have already thought, – they do not think for themselves any more . . . Their instinct for self-defence has worn out, otherwise they would be defending themselves from books. The scholar – a decadent. – I have seen it with my own eyes: natures that are gifted, rich, and disposed to be free, already 'ruined by reading' in their thirties, just matches that have to be struck to emit sparks – 'thoughts'. Early in the morning, at the break of day, when everything is fresh, in the dawn of your strength, to read a *book* – that is what I call depraved! – –

9

It cannot be avoided any more, at this point there needs to be a genuine answer to the question of *how you become what you are*. And this leads me to that masterpiece in the art of survival – *selfishness* . . . Assuming, of course, that the task, the vocation, the *destiny* of the task is far from ordinary, then nothing is more dangerous than catching sight of yourself *with* this task. Becoming what you are presupposes that you do not have the slightest idea *what* you are. If you look at it this way, even life's *mistakes* have their own meaning and value, the occasional side roads and wrong turns, the delays, the 'modesties', the seriousness wasted on tasks that lie beyond *the* task. All these could be very clever moves, even as clever as it gets: where *nosce te ipsum*[29] is the recipe for decline, then forgetting yourself, *misunderstanding* yourself, belittling, narrowing yourself, making yourself mediocre would

---

[29] Know thyself.

be the essence of reason. In moral terms: neighbour love, living for other people and other things, *can* be a form of precautionary discipline for maintaining the toughest selfishness. Here I make an exception to my rule and conviction, and side with 'selfless drives': in this case, they are working in the service of *selfishness* and *self-discipline*.[30] The whole surface of consciousness – consciousness *is* a surface – has to be kept free from all of the great imperatives. Be careful even of great words, great attitudes. They pose the threat that instinct will 'understand itself' too early. – – In the mean time, the organizing, governing 'idea' keeps growing deep inside, – it starts commanding, it slowly leads *back* from out of the side roads and wrong turns, it gets the *individual* qualities and virtues ready, since at some point these will prove indispensable as means to the whole, – one by one, it develops all the *servile* faculties before giving any clue as to the domineering task, the 'goal', the 'purpose', the 'meaning'. – Viewed in this light, my life is just fantastic. The task of *revaluing values* might have required more abilities than have ever been combined in any one individual, and in particular contradictory abilities that could not be allowed to disturb or destroy one another. Rank order of abilities; distance; the art of separating without antagonizing; not mixing anything, not 'reconciling' anything; an incredible multiplicity that is nonetheless the converse of chaos – this was the precondition, the lengthy, secret work and artistry of my instinct. Its *higher protection* manifested itself so strongly that I had absolutely no idea what was growing inside me, – and then one day all my capabilities suddenly *leapt out*, ripened to ultimate perfection. I have no memory of ever having made an effort, – you will not detect any trace of *struggle* in my life, I am the opposite of a heroic nature. To 'will' anything, to 'strive' after anything, to have a 'goal', a 'wish' in mind – I have never experienced this. Right now I am still looking out over my future – an immense future! – as if it were a calm sea: there is not a ripple of longing. I do not have the slightest wish for anything to be different from how it is; I do not want to become anything other than what I am. But this is how my life has always been. I have never wished for anything. Someone over the age of forty-four who can say that he never tried to get *honour, women,* or *money*! – Not that I would have enjoyed them . . . So, for instance, one day I found myself a university professor, – nothing like this had ever crossed my mind, as I was barely twenty-four years old. And

---

[30] Nietzsche is playing with the similarity between the two words *Selbstsucht* and *Selbstzucht.*

97

one day, two years earlier, I found myself a philologist: in the sense that my teacher Ritschl asked if he could publish my *first* philological work, my starting point in every sense, in his *Rheinisches Museum*.[31] (*Ritschl* – I say it with admiration – the only brilliant scholar I have ever come across. He had that pleasant corruption characteristic of us Thuringians, that makes even Germans sympathetic: – we still prefer surreptitious paths, even to reach the truth. In saying this, I have absolutely no intention of underestimating my close compatriot, the *clever* Leopold von Ranke . . .)

10

At this point, a more general reflection is called for. I will be asked why I have been talking about all these petty matters that people usually think are not worth worrying about; I am not doing myself any good, particularly if I am destined to take on great tasks. Answer: these petty concerns – nutrition, location, climate, recuperation, the whole casuistry of selfishness – are far more important than all the concepts people have considered important so far. This is exactly where people have to start *re-educating* themselves. The things that humanity used to think seriously about are not even realities, just figments of the imagination or, to put it more strongly, *lies* from the bad instincts of sick natures who were harmful in the deepest sense – all the concepts of 'God', the 'soul', 'virtue', 'sin', the 'beyond', 'truth', 'eternal life' . . . But this is where people used to look for the greatness of human nature, its 'divinity' . . . All questions of politics, of social organization, of education are shown up as forgeries at a very basic level when the most harmful people are taken for great human beings, – when people are taught to despise 'petty' matters, by which I mean the fundamental concerns of life itself . . . Contemporary culture is ambiguous in the highest degree . . . The German emperor makes deals with the Pope, as if the Pope did not represent a deadly hostility to life! . . . Things that are built today are gone in three years' time. – When I measure myself by what I *can* do, not to mention what will come after me, a revolution, a construction without equal, I have better claims to the word 'great' than any other mortal. When I compare myself with people who have been honoured as *first* so far, then the difference is palpable. I do not even consider these supposedly 'first' people to be people at all, – to my mind they are human waste, excrescences of disease and vengeful

---

[31] A professional journal.

instincts: they are nothing but disastrous, fundamentally incurable non-humans who take revenge on life . . . I want to be the opposite of all this: it is my privilege to have the finest sense for all signs of healthy instincts. I do not have any sickly features; even in times of widespread illness I do not get sick; you won't find a single trace of fanaticism in my character. You will not find any signs of presumptuous or pathetic behaviour at any point in my life. The pathos of poses is *not* a component of greatness; anyone who needs poses is *false* . . . Beware of picturesque people! – Life has become easy for me, and easiest when it is demanding the most difficult things. Anyone who saw me during the seventy days this fall when, working without a break, I created things of only the highest calibre, things that nobody will surpass – or anticipate – with a responsibility for all the millennia to come; nobody who saw me then would have noticed a single trace of tension, but rather an overflowing freshness and cheerfulness. I never ate more happily, I never slept better. – I do not know any other way of handling great tasks than as *play*: as a sign of greatness, this is an essential presupposition. The slightest compulsion, a gloomy look, any sort of harsh tone in the throat, all these are objections to a person and even more to his work . . . You cannot have any nerves . . . Even *suffering* from solitude is an objection, – I have only ever suffered from multitudes . . . At an absurdly early age, when I was seven, I already knew that no human word would ever reach me: has anyone ever seen me sad about this? – And I still have the same affable approach to everyone, I even treat the lowest with distinction: there is never any hint of arrogance, of secret loathing. *Whoever* I hate can *tell* that I hate him: my mere existence infuriates anything with bad blood in its body . . . My formula for human greatness is *amor fati*:[32] that you do not want anything to be different, not forwards, not backwards, not for all eternity. Not just to tolerate necessity, still less to conceal it – all idealism is hypocrisy towards necessity –, but to *love* it . . .

WHY I WRITE SUCH GOOD BOOKS

I

I am one thing, my writings are another. – Before turning to them, I will touch on the question of their intelligibility or *un*intelligibility. I will do

---

[32] Love of fate.

this with all the carelessness it warrants: because the time has certainly not come for this question. The time has not come for me either. Some people are born posthumously. – At some point people will need institutions where they can live and teach the way I understand living and teaching; perhaps there will be endowed chairs dedicated to *Zarathustra* interpretation. But it would be completely inconsistent of me to expect ears *and hands* to already exist for *my* truths: the fact that people do not hear me these days, that they do not know how to accept anything I say, these facts are not only understandable, they even strike me as the way things should be. I do not want to be mistaken for anyone else, – which also means that *I* should not mistake myself for anyone else either. – To say it again, you can find very little 'ill will' in my life; I can hardly think of a single case of literary 'ill will' either. By contrast, there is too much *pure stupidity* . . . It seems to me that someone confers a very uncommon distinction on himself when he takes a book of mine in his hands, – I will even assume that he takes his shoes off first, – not to mention his boots . . . Dr Heinrich von Stein once complained in all honesty that he could not understand a single word of my *Zarathustra*, and I told him that that was fair enough: to understand six sentences from it – that is, to have *experienced* six sentences from it – would raise you to a higher level of existence than 'modern' men are capable of achieving. With *this* feeling of distance, how could I even *wish* to be read by the 'moderns' I know –! My triumph is precisely the opposite of Schopenhauer's, – I say 'non *legor*, non legar'.[33] – Not that I underestimate the pleasure I have often felt when *innocents* say no to *my* writings. Just this summer, at a moment when I might have been able to throw every other piece of literature off balance with my own weighty, too-weighty literature, a kindly professor at the University of Berlin gave me to understand that I should devote myself to a different form: nobody reads this sort of thing. – In the end, it was Switzerland rather than Germany that came up with the two extreme cases. An essay by Dr V. Widmann in the *Bund* about *Beyond Good and Evil* under the title 'Nietzsche's Dangerous Book', and an overview of my books by one Herr Karl Spitteler, also in the *Bund*, represent a maximum in my life – I will be careful not to say what they are a maximum of . . . For instance, the latter treated my *Zarathustra* as a 'superior stylistic exercise' with the wish that I concern myself with content too, at some point in the

---

[33] 'I am *not* read, I will *not* be read.'

future; Dr Widmann conveys his admiration for my courage in endeavouring to do away with all decent feelings. – Through some small accident of fate, every sentence was, with remarkable consistency, a truth standing on its head: basically, just by 'revaluing the values' you can really hit the nail right on the head – instead of hitting a nail into *my* head . . . All the more reason for trying to find an explanation. – Ultimately, nobody can get more out of things – including books – than they already know. You will not have an ear for something until experience has given you some headway into it. Let us take the most extreme case, where a book talks only about events lying completely outside the possibility of common, or even uncommon, experience, – where it is the *first* language of a new range of experiences. In this case, absolutely nothing will be heard, with the associated acoustic illusion that if nothing is heard, *nothing is there*. At the end of the day, this has been my usual experience and, if you will, the *originality* of my experience. Anyone who thinks that they have understood me has made me into something after their own image, – often enough they make me into my opposite, an 'idealist', for example; anyone who has not understood me at all denies that I deserve any sort of consideration. The word '*overman*', as a designation for a type that has the highest constitutional excellence, in contrast to 'modern' people, to 'good' people, to Christians and other nihilists – a word that really makes you think when it comes from the mouth of a Zarathustra, a *destroyer* of morals; this word '*overman*' is understood almost everywhere with complete innocence to mean values that are the *opposite* from the ones appearing in the figure of Zarathustra, which is to say the 'idealistic' type of the higher sort of humanity, half 'saint', half 'genius' . . . Other scholarly cattle have suspected me of Darwinism for this reason; they even read into it the 'cult of the hero' that I condemn so bitterly, the invention of that unknowing and involuntary counterfeiter Carlyle. If I whisper to people that this type would look more like a Cesare Borgia than a Parsifal, they do not believe their ears. – You will have to forgive my complete lack of curiosity about reviews of my books, in particular those in the newspapers. My friends, my publishers, know this and do not talk to me about this sort of thing. In one particular case I was confronted with all the sins committed against one book – it was *Beyond Good and Evil*; I could produce a nice little report about that. Would you believe it, the *Nationalzeitung* – a Prussian newspaper, to keep my foreign readers informed: for my own part, I only read the *Journal des Débats* – seriously knew enough to see the book as a 'sign of the times', as the true blue *Junker philosophy* that the *Kreuzzeitung*[34] was not brave enough for? . . .

2

This was said for the benefit of Germans: because I have readers every-where else – nothing but *select* intelligences and proven characters, edu-cated to high positions and duties; I even have real geniuses among my readers. In Vienna, in St Petersburg, in Stockholm, in Copenhagen, in Paris and New York – I have been discovered everywhere: *not*, however, in Germany, the flatlands of Europe . . . And, I confess, I am even more pleased about my non-readers, people who have never heard either my name or the word 'philosophy'; but wherever I go, here in Turin, for exam-ple, every face lights up at the sight of me. I have felt most flattered so far by the old pedlar women who will not be happy until they have picked out the sweetest grapes for me. *This* is the extent to which you have to be a philosopher . . . It is not for nothing that people call Poles the French among the Slavs. A charming Russian woman would not have a moment's doubt as to where I belong. I cannot make myself solemn, I can achieve embarrassment at best . . . To think German, to feel German – I am capable of anything, but *this* is too much for me . . . My old teacher Ritschl once said that I drafted even my philology articles like a Parisian novelist – absurdly gripping. Even in Paris people are astonished over '*toutes mes audaces et finesses*'[35] – the expression comes from Monsieur Taine –; I am afraid that even in the highest forms of the dithyramb you will find that I have added a dose of *esprit*, the spice that can never be dull – 'German' – . . . I can do no other. So help me God! Amen.[36] – We all know what long ears a jackass has, some of us even know from expe-rience. Well then, I will bet that I have the shortest ears of all. This is of no little interest to women –, they seem to think that I understand them better? . . . I am the *anti-jackass par excellence*, which makes me a world-historical monster, – I am, in Greek, and not just Greek, the *Anti-Christ* . . .

---

[34] A very right-wing newspaper.
[35] All my audacities and finesses.   [36] Luther's words at the Diet of Worms.

3

I have some idea of my privileges as a writer; in a few cases I also know the extent to which familiarity with my writings 'spoils' your taste. You just cannot stand other books any more, philosophy books in particular. It is an honour beyond compare to enter into this noble and delicate world, – you cannot under any circumstances be German; ultimately, it is an honour you have to earn. But anyone related to me – by virtue of the *height* of their will – experiences true ecstasies of learning: because I come from heights that no bird has ever reached, I know abysses where no foot has ever strayed. I am told that it is not possible to put down any of my books, – I even disrupt sleep . . . This is the proudest, most refined type of book in existence: – they sometimes reach the highest elevation you will find anywhere on earth, cynicism; you need the most delicate fingers as well as the bravest fists to conquer them. Any infirmity of the soul will permanently disqualify you – even dyspepsia: you do not need nerves, you need a joyful stomach. Not just poverty, the stale air of a soul will bar you from them too, and cowardice, uncleanliness, secret vengefulness of the intestines even more so: one word from me will drive all your bad instincts into your face. I know a number of guinea pigs who provide me with a variety – a very instructive variety – of reactions to my writings. People – my so-called friends, for instance – become 'impersonal' when they do not want anything to do with the content of my writings: they congratulate me on having come 'so far' again, and find progress in a greater cheerfulness of tone . . . Completely depraved 'spirits', the 'beautiful souls', who are liars through and through, have no idea how even to approach these books, – which is why they see them as *beneath* themselves, the beautiful logic of all 'beautiful souls'. The cattle I know – pure Germans, if I may – give me to understand that people won't always agree with me, except sometimes, for instance . . . I have even heard this said about my *Zarathustra* . . . In addition, I regard every type of 'feminism' espoused by people, men as well as women, as the closing of a door: you will never enter this labyrinth of daring knowledge. You need to never have gone easy on yourself, you need to have *harshness* in your habits, if you are going to be cheerful among harsh truths. When I imagine a perfect reader, I always think of a monster of courage and curiosity who is also supple, cunning, cautious, a born adventurer and discoverer. Finally: when it comes to the question of *who*

I am speaking to, I cannot put it any better than Zarathustra does; *who* is the only one he wants to tell his riddles to?

> To you, the bold seekers, experimenters,[37] and anyone who has ever
> embarked with cunning sails on terrible seas, –
> to you, the riddle-drunk, twilight-glad, whose souls are seduced by
> flutes to every wild abyss:
> – because you do not want to fumble for a thread with a cowardly
> hand; and you hate to *guess* where you can *discern* . . .[38]

4

At the same time, I will say a general word about my *art of style*. To *communicate* a state, an inner tension of pathos, with signs, including the tempo of these signs – that is the meaning of every style; and considering that I have an extraordinary number of inner states, I also have a lot of stylistic possibilities – the most multifarious art of style that anyone has ever had at his disposal. Every style that really communicates an inner state is *good*, every style that is not wrong about signs, about the tempo of signs, about *gestures* – all laws concerning periods involve the art of gesture. My instinct here is unfailing. Good style *in itself* – this is *pure stupidity*, just 'idealism', somewhat like 'Beauty *in itself*', 'the Good *in itself*', the 'thing *in itself*' . . . Always supposing that there are ears – that there are people capable and worthy of a similar pathos, that there are people you *can* communicate with. – Meanwhile, my Zarathustra, for instance, looks for people like this – and oh! he will have to look for a long time! – You need to be *worthy* of hearing him . . . And until then nobody will understand the *art* that has been wasted here: nobody has ever wasted a greater number of new and unheard of artistic devices, devices created for this very purpose. It remained to be shown that this sort of thing was possible in German, of all languages: I myself would have been the first to deny it. Before I came along, no one knew what the German language was capable of, – what was possible with language in general. – I was the first to discover the art of *great* rhythm, the *great style* of the period, to express an incredible up and down of sublime, of overmanly passion; with a dithyramb like the last one in the *third part* of *Zarathustra*, entitled 'The

---

[37] *Suchern, Versuchern.*   [38] *Z*, Part III, 'Of the Vision and the Riddle', 1.

Seven Sails', I soared a thousand miles above anything called poetry so far.

5

– The fact that a *psychologist* without equal is speaking in my works, this is perhaps the first thing a good reader will realize – the sort of reader I deserve, who reads me as good old philologists read their Horace. Claims that everyone basically agrees with, not to mention commonplace philosophers, moralists, and other dunces and dimwits – I show that these claims are naïve mistakes: for instance, the belief that 'unegoistic' and 'egoistic' are opposites, when the ego is itself just a 'higher lie', an 'ideal' . . . There are *neither* egoistic *nor* un-egoistic acts: both concepts are psychological absurdities. Or the claim 'people strive for happiness' . . . Or the claim 'happiness is the reward for virtue' . . . Or the claim 'pleasure and pain are opposites' . . . Morality, the Circe of humanity, has fundamentally falsified – *moralified* – all *psychologica* – to the point where you get complete nonsense like the claim that love is something 'unegoistic' . . . You have to be firmly grounded in *yourself*, you have to stand bravely on your own two feet to be *able* to love at all. At the end of the day, this is something women know all too well: they could not care less about selfless, purely objective men . . . Do I dare to suggest that I *know* women? This is part of my Dionysian dowry. Who knows? perhaps I am the first psychologist of the eternal-feminine.[39] They all love me – an old story: not counting *unsuccessful* women, the 'emancipated' who do not have what it takes to have children. Luckily, I have no desire to let myself be torn apart: the perfect woman tears apart what she loves . . . I know these obliging maenads . . . Oh, what dangerous, insidious, subterranean little beasts of prey they are! And so pleasant into the bargain! A little woman in search of revenge would knock down fate itself. – Woman is incomparably more evil than man, cleverer too; goodness in woman is a form of *degeneration* . . . There is a physiological disaster at the bottom of all so-called 'beautiful souls', – I won't say everything or else I will become medi-cynical. The struggle for *equal* rights is actually a symptom of disease: every doctor knows this. – The woman, the more of a woman she is, fights tooth and nail against rights in general: after all, the natural

---

[39] A phrase from the last line of Goethe's *Faust*, Part II: 'The Eternal-Feminine / leads us on high.'

state of things, the eternal *war* between the sexes, gives her the highest rank by far. – Did anyone have ears for my definition of love? It is the only one worthy of a philosopher. – Love – its method is warfare, its foundation is the deadly hatred between the sexes. – Did anyone hear my answer to the question of how to *cure* – 'redeem' – a woman? Give her a baby. Women need children, the man is only ever the means: thus spoke Zarathustra. – 'Emancipation of women' – that is the instinctive hatred of *failed* women, which is to say infertile women, against those who have turned out well, – the fight against 'men' is only ever a means, pretext, tactic. By elevating *themselves* as the 'women *an sich*',[40] as the 'higher women', as the 'idealists' of women, they want to *lower* the rank of women in general; there is no surer means of doing this than secondary education, trousers, and the right to belong to the political herd of voters. Emancipated women are basically *anarchists* in the world of the 'eternal-feminine', people in bad shape whose bottom-most instinct is revenge . . . An entire species of the most vicious 'idealism' – you find this in men as well, by the way, in Henrik Ibsen, for instance, this typical old maid – sets out to *poison* the good conscience, the natural aspects of sexual love . . . And to leave no doubt as to my convictions, which are as principled as they are strict in this matter, I will communicate another proposition against *vice* from out of my moral code: I use the word 'vice' to fight against every type of anti-nature or, if you like pretty words, idealism. The proposition reads: 'preaching chastity is a public incitement to anti-nature. Every contempt for sex, every effort to dirty it through the concept of "impurity" is a crime against life itself – it is the true sin against the holy spirit of life.' –

6

To give some idea of me as a psychologist, I will take an odd bit of psychology from *Beyond Good and Evil*, – incidentally, I won't allow any speculation as to who I am describing here. 'The genius of the heart, as it is possessed by that great hidden one, the tempter-god[41] and born pied piper of consciences, whose voice knows how to descend into the underworld of every soul, whose every word and every glance conveys

---

[40] In-itself (or in-themselves).
[41] In German: *Versucher-Gott*. This could also mean the 'experimenting god'.

both consideration and a wrinkle of temptation, whose mastery includes an understanding of how to seem – not like what he is but rather like one *more* compulsion for his followers to keep pressing closer to him, to keep following him more inwardly and thoroughly . . . The genius of the heart, that makes everything loud and complacent fall silent and learn to listen, that smoothes out rough souls and gives them the taste of a new desire, – to lie still, like a mirror that the deep sky can mirror itself upon . . . The genius of the heart, that teaches the foolish and over-hasty hand to hesitate and reach out more delicately; that guesses the hidden and forgotten treasure, the drop of goodness and sweet spirituality under thick, dull ice, and is a divining rod for every speck of gold that has long been buried in a prison of mud and sand . . . The genius of the heart, that enriches everyone who has come into contact with it, not making them blessed or surprised, or leaving them feeling as if they have been gladdened or saddened by external goods; rather, they are made richer in themselves, newer than before, broken open, blown on and sounded out by a thawing wind, perhaps less certain, more gentle, fragile and broken, but full of hopes that do not have names yet, full of new wills and currents, full of new indignations and countercurrents . . .'[42]

THE BIRTH OF TRAGEDY

I

You need to forget about a couple of things if you are going to be fair to *The Birth of Tragedy* (1872). The book owed its *effectiveness* and even its fascination to what was wrong with it – its practical application to *Wagnerianism*, as if that were a symptom of *ascent*. This is why the book was an event in Wagner's life: it was at this point that Wagner's name began to give rise to great hopes. People still remind me of this, sometimes in the context of *Parsifal*: how it is on *my* conscience that there are such high opinions of the *cultural value* of this movement. – Several times I have found the essay cited as *The Rebirth of Tragedy Out of the Spirit of Music*: there were only ears for a new formula for *Wagner's* art, *Wagner's* intentions, *Wagner's task*, – and this is why people failed to hear what was really valuable in the essay. *Hellenism and Pessimism*: that would have

[42] *BGE* 295.

been an unambiguous title: that is, as the first lesson in how the Greeks put pessimism behind them, – how they *overcame* it . . . Tragedy in particular proves that the Greeks were *not* pessimists: Schopenhauer was wrong about this as he was wrong about everything. – Viewed impartially, *The Birth of Tragedy* looks very untimely: you would never dream that it was *begun* in the thunder of the battle of Wörth. I thought these problems out in front of the walls of Metz during the cold September nights when I was serving as a medical orderly; you would sooner believe that the essay was fifty years older. It is politically indifferent, – 'un-German' people would say nowadays – it smells offensively Hegelian and only a few formulas are tainted with the cadaverous fragrance of Schopenhauer. One 'idea' – the opposition between Dionysian and Apollonian – translated into metaphysics; history itself as the development of this 'idea'; the opposition sublated into a unity in tragedy; viewed through this optic, things never before confronted with each other are suddenly juxtaposed, used to clarify each other, and *understood*. Opera, for instance, and the revolution . . . The two crucial *innovations* of the book are, first, the understanding of the *Dionysian* phenomenon among the Greeks: the book gives the first psychology of this phenomenon, it sees it as the single root of the whole of Greek art. The other innovation is the understanding of Socratism: Socrates, recognized for the first time as the instrument of Greek disintegration, as a typical decadent. 'Rationality' *against* instinct. 'Rationality' at any price as dangerous, as a form of violence that undermines life! – Deep, hostile silence about Christianity throughout the whole book. It is neither Apollonian nor Dionysian; it *negates* all *aesthetic* values – the only values the *Birth of Tragedy* acknowledges: it is nihilistic in the deepest sense, while the furthest limits of *affirmation* are achieved in the Dionysian symbol. At one point Christian priests are alluded to as an 'insidious type of dwarf', of 'subterranean' . . .

2

This is an extremely strange beginning. I had *discovered* the only historical simile and facsimile of my own innermost experience, – and this led me to understand the amazing phenomenon of the Dionysian, the first person ever to have done so. At the same time, the fact that I recognized Socrates as a decadent proved beyond a doubt that my psychological grasp was firm enough not to be endangered by any moral idiosyncrasy: – to understand morality itself as a symptom of decadence is an innovation, a unique event of the highest rank in the history of knowledge. These two insights catapulted me high above any pathetic, idiot gossip about optimism *contra* pessimism! – I was the first to see the real opposition: – the *degenerate* instinct that turns against life with subterranean vindictiveness (– Christianity, Schopenhauer's philosophy, and in a certain sense even Plato's philosophy, the whole of idealism as typical forms) and a formula of the *highest affirmation* born out of fullness, out of overfullness, an unreserved yea-saying even to suffering, even to guilt, even to everything questionable and strange about existence . . . This final, most joyful, effusive, high-spirited yes to life is not only the highest insight, it is also the most *profound*, the most rigorously confirmed and supported by truth and study. Nothing in existence should be excluded, nothing is dispensable – the aspects of existence condemned by Christians and other nihilists rank infinitely higher in the order of values than anything the instinct of decadence is able to approve, to *call good*. To understand this requires *courage* and, as its condition, a surplus of *force*: because the forcefulness with which you approach truth is proportionate to the distance courage dares to advance. Knowledge, saying yes to reality, is just as necessary for the strong as cowardice and *fleeing* in the face of reality – which is to say the 'ideal' – is for the weak, who are inspired by weakness . . . They are not free to know: decadents *need* lies, it is one of the conditions for their preservation. – Anyone who does not just understand the word 'Dionysian' but understands *himself* in the word 'Dionysian' does not need to refute Plato or Christianity or Schopenhauer – *he smells the decay* . . .

3

In *Twilight of the Idols* I discussed how this led me to discover the concept of the 'tragic' and finally come to understand the psychology of tragedy. 'Saying yes to life, even in its strangest and harshest problems; the will to life rejoicing in its own inexhaustibility through the *sacrifice* of its highest types – *that* is what I called Dionysian, *that* is what I understood as the bridge to the psychology of the *tragic* poet. *Not* in order to escape fear and pity, not in order to cleanse yourself of a dangerous affect by violent discharge – as Aristotle mistakenly thought –: but instead, over and above all fear and pity, in order for *you yourself to be* the eternal joy in becoming, – the joy that includes even the eternal *joy in negating* . . .'[43] In this sense, I have the right to understand myself as the first *tragic philosopher* – which is to say the most diametrically opposed antipode of a pessimistic philosopher. Nobody had ever turned the Dionysian into a philosophical pathos before: *tragic wisdom* was missing, – I could not find any sign of it, even among the *eminent* Greek philosophers, those from the two centuries *before* Socrates. I had some doubts in the case of *Heraclitus*; I generally feel warmer and in better spirits in his company than anywhere else. The affirmation of passing away *and destruction* that is crucial for a Dionysian philosophy, saying yes to opposition and war, *becoming* along with a radical rejection of the very concept of 'being' – all these are more closely related to me than anything else people have thought so far. The doctrine of the 'eternal return', which is to say the unconditional and infinitely repeated cycle of all things – this is Zarathustra's doctrine, but ultimately it is nothing Heraclitus couldn't have said too. At least the Stoics have traces of it, and they inherited almost all of their fundamental ideas from Heraclitus. –

4

A tremendous hope is speaking from out of this essay. Ultimately, I have no reason to take back my hope that music will have a Dionysian future. Let us look forward a century and assume that I have succeeded in my attempts to assassinate two thousand years of anti-nature and desecration of humanity. The new faction in favour of life that takes on the greatest task of all, that of breeding humanity to higher levels (which includes the ruthless extermination of everything degenerate and parasitical), will make possible a *surplus of life* on earth that will necessarily regenerate the Dionysian state. I promise a *tragic* age: tragedy, the highest art of saying yes to life, will be reborn when humanity has moved beyond consciousness of the harshest though most necessary wars *without suffering from it* . . . A psychologist might add that what I heard in Wagner's music when I was young had absolutely nothing to do with Wagner; and that when I described Dionysian music I described what *I* had heard, – that I instinctively had to translate and transfigure everything into the new

---

[43] 'What I Owe the Ancients', section 5, with minor changes.

spirit I was carrying inside me. The proof of this is *as strong as any proof could be*: my essay 'Wagner in Bayreuth': at every psychologically decisive spot I am only talking about myself, – you can put my name or the word 'Zarathustra' without hesitation wherever the text has the word 'Wagner'. The whole picture of the *dithyrambic* artist is the picture of the *not-yet-existing* author of *Zarathustra*, sketched out with abysmal profundity; it does not come into contact with Wagnerian reality for even a moment. Wagner himself sensed this; he did not recognize himself in the text. – At the same time, the 'idea of Bayreuth' had transformed itself into something that will be no great mystery to anyone who knows my *Zarathustra*: it had transformed itself into that *great noon* when the most select people will devote themselves to the greatest tasks of all – who knows? the vision of a celebration that I will live to see some day . . . The pathos of the first pages is world-historical; the *glance* that is spoken of on the seventh page[44] is the true glance of a Zarathustra; Wagner, Bayreuth, the whole pathetic little German spectacle of misery is a cloud in which an infinite *fata morgana*[45] reflects the future. Even psychologically, all the decisive features of my own nature are projected onto Wagner – the juxtaposition of the brightest and most disastrous forces, the will to power as no man has possessed it before, the reckless courage in spiritual matters, the boundless energy for learning that does not overwhelm the will to act. Everything is announced in advance in this essay: the imminent return of the Greek spirit, the need for *counter-Alexanders* to *retie* the Gordian knot of Greek culture after it had been undone . . . Listen to the world-historical accent that introduces the concept of 'tragic attitude' at the end of section 4: all the accents in this essay are world-historical ones. This is the strangest 'objectivity' possible: absolute certainty about what I *am* projects itself onto some arbitrary piece of reality, – the truth about myself speaks from out of an awe-inspiring depth. At the beginning of section 9, the *style* of *Zarathustra* is described and anticipated with decisive assurance; and you will never find a more magnificent expression for the *event* of *Zarathustra*, the act of an incredible purification and consecration of humanity, than you find in section 6. –

[44] Nietzsche is citing the original edition of *Untimely Meditations* (*UM*) IV, 'Richard Wagner in Bayreuth'.
[45] A fairy enchantress, after whom an especially complex type of mirage is named.

THE UNTIMELY ONES

I

The four *Untimely* ones are utterly belligerent. They prove that I was no 'John-a-dreams', that I enjoy brandishing a sword, perhaps even that I am dangerously free with my wrist. The *first* thing I attacked (1873) was German culture, which I already viewed with pitiless contempt. Without meaning, without substance, without any goal; just 'public opinion'. No misunderstanding is more malicious than the belief that Germany's great military success proves anything in favour of its culture – or establishes anything like a cultural victory over France . . . The *second Untimely* one (1874) sheds light on the danger inherent in the way we conduct our scholarship, which gnaws away at life and poisons it –: life is *sick* from this dehumanized cog-grinding and mechanism, from the '*im*personal' nature of the worker, from the false economy of the 'division of labour'. The *goal*, culture, disappears – the means, modern scholarly practice, *barbarizes* . . . In this essay, the 'historical sense' that this century is so proud of is recognized for the first time as a disease, as a typical sign of decay. – The *third* and *fourth Untimely* ones use two images of the harshest *selfishness, self-discipline*[46] to point to a *higher* concept of culture, to re-establish the concept of 'culture' – these are images of untimely types *par excellence*, full of sovereign contempt for everything around them called '*Reich*', 'culture', 'Christianity', 'Bismarck', 'success', – Schopenhauer and Wagner *or*, in a word, Nietzsche . . .

2

The first of these four assassination attempts was a tremendous success. The uproar it caused was magnificent in every sense. I had found the sore spot of a victorious nation – the fact that its victory was *not* a cultural event but maybe, just maybe, something else entirely . . . The response came from all sides and *not* just from the old friends of David Strauss, who I had made fun of as the type of a German cultural philistine and *satisfait*,[47] as the author, in short, of that beer-bench gospel *The Old and the New Faith* (my essay introduced the term 'cultural philistine' into the

---

[46] Nietzsche is again playing with the similarity between the words *Selbstsucht* and *Selbstzucht*.
[47] Self-satisfied.

German language). These old friends, Würtenbergers and Swabians who were cut to the quick by my poking fun at their prodigy, their Strauss, answered as self-righteously and crudely as I could have wanted; the replies from Prussia were cleverer, – they had more 'Berliner blue' in them. The most indecent reply was provided by a newspaper in Leipzig, the famous *Grenzboten*; I had a hard time keeping the infuriated Baslers from taking action. Only a few old men were completely on my side, for mixed and partly indiscernible reasons. Among them was Ewald in Göttingen, who let it be known that my assassination attempt had had deadly results. Also the old Hegelian Bruno Bauer, who was one of my most attentive readers from then on. He loved to refer to me in later years, for instance by telling Herr von Treitschke, the Prussian historiographer, who he could turn to if he wanted to learn about the concept of 'culture', a concept he (von Treitschke) was lacking. The most thoughtful and also the longest thing written about the essay and its author was by one Professor Hoffmann in Würzburg, an old student of the philosopher von Baader. He predicted on the basis of the piece that I would have a great destiny – that I would precipitate a type of crisis and highest decision in the problem of atheism, having pegged me as its most instinctive and ruthless type. Atheism was what led me to Schopenhauer. – Nothing was heard as well – or received as bitterly – as an extraordinarily strong and bold intervention by the otherwise so mild Karl Hillebrand, this last *humane* German, and one who had a real way with his pen. His essay could be read in the *Augsburger Zeitung*; he can be read today in the somewhat more cautious form of his collected writings. Here, my essay was presented as an event, a turning point, an initial self-examination, as the very best sign, as a real *return* of German seriousness and German passion in spiritual matters. Hillebrand was full of high praise for the form of the work, for its mature taste, for its perfect tact in distinguishing between the person and the issue: he praised it as the best polemical work in German, – the art of polemic that is so dangerous, so inadvisable for Germans in particular. Unreservedly affirmative, even strengthening what I had dared to say about the neglect of language in Germany (– these days Germans play the purist and cannot formulate a single sentence –), equally contemptuous of the 'foremost authors' of the nation, he finishes by expressing his admiration for my *courage* – that 'highest courage that specifically indicts a people's favourites' . . . This review had an almost inestimable effect on my life. People have left me alone. They do not say anything, people in Germany treat me with a gloomy caution: for years I have taken advantage of an absolute freedom of speech that nobody today is free enough for, least of all in the '*Reich*'. Heaven for me is 'in the shadow of my sword' . . . Basically, I had put into practice one of Stendahl's maxims: he suggests entering society with a *duel*. And how I chose my opponent! The leading free spirit[48] in Germany . . . In fact, the essay introduced an entirely *new* type of free-spiritedness: to this day, nothing is more foreign and unrelated to me than this whole European and American species of '*libres penseurs*'.[49] Just with dyed-in-the-wool idiots and clowns of 'modern ideas', I find myself even more in conflict with representatives of this Anglo-American species than with any of their opponents. They also want to 'improve' humanity in their own way, in their own image; they would wage irreconcilable war against what I am, what I *will*, if only they understood it, – they all still believe in the 'ideal' . . . I am the first *immoralist* –

3

That the *Untimely* ones featuring the names of Schopenhauer and Wagner could be particularly useful for understanding, or even just posing, psychological questions in both cases – I do not want to claim this, except, of course, in a few small points. So, for instance, I showed a profound assurance of instinct by having already characterized the most elementary aspect of Wagner's nature as a talent for acting; Wagner's means and intentions are only the logical results of this talent. Basically, I wanted to do something completely different from psychology: – in this piece, a problem of education without equal, a new concept of *self-discipline*, *self-defence* to the point of harshness, a path to greatness and to world-historical tasks wanted to make themselves heard for the very first time. Broadly speaking, I took hold of two famous and completely undiagnosed types the way you take hold of an opportunity, in order to express something, in order to have another couple of formulas, signs, means of expression. And with absolutely uncanny sagacity, this is even hinted in section 7 of the third *Untimely* one. This is the way Plato used Socrates, as a semiotic for Plato. – Now that I am looking back from some distance at

---

[48] The German term *Freigeist* can be translated as both 'free thinker' and 'free spirit', and Nietzsche often trades on this ambiguity.

[49] Free thinkers.

the situations witnessed by these writings, I would not want to deny that they are basically only talking about me. The essay 'Wagner in Bayreuth' is a vision of my future; by contrast, 'Schopenhauer as Educator' registers my innermost history, my *becoming*. Above all my *pledge*! . . . *What* I am today, *where* I am today – at a height where I have stopped speaking with words and now speak with lightning –, oh, how far from all this I still was at that time! But I *saw* the land, – I did not deceive myself for a minute about the path, the sea, the danger – *and* the success! The great calm in promising, this happy gaze out onto a future that won't remain just a promise! – Here every word is experienced, deep, inward; the most painful things are not missing either, there are words here that would almost curdle your blood. But a wind of *great* freedom blows over everything; even wounds do not have the character of objections. – The way I understand the philosopher, as a terrible explosive that is a danger to everything, how remote my idea of a philosopher is from anything that includes even a Kant, let alone academic 'ruminants' and other professors of philosophy. The piece gives an invaluable lesson here, if we admit that what is basically at issue is not 'Schopenhauer as Educator' but instead its *opposite*, 'Nietzsche as Educator'. – Considering that my craft at that time was that of a scholar, and perhaps that I *understood* my craft, the brutal psychology of the scholar that suddenly emerges in the piece is not without significance: it expresses the *feeling of distance*,[50] the profound assurance about what my *task* might be, what could only be a means, an *entr'acte*, a secondary project. It is clever of me to have been many things and to many places so I can become one thing, – can come to one thing. For a long time I even *had to* be a scholar. –

HUMAN, ALL TOO HUMAN

With two sequels

I

Human, All Too Human is the monument to a crisis. It calls itself a book for *free* spirits: almost every sentence is the manifestation of a victory – I used it to liberate myself from things that *did not belong* to my nature. Idealism is one of them: the title says 'where *you* see ideal things, *I*

---

[50] Cf. *BGE* 257.

see – human, oh, only all too human!' . . . I know people *better* . . . The term 'free spirit' does not want to be understood in any other way: a spirit *that has become free*, that has taken hold of itself again. The tone, the sound, has completely changed: you will find the book clever, bold, under certain circumstances harsh and sarcastic. A certain spirituality of *noble* taste seems to be constantly fighting a more passionate current in order to stay on top. In this context, it is significant that the hundredth anniversary of the death of *Voltaire* is an excuse, as it were, for the book appearing in 1878.[51] Because Voltaire, in contrast to all subsequent writers, is, above all, a *grandseigneur* of the spirit: which is precisely what I am too. – The name 'Voltaire' on one of my writings – that was true progress – *towards myself* . . . If you look more closely you will find a merciless spirit who knows all the hiding-places where the ideal is at home, – the mountain where its dungeon lies and, as it were, its ultimate security. With a steady torch in hand, this *underworld* of the ideal is illuminated with a searing clarity. It is war, but a war without powder or fumes, without belligerent posturing, without pathos and contorted limbs – all this would still be 'idealism'. One mistake after another is calmly put on ice, the ideal is not refuted, it is *frozen to death* . . . Here, for instance, 'genius' is frozen; in another *corner* 'the saint' is frozen: 'the hero' is frozen underneath a thick layer of ice; in the end, 'faith' freezes, so-called 'conviction', and 'pity' is getting cold fast – 'the thing-in-itself' is frozen to death almost everywhere . . .

2

The beginnings of this book belong in the middle of the first Bayreuth festival; it presupposes a deep sense of alienation from everything around me there. Anyone who knows the sort of visions I was already having can guess what I felt when I woke up in Bayreuth one day. Just like a dream . . . And where was I? I did not recognize anything, I hardly recognized Wagner. I sifted through my memories in vain. Tribschen – a distant island of blissfulness: not a shadow of similarity. The incomparable days when the cornerstone was laid, the small society of people who *belonged* there, who celebrated, and who already had fingers for delicate matters: not a shadow of similarity. *What had happened?* – Wagner had

---

[51] Voltaire was the original dedicatee of *Human, All Too Human*.

been translated into German! The Wagnerians had gained control over Wagner! – *German* art! the *German* master! *German* beer! . . . We who are different, we know all too well the sort of refined artists, the sort of cosmopolitanism Wagner's taste is aimed at, we were beside ourselves when we found Wagner decked out in German 'virtues'. – I think I know Wagnerians, I have '*experienced*' three generations of them from the late Brendel, who confused Wagner with Hegel, to the 'idealists' of the *Bayreuter Blätter*, who confused Wagner with themselves, – I have heard all sorts of confessions of 'beautiful souls' about Wagner. A kingdom for a sensible word! – It was truly a hair-raising group! Nohl, Pohl, *Kohl*,[52] with grace evermore! No freak of nature was missing, not even the anti-Semite. – Poor Wagner! What had he got himself into! If only he had fallen among swine! But among Germans! . . . As a lesson for generations to come, someone should take a real Bayreuther and have him stuffed, or even better, preserve him in spirits, since spirits are what he is lacking –, with the label: this is the sort of 'spirit' the '*Reich*' was based on . . . Enough, I left for a couple of weeks in the middle of it all, very suddenly too, in spite of the fact that a charming Parisienne was trying to cheer me up; I excused myself with Wagner using only a fateful telegram. In Klingenbrunn, deep in the forests of the Böhmerwald, I carried my melancholy and Germanophobia around with me like a disease – *and* from time to time wrote a sentence in my notebook under the heading 'The Ploughshare', pure, *hard psychologica*, which can perhaps still be found in *Human, All Too Human*.

3

What decided me then was not a break with Wagner or anything like that – I felt a complete displacement of my instincts; the occasional mistake, whether it is called 'Wagner' or the professorship in Basle, was just a symptom. I was overcome by *impatience* with myself: I saw that it was high time to reconsider *myself*. All at once I realized to my horror how much time had already been wasted, – how useless, how arbitrary my whole existence as a philologist seemed with respect to my task. I was ashamed of this *false* modesty . . . Ten years had gone by, and during that time the *nourishment* of my soul had come to a complete standstill, I

---

[52] Cabbage – but also nonsense or rubbish.

had not learned anything useful, and I had forgotten an absurd amount for the sake of some scrap of dusty, scholarly junk. To creep through ancient metrists with diligence and bad eyes – that is what I had come to! I was worried how thin and starved I had become: my knowledge was completely devoid of *realities*, and 'idealities' were not worth a damn! – I was seized with an almost burning thirst: and in fact, from that point on, I pursued nothing more than physiology, medicine, and the natural sciences, – I did not return, even to genuine historical studies, until the *task* forced me to. That is when I first understood the connection between, on the one hand, an activity chosen against your instinct, a so-called 'calling' that you are not *remotely* called to – and, on the other hand, the need to *anaesthetize* feelings of hunger and monotony using a narcotic art, – the Wagnerian art, for example. A careful look revealed to me that the same type of distress obtains for a large number of young men: one piece of anti-nature virtually *forces* another. In Germany, in the '*Reich*' (to be unambiguous), too many people are condemned to make up their minds before they are ready, and then to *waste away* under a burden that has become impossible to throw off, . . . They crave Wagner like an *opiate*, – they forget themselves, they lose themselves for a moment . . . What am I saying! *for five or six hours!* –

4

That was the moment my instinct made the inexorable decision to stop giving in, going along, and confusing me with other people. Any type of life, the most unfavourable conditions, illness, poverty – everything seemed preferable to that degrading 'selflessness' I had first fallen into out of ignorance, out of *youth*, and later remained in out of inertia, out of a so-called 'sense of duty'. – Here, at precisely the right moment, that *bad* inheritance from my father came to my aid, and in a manner I cannot admire enough, – basically, a predetermination of an early death. The illness *slowly pulled me away*: it spared me any break, any brusque or offensive measures. I did not lose any good will and I gained quite a bit of it. At the same time, the illness gave me the right to change all my habits completely; it permitted, it *required* me to forget; it gave me the *need* to lie still, to be idle, to wait and be patient . . . But that would certainly mean thinking! . . . My eyes alone put an end to any bookworm behaviour, in plain language: philology: I was redeemed from the 'book', I did not read anything else for years – the *greatest* blessing I ever conferred on myself! – That lowermost self, buried and silenced by constantly *having* to listen to other selves (– and that would certainly mean reading!), slowly woke up, shyly and full of doubts, – but it finally *started talking again*. I have never felt as happy with myself as I was in the sickest and most painful times of my life: you just need to look at something like *Daybreak* or *The Wanderer and His Shadow* to see what this 'return *to myself*' really was: the highest type of *convalescence*! . . . Others just follow from this. –

5

Human, All Too Human, this monument of rigorous self-discipline, was what I used to put an abrupt end to all the 'higher lies', 'idealism', 'beautiful feelings', and other femininities I had taken on board; most of it was written in Sorrento; it was finished and put into final form during a winter in Basle under far less favourable conditions than in Sorrento. Basically, Herr *Peter Gast*, who was then a student at the University of Basle and very devoted to me, has the book on his conscience. I dictated with my head wrapped in a bandage and hurting very badly, he wrote it down and corrected it too, – he was essentially the actual writer while I was just the author. When the finished book finally came into my hands – a profound surprise for a very sick man –, I sent two copies to Bayreuth, along with some other things. By some miraculous coincidence, pregnant with meaning, a beautiful copy of the text to *Parsifal* arrived simultaneously at my door, with Wagner's personal inscription, 'for his dear friend, Friedrich Nietzsche, Richard Wagner, Church Counsellor'. – These two books crossing paths – it was as if I had heard some ominous sound. Didn't it sound as if *swords* were crossing? . . . At any rate, that is how we both thought of it: because neither of us said anything. – This was when the first *Bayreuther Blätter* appeared: I saw *what* it was high time for. – Unbelievable! Wagner had become pious . . .

6

What I thought about myself at that time (1876), the tremendous assurance with which I took my task and its world-historical aspect in hand, the whole book bore witness to this, but one very explicit passage in particular: it is just that with my instinctive deviousness, I dodged the word 'I' again; this time it was not Schopenhauer or Wagner, but instead a friend of mine, the excellent Dr Paul Rée, who I showered in rays of world-historical glory – luckily, much too subtle a creature to . . . *Others* were less subtle: I have always been able to recognize my helpless readers, typical German professors, for instance, because they thought that they had to understand the whole book as higher Reé-alism on the basis of this passage . . . As a matter of fact, the passage contradicts five or six claims my friend makes: you can read about this in the Preface to the *Genealogy of Morality*. – The passage reads: 'What is the chief claim made by one of the boldest and coolest thinkers, the author of the book *On the Origin of Moral Sensations* [*lisez*[53]: Nietzsche, the first *immoralist*], thanks to his incisive and decisive analysis of human action? "The moral man is no closer to the intelligible world than the physical man – *because* there is no intelligible world . . ." This claim, which has become hard and pointed under the hammer blow of historical knowledge [*lisez: revaluation of all values*] might one day, at some future time – 1890! – be the axe that will chop at the root of humanity's "metaphysical need", – whether this will prove more of a blessing or a curse for humanity, who can say? But at any rate as a claim of the gravest consequences, at once fruitful and frightful, looking into the world with that *two-sided gaze* that all great pieces of knowledge share . . .'[54]

DAYBREAK

Thoughts on the prejudices of morality

I

My campaign against *morality* begins with this book. Not that it has the slightest scent of gunpowder: – if you have some subtlety in your nostrils, you will smell very different and much pleasanter odours in it. Neither big guns nor small ones: if this book has a negative effect, its means are anything but that; the effect follows from these means like an inference, *not* like cannon fire. If you take leave of this book with a sort of timid caution towards everything that has been honoured and even adorned under the aegis of morality, this is not at odds with the fact that there is not a single negative word in the entire book, not a single attack or piece of malice, – that instead it lies in the sun, round and happy like a sea

---

[53] Read.   [54] The passage is taken from *Human, All Too Human* (*HAH*) 37, with minor changes.

creature sunning itself between rocks. Ultimately, this is what *I* was, this sea creature: almost every sentence in the book was thought, *hatched*, in that jumble of rocks near Genoa where I was alone and still had secrets with the sea. Even now, whenever I happen to come into contact with this book, almost every sentence turns into a hook, pulling something incomparable from out of the depths: its whole skin trembles with gentle shudders of memory. It shows considerable artistry in taking things that are light, that slip by without a sound, moments I call divine lizards, and fastening them down a little – not with the sort of cruelty shown by that young Greek god who just impaled the poor lizard, but nonetheless with something pointed, with a pen . . . 'There are so many dawns that have not begun to shine' – this *Indian* inscription is written on the doorway to the book. Where does its author *look* for that new morning, that gentle shade of red, undiscovered until now, that marks the start of a new day – oh, a whole series, a whole world of new days! In a *revaluation of all values*, in an escape from all moral values, in an affirmation and trust in everything that had been forbidden, despised, cursed until now. This *affirmative* book saves its light, its love, its tenderness for bad things alone, it gives them back their 'soul', a good conscience, the high right and *privilege* to exist. Morality is not attacked, it just does not come into consideration any more . . . This book ends with an 'Or?', – it is the only book to end with an 'Or?' . . .

2

My task, preparing for humanity's moment of highest self-examination, a *great noon* when it will look back and look out, when it will escape from the domination of chance and priests and, for the first time, pose the question 'why?', the question 'what for?' *as a whole* –, this task follows necessarily from the insight that humanity has *not* put itself on the correct path, that it has absolutely *no* divine governance, that instead, the instinct of negation, of corruption, the decadence-instinct, has been seductively at work, and precisely under humanity's holiest value concepts. The question of the origin of moral values is a question of the *first rank* for me because it determines the future of humanity. The demand that people *believe* that everything is really in the best hands, that one book, the Bible, gives us definitive assurances of the divine control and wisdom presiding over the fate of humanity – translated back into reality, this is the will to suppress the fact that the pathetic opposite has been the case so far, that humanity has been in the *worst* hands, that it has been governed by people who are in bad shape and full of malice and revenge, the so-called 'saints', these slanderers of the world and desecraters of humanity. The decisive sign that priests (– including the *hidden* priests, the philosophers) have not just become dominant within a certain religious community, but overall, and that decadence morality, the will to an end, passes for morality *as such*, is that absolute value is conferred on the absence of egoism, while egoism meets with hostility. I consider anyone who disagrees with me about this to be *infective* . . . But everyone disagrees with me. For a physiologist, this sort of value contrast leaves no doubts. When the least organ inside an organism shows even the slightest neglect for its self-preservation, and rejuvenates its energies or asserts its 'egoism' with anything less than complete assurance, the whole organism will degenerate. The physiologist demands that the degenerate part be *cut out*, he refuses solidarity with anything degenerate, pity is the last thing on his mind. But what the priests *want* is precisely the degeneration of the whole, of humanity: that is why they *preserve* degenerates – this is the price of ruling over them . . . What do those deceitful concepts mean, the *supporting* concepts of morality – 'soul', 'spirit', 'free will', 'God' – if not the physiological ruin of humanity? . . . When you divert seriousness from the self-preservation and energy accumulation of the body, *which is to say: of life*, when you construct an ideal out of anaemia and 'salvation of the soul', out of contempt for the body, what is that if not a *recipe* for decadence? – The loss of a centre of gravity, resistance to natural instincts, in a word 'selflessness' – this is what has been called '*morality*' so far . . . In *Daybreak* I first took up the fight against the morality of 'unselfing'. –

THE GAY SCIENCE

('la gaya scienza')

Daybreak is an affirmative book, deep but bright and good-natured. The same is true once again and in the highest degree for the *gaya scienza*: in almost every sentence, profundity gently joins hands with headstrong passion. One verse that expresses gratitude for the most wonderful January I ever experienced – the whole book is its gift – gives ample evidence of the depths from which the 'science' emerged into *gaiety*:

Oh, my icy soul you sundered
With a spear of flaming beams,
To the ocean now it thunders
To the sea of highest dreams:
Free in the most loving duties,
Ever healthier and bright,
January, how your beauties
Give my praiseful soul delight!

What I mean here by 'highest dreams', how could anyone have any doubts about this after they have seen the diamond beauty of the first words of *Zarathustra* shining at the end of the fourth book? – Or after they have read the granite sentences at the end of the third book, where a destiny *for all ages* formulates itself for the very first time? – The *Songs of Prince Vogelfrei*,[55] composed for the most part in Sicily, are very clearly reminiscent of the Provençal concept of a *gaya scienza*, that unity of *singer, knight,* and *free spirit* that is distinctive of the wonderful early culture of Provence over and against all ambiguous cultures; the very last poem above all, 'To the Minstrel', an exuberant dance song in which (if I may say so!) you dance over morality, is a perfect piece of Provençalism. –

THUS SPOKE ZARATHUSTRA

A book for all and for none

I

Now I will tell the history of *Zarathustra*. The basic idea of the work, *the thought of eternal return*, the highest possible formula of affirmation –, belongs to August of the year 1881: it was thrown onto paper with the title '6,000 feet beyond people and time'. That day I went through the woods to the lake of Silvaplana; I stopped near Surlei by a huge, pyramidal boulder. That is where this thought came to me. – Counting backwards a couple of months from that day, I see it was foreshadowed by a sudden and most profoundly fatal change in my taste, above all in music. Perhaps the whole of *Zarathustra* can be considered music; – certainly a rebirth in the art of *hearing* was one of its preconditions. In a small mountain spa not far from Vicenza, Recoaro, where I spent the spring of the year

---

[55] 'Free as a bird'.

1881, I discovered, along with my maestro and friend Peter Gast (who was 'reborn' as well), that the phoenix of music flew over us with lighter and more luminous feathers than it had ever displayed before. Alternatively, if I count forwards from that day up to the sudden birth that took place in February 1883 under the most improbable of circumstances – the closing section (I quoted a few sentences from it in the Preface) was completed at exactly the sacred hour when Wagner died in Venice – this gives eighteen months for the pregnancy. This figure of exactly eighteen months might suggest, at least among Buddhists, that I am really a female elephant. – The '*gaya scienza*' belongs to the intervening period; there are a hundred signs in it that something incomparable was close at hand; it even has the beginnings of *Zarathustra*, the second to last section of the fourth book contains the fundamental thought of *Zarathustra*.[56] – The *Hymn to Life* (for mixed chorus and orchestra) also belongs to that intervening period – the score was published two years ago by E. W. Fritzsch in Leipzig: not an insignificant symptom for the situation of that year, when the *affirmative* pathos *par excellence*, which I have named the tragic pathos, was alive in me to the highest degree. In the future it will be sung in my memory. – Since a misunderstanding has been circulating, I will say at once that I did not write the text: it is the astonishing inspiration of a young Russian woman who was my friend at that time, Miss Lou von Salomé. If you can glean any meaning at all from the last words of the poem, you will guess why I admired it: these words achieve greatness. Pain is *not* considered an objection to life: 'If you do not have any more happiness to give me, well then! *You still have pain* . . .' Perhaps my music also achieves greatness at this point. (The last note on the oboe is C flat, not C. Misprint.) – The following winter I lived in that charming, quiet bay of Rapallo, close to Genoa, between Chiavari and the foothills of Portofino. I was not in the best of health; the winter was cold, and rainier than usual; a small *albergo* (right on the lake so that high tides made it impossible to get to sleep at night) was pretty much the opposite of what I could have wanted. Nevertheless, and as if to prove my claim that everything decisive comes into being 'nevertheless', it was during this winter and in these adverse conditions that my *Zarathustra* came into being. – In the mornings I would go south, up along the wonderful street to Zoagli, climbing past pine trees and looking out far over the lake; in the afternoons, whenever my health

[56] *GS* 341, 342.

permitted, I would walk around the entire bay from Santa Margherita down to Portofino. This place and this landscape came even closer to my heart because of the great love that the unforgettable German emperor Friedrich III felt for it; I happened to be on that coast again in the fall of 1886 when he visited this small forgotten world of happiness for the last time. – It was on these two walks that the whole of the first book of *Zarathustra* occurred to me, and above all Zarathustra himself, as a type: it would be more accurate to say he *overtook me . . .*

2

In order to understand this type, you first need to be clear about what he presupposes physiologically: it is what I call *great health*. I do not know how to explain this idea better or more *personally* than I already did in one of the concluding sections of the fifth book of the '*gaya scienza*'. 'We who are new, nameless, hard to understand; we premature births of an as yet unproved future – for a new end, we also need a new means, namely, a new health that is stronger, craftier, tougher, bolder, and more cheerful than any previous health. Anyone whose soul thirsts to experience the whole range of previous values and aspirations, to sail around all the coasts of this "inland sea" (*Mittelmeer*) of ideals, anyone who wants to know from the adventures of his own experience how it feels to be the discoverer or conqueror of an ideal, or to be an artist, a saint, a lawmaker, a sage, a scholar, a pious man, an old-style divine loner – any such person needs one thing above all – *the great health*, a health that one doesn't only have, but also acquires continually and must acquire because one gives it up again and again, and must give it up . . . And now, after being on our way in this manner for a long time, we argonauts of the ideal – braver, perhaps, than is prudent and often suffering shipwreck and damage but, to repeat, healthier than one would like to admit, dangerously healthy; ever again healthy – it seems to us as if, in reward, we face an as yet undiscovered land the boundaries of which no one has yet surveyed, beyond all the lands and corners of the ideal heretofore, a world so over-rich in what is beautiful, strange, questionable, terrible, and divine that our curiosity and our thirst to possess it have veered beyond control – alas, so that nothing will sate us any more! . . . After such vistas and with such a burning hunger in our conscience and science, how could we still be satisfied with *modern-day man*? Too bad – but it's inevitable that we look at his worthiest goals and hopes with a seriousness which is difficult to maintain; maybe we don't even look at all any more . . . Another ideal runs before us, a peculiar, seductive, dangerous ideal to which we wouldn't want to persuade anyone, since we don't readily concede *the right to it* to anyone: the ideal of a spirit that plays naïvely, i.e. not deliberately but from an overflowing abundance and power, with everything that was hitherto called holy, good, untouchable, divine; a spirit which has gone so far that the highest thing which the common people quite understandably accepts as its measure of value would signify for it danger, decay, debasement, or at any rate recreation, blindness, temporary self-oblivion: the ideal of a human, superhuman well-being and benevolence that will often enough appear *inhuman* – for example, when it places itself next to all earthly seriousness heretofore, all forms of solemnity in gesture, word, tone, look, morality, and task as if it were their most incarnate and involuntary parody – and in spite of all this, it is perhaps only with it that *the great seriousness* really emerges; that the real question mark is posed for the first time; that the destiny of the soul changes; the hand of the clock moves forward; the tragedy *begins* . . .'[57]

3

– Does anyone at the end of the nineteenth century have a clear idea of what poets in strong ages called *inspiration*? If not, I will describe it. – If you have even the slightest residue of superstition, you will hardly reject the idea of someone being just an incarnation, mouthpiece, or medium of overpowering forces. The idea of revelation in the sense of something suddenly becoming *visible* and audible with unspeakable assurance and subtlety, something that throws you down and leaves you deeply shaken – this simply describes the facts of the case. You listen, you do not look for anything, you take, you do not ask who is there; a thought lights up in a flash, with necessity, without hesitation as to its form, – I never had any choice. A delight whose incredible tension sometimes triggers a burst of tears, sometimes automatically hurries your pace and sometimes slows it down; a perfect state of being outside yourself, with the most distinct consciousness of a host of subtle shudders and shiverings down to the tips of your toes; a profound joy where the bleakest and most painful things

---

[57] From *GS* 382.

do not have the character of opposites, but instead act as its conditions, as welcome components, as *necessary* shades within this sort of excess of light; an instinct for rhythmic relations that spans wide expanses of forms – the length, the need for a rhythm that *spans wide distances* is almost the measure of the force of inspiration, something to balance out its pressure and tension . . . All of this is involuntary to the highest degree, but takes place as if in a storm of feelings of freedom, of unrestricted activity, of power, of divinity . . . The most remarkable thing is the involuntary nature of the image, the metaphor; you do not know what an image, a metaphor, is any more, everything offers itself up as the closest, simplest, most fitting expression. It really seems (to recall something Zarathustra once said) as if things approached on their own and offered themselves up as metaphors (– 'here all things come caressingly to your speech and flatter you: because they want to ride on your back. Here you ride on every metaphor to every truth. Here words and word-shrines of all being jump up for you; all being wants to become a word here, all becoming wants to learn to speak from you –'⁵⁸). This is *my* experience of inspiration; I do not doubt that you would need to go back thousands of years to find anyone who would say: 'it is mine as well'. –

4

I stayed in Genoa for a couple of weeks after that, in bad health. Then came a melancholy springtime in Rome, where I submitted to life – it was not easy. I was deeply upset with the place, the most indecent spot on earth for the poet of *Zarathustra*, and I did not want to be there; I tried to get away, – I wanted to go to *Aquila*, the opposite of Rome, founded out of hostility to Rome, just as I will someday found a city in memory of an atheist and hater of the church *comme il faut*,⁵⁹ one of the people most closely related to me, the great Hohenstaufen emperor, Friedrich II. But some piece of fate was at work, I had to go back. In the end, I had to be content with the Piazza Barberini after my search for somewhere *anti-Christian* had worn me out. In my efforts to avoid bad smells as much as possible, I am afraid that I even asked in the Palazzo del Quirinale itself if they had a quiet room for a philosopher. – On a *loggia* high above that *piazza* where you can look out over Rome and hear the *fontana* roaring far

---

⁵⁸ *Z*, Part III, 'The Home-Coming'.   ⁵⁹ As is necessary.

below, the loneliest song ever written came into being, the 'Night Song'; a tune of unspeakable melancholy was always floating around me at that time – I found its refrain in the words 'dead of immortality . . .'.[60] In the summer, coming back to the holy spot where I had been hit by the first lightning flash of the thought of *Zarathustra*, I discovered the second book of *Zarathustra*. Ten days were enough; I did not need any more time than this for the others, for the first or the third and last books. The following winter, under Nice's halcyon skies (which were shining for the first time in my life), I discovered the third book of *Zarathustra* – and was finished. The whole thing took hardly a year. Many hidden spots and heights in Nice's landscape are made holy to me by unforgettable moments; the crucial section that bears the title 'Old and New Tablets' was composed during the most tiring climb from the station up to the glorious Moorish eyrie of Eza, – my muscular dexterity has always been at its best when the richest creative energies were flowing through me. The *body* is inspired: let us leave the 'soul' out of it . . . I could often be seen dancing; at that time, I could hike in the mountains for seven or eight hours at a time without any thought of tiredness. I slept well, I laughed a lot –, I had the most perfect vigour and patience.

5

Apart from these ten-day works, the years during and above all *after* *Zarathustra* were spent in a state of unparalleled distress. You pay a high price for being immortal: you have to die several times during your life. – There is something I call the *rancune*[61] of the great: once completed, every-thing great – a work, an act – immediately turns *against* the one who did it. By virtue of having done it, the doer becomes *weak*, – he cannot sustain the action any more, he cannot look it in the face any more. To have something *behind* you that you were never allowed to will, something the fate of humanity was knotted up in – and now to have it hanging *over* you! . . . It almost crushes you . . . The *rancune* of the great! – Another thing is the horrible silence you hear around you. Solitude has seven skins; nothing can come through them any more. You go up to people, you greet your friends: new wastelands, there is nothing welcoming in any of their looks. At best, a type of revolt. I have experienced revolts

---

[60] *Z*, Part II, 'The Night Song'.   [61] Rancour.

like this from almost everyone who has ever been close to me, although to very different degrees; it seems that nothing is more insulting than suddenly letting a distance be felt, – *noble* natures who do not know how to live without admiring are few and far between. – A third thing is having absurdly sensitive skin for little digs, a type of helplessness in the face of everything small. This seems to be conditioned by the incredible wastefulness of all the defensive forces presupposed by every *creative* act, every act that is lowest down, most intimate, most your own. The *small* defensive capabilities are also suspended, as it were; energy stops flowing to them. – I will hazard a suggestion that digestion gets worse, movement is reluctant, and feelings of cold and mistrust become far too apparent, – mistrust, which in many cases is just an aetiological mistake. In a state like this I once sensed the presence of a herd of cows even before I saw them, by virtue of the milder, more philanthropic thoughts that returned to me: *they* had warmth . . .

6

This work stands entirely on its own. Leaving aside the poets: perhaps nothing has ever been done with such an excess of energy. Here, my concept of the 'Dionysian' became the *highest deed*; all the rest of human activity looks poor and limited in comparison. The fact that a Goethe, a Shakespeare, would not know how to breathe for a second in this incredible passion and height, that compared to Zarathustra, Dante is just another one of the faithful and not one who first *creates* truth, a *world-governing* spirit, a destiny –, that the poets of the Veda are priests and do not deserve even to tie the shoelaces of a Zarathustra, all this is the least that can be said, and does not give you any real idea of the distance, of the *azure* solitude this work lives in. Zarathustra has an eternal right to say: 'I draw circles around myself and sacred boundaries; decreasing numbers of people climb with me up increasingly large mountains, – I am building mountain ranges out of mountains that are becoming increasingly holy.'[62] The collective spirit and goodness of all great souls would not be capable of producing a single one of Zarathustra's speeches. The ladder he climbs up and down is enormous; he has seen further, willed further, had further *abilities* than anyone else. This most affirmative of all spirits contradicts with every

---

[62] *Z*, Part III, 'Of Old and New Law-Tables', 19.

word he speaks; all oppositions are combined into a new unity in him. The highest and the lowest forces of human nature, everything that is sweetest, most carefree, and most terrible, radiates from a single fountain with undying assurance. Until then, you do not know what height, what depth really is; you know even less what truth is. Not a single moment of this revelation of truth has been anticipated or hinted at by any of the greatest people. Wisdom, investigations of the soul, the art of speaking – none of this existed before Zarathustra; here, what is closest and most everyday speaks about things the likes of which have never been heard. Sayings trembling with passion; eloquence become music; bold strokes of lightning hurled forwards into futures never before anticipated. The most powerful force of metaphor that has ever existed is poor and trivial compared to this return of language to the nature of imagery. – And how Zarathustra descends and says the most gracious things to everybody! How gently he handles even his adversaries, the priests, and suffers with them and from them! – At every moment here, humanity has been overcome, the idea of 'overman' has become the highest reality, – everything that was considered great about people lies infinitely far *beneath* him. Light feet, the halcyon, the omnipresence of malice and high spirits, and everything else typical of the Zarathustra type – no one had ever dreamed that these were essential components of greatness. In just this expansiveness, this willingness to accept oppositions, Zarathustra feels himself to be the *highest type of everything that exists*; and when you hear how he defines this, you will stop looking for any similes or similarities to him.

> – the soul that has the longest ladder and can go down the furthest,
> the most extensive soul that can go the furthest into itself and drift
> and wander,
> the most necessary, that plunges joyfully into chance,
> the soul that is, that *wills* itself into becoming, the soul that has, that
> *wills* itself into wanting and longing –
> the one that flees from itself, that gathers itself in the furthest circles,
> the wisest soul, that idiocy speaks to most sweetly,
> the one that loves itself the most, in which all things have their
> current and counter-current and ebb and flow – –[63]

But this is the concept of Dionysus himself. – Another consideration also leads to this conclusion. The psychological problem apparent in the Zarathustra

---

[63] *Ibid.*

type is how someone who to an unprecedented degree says no and *does*
no to everything everyone has said yes to so far, – how somebody like this
can nevertheless be the opposite of a no-saying spirit; how a spirit who
carries everything that is most difficult about fate, a destiny of a task, can
nonetheless be the lightest, spinning out into the beyond – Zarathustra is
a dancer –; how someone with the hardest, the most terrible insight into
reality, who has thought 'the most abysmal thought', can nonetheless see
it *not* as an objection to existence, not even to its eternal return, – but
instead find one more reason in it for *himself to be* the eternal yes to all
things, 'the incredible, boundless yes-saying, amen-saying' . . .[64] 'I still
carry my blessed yea-saying into all abysses' . . . *But this is the concept of
Dionysus once more.*

7

What language will a spirit like this speak when he speaks to himself?
The language of the *dithyramb*. I am the inventor of the dithyramb. You
can hear how Zarathustra speaks to himself *before sunrise* (III[65]): before
I came along there was no tongue for this sort of emerald happiness,
this sort of divine tenderness. Even the deepest melancholy of such a
Dionysus becomes a dithyramb; I will prove this with the 'Night Song',
the immortal lament at being condemned never to love by an excess of
light and power, by a *sun-like* nature.

> It is night: all leaping fountains speak louder now. And my soul is
> a leaping fountain too.
> It is night: all lovers' songs awaken for the first time now. And my
> soul is the song of a lover too.
> There is something unquenched and unquenchable in me that
> wants to speak up. A desire for love is in me that speaks the language
> of love.
> I am light: oh, that I were night! But this is my solitude, that I am
> sheathed by light.
> Oh, that I were dark and night-like! How I would want to suckle
> at the breast of light!
> And I wanted to bless you too, you little shining stars and glow
> worms above! – and be blessed with your gifts of light.

[64] Cf. *Z*, Part III, 'The Seven Seals', which is subtitled 'or: The Song of Yes and Amen'.
[65] *Z*, Part III, 'Before Sunrise'.

But I live in my own light, I drink back the flames that break out from myself.

I do not know the happiness of the taker; and I often dream that stealing is even more blessed than taking.

That is my poverty, that my hand never rests from giving; that is my envy, that I see waiting eyes and illuminated nights of longing.

Oh, the misfortune of all givers! Oh, the darkening of my sun! Oh, longings for desire! Oh, ardent hunger in satisfaction!

They take from me: but do I still touch their souls? There is a gap between taking and giving; and the smallest gap is the last to be bridged.

A hunger grows from my beauty: I would like to hurt those I illuminate, I would like to rob those I have given to, – and so I hunger for malice.

To pull back my hand when the hand reaches out for it; like the waterfall that hesitates in its downward plunge: and so I hunger for malice.

My fullness devises this sort of vengeance, my solitude pours out this sort of spite.

My happiness in giving died in giving, my virtue grew tired of itself in its excess!

Anyone who gives is in danger of losing his shame; anyone who distributes his hand and heart has calluses from sheer distribution.

My eyes have stopped brimming over at the shame of beggars; my hand has become too hard for the trembling of filled hands.

Where have the tears of my eyes gone and the down feathers of my heart? Oh, the solitude of all givers! Oh, the silence of everything that shines!

Many suns circle through desert spaces: they speak with their light to everything dark – they say nothing to me.

Oh, this is the enmity of light to the luminous: it traces its orbit without mercy.

Unjust in its deepest heart to anything luminous, cold to suns – that is how every sun travels.

Suns trace their orbits like storms, they follow their inexorable will, that is their coldness.

Oh, you are the first, you dark ones, you night ones, to create your heat out of things that shine! Oh, you are the first to drink your milk and take refreshment from the udders of the light!

Oh, ice is all around me, my hand burns itself on icy things! Oh, thirst is in me that pines for your thirst.

It is night: oh, that I have to be light! And thirst for the nightly ones! And solitude!

It is night: now my longing erupts from me like a fountain, – and longs for me to speak.

It is night: all leaping fountains speak louder now. And my soul is a leaping fountain too.

It is night: all lovers' songs awaken for the first time now. And my soul is the song of a lover too. –[66]

8

Nothing like this has ever been composed, ever been felt, ever been *suffered* before: this is how a god suffers, a Dionysus. The answer to this sort of dithyramb of solar solitude in the light would be Ariadne . . . Who besides me knows what Ariadne is! . . . Nobody until now has been able to solve riddles like this, I doubt anyone has even seen riddles here. – Zarathustra rigorously determines his task – it is mine as well –, and there can be no mistake about what he *means*: he is *affirmative* to the point of justification, to the point of salvation, even for everything past.

> I wander among people as among fragments of the future: the future that I see.
>
> This is my every writing and every wish, that I write and unite every riddle, everything that is fragmentary and at the terrible whims of chance.
>
> And how could I bear to be human if humans were not also writers and riddle solvers and redeemers of chance?
>
> *To redeem what is past* and transform all 'it was' into 'that is what I willed!' – that is the only thing I would consider redemption.[67]

In another passage, he determines as rigorously as possible what 'the human' could be for him alone – *not* an object of love or, even worse, of pity – and Zarathustra has control over the *great disgust* at people: people for him are something unformed, matter, an ugly stone that needs a sculptor.

> Not *willing* any more and not *esteeming* any more and not *creating* any more: oh, for this great exhaustion always to stay far away from me!

---

[66] *Z*, Part II, 'The Night Song'.   [67] *Z*, Part II, 'Of Redemption'.

Even in knowing I only feel my will's joy in procreating and becoming; and if there is innocence in my knowledge, this is because it has a *will to procreate*.

This will seduced me away from God and gods: what would there be to create if gods – were there?

But my fervent will to create always drives me back to humanity; just as the hammer is driven to the stone.

Oh, you humans, I see an image lying asleep in the stone, the image of images! Oh, but it would have to sleep in the hardest and ugliest stone!

Now my hammer pounds on its prison with fury and cruelty. Pieces chip away from the stone: what do I care!

I want to finish it, because a shadow came to me, - the stillest and lightest of all things once came to me!

The beauty of the overman came to me as a shadow: now what do I care – about gods! . . .[68]

I will stress one last point: the italicized verse provides the occasion for this. One of the preconditions of a *Dionysian* task is, most crucially, the hardness of a hammer, the *joy even in destruction*. The imperative 'become hard!', the deepest certainty that *all creators are hard*[69] is the true sign of a Dionysian nature. –

BEYOND GOOD AND EVIL

Prelude to a Philosophy of the Future

I

The task for the years that followed was as clear as could be. After the yea-saying part of my task had been solved it was time for the no-saying, *no-doing* half: the revaluation of values so far, the great war, – summoning a day of decision. This involved slowly looking around for anyone related to me, for anyone who, out of strength, would give me a hand with *destruction*. – All my writings from this point on have been fish hooks: perhaps I know how to fish as well as anyone? . . . It was not my fault if nothing was *caught*. *There weren't any fish* . . .

---

[68] *Z*, Part II, 'On the Blissful Islands'.   [69] *Z*, Part III, 'Of Old and New Law-Tables', 29.

2

This book (1886) is in essence a *critique of modernity*, including modern science, modern art – even modern politics –, along with indications of an opposite type who is as un-modern as possible, a noble, affirmative type. In the latter sense the book is a *school of the gentilhomme*, taking the concept more spiritually and radically than it has ever been taken before. You need courage in your body in order just to stand it, you need to never have learned fear . . . All the things this age is proud of are viewed as conflicting with this type, almost as bad manners, the famous 'objectivity', for example, 'sympathy with all sufferers', the 'historical sense' that subordinates itself to alien tastes, prostrating itself before *petits faits*,[70] the 'scientific attitude'. – If you stop and think that this book came *after Zarathustra*, you might guess what dietetic regime brought it about. The eye that had been spoiled by an incredible need to see into the *distance – Zarathustra* is even more far-sighted than the Tsar –, is forced to focus on things that are closest to it, the age, our *surroundings*. In every respect, particularly in its form, you will find a *deliberate* turning away from the sort of instincts that make a *Zarathustra* possible. Subtlety in form and intention, in the art of *remaining silent* – these are in the foreground, and psychology is applied with avowed hardness and cruelty, – there is not a single good-natured word in the whole book . . . All this is a recuperation: who in the end can guess *what* type of recuperation is needed after a squandering of goodness like Zarathustra? . . . Theologically speaking – listen carefully, because I do not speak like a theologian very often – it was God himself who assumed the form of a serpent and lay under the tree of knowledge at the end of his day's work: this is how he recuperated from being God . . . He had made everything too nice . . . The devil is just God's leisure every seventh day . . .

THE GENEALOGY OF MORALITY

A Polemic

With regard to expression, intention, and the art of surprise, the three essays that make up this *Genealogy* are perhaps the most uncanny things written so far. Dionysus, as is known, is also the god of darkness. – In

---

[70] Little facts.

each case, a beginning that *should* be deceptive: cool, scientific, even ironic, intentionally foreground, intentionally evasive. Gradually increasing unrest; scattered moments of sheet lightning; the muffled roar of very unpleasant truths becoming increasingly audible in the distance, – until finally a *tempo feroce* is reached where everything presses forward with a tremendous tension. In each case, an ending with absolutely terrible detonations, a *new* truth visible between thick clouds. – The truth of the *first* essay is the psychology of Christianity: the birth of Christianity out of the spirit of *ressentiment*, *not*, as is believed, out of the 'spirit', – a counter-movement in its very essence, the great revolt against the dominance of *noble* values. The *second* essay gives the psychology of the *conscience*: conscience is *not*, as is believed, 'the voice of God in man', – it is the instinct of cruelty that is turned inwards after it cannot discharge itself outwards anymore. Cruelty is first brought to light here as one of the oldest and most persistent underpinnings of culture. The *third* essay gives the answer to the question of how the ascetic ideal, the priestly ideal, acquired such incredible *power* despite the fact that it is the *detrimental* ideal *par excellence*, a will to the end, a decadence ideal. Answer: *not* because God is at work behind priests, as is believed, but instead *faute de mieux*,[71] – because it has been the only ideal so far, because it has not had any competition. 'Because people would rather will nothingness than *not* will' . . . Above all, there was no *counter-ideal – until Zarathustra*. – I have been understood. A psychologist's three crucial preparatory works for a revaluation of all values. – This book contains the first psychology of the priest.

TWILIGHT OF THE IDOLS

How to Philosophize with a Hammer

I

This essay, less than 150 pages long, cheerful and fateful in tone, a demon that laughs –, the work of so few days that I hesitate to say how many, is an exception among books: nothing has greater substance or more independence, nothing is more liable to overthrow, – nothing is more evil. If you want a quick idea of the extent to which everything was standing

---

[71] For want of anything better.

on its head before I came along, just begin with this essay. What the word 'idols' on the title page means is quite simply what had been called truth so far. *Twilight of the Idols* – in plain language: the end of the old truth . . .

2

There is no reality, no 'ideality' this work does not touch (– touch: what a cautious euphemism! . . .) Not just the *eternal* idols, also the very youngest, with all the infirmities of their age. 'Modern ideas', for instance. A mighty wind blows between the trees and fruit is falling everywhere – truths. The work contains the squandering of an all too rich autumn: you stumble over the truths, you even crush a couple to death, – there are too many of them . . . But you do not get hold of things that are questionable any more, you get hold of decisions. I am the first to have a measure for 'truths', I am the first to be *able* to decide. As if I had grown a *second consciousness*, as if 'the will' had struck a light in me to illuminate the *oblique* course it had gone down so far . . . The *oblique* course – this is what people call the path to the 'truth' . . . All the 'dark impulses' are at an end, '*good* people' had even less of an idea than anyone else of the right way . . . And in all seriousness, nobody before me knew the right way, the way *up*: only starting with me did hopes, tasks, prescribed paths for culture exist again – *I am the bearer of these glad tidings* . . . This also makes me a destiny. – –

3

As soon as I finished this work, and without losing a single day, I grasped the tremendous task of the *Revaluation*[72] with a sovereign feeling of pride, an incomparable feeling; I was certain of my immortality at every moment, engraving sign after sign on iron tablets with the assurance of a destiny. The Preface was written 3 September 1888: on the morning after writing it down, I walked outside to discover the most beautiful day Upper Engadine had ever shown me – transparent, glowing in colours, containing all opposites, everything between ice and the South. – I did not leave Sils-Maria until 20 September, held back by floods; in the end I was the only guest left in this wonderful place: my gratitude wants to give it the gift of an immortal name. After an eventful journey – it was even life-threatening because of flooding in Como, which I only reached

---

[72] *The Anti-Christ.*

late at night – I arrived in Turin on the afternoon of the 21st, my *proven* place, my residence from then on. I took the same apartment that I had in the spring, via Carlo Alberto 6, III, across from the enormous Palazzo Carignano where Vittore Emanuele was born, with a view of the Piazza Carlo Alberto and the hills beyond. I went back to work without delay: only the last quarter of the work was left to be done. Great victory on 30 September; the conclusion of the *Revaluation*; the leisure of a god walking along the river Po. That same day, I wrote the Preface to *Twilight of the Idols*: I had corrected the manuscript for it in September, as my recuperation. – I never experienced an autumn like this before, I never thought anything like this could happen on earth, – a Claude Lorrain projected out to infinity, every day having the same tremendous perfection. –

THE CASE OF WAGNER

A Musician's Problem

I

To be fair to this work, you need to suffer from the destiny of music as if it were an open wound. – *What* do I suffer from when I suffer from the destiny of music? From the fact that music has been robbed of its world-transfiguring, affirmative character – that it has become decadent and is not the flute of Dionysus any more . . . But if you experience the problems of music as if they were your *own* problems, your *own* tale of woe, you will find this text very considerate and unusually mild. In cases like this, to be cheerful and to have a sense of humour about yourself too – *ridendo dicere severum*,[73] where the *verum dicere*[74] would justify any hardness – is humaneness itself. Who really doubts that I, old artillerist that I am, had it in me to use my *heavy* guns against Wagner? – I held back everything decisive in this matter, – I loved Wagner. – Ultimately, the meaning and pathway of my task entailed an attack on a subtler 'unknown', one whose identity will not be readily apparent, – oh, I have 'unknowns' to expose of a very different kind than some Cagliostro of music – even more, of course, an attack on a German nation that keeps getting lazier, losing its instinct in spiritual matters and becoming more and more *honest*, a nation with an enviable appetite that keeps nourishing itself on oppositions, swallowing

---

[73] Saying what is sombre through what is laughable.   [74] Speaking the truth.

'faith' as well as science, 'Christian love' as well as anti-Semitism, the will to power (to '*Reich*') as well as the *évangile des humbles*,[75] and all this without any indigestion . . . This failure to take sides when presented with opposites! This neutrality and 'selflessness' of the stomach! This sense of justice of the German *palate* that gives everything equal rights, – that likes everything it tastes . . . There is no doubt about it, Germans are idealists . . . The last time I visited Germany, I found the German taste busy conferring equal rights on Wagner and the *Trumpeter of Säckingen*;[76] in Leipzig, I *personally* witnessed the founding of a Liszt Society in honour of one of the most authentic and German musicians (in the old sense of the word 'German', not just an imperial German), the master *Heinrich Schütz*, with the goal of cultivating and disseminating *sly* church music[77] . . . There is no doubt about it, Germans are idealists . . .

2

But at this point, nothing should stop me from becoming blunt and telling the Germans a couple of harsh truths: *who else would do it?* – I am talking about their indecency *in historicis*. It is not just that German historians have entirely lost the *greater perspective* on the workings and value of culture, that they are all political (or ecclesiastical –) clowns: they have actually *banned* this greater perspective. First you need to be 'German', you need to have 'breeding', then you can make decisions about all values and un-values *in historicis* – you determine them . . . 'German' is an argument, '*Deutschland, Deutschland über Alles*'[78] is a principle, the Teutons represent the 'moral world order' in history; in relation to the *imperium romanum* they are the bearers of freedom, in relation to the eighteenth century they bring back morality, the 'categorical imperative' . . . There is a German, imperial way of writing history, I am afraid there is even an anti-Semitic way, – there is a *courtly* way of writing history and Herr von Treitschke is not ashamed . . . An idiotic judgment *in historicis*, a claim made by Vischer – an aesthetic Swabian, fortunately a deceased one – recently made the rounds of the German newspapers as a 'truth' that every German *has to assent to*: 'The Renaissance *and* the Reformation, only together do they form a whole – aesthetic rebirth *and* ethical

---

[75] Gospel of the humble.
[76] Epic poem by Josef Viktor Scheffel. [77] A pun on 'Liszt': *listig* is German for sly.
[78] '*Germany, Germany above everything*', the first line of the German national anthem.

rebirth.' – I do not have any patience for this sort of assertion, and I feel the need, I even feel it is my duty, to tell the Germans *just what* they have on their conscience. *They have all the great cultural crimes of the past four hundred years on their conscience!* . . . And always for the same reason, their innermost *cowardice* in the face of reality, which is also cowardice in the face of the truth; untruthfulness that has become instinctive for them, their 'idealism' . . . The Germans have robbed Europe of the harvest, the meaning, of the last *great* age, the age of the Renaissance, at a moment when a higher order of values, the noble, life-affirming values, the values that guarantee the future, had triumphed; they had triumphed, moreover, at the very spot where the opposing values reside, the *values of decline* – they had even triumphed *in the instincts of those who reside there*! Luther, this disaster of a monk, re-established the church and – what is a thousand times worse – Christianity, just when it had been *defeated* . . . Christianity, *this denial of the will to life* made into a religion! . . . Luther, an impossible monk who attacked the church because of his own 'impossibility' and – consequently! – restored it . . . The Catholics would have good reason to celebrate Luther festivals, to write Luther plays . . . Luther – and the 'moral rebirth'! The whole of psychology can go to hell! – There is no doubt about it, Germans are idealists. – Twice already, just when an honest, unequivocal, perfectly scientific way of thinking had been achieved, and with incredible courage and self-overcoming, the Germans knew how to find a secret path back to the old 'ideal', ways of reconciling truth and the 'ideal', basically formulas for a right to reject science, a right to *lie*. Leibniz and Kant – these two great bumps in the path to Europe's sense of intellectual integrity! – Finally, when a *force majeure*[79] of genius and will became visible on the bridge between two centuries of decadence, one strong enough to make Europe into a unity, a political *and economic* unity for the purpose of world governance, the Germans with their 'Wars of Liberation' cheated Europe out of the meaning, the miracle of meaning, in the existence of Napoleon. – As a result, they have everything that has happened on their conscience, everything that is the case today, the most *anti-cultural* sickness and unreason there is, nationalism, this *névrose nationale*[80] that Europe is sick from, this immortalizing of Europe's provincial character, of *petty* politics. They have even robbed Europe of its sense, its *rationality* – they have steered it into a dead end. – Does anyone

---

[79] Superior force.   [80] National neurosis.

except me know a *way* out of this dead end? . . . A task big enough to *reunite* peoples? . . .

3

– And finally, why shouldn't I voice my suspicions? In my case too, the Germans will do everything they can to take an incredible destiny and give birth to a mouse. They have been compromising themselves up to now as far as I am concerned, and I doubt whether they will do any better in the future. – Oh, to be a *bad* prophet here! . . . My natural readers and listeners now are the Russians, Scandinavians, and French, – will it always be this way? – Germans are only ever inscribed in the annals of epistemology under equivocal names, they have only ever produced 'unconscious' counterfeiters (– Fichte, Schelling, Schopenhauer, Hegel, Schleiermacher deserve this epithet as much as Kant and Leibniz, they are all just *Schleiermachers*[81]–): they will never have the honour of being able to consider the first *honest* spirit in the history of spirit, the spirit in which truth comes to pass judgment over four thousand years of counterfeit, as united with the German spirit. The 'German spirit' is *my* bad air: I have trouble breathing when I am around the instinctive uncleanliness *in psychologicis* that is revealed in a German's every word, every expression. They never went through a seventeenth century of hard self-examination as the French did – a La Rochefoucauld, a Descartes has a hundred times more integrity than the best of the Germans, – they have not produced a psychologist to this day. But psychology is almost the measure of the *cleanliness* or *uncleanliness* of a race . . . And how can you be expected to be *profound* if you are not even clean? With Germans, as with women, you never plumb their depths – *they do not have any*: that is all. But this means that they are not even shallow. – What is considered 'deep' in Germany is precisely this sort of instinctive uncleanliness with respect to oneself: people do not even *want* to be clear about themselves. Can I suggest 'German' as an international coinage for *this* psychological depravity? – For instance, right now the German emperor calls it his 'Christian duty' to free the slaves in Africa: but among ourselves, we *other* Europeans just call it 'being German' . . . Have the Germans produced a single deep book? They do not even have an idea of what counts as depth in a book. I have met scholars who consider Kant deep; I am afraid that in the Prussian

---

[81] A metaphysical pun: *Schleiermacher* means veil-maker.

court people think of Herr von Treitschke as deep. And occasionally when I praise Stendhal as a deep psychologist, German university professors ask me how to spell the name . . .

4

– And why shouldn't I see this through to the end? I like to make a clean sweep of things. It is even my ambition to be considered the despiser of the Germans *par excellence*. I had already expressed my *mistrust* of the German character when I was just twenty-six (third *Untimely*, 6) – I find Germans impossible. When I imagine the type of person who runs counter to all my instincts, it is always a German. The first thing I test someone on is whether his body has a feeling for distance, whether he sees rank, degree, an ordering system between people all around him, whether he *makes distinctions*: this makes you a *gentilhomme*; in every other case, you fall hopelessly into the broadminded, oh-so-good-natured category of the *canaille*.[82] But Germans are *canaille* – oh! they are so good-natured . . . You abase yourself by having anything to do with Germans: Germans are *levellers* . . . Apart from my relationships with a couple of artists, with Richard Wagner above all, I have never spent a single good hour among Germans . . . If the deepest spirit of all the millennia were to appear among Germans, some lady saviour of the capitol would opine that her very unbeautiful soul was at least as worthy of consideration . . . I cannot stand this race, you are always in bad company when you are with them. They do not have a finger for nuances – poor me! I am a nuance –, they do not have any *esprit* in their feet, they cannot even walk . . . Ultimately, the Germans do not have feet at all, they just have legs . . . Germans have no idea how vulgar they are, but that is the superlative of vulgarity, – they are not even *ashamed* of being merely German . . . They talk about everything, they consider themselves decisive, I am afraid they have reached a decision about me . . . – My whole life is the proof *de rigueur* of these propositions. I have looked back through my life for any sign of tact, of *délicatesse*, in their treatment of me, and I have found nothing. From Jews, yes, but never from Germans. My character forces me to be gentle and benevolent to everyone – I have the *right* not to make distinctions –: this does not stop me from keeping my eyes open. I do not make exceptions, least of all for my

---

[82] Riff-raff.

friends, – I hope this does not ultimately prevent me from being humane towards them! There are five or six things that have always been particular points of honour with me. – It is nonetheless true that for the past few years I have regarded almost every letter I have received as a piece of cynicism: there is more cynicism in wishing me well than in any sort of hatred . . . I tell all my friends to their faces that they never thought it worth their while to *study* any of my writings; I can guess from the smallest signs that they do not even know what is written in them. As far as my *Zarathustra* goes, which of my friends has seen it as anything more than a forbidden piece of arrogance which, luckily, makes absolutely no difference? . . . Ten years: and nobody in Germany has felt bound by conscience to defend my name against the absurd silence it has been buried under: a foreigner, a Dane, was the first to have enough subtlety of instinct and *courage*, and he became angry at my supposed friends . . . What German university could you go to today to hear lectures on my philosophy like the lectures held last spring in Copenhagen by Dr Georg Brandes (proving once again what a psychologist he is) – I myself never suffered from any of this; *necessity* does not hurt me; *amor fati* is my innermost nature. But this does not prevent me from loving irony, even world-historical irony. And so, about two years before the shattering lightning bolt of the *Revaluation*, a book that will rack the earth with convulsions, I sent the *Case of Wagner* into the world: let the Germans commit one more immortal act of misappropriation and *eternalize* me! There is just enough time for it! – Has that been achieved? Most beautifully, my dear Germans! My compliments . . . Just to include my friends in this as well, an old friend has just written to say that she is *laughing* at me . . . And this at a moment when an unspeakable responsibility rests on me, – when no word can be too gentle, no look respectful enough for me. Because I am carrying the destiny of humanity on my shoulders. –

WHY I AM A DESTINY

I

I know my lot. One day my name will be connected with the memory of something tremendous, – a crisis such as the earth has never seen, the deepest collision of conscience, a decision made *against* everything that has been believed, demanded, held sacred so far. I am not a human being,

I am dynamite. – And yet I am not remotely the religion-founding type – religions are the business of the rabble, I need to wash my hands after coming into contact with religious people . . . I do not *want* any 'true believers', I think I am too malicious to believe in myself, I never speak to the masses . . . I have a real fear that someday people will consider me *holy*: you will guess why I am publishing this book *beforehand*; it is supposed to stop any nonsense as far as I am concerned . . . I do not want to be a saint, I would rather be a buffoon . . . Perhaps I am a buffoon . . . And yet in spite of this or rather *not* in spite of this – because nothing to date has been more hypocritical than saints – the truth speaks from out of me. – But my truth is *terrible*: because *lies* have been called truth so far. – *Revaluation of all values*: that is my formula for an act of humanity's highest self-examination, an act that has become flesh and genius in me. My lot would have it that I am the first *decent* human being, that I know myself to be opposing the hypocrisy of millennia . . . I was the first to *discover* the truth because I was the first to see – to *smell* – lies for what they are . . . My genius is in my nostrils . . . I contradict as nobody has ever contradicted before, and yet in spite of this I am the opposite of a nay-saying spirit. I am a *bearer of glad tidings* as no one ever was before; I am acquainted with incredibly elevated tasks, where even the *concept* of these tasks has been lacking so far; all hope had disappeared until I came along. And yet I am necessarily a man of disaster as well. Because when truth comes into conflict with the lies of millennia there will be tremors, a ripple of earthquakes, an upheaval of mountains and valleys such as no one has ever imagined. The concept of politics will have then merged entirely into a war of spirits, all power structures from the old society will have exploded – they are all based on lies: there will be wars such as the earth has never seen. Starting with me, the earth will know *great politics* –

2

Do you want a formula for a destiny like this, one *that becomes a human being*? – You will find it in my *Zarathustra*.

> – *and whoever wants to be a creator in good and evil first has to be a destroyer and smash values.*
> *Thus the highest evil is part of the highest good: but this is the creative good.*[83]

---

[83] *Z*, Part II, 'Of Self-Overcoming'.

I am by far the most terrible human being who has ever existed; this does not mean that I will not be the most charitable. I know the joy of *destruction* to a degree proportionate to my *strength* for destruction, – In both cases I obey my Dionysian nature, which does not know how to separate doing no from saying yes. I am the first *immoralist*: which makes me the *destroyer par excellence*. –

3

I have not been asked as I should have been asked what the name *Zarathustra* means coming from *my* mouth, the mouth of the first immoralist: because it is precisely the opposite of what constitutes that Persian's monumental and unique place in history. Zarathustra was the first to see the struggle of good and evil as the true wheel in the machinery of things, – morality translated into metaphysics as force, cause, goal in itself, is *his* work. But this question essentially answers itself. Zarathustra *created* this fateful error of morality: this means that he has to be the first to *recognize* it. Not only has he spent longer and had more experience here than any other thinker – the whole of history is in fact the experimental refutation of the principle of the so-called 'moral world order' –: more importantly, Zarathustra is more truthful than any other thinker. His teaching is the only one that considers truthfulness to be the highest virtue – that means the opposite of the *cowardice* of 'idealists', who take flight in the face of reality; Zarathustra has more courage in his body than all thinkers put together. To speak the truth and *shoot well with an arrow*, this is the Persian virtue. – Have I been understood? . . . The self-overcoming of morality from out of truthfulness, the self-overcoming of moralists into their opposite – *into me* – that is what the name Zarathustra means coming from my mouth.

4

My word *immoralist* essentially entails two negations. First, I am negating a type of person who has been considered highest so far, the *good*, the *benevolent*, the *charitable*; second, I am negating a type of morality that has attained dominance and validity in the form of morality as such, – decadence morality or, to put it plainly, *Christian* morality. The second opposition may be considered decisive, since in general I see the

overestimation of goodness and benevolence as a consequence of decadence, as a symptom of weakness, as incompatible with an ascending and
affirmative life: negation and *destruction* are conditions of affirmation. –
For the moment I will stay on the subject of the psychology of the good
man. To estimate the value of any given type of person you need to work
out how much it costs to maintain him, – you need to know the conditions
of his existence. The condition for the good man's existence is the *lie*: –
to put it another way, taking all measures to *avoid* seeing that reality is
not constituted in a way that always invites benevolent instincts, much
less puts up with the interference of short-sighted, good-natured hands.
To consider all forms of *distress* as objections, as things that need to be
done *away* with, is the *niaiserie*[84] *par excellence*, a real disaster in its consequences, a destiny of stupidity –, almost as stupid as the desire to get
rid of bad weather – maybe out of pity for poor people . . . In the great
economy of the whole, the horrors of reality (in the affects, in the desires,
in the will to power) are incalculably more necessary than that form of
petty happiness called 'goodness'; you need to be lenient to think that the
latter has any place at all, since it is conditioned by instinctive hypocrisy. I
will have a major opportunity to demonstrate the unusually uncanny historical consequences of *optimism*, that excrescence of the *homines optimi*.[85]
Zarathustra, the first to comprehend that the optimist is just as decadent
as the pessimist and perhaps more harmful, says: '*good people never speak
the truth. Good people have taught you false coasts and assurances; you were
born and hidden in the lies of the good. The good lie about everything and conceal it completely.*'[86] Luckily, the world is not built on instincts such that
only good-natured herd animals can find their narrow bit of happiness in
it; to demand that everyone should become 'good', herd animals, blue-
eyed, benevolent 'beautiful souls' – or altruistic, as Mr Herbert Spencer
would have it, – would mean robbing existence of its *great* character, would
mean castrating humanity and bringing it down to a miserable, Chinese
level. – *And this is what people have tried to do!* . . . *This is precisely what
people have called morality* . . . In this sense Zarathustra sometimes calls
the good men 'the last men',[87] and sometimes the 'beginning of the end';
above all he sees them as *the most harmful type of person* because they exist

---

[84] Folly.   [85] Best men.
[86] *Z*, Part III, 'Of Old and New Law-Tables', 7, 28.   [87] *Z*, Prologue, 5.

at the expense of the *truth* as much as they exist at the expense of the *future*.

> The good – they cannot *create*, they are always the beginning of the end –
> – they crucify those who write *new* values on new tablets, they sacrifice the future to *themselves*, they crucify all the futures of mankind!
> The good – they have always been the beginning of the end . . .
> And whatever other harm the slanderers of the world might do, the harm of the good is the most harmful of harms.[88]

5

Zarathustra, the first psychologist of the good, is – consequently – a friend of the evil. When a decadent type of person is raised to the highest rank, this can only happen at the expense of the opposing type, the type of person who is strong and sure of life. When the herd animal shines forth with the brilliance of the purest of virtue, the exceptional type of person will necessarily be devalued down into evil. When hypocrisy takes every step to claim the word 'truth' for its optic, genuine truthfulness will necessarily be found under the worst names. Zarathustra leaves no doubt about this: he says that knowledge of the good, of the 'best', is precisely what terrifies him about humanity in general; *this* was the revulsion that gave him wings 'to glide off into distant futures', – he does not conceal the fact that *his* type of person – a type that is an overman in comparison – is an overman specifically when compared to the *good*, that the good and just would call his overmen *devils* . . .

> You highest men that strike my eye, that is my doubt about you and my secret laughter: I am guessing that you would call my overmen – devils!
> Greatness is so foreign to you with your souls that the overman would be *terrible* to you in his goodness . . .[89]

At this point and nowhere else, you need to make an effort to understand what Zarathustra *wants*: the type of person he conceives of is the type that

[88] *Z*, Part II, 'Of Old and New Law-Tables', 26.   [89] *Z*, Part II, 'Of Manly Prudence'.

conceives of reality *as it is*: his type has the strength to do this –, it is not alienated, removed from reality, it is *reality itself*, it contains in itself everything terrible and questionable about reality, *this is the only way someone can achieve greatness* . . .

6

– But there is another sense in which I have chosen the word *immoralist* for myself as an emblem, a badge of honour; I am proud of having a word that pits me against the whole of mankind. Nobody so far has felt *Christian* morality to be *beneath* him: this would involve a height, a vista, an unheard-of psychological depth and abyss. Christian morality has been the Circe of all thinkers so far, – they were in service to her. – Who before me has climbed into the caves that spew out the poisoned breath of this type of ideal – the ideal of *slandering the world*? Who has even dared to suppose *that* such caves existed? What philosopher before me was a *psychologist* instead of its opposite, a 'higher fraud', an 'idealist'? Psychology did not exist until I appeared. – It can be a curse to be first here, it is at any rate a destiny: *because you are also the first to despise* . . . My danger is *disgust* with people . . .

7

Have I been understood? – What sets me apart, what singles me out over and above the rest of humanity is the fact that I *uncovered* Christian morality. That is why I needed a word whose significance lay in challeng-ing everyone. The fact that humanity did not open its eyes to this earlier is, to my mind, the greatest uncleanliness it has on its conscience; this fact is a self-deception that has become instinctive, it is a fundamental will *not* to see any event, any causality, any actuality, it is a piece of coun-terfeit *in psychologicis* that verges on criminality. Blindness when it comes to Christianity is *criminality par excellence* – the crime *against life* . . . The millennia, the peoples, the first and the last, the philosophers and the old women – apart from five or six moments in history, with me as the seventh – they are all worthy of each other on this point. Until now, the Christians have been *the* 'moral beings', a *curiosum* without equal – and *as* 'moral beings', more absurd, bigger liars, more vain and frivolous, *more harmful to themselves* than even the greatest despiser of humanity could ever dream possible. Christian morality – the most malicious form of the will to lie, the true Circe of humanity: the thing that has *corrupted* humanity. What horrifies me when I look at this is *not* the error as an error, *not* the thousands of years without a 'good will', discipline, decency, courage in spiritual matters that are apparent in its victory: – it is the absence of nature, it is the absolutely horrible state of affairs where *anti-nature* itself has been given the highest honour as morality and hangs over humanity as law, as categorical imperative! . . . To make this big a mistake, *not* as an individual, *not* as a people, but as humanity! . . . The fact that people were taught to hate the very first instincts of life; that a 'soul', a 'spirit', was *invented* to disgrace the body; the fact that people were taught that there is something unclean about sexuality, the presupposition of life; the fact that people looked for the evil principle in *rigorous* selfishness (– even the word is a slander!), which is the very thing you need the most if you are going to thrive; on the other hand, the fact that people found *higher* value – what am I saying! *value in itself*! – in the typical signs of decline and conflicting instincts, in 'selflessness', in the loss of a centre of gravity, in 'depersonalization' and 'love of the neighbour' (– *addiction* to the neighbour!) . . . What! Is humanity itself decadent? Has it always been? – What is certain is that it has been *taught* decadence values, and *only* decadence values, as the highest values. The morality of un-selfing is the morality of decline *par excellence*, the fact 'I am in decline' translated into the imperative 'thou *shalt* decline' – and *not only* into an imperative! . . . This, the only morality that has been taught so far, the morality of un-selfing, demonstrates a will to the end, it *negates* life at the most basic level. – There remains the possibility here that humanity is not what is in degeneration, only that parasitical type of human, *priests*, who, with their morality, have lied themselves into the position of determining values, – who see Christian morality as their means of wielding *power* . . . And in fact, that is *my* insight: the teachers, the leaders of humanity, all of them theologians, were also all decadents: *this* explains why all values were revalued into ones hostile to life, *this* explains morality . . . *Definition of morality*: morality, the idiosyncrasy of decadents with the ulterior motive of taking revenge *on life* – *and* successfully. I attach value to *this* definition. –

8

– Have I been understood? – I have not said anything that I would not have said five years ago through the mouth of Zarathustra. – The *uncovering* of Christian morality is an event without equal, a real catastrophe. Anyone who knows about this is a *force majeure*, a destiny, – he splits the history of humanity into two parts. Some live *before* him, some live *after* him ... The lightning bolt of truth strikes precisely those things that have stood the highest so far: whoever understands *what* has been destroyed here can see if they are left with anything in their hands. Everything that has been called 'truth' so far is recognized as the most harmful, treacherous, subterranean form of lie; the holy pretext of 'improving' humanity is recognized as the ruse to *suck the blood* out of life itself, to make it anaemic. Morality as *vampirism* ... Anyone who uncovers morality also discovers the worthlessness of all values people believe in or have believed in; he stops seeing anything admirable in the most venerated types of people, in types of people who have even been called *holy*, he sees them as the most disastrous type of deformity, disastrous *because fascinating* ... The concept 'God' invented as a counter-concept to life, – it makes a terrible unity of everything that is most harmful, poisonous, slanderous, the whole deadly hostility to life! The concept of the 'beyond', the 'true world', invented to devalue the *only* world there is, – to deprive our earthly reality of any goal, reason or task! The concept 'soul', 'spirit', finally even 'immortal soul' invented in order to make the body despised, to make it sick – 'holy' –, to treat as frivolous all the things about life that deserve to be taken very seriously – questions of nutrition, residence, spiritual diet, treatment of the sick, cleanliness, weather! 'Salvation of the soul' instead of health – I mean a *folie circulaire*[90] between spasms of atonement and hysteria over redemption! The concept of 'sin' invented along with the associated instrument of torture, the concept of 'free will', in order to confuse the instincts, in order to make mistrust of the instincts second nature! In the concept of 'selflessness', of 'self-renunciation', the true sign of decadence, being *seduced* by what is harmful, not being *able* to find your advantage any more, self-destruction made into the sign of value in general, into 'duty', into 'holiness', into something 'divine' in people! Finally – this is the most terrible thing of all – in the concept of the *good* person,

[90] Manic depression.

the defence of everything weak, sick, badly formed, suffering from itself, everything *that should be destroyed* –, defiance of the law of *selection*, an ideal constructed by opposing people who are proud and well constituted, who are affirmative, who are certain of a future, who guarantee a future – they are now called *evil* . . . And all this is believed, *as morality!* – *Ecrasez l'infâme!*[91] – –

9

– Have I been understood? – *Dionysus versus the crucified* . . .

[91] 'Crush the infamy!' – an anti-clerical motto of Voltaire's.

Twilight of the Idols
or How to Philosophize with a Hammer

.

PREFACE

It is quite an achievement to stay cheerful in the middle of a depressing business, one that has more than the usual number of responsibilities: but what could be more important than cheerfulness? Nothing gets done without a dose of high spirits. The only proof of strength is an excess of strength. – A *revaluation of all values*: this question mark is so dark and so huge that it casts shadows over anyone who puts it forward – this sort of destiny of a task forces him to keep running out into the sunlight to shake off a seriousness that has become heavy, all too heavy. All means are justified, every 'case' is a case of luck. Especially *war*. War has always been the most sensible measure for spirits who have become too inward-looking and profound; even wounds have the power to heal. I have had a motto for a long time (and I won't gratify scholarly curiosity as to its source):

> *increscunt animi, virescit volnere virtus.*[1]

Another form of convalescence, which I sometimes even prefer, is *sounding out idols* . . . The world has more idols than realities: this is *my* 'evil eye' on the world, this is my 'evil *ear*' as well . . . Posing questions with a *hammer* and, perhaps, hearing in reply that famous hollow sound that indicates bloated intestines – what a pleasure for someone with ears even behind his ears, – what a pleasure for me, an old psychologist and pied piper; in my presence, the very things that want to keep quiet are *made to speak out* . . .

Even this work – the title gives it away – is above all a recuperation, a sunspot, a little light adventure into a psychologist's idle hours. And perhaps a new war too? And will new idols be sounded out? . . . This little work is a *great declaration of war*; and as far as sounding out idols is concerned, this time they are not just idols of our age but *eternal* idols, and they will be touched here with a hammer as with a tuning fork, – these are the oldest, most convinced, puffed-up, and fat-headed idols you will ever find . . . . And also the most hollow . . . But that does not stop

---

[1] 'The spirit soars, valour thrives by wounding.' The source is in fact the Roman poet Furius of Antium.

them from being the *most fervently believed*. And even in the noblest of cases they are never, ever called idols. . .

Turin, on 30 September 1888,
the day that the first book of the *Revaluation
of All Values* was finished.[2]

FRIEDRICH NIETZSCHE.

ARROWS AND EPIGRAMS

1

All psychology begins with idleness. What? So psychology would be – a vice?

2

Even the bravest among us only rarely has courage for what he really *knows* . . .

3

To live alone, you need to be either an animal or a god – says Aristotle. But he left out the third case: you can be both – a *philosopher* . . .

4

'All truth is simple.' – Isn't that a double lie? –

5

For once and for all, I want *not* to know many things. – Wisdom sets limits on knowledge too.

6

Our own wild nature is the best place to recover from our un-nature, from our spirituality . . .

---

[2] Nietzsche is referring to *The Anti-Christ*.

7

What? Is man just God's mistake? Or is God just man's mistake? –

8

From life's school of war. – What doesn't kill me makes me stronger.

9

Help yourself: then everyone will help you. Principle of neighbour-love.

10

Don't be cowardly about your actions! Don't abandon them afterwards! – The pang of conscience is obscene.

11

Can an *ass* be tragic? – Can someone be destroyed by a weight he cannot carry or throw off? . . . The case of the philosopher.

12

If you have your '*why?*' in life, you can get along with almost any '*how?*'. People *don't* strive for happiness, only the English do.

13

Man created woman – but out of what? Out of a rib from his God, – from his 'ideal' . . .

14

What? You are looking for something? You want to multiply yourself by ten, by a hundred? You are looking for disciples? – Look for *zeros!* –

15

Posthumous people (me, for instance) are understood worse than contemporary ones but *heard* better. More precisely: no one ever understands us – and *that's* what gives us our authority . . .

16

Between women. – 'Truth? Oh, you don't know truth! Isn't it an attempt to assassinate all our *pudeurs*?[3]' –

17

This is the sort of artist I love, modest in his needs: he really only wants two things, his bread and his art, – *panem et* Circen . . .[4]

18

Whoever doesn't know how to put his will into things can at least put *meaning* into them: that means, he has faith that a will is already there (principle of 'faith').

19

What? You choose virtue and a puffed-up chest and at the same time glance sideways at the advantages of having neither? – But virtue means *renouncing* 'advantages' . . . (for the door of an anti-Semite's house.)

20

The perfect woman commits literature the way she commits a small sin: as an experiment, in passing, looking around to see whether anyone noticed and to make sure someone *has* noticed . . .

21

To enter into only those situations where you cannot have any counterfeit virtues, where instead, like the tightrope walker on his tightrope, you either fall down or remain standing – or come away . . .

22

'Evil men have no songs.' – So why do the Russians have songs?

[3] Modesties. [4] A pun on 'bread and *circuses*'.

23

'German Spirit': a *contradictio in adjecto*[5] for eighteen years now.

24

When you look for beginnings, you become a crab. Historians look backwards; and they end up *believing* backwards too.

25

Contentment protects you, even from colds. Has a woman who knew she was well dressed ever caught a cold? – I'm even assuming that she was hardly dressed at all.

26

I distrust all systematizers and avoid them. The will to a system is a lack of integrity.

27

Women are considered deep – why? Because you never get to the bottom of them. Women aren't even shallow.

28

When a woman has masculine virtues, you feel like running away; and when she doesn't have masculine virtues, she runs away herself.

29

'How much did conscience use to have to bite? And how good were its teeth? – And these days? What's missing?' A dentist's question.

30

People rarely rush into things only once. The first time you rush into things, you always do too much. That's why you usually do the same thing again – and then you do too little . . .

---

[5] Contradiction in terms.

31

A worm will twist back on itself when it is stepped on. This is shrewd. It lessens the chance of being stepped on again. In the language of morality: *humility.* –

32

There is a hatred of lying and disguise that comes from a delicate sense of honour; there is also a hatred that comes from cowardice, since lying is *forbidden* by divine commandment. Too cowardly to lie . . .

33

How little is required for happiness! The sound of a bagpipe. – Without music, life would be a mistake. Germans even imagine God singing songs.

34

On ne peut penser et écrire qu'assis[6] (G. Flaubert). – I've caught you, nihilist! Sitting still is the very *sin* against the Holy Spirit. Only *peripatetic* thoughts have any value.

35

There are times when we're like horses, we psychologists, and get restless: we see our own shadows bobbing up and down in front of us. Psychologists need to stop looking at *themselves* if they want to see anything at all.

36

Are we *harming* virtue, we immoralists? – Just as little as anarchists harm princes. Princes sit securely on their thrones only after they've been shot at. Moral: *morality must be shot at.*

---

[6] One cannot think and write except while sitting down.

37

You are running *ahead*? – Are you doing it as a shepherd? Or as an exception? A third case would be when someone is running away . . . *First* question of conscience . . .

38

Are you for real? Or only an actor? A representative? Or the represented? – In the end, you are really only an imitation of an actor . . . *Second* question of conscience.

39

The *disappointed one speaks.* – I looked for great men, and all I could find were the *apes* of their ideals.

40

Are you someone who looks on? Or who lends a hand? – Or who looks the other way, goes off to the side? . . . *Third* question of conscience.

41

Do you want to come along? Or go ahead? Or go by yourself? . . . People need to know *what* they want and *that* they want. *Fourth* question of conscience.

42

Those were steps for me, and I climbed them, – to do it, I had to get over them. But they thought that I wanted to come to rest on them . . .

43

Who cares if *I* am right! I am much *too* right. – And whoever laughs best today also laughs last.

44

Formula for my happiness: a yes, a no, a straight line, a *goal* . . .

THE PROBLEM OF SOCRATES

I

The wisest men in every age have reached the same conclusion about life: *it's no good* . . . Always and everywhere, you hear the same sound from their mouths, – a sound full of doubt, full of melancholy, full of exhaustion with life, full of resistance *to* life. Even Socrates said as he died: 'living – that means being sick for a long time: I owe Asclepius the Saviour a rooster.' Even Socrates had had enough. – What does this *prove*? What does it *demonstrate*? – There was a time when people would have said (–oh, people have said it, and loud enough too, with our pessimists first in line!): 'There has to be some truth here! The *consensus sapientium*[7] is proof of truth.' – And nowadays, are we going to keep talking like this? Are we even *allowed* to? 'There has to be some *sickness* here' – is what *we* will reply: these wisest men of all ages, let us start looking at *them* more closely! Perhaps they had become a bit unsteady on their feet? Perhaps they were late? doddering? decadent? Perhaps wisdom appears on earth as a raven, inspired by a little scent of carrion? . . .

2

This piece of irreverence, that the great sages are *types of decline*, first dawned on me in just the sort of case where scholarly and unscholarly prejudice would be working most strongly to prevent it: I recognized Socrates and Plato as symptoms of decay, as agents of Greek disintegration, as pseudo-Greek, as anti-Greek (*Birth of Tragedy*, 1872). The *consensus sapientium* – I see this with increasing lucidity – proves least of all that the wisest men were right about what they agreed on: instead, it proves that they were in *physiological* agreement about something, and consequently adopted – *had* to adopt – the same negative attitude towards life. Judgments, value judgments on life, for or against, can ultimately never be true: they have value only as symptoms, they can be taken seriously only as symptoms, – in themselves, judgments like these are stupidities. You really have to stretch out your fingers and make a concerted attempt to grasp this amazing piece of subtlety, that *the value of life cannot be estimated*. Not by the living, who are an interested party, a bone of contention,

---

[7] Consensus of the wise.

even, and not judges; not by the dead for other reasons. – It is an objection to a philosopher if he sees a problem with the *value* of life, it is a question mark on his wisdom, an un-wisdom. – What? So not only were the great sages all decadents but – they weren't even sages? – But let me return to the problem of Socrates.

3

Socrates was descended from the lowest segment of society: Socrates was plebeian. We know, we can still see how ugly he was. But ugliness, an objection in itself, was almost a refutation for the Greeks. Was Socrates Greek at all? Often enough, ugliness is a sign of crossbreeding, of *arrested* development due to crossbreeding. In other cases it appears as a *declining* development. Anthropologists specializing in crime tell us that the typical criminal is ugly: *monstrum in fronte, monstrum in animo.*[8] But criminals are decadents. Was Socrates a typical criminal? – At the very least, this is not contradicted by that famous physiological judgment that sounded so offensive to Socrates' friends. A foreign expert in faces who had come to Athens told Socrates to his face that he was a *monstrum*, – that he was a repository for all the vices and bad appetites. And Socrates simply replied: 'you know me, sir!' –

4

We see signs of Socrates' decadence not only in the admitted chaos and anarchy of his instincts, but in the hypertrophy of logic as well as in his emblematic rachitic spite. And let us not forget those auditory hallucinations, interpreted religiously as 'Socrates' daemon'. Everything about him is exaggerated, *buffo*, a caricature – and, at the same time, hidden, subterranean, and full of ulterior motives. – I am trying to figure out which idiosyncrasy gave rise to that Socratic equation of reason = virtue = happiness: the most bizarre of all equations, which is opposed to all the instincts of the earlier Greeks.

5

With Socrates, Greek taste suddenly changed in favour of dialectics: what really happened here? Above all, a *noble* taste was defeated; with dialectics,

---

[8] Monster in face, monster in soul.

the rabble rises to the top. Before Socrates, dialectical manners were rejected in good society: they were seen as bad manners, they humiliated people. The young were warned against them. People were generally distrustful of reasons being displayed like this. Honourable things, like honourable people, do not go around with their reasons in their hand. It is indecent to show all five fingers. Nothing with real value needs to be proved first. Wherever authority is still part of the social fabric, wherever people give commands rather than reasons, the dialectician is a type of clown: he is laughed at and not taken seriously. – Socrates was the clown who *made himself be taken seriously*: what really happened here?

6

You choose dialectics only as a last resort. You know that it will be viewed with suspicion, that it won't be very convincing. Nothing is easier to shake off than a dialectical effect: this is proved by the experience of any meeting where people make speeches. Dialectics is a type of *self-defence* used only by people who do not have any other weapons. You would need to be in a position of having to *enforce* your right: you would not use it for anything short of that. This is why the Jews were dialecticians; Reynard the Fox was one: what? and Socrates was too? –

7

– Is Socratic irony an expression of revolt? of plebeian *ressentiment*? As the member of an oppressed group, did Socrates take pleasure in the ferocity with which he could thrust his syllogistic knife? Did he avenge himself on the nobles he fascinated? – As a dialectician, you have a merciless tool in your hands; dialectics lets you act like a tyrant; you humiliate the people you defeat. The dialectician puts the onus on his opponent to show that he is not an idiot: the dialectician infuriates people and makes them feel helpless at the same time. The dialectician *undermines* his opponent's intellect. – What? Is dialectics just a form of *revenge* for Socrates?

8

I have shown how Socrates could be repulsive: which makes it even more important to explain the fact that he fascinated. – That he discovered a new type of *agon*,[9] that he was its first fencing master in the noble circles of Athens – this is one thing. He fascinated by appealing to the agonistic drive of the Greeks, – he introduced a variation into the wrestling matches between young men and youths. Socrates was a great *erotic* too.

9

But Socrates suspected even more. He looked *behind* his noble Athenians; he understood that *his* case, his idiosyncrasy of a case was not an exception any more. The same type of degeneration was quietly gaining ground everywhere: old Athens was coming to an end. – And Socrates understood that the world *needed* him, – his method, his cure, his personal strategy for self-preservation . . . Everywhere, instincts were in anarchy; everywhere, people were five steps away from excess: the *monstrum in animo*[10] was a universal danger. 'The drives want to act like tyrants; an even stronger *counter-tyrant* needs to be invented' . . . When the physiognomist revealed Socrates to himself as a pit of bad appetites, the great ironist dropped another clue that gives us the real key to his nature. 'This is true', he replied, 'but I have mastered them all.' *How* did Socrates master *himself*? – Basically, his case was only the most extreme and eye-catching example of what was turning into a universal affliction: people had stopped being masters of themselves and the instincts had turned *against* each other. Socrates was fascinating as an extreme case – his awe-inspiring ugliness showed everyone just what he was. Of course, his fascination lay mainly in the fact that he was an answer, a solution, the manifestation of a *cure* for this case. –

10

When people need *reason* to act as a tyrant, which was the case with Socrates, the danger cannot be small that something else might start acting as a tyrant. Rationality was seen as the *saviour*, neither Socrates nor his 'patients' had any choice about being rational, – it was *de rigueur*, it was their *last* resort. The fanaticism with which all of Greek thought threw itself on rationality shows that there was a crisis: people were in danger, they had only one option: be destroyed or – be *absurdly rational* . . .

---

[9] Contest.   [10] Monster in soul.

The moralism of Greek philosophers from Plato onwards is pathologically conditioned; the same is true for the value they give to dialectics. Reason = virtue = happiness only means: you have to imitate Socrates and establish a permanent state of *daylight* against all dark desires – the daylight of reason. You have to be clever, clear, and bright at any cost: any concession to the instincts, to the unconscious, leads *downwards* . . .

II

I have shown how Socrates fascinated: he seemed to be a doctor, a saviour. Do we really need to point out the errors inherent in his belief in 'rationality at any cost'? – Philosophers and moralists are lying to themselves when they think that they are going to extricate themselves from decadence by waging war on it. Extrication is not in their power: what they choose as a remedy, as an escape, is itself only another expression of decadence – they *change* the way it is expressed but do not get rid of the thing itself. Socrates was a misunderstanding; *the whole morality of improvement, including that of Christianity, was a misunderstanding* . . . The most glaring daylight, rationality at any cost, a cold, bright, cautious, conscious life without instinct, opposed to instinct, was itself just a sickness, another sickness – and in no way a return to 'virtue', to 'health', to happiness . . . To *have* to fight the instincts – that is the formula for decadence: as long as life is *ascending*, happiness is equal to instinct. –

12

– Did he understand this, that cleverest of all self-deceivers? Did he say this to himself in the end, in the *wisdom* of his death-bed courage? . . . Socrates *wanted* to die: – Athens did not give him the poisoned drink, he took it *himself*, he forced Athens to give it to him . . . 'Socrates is no doctor', he said quietly to himself: 'death is the only doctor here . . . Socrates was only sick for a long time . . .'

'REASON' IN PHILOSOPHY

I

You want to know what the philosophers' idiosyncrasies are? . . . Their lack of historical sense for one thing, their hatred of the very idea of becoming, their Egypticity. They think that they are showing *respect* for something when they dehistoricize it, *sub specie aeterni*,[11] – when they turn it into a mummy. For thousands of years, philosophers have been using only mummified concepts; nothing real makes it through their hands alive. They kill and stuff the things they worship, these lords of concept idolatry – they become mortal dangers to everything they worship. They see death, change, and age, as well as procreation and growth, as objections, – refutations even. What is, does not *become*; what becomes, *is* not . . . So they all believe, desperately even, in being. But since they cannot get hold of it, they look for reasons why it is kept from them. 'There must be some deception here, some illusory level of appearances preventing us from perceiving things that have being: where is the deceiver?' – 'We've got it!' they shout in ecstasy, 'it is in sensibility! These senses *that are so immoral anyway*, now they are deceiving us about the *true* world. Moral: get rid of sense-deception, becoming, history, lies, – history is nothing but a belief in the senses, a belief in lies. Moral: say no to everyone who believes in the senses, to all the rest of humanity: they are all "rabble". Be a philosopher, be a mummy, put on your gravedigger's face and show the world what monotono-theism is all about! – And above all, get rid of the *body*, this miserable *idée fixe* of the senses! full of all the errors of logic, refuted, impossible even, although it is impudent enough to act as if it were real!' . . .

2

With the greatest respect, I will make an exception for the name of *Heraclitus*. When all the other philosophical folk threw out the testimony of the senses because it showed multiplicity and change, Heraclitus threw it out because it made things look permanent and unified. Heraclitus did not do justice to the senses either. The senses do not lie the way the Eleatics[12] thought they did, *or* the way Heraclitus thought they did, – they do not lie at all. What we *do* with the testimony of the senses, that is where the lies begin, like the lie of unity, the lie of objectification, of substance, of permanence . . . 'Reason' makes us falsify the testimony of the senses. The senses are not lying when they show becoming, passing away, and

---

[11] From the standpoint of eternity.
[12] The school of Parmenides, who denied the reality of change.

change, . . . But Heraclitus will always be right in thinking that being is an empty fiction. The 'apparent' world is the only world: the 'true world' is just a *lie added on to it* . . .

3

– And what excellent tools for observation we have in our senses! Take the nose, for instance – no philosopher has ever mentioned the nose with admiration and gratitude, even though it is the most delicate instrument we have at our disposal: noses can detect tiny differences in motion that even spectroscopes do not notice. We have science these days precisely to the extent that we have decided to *accept* the testimony of the senses, – to the extent that we have learned to sharpen them, arm them, and think them through to the end. Everything else is deformity and pre-science: I mean metaphysics, theology, psychology, epistemology. *Or* formal science, a system of signs: like logic and that application of logic, mathematics. They do not have anything to do with reality, not even as a problem; they are equally distant from the question of whether a sign-convention like logic has any value at all. –

4

The *other* idiosyncrasy of the philosophers is just as dangerous: they confuse what comes first with what comes last. They take what comes at the end (unfortunately! since it should not come at all!), the 'highest ideas', which means the emptiest, most universal ideas, the last wisps of smoke from the evaporating end of reality – and they put it at the beginning, *as* the beginning. But again, this is just their way of showing respect: the highest should *not* grow out of the lowest, it should *not* grow at all . . . Moral: everything from the first rank must be a *causa sui*.[13] It is an objection for something to come from something else, it casts doubt on its value. All the supreme values are of the first rank, all the highest concepts, Being, the Unconditioned, the Good, the True, the Perfect – none of these could have become, and so they *must* be *causa sui*. But also, none of these things can be different from the others or opposed to

---

[13] Cause of itself.

them . . . This is how they get their stupendous concept of 'God' . . . It is the last, emptiest, most meagre idea of all, and it is put first, as cause in itself, as *ens realissimum*[14] . . . Why did humanity have to take the brain diseases of sick cobweb-weavers so seriously? – It has certainly paid the price! . . .

5

Finally, let us contrast this with the very different way that *we* (– I say 'we' to be polite) treat the problem of error and illusory appearances. People used to consider change, alteration, and becoming in general as proof that appearances were illusory, as a sign that something must be misleading us. These days, on the other hand, we see ourselves mired in error, drawn *necessarily* into error, precisely to the extent that the prejudice of reason forces us to make *use* of unity, identity, permanence, substance, cause, objectification, being; we have checked this through rigorously and are sure that this is where the error lies. This is no different than the movement of the sun, where our eye is a constant advocate for error, here it is *language*. Language began at a time when psychology was in its most rudimentary form: we enter into a crudely fetishistic mindset when we call into consciousness the basic presuppositions of the metaphysics of language – in the vernacular: the presuppositions of *reason*. It sees doers and deeds all over: it believes that will has causal efficacy: it believes in the 'I', in the I as being, in the I as substance, and it *projects* this belief in the I-substance onto all things – this is how it *creates* the concept of 'thing' in the first place . . . Being is imagined into everything – *pushed under everything* – as a cause; the concept of 'being' is only derived from the concept of 'I' . . . In the beginning there was the great disaster of an error, the belief that the will is a thing with *causal efficacy*, – that will is a *faculty* . . . These days we know that it is just a word . . . Much, much later, in a world more enlightened in thousands of ways, philosophers, to their great surprise, became conscious of a *certainty*, a subjective *assurance* in the way the categories of reason were applied: they concluded that these categories could not have come from the empirical world, – in fact, the entirety of the empirical world stood opposed to them. *So where did they*

---

[14] The most real thing.

come from? – And in India people made the same mistake they made in Greece: 'we must have lived in a higher world at some point' (rather than *in a much, much lower one*: which would have been true!), 'we must have been divine, *because* we have reason!' . . . In fact, nothing has ever had a more naïve power of persuasion than the error of being, as formulated by the Eleatics, for example: after all, every word we say, every sentence we use, speaks in its favour! – Even the Eleatics' adversaries succumbed to the seduction of the Eleatic concept of being: Democritus, for instance, when he invented his *atom* . . . 'Reason' in language: oh, what a deceptive old woman this is! I am afraid that we have not got rid of God because we still have faith in grammar . . .

6

You will be glad to know that I am compressing this key and novel insight into four theses: I am helping everyone to understand it and daring anyone to oppose it.

First proposition: The reasons people give for calling 'this' world an illusion argue much more convincingly in favour of its reality, – no *other* reality could ever be proven.

Second proposition: The criteria that people think indicate the 'true being' of things actually indicate non-being, *nothing*, – people have based the 'true world' on an opposition to the actual world: in fact it is an illusory world to the extent that it is just a *moral–optical* illusion.

Third proposition: It would not make any sense to fabricate a world 'other' than this one unless we had a powerful instinct for libelling, belittling, and casting suspicion on life: in that case, we would be using the phantasmagoria of an 'other', a 'better' life to *avenge* ourselves on life.

Fourth proposition: To divide the world into a 'true' half and an 'illusory' one, whether in the manner of Christianity or in the manner of Kant (an *underhanded* Christian, at the end of the day), is just a sign of decadence, – it is a symptom of life *in decline* . . . The fact that artists have valued appearance more highly than reality is not an objection to this proposition. Because 'appearance' here means reality *once again*, only selected, strengthened, corrected . . . The tragic artist is *not* a pessimist, – he says *yes* to the very things that are questionable and terrible, he is *Dionysian* . . .

HOW THE 'TRUE WORLD' FINALLY
BECAME A FABLE

The history of an error

1   The true world attainable for a man who is wise, pious, virtuous, – he lives in it, *he is it*. (Oldest form of the idea, relatively coherent, simple, convincing. Paraphrase of the proposition 'I, Plato, *am* the truth.')

2   The true world, unattainable for now, but promised to the man who is wise, pious, virtuous ('to the sinner who repents'). (Progress of the idea: it gets trickier, more subtle, less comprehensible, – *it becomes female*, it becomes Christian . . .)

3   The true world, unattainable, unprovable, unpromisable, but the very thought of it a consolation, an obligation, an imperative. (Basically the old sun but through fog and scepticism; the idea become elusive, pale, Nordic, Königsbergian.[15])

4   The true world – unattainable? At any rate, unattained. And as unattained also *unknown*. Consequently not consoling, redeeming, obligating either: how could we have obligations to something unknown? . . . (Gray morning. First yawn of reason. Cockcrow of positivism.)

5   The 'true world' – an idea that is of no further use, not even as an obligation, – now an obsolete, superfluous idea, *consequently* a refuted idea: let's get rid of it! (Bright day; breakfast; return of *bon sens*[16] and cheerfulness; Plato blushes in shame; pandemonium of all free spirits.)

6   The true world is gone: which world is left? The illusory one, perhaps? . . . But no! *we got rid of the illusory world along with the true one!* (Noon; moment of shortest shadow; end of longest error; high point of humanity; INCIPIT ZARATHUSTRA.[17])

MORALITY AS ANTI-NATURE

I

All passions go through a phase where they are just a disaster, where they drag their victim down with the weight of their stupidity – and

---

[15] Königsberg is the Prussian city where Kant lived.   [16] Good sense.   [17] Zarathustra begins.

a later, much later phase where they marry themselves to spirit, where they 'spiritualize' themselves. People used to fight against the passions because the passions were so stupid: people conspired to destroy them, – all the old moral monsters are unanimous on that score: '*il faut tuer les passions*'.[18] The most famous formula for this is in the New Testament, in that Sermon on the Mount, where, incidentally, things are certainly not viewed *from a higher perspective*. When it comes to sexuality, for instance, it says: 'if your eye offends you, pluck it out':[19] fortunately, Christians do not follow this rule. Nowadays, to *destroy* the passions and desires just to guard against their stupidity and its unpleasant consequences strikes us as itself a particularly acute form of stupidity. We have stopped admiring dentists who *pluck out* people's teeth just to get rid of the pain . . . But it is reasonable to admit that the idea of '*spiritualizing* the passions' could never have arisen on the soil where Christianity grew. It is well known that the first church even fought *against* the 'intelligent' for the sake of the 'poor in spirit': how could we expect it to have waged an intelligent war on the passions? – The church combats the passions by cutting them off in every sense: its technique, its 'cure', is *castration*. It never asks: 'how can a desire be spiritualized, beautified, deified?' – it has always laid the weight of its discipline on eradication (of sensuality, of pride, of greed, of the thirst to dominate and exact revenge). – But attacking the root of the passions means attacking the root of life: the practices of the church are *hostile to life* . . .

2

The same methods – castration, eradication – are instinctively chosen by people whose wills are too weak and degenerate to exercise any restraint in a struggle against a desire: by people with the sort of nature that needs *La Trappe*,[20] to use an allegory (and not allegorically –), they need some sort of definitive declaration of hostilities, they need a *gap* between themselves and the passion. Radical means are only indispensable for degenerates; weakness of the will or, to be exact, the inability *not* to react to a stimulus, is itself just another form of degeneration. A radical antagonism, a deadly hostility, to the senses is a telling symptom: it raises suspicions about

[18] 'It is necessary to kill the passions.'   [19] Matt. 5:29.
[20] The abbey after which the Trappist order of monks is named.

the overall state of anyone who is excessive like this. – Incidentally, this hostility, this hatred, reaches its climax only when natures like this do not even have enough strength to adopt this radical cure and renounce their 'devil'. Looking through the whole history of priests and philosophers (and artists as well): it is not the ascetics or the impotent who say the most poisonous things about the senses, it is the impossible ascetics, people who really *should* be ascetics . . .

3

The spiritualization of sensuality is called *love*: it represents a great triumph over Christianity. Another triumph is our spiritualization of *hostility*. It involves a deep appreciation of the value of having enemies; basically, it means acting and reasoning in ways totally at odds with how people used to act and reason. The church has always wanted to destroy its enemies: but we, on the other hand, we immoralists and anti-Christians, think that we benefit from the existence of the church. Even in politics, hostility is becoming more spiritual, – much cleverer, much more thoughtful, much more *careful*. Almost every party knows that its self-preservation depends on its opposition not losing too much strength: and the same is true in power politics. A new creation in particular, like the new *Reich*, needs enemies more than it needs friends: it only feels necessary when it faces opposition, it only *becomes* necessary when it faces opposition . . . We act the same way towards the 'inner enemy': we have spiritualized hostility there too, and have come to appreciate its *value*. The price of *fertility* is to be rich in contradictions; people stay *young* only if their souls do not stretch out languidly and long for peace . . . Nothing is more foreign to us than that one-time desideratum of 'peacefulness of the soul', the *Christian* desideratum; there is nothing we envy less than the moral cow and the fat happiness of good conscience. You give up the *great* life when you give up war . . . In many cases, of course, 'peacefulness of the soul' is just a misunderstanding, – something *else* is really happening, but without knowing what to call itself. A couple of cases, bluntly and without bias. 'Peacefulness of the soul', for instance, can be the gentle diffusion of a rich, animal nature into a moral (or religious) sphere. Or the beginning of fatigue, the first shadow of evening, of any type of evening. Or a sign of humidity in the air, of south winds approaching. Or an unselfconscious gratitude for a good digestion (sometimes called 'love of humanity'). Or the quieting down of a convalescent who is tasting everything as if for the first time and who waits . . . Or the condition following an intense gratification of our ruling passions, the well-being of rare satisfaction. Or the sort of weakness that age brings to our will, our desires, our vices. Or laziness that has been persuaded by vanity to dress itself up as morality. Or the emergence of certainty, even a terrible certainty, after the suspense and torture of a long uncertainty. Or the expression of maturity and mastery in the middle of doing, making, effecting, willing, a tranquil breathing, an *attained* 'freedom of the will' . . . *Twilight of the Idols*: who knows? Perhaps this is just a type of 'peacefulness of the soul' too . . .

4

– I will formulate a principle. Every naturalism in morality – which is to say: every *healthy* morality – is governed by an instinct of life, – some rule of life is served by a determinate canon of 'should' and 'should not', some inhibition and hostility on the path of life is removed this way. But *anti-natural* morality, on the other hand, which is to say almost every morality that has been taught, revered, or preached so far, explicitly turns its back on the instincts of life, – it *condemns* these instincts, sometimes in secret, sometimes in loud and impudent tones. By saying 'God sees into the heart', it says no to both the lowest and the highest desires of life, and treats God as the *enemy of life* . . . The saint who is pleasing to God is the ideal eunuch . . . Life comes to an end where the 'kingdom of God' *begins* . . .

5

If you have understood how sacrilegious it is to rebel against life (and this sort of rebellion is practically sacrosanct for Christian morality), then, fortunately, you have understood something else as well: the futility, fallacy, absurdity, *deceitfulness* of a rebellion like this. A condemnation of life on the part of the living is, in the end, only the symptom of a certain type of life, and has no bearing on the question of whether or not the condemnation is justified. Even to raise the problem of the *value* of life, you would need to be both *outside* life and as familiar with life as someone, anyone, everyone who has ever lived: this is enough to tell us that the problem is inaccessible to us. When we talk about values we are under the inspiration, under the optic, of life: life itself forces us to posit values, life itself evaluates through us, *when* we posit values. It follows from this that even the *anti-natural morality* that understands God as the converse of life, the condemnation of life, is only a value judgment made by life – but *which* life? Which type of life is making value judgments here? – But I have already answered this: it is the judgment of a declining, weakened, exhausted, condemned life. Morality as it has been understood so far, as it was finally summed up by Schopenhauer with the formula: 'negation of the will to life' – is the *instinct of decadence* making an imperative of itself: it says: '*be destroyed*!' – it is the judgment of the condemned.

6

Finally, let us think how naïve it is to say 'this is the way people *should* be!'. Reality shows us an enchanting abundance of types, a lavish profusion of forms in change and at play: and some worthless idiot of a moralist sees all this and says: 'no! people should be *different from the way they are*'!? . . . He even knows what people should be like, this miserable fool, he paints a picture of himself on the wall and says '*ecce homo*!'.[21] . . . But even when a moralist picks out a single individual and says: 'this is the way *you* should be!', he is still making a fool of himself. An individual is a piece of fate, from the front and from the back; an individual is one more law, one more necessity imposed on everything that is coming and going to be. To say to an individual: 'change yourself' means demanding that everything change, even retroactively . . . And in fact there have been consistent moralists who wanted people to be different, namely virtuous, who wanted to have people in their own image, which is that of a idiot: and to this end they *negated* the world! This is no minor piece of insanity! This is no modest type of immodesty! Morality, to the extent that it is just *condemnation*, without *any* attention to, interest in, or concern for life, is a specific error that you should not pity, an *idiosyncrasy of degenerates* that has caused incalculable damage! . . . But we who are different, we immoralists, have opened our hearts to all types of understanding, comprehension, *approval*. We do not negate easily, we stake our honour on being *affirmative*. We are increasingly opening our eyes to that economy that both needs and knows how to make use of everything rejected by the holy insanity of the priests,

---

[21] 'Behold the man!'

the *sick* reason of the priests – to that economy in the law of life that that can take advantage of even the disgusting species of idiot, the priests, the virtuous, – *what* advantage? – But we ourselves, we immoralists, are the answer to this . . .

THE FOUR GREAT ERRORS

I

The error of confusing cause and effect. – No error is more dangerous than that of *confusing the cause with the effect*: I call it the genuine destruction of reason. Nevertheless, this error can be found in both the oldest and the newest habits of humanity: we even sanctify it and call it 'religion' and 'morality'. It can be found in every single claim formulated by religion and morality; priests and legislators of moral law are the authors of this destruction of reason. – Here is an example: everyone has heard of the book in which the famous Cornaro recommends his meagre diet as a recipe for a long and happy – and virtuous – life. This is one of the most widely read books, and several thousand copies are still being printed in England every year. There is no doubt in my mind that few books (except of course the Bible) have wreaked as much havoc, have *shortened* as many lives as this well-meaning curiosity has done. The reason: confusion of cause and effect. This conscientious Italian thought that his diet was the *cause* of his longevity: but the preconditions for a long life – an exceptionally slow metabolism and a minimal level of consumption – were in fact the cause of his meagre diet. He was not free to eat *either* a little *or* a lot, his frugality was *not* 'freely willed': he got sick when he ate more. But unless you are a carp, it is not only advisable but necessary to have *decent meals*. Scholars in *this* day and age, with their rapid consumption of nervous energy, would be destroyed by a regimen like Cornaro's. *Crede experto.*[22] –

2

The most general formula at the centre of all religions and moralities is: 'do this, don't do that – and then you'll be happy! Otherwise . . .'.

---

[22] Believe one with experience.

Every morality, every religion, *is* this imperative, – I call it the great original sin of reason, the *immortal unreason*. In my mouth, this formula changes into its opposite – *first* example of my 'revaluation of all values' – someone who has turned out well, a 'happy one', *has to* perform certain acts and will instinctively avoid others, he is the physiological representative of the system he uses in dealing with people and things. In a word: his virtue is the *effect* of his happiness . . . Leading a long life, having many descendants, these are *not* the rewards of virtue; rather, virtue is itself a deceleration of the metabolism that brings about (among other things) a long life with many descendants – in short, *Cornarism*. – Church and morality say: 'a generation, a people destroys itself through vice and luxury'. My *restored* reason says: when a people is destroyed and becomes physiologically degenerate, this *leads* to vice and luxury (which is to say the need for increasingly strong and more frequent stimuli, as anyone with an exhausted nature can tell you). A young man becomes prematurely pale and wrinkled. His friends say: some illness or another is to blame. I say: *the fact that* he became sick, *the fact that* he could not fight the illness off, this was already the effect of an impoverished life, a hereditary exhaustion. Someone reading the newspapers says: this party is destroying itself with mistakes like this. But according to my *higher* politics: a party that makes mistakes like this is finished – it has lost its instinctive certainty. Every mistake in every sense is the effect of a degeneration of the instincts, of a disintegration of the will: this is almost a definition of what it means to be *bad*. Everything *good* is instinctive – and consequently light, necessary, free. Effort is an objection, gods and heroes belong to different types (in my language: *light* feet are the first attribute of divinity).

3

Error of false causation. – People have always believed that they knew what a cause was: but how did we get this knowledge – or, more precisely, how did we get this belief that we have knowledge? From the famous realm of 'inner facts', none of which has ever proven factual. We believed that our acts of will were causally efficacious; we thought that here, at least, we had caught causality *in the act*. Nobody doubted that consciousness was the place to look for all the *antecedentia* of an act, its causes, and that you would be able to *find* these causes there as well – under the rubric of 'motives': otherwise the action could hardly be considered free, and nobody could really be held responsible for it. Finally, who could deny that thoughts have causes? that the 'I' is what causes thoughts? . . . Of all these three 'inner facts' that together seem to guarantee causation, the first and most convincing is that of *will as causal agent*; the conception of a consciousness ('mind') as cause, and then that of the I (the 'subject') as cause are just latecomers that appeared once causality of the will was established as given, as *empirical* . . . Meanwhile, we have thought better of all this. Nowadays we do not believe a word of it. The 'inner world' is full of illusions and phantasms: will is one of them. The will does not do anything any more, and so it does not explain anything any more either – it just accompanies processes, but it can be absent as well. The so-called 'motive': another error. Just a surface phenomenon of consciousness, an 'after-the-fact' that hides the *antecedentia* of an act more than it reveals them. Not to mention the I! That has become a fairy tale, a fiction, a play on words: it has stopped thinking, feeling, and willing altogether! . . . What follows from this? There are no mental causes whatsoever! All the would-be empirical evidence for this goes to hell! *That's* what follows! – And we really botched this 'empiricism' – we used it to *create* the world as a world of causes, wills, and minds. The oldest and most enduring psychology was at work here, doing absolutely nothing but this: it considered all events to be deeds, all deeds to be the result of a will, the world became a multitude of doers, a doer ('subject') pushed its way under all events. People projected their three 'inner facts' out of themselves and onto the world – the facts they believed in most fervently, the will, the mind, and the I. They took the concept of being from the concept of the I, they posited 'things' as beings in their own image, on the basis of their concept of I as cause. Is it any wonder that what they rediscovered in things later is only *what they had put into them in the first place*? – Even the 'thing', to say it again, the concept of a thing, is just a reflex of the belief in the I as cause . . . And even your atom, my dear Mr Mechanist and Mr Physicist, how many errors, how much rudimentary psychology is left in your atom! Not to mention the 'thing-in-itself', the *horrendum pudendum*[23] of metaphysicians! The error of thinking that the mind caused reality! And to make it the measure of reality! And to call it *God*! –

[23] Shameful part.

4

The error of imaginary causes. – Beginning with dreams: we experience a certain sensation (following the sound of cannon fire in the distance, for example) and then retrospectively supply a cause for it (which often takes the form of a whole little novel with the dreamer as the protagonist). Meanwhile, the sensation remains in a type of resonance: it waits, as it were, until our causal instinct allows it to come into the foreground, – at which point it has stopped being accidental, it is 'meaningful'. The cannon fire takes place inside a *causal* nexus, in what seems like a temporal reversal. The later event, the motivation, is experienced first, often with hundreds of details that flash past, followed by the shot . . . What has happened? The ideas that were *created* by a certain physical condition were mistaken for the cause of that condition. – In fact, we do the same thing when we are awake. Most of our general feelings – every type of inhibition, pressure, tension, explosion in the give and take of our organs, and particularly the state of *nervus sympathicus*[24] – excite our causal instinct: we want there to be a *reason why* we are in the particular state we are in, – why we are feeling good or bad. It is never enough just to establish the fact that we *are* in a particular state: we only let this state register, – we only become *conscious* of it –, once we have assigned it a type of motivation. – The memory that unconsciously becomes activated in such cases is what leads back to earlier states of the same type and the associated causal interpretation, – *not* their causality. Of course, memory also interjects the belief that the ideas, the accompanying train of consciousness, had been the cause. This is how a particular causal interpretation comes to be *habituated*; this interpretation in fact inhibits an *investigation* into the cause and even precludes it.

5

Psychological explanation for this. – Familiarizing something unfamiliar is comforting, reassuring, satisfying, and produces a feeling of power as well. Unfamiliar things are dangerous, anxiety-provoking, upsetting, – the primary instinct is to *get rid* of these painful states. First principle: any explanation is better than none. Since it is basically a matter of wanting to get rid of unpleasant thoughts, people are not exactly particular about how

[24] Sympathetic nervous system.

to do it: the first idea that can familiarize the unfamiliar feels good enough to be 'considered true'. Proof of *pleasure* ('strength') as the criterion of truth. – So the causal instinct is conditioned and excited by feelings of fear. Whenever possible, the question 'why?' won't point to the cause as such, but instead will point to a *particular type of cause* – a reassuring, comforting cause. The first consequence of this need is that causation gets attributed to something we are already *familiar* with, something we have already encountered and registered in memory. This forecloses the possibility that anything novel, alien, or previously unencountered can be a cause. – So we are not looking for just any type of explanatory cause, we are looking for a *chosen, preferred* type of explanation, one that will most quickly and reliably get rid of the feeling of unfamiliarity and novelty, the feeling that we are dealing with something we have never encountered before, – the *most common* explanation. – Result: a certain type of causal attribution becomes increasingly prevalent, gets concentrated into a system, and finally emerges as *dominant*, which is to say it completely rules out *other* causes and explanations. – The banker thinks immediately of his 'business', the Christian of 'sin', the girl of her love.

6

The entire realm of morality and religion belongs to this concept of imaginary cause. – 'Explanation' for generally *unpleasant* feelings. They come from unfriendly beings (evil spirits: the most famous case – hysterics thought to be witches). They come from illicit acts (the feeling of 'sin', of 'sinfulness', insinuated into a sense of physiological unease – people will always find reasons for feeling unhappy with themselves). They are punishments, payments for something we should not have done, should not have *been* (shamelessly generalized by Schopenhauer into a statement that shows morality for what it really is, the true poisoner and slanderer of life: 'every great pain, whether mental or physical, shows us what we deserve; since it could not have happened unless we deserved it'. *The World as Will and Representation*, II, p. 580). They come from thoughtless acts that ended badly (– the affects, the senses are considered as causes, as 'guilty'; physiological emergencies are interpreted as 'deserved', with the help of *other* emergencies). – 'Explanation' for generally *pleasant* feelings. They come from faith in God. They come from a consciousness of good acts (the so-called 'good conscience', a physiological state similar to a good digestion and often confused with it). They come from things turning out well (– a naïve fallacy: a hypochondriac or a Pascal does not experience anything like pleasant feelings when things turn out well). They come from faith, love, hope – the Christian virtues. – In fact, all these supposed explanations are *results* and, as it were, the translation of feelings of pleasure or pain into a false dialect: people experience hope *because* their fundamental physiological feeling is strong and rich again; people have faith in God *because* the feeling of fullness and strength gives them peace. – Morality and religion can be exhaustively accounted for by *the psychology of error*: in every single case, cause and effect are confused; or truth is confused with the effects of *believing* that something is true; or a state of consciousness is confused with its causes.

7

Error of free will. – People have lost sympathy for the concept of 'free will': we know all too well what it is – the shadiest trick theologians have up their sleeves for making humanity 'responsible' in their sense of the term, which is to say *dependent on them* . . . I am just describing the psychology that comes into play whenever people are held responsible. – Wherever responsibilities are assigned, an instinct to *punish and judge* is generally at work. Whenever a particular state of affairs is traced back to a will, an intention, or a responsible action, becoming is stripped of its innocence. The notion of will was essentially designed with punishment in mind, which is to say the desire to *assign guilt*. The whole of ancient psychology, the psychology of will, was conditioned by the desire of its architects (the priests at the head of the ancient community) to establish their *right* to inflict punishment – or to assign the right to God . . . People were considered 'free' so that they could be judged and punished – so that they could be *guilty*: consequently, every act *had* to be thought of as willed, every act *had* to be seen as coming from consciousness (– which made the *most fundamental* counterfeit *in psychologicis* into the very principle of psychology . . .). But now that we have set off in the *opposite* direction, now that we immoralists in particular are trying as hard as we can to rid the world of the concepts of guilt and punishment and cleanse psychology, history, nature, and social institutions and sanctions of these concepts, the most radical opponents we face are the theologians who use the concept of the 'moral world order' to keep infecting the innocence of becoming with 'punishment' and 'guilt'. Christianity is a hangman's metaphysics.

8

What is the only teaching *we* can have? – That no one *gives* people their qualities, not God or society, parents or ancestors, not even *people themselves* (– this final bit of nonsense was circulated by Kant – and maybe even by Plato – under the rubric of 'intelligible freedom'). *Nobody* is responsible for people existing in the first place, or for the state or circumstances or environment they are in. The fatality of human existence cannot be extricated from the fatality of everything that was and will be. People are *not* the products of some special design, will, or purpose, they do *not* represent an attempt to achieve an 'ideal of humanity', 'ideal of happiness', or 'ideal of morality', – it is absurd to want to *devolve* human existence onto some purpose or another. We have invented the concept of 'purpose': there *are* no purposes in reality . . . A person is necessary, a person is a piece of fate, a person belongs to the whole, a person only *is* in the context of the whole, – there is nothing that can judge, measure, compare, or condemn our being, because that would mean judging, measuring, comparing, and condemning the whole . . . *But there is nothing outside the whole!* – The fact that nobody is held responsible any more, that being is not the sort of thing that can be traced back to a *causa prima*,[25] that the world is not unified as either a *sensorium* or a 'spirit', *only this can constitute the great liberation*, – only this begins to restore the *innocence* of becoming . . . The concept of 'God' has been the biggest *objection* to existence so far . . . We reject God, we reject the responsibility in God: *this* is how we begin to redeem the world. –

'IMPROVING' HUMANITY

1

You have heard me call for philosophers to place themselves *beyond* good and evil, – to rise *above* the illusion of moral judgment. This call is the result of an insight that I was the first to formulate: *there are absolutely no*

---

[25] First cause.

moral facts. What moral and religious judgments have in common is the belief in things that are not real. Morality is just an interpretation of certain phenomena or (more accurately) a *mis*interpretation. Moral judgments, like religious ones, presuppose a level of ignorance in which even the concept of reality is missing and there is no distinction between the real and the imaginary; a level where 'truth' is the name for the very things that we now call 'illusions'. That is why moral judgments should never be taken literally: on their own, they are just absurdities. But *semiotically*, they are invaluable: if you know what to look for, moral judgments reveal the most valuable realities of the cultures and interiorities that did not *know* enough to 'understand' themselves. Morality is just a sign language, just a symptomatology: you have to know *what* it means in order to take advantage of it.

2

A first example, just in passing. People have always wanted to 'improve' human beings; for the most part, this has been called morality. But this one term has stood for vastly different things. The project of *domesticating* the human beast as well as the project of *breeding* a certain species of human have both been called 'improvements': only by using these zoological terms can we begin to express the realities here – realities, of course, that the typical proponents of 'improvement', the priests, do not know anything about, do not *want* to know anything about . . . To call the domestication of an animal an 'improvement' almost sounds like a joke to us. Anyone who knows what goes on in a zoo will have doubts whether beasts are 'improved' there. They become weak, they become less harmful, they are *made ill* through the use of pain, injury, hunger, and the depressive affect of fear. – The same thing happens with domesticated people who have been 'improved' by priests. In the early Middle Ages, when the church was basically a zoo, the choicest specimens of the 'blond beast'[26] were hunted down everywhere, – people like the Teuton nobles were subjected to 'improvement'. But what did an 'improved' Teuton look like after being seduced into a cloister? He looked like a caricature of a human being, like a miscarriage: he had turned into a 'sinner', he was

---

[26] Nietzsche first speaks of the 'blond beast' in *GM* I.11 and means by it any rapacious, warlike (lion-like) people.

stuck in a cage, locked up inside all sorts of horrible ideas . . . There he lay, sick, miserable, full of malice against himself, hating the drive for life, suspicious of everything that was still strong and happy. In short, a 'Christian' . . . To put the matter physiologically: when struggling with beasts, making them sick *might* be the only way to make them weak. The church understood this: it has ruined people, it has weakened them, – but it claims to have 'improved' them . . .

3

Let us take the other case of so-called morality, the *breeding* of a particular race or type. The most magnificent example can be found in Indian morality, where it is given religious sanction as the 'law of Manu'. This law sets the task of breeding no fewer than four races at once: a priestly race, a warrior race, a merchant and agricultural race, and finally a servant race, the Sudras. Clearly, we are not talking about taming animals any more: even to conceive of a breeding scheme like this presupposes a type of person who is a hundred times gentler and more reasonable. You breathe freely again when you leave the Christian atmosphere of disease and dungeon and enter this healthier, higher, more *expansive* world. What a miserable book the New Testament is in comparison with Manu, how bad it smells! – But even this system found it necessary to be *terrible* – not (as before) in the struggle against beasts, but rather with its *own* opposite, the unbred people, the human hodgepodge, the Chandala.[27] And again, the only way it was able to render these people harmless, to make them weak, was to make them *sick*, – it was a fight against the 'great number'. Perhaps nothing is more opposed to our sensibility than *these* protective measures of Indian morality. The third edict, for example (Avadana-Sastra I), 'on impure vegetables', decrees that the only foods the Chandala are allowed to have are garlic and onions, since the holy scripture says that they cannot be given grain, or fruits with grains, or *water* or fire. The same edict proclaims that they cannot get their water from rivers or wells or ponds, but only from the entrances to swamps or from pits formed by animal footprints. They are also forbidden from washing their laundry or even *washing themselves*, since any water that is conceded to them as an act of special mercy can only be used to quench thirst. Finally, the

---

[27] The untouchables.

184

Sudra women are forbidden to come to the aid of Chandala women in childbirth, who are, furthermore, not even allowed *to help each other* . . . – Sanitary policing like this is bound to succeed: – deadly epidemics, hideous sexual diseases, followed again by the 'law of the knife', ordering circumcision for male children, removal of the labia for female children. – Manu himself says: 'the Chandalas are the fruits of adultery, incest and crime [– these as the *necessary* consequence of the concept of breeding]. The only clothes they can have are rags from corpses, the only dishes are broken pots, the only jewelry is old iron, and they can only worship evil spirits; they will wander perpetually from one place to the next. They are not allowed to write from left to right and cannot write with their right hand: the use of the right hand and writing from left to right is reserved for the *virtuous*, for people with *breeding*.' –

4

These decrees are instructive enough: they present us with *Aryan* humanity for once, in its pure and primordial form, – we learn that the concept of 'pure blood' is anything but harmless. On the other hand, it is clear *which* people represent the eternal hatred, the Chandala-hatred of this 'humanity', where this hatred has become a religion, where it has become *genius* . . . From this perspective, the Gospels are first-rate documents; the book of Enoch even more so. – Christianity, which has sprung from Jewish roots and can only be understood as a plant that has come from this soil, represents the *counter-movement* to every morality of breeding, race, or privilege: – it is the *anti-Aryan* religion *par excellence*: Christianity, the revaluation of all Aryan values, the victory of Chandala values, the gospel preached to the poor and the base, the general revolt of the downtrodden, the miserable, the malformed, the failures, against anyone with 'breeding', – the eternal vengeance of the Chandala as a *religion of love* . . .

5

In the methods they have employed, the morality of *breeding* and the morality of *domestication* are fully worthy of each other: we can put down as our highest principle that to *make* morality you must have the unconditional will to its opposite. This is the great, *uncanny* problem, and the one

I have spent the longest time pursuing: the psychology of the 'improvers' of humanity. An essentially modest little fact, the so-called *pia fraus*,[28] gave me my first inroad into this problem: the *pia fraus*, the bequest of all philosophers and priests who have 'improved' humanity. Neither Manu nor Plato nor Confucius nor the teachers of Judaism and Christianity have ever doubted their *right* to lie. They never doubted that they had *very different rights* . . . Boiling this down to a formula, you could say: *all the methods* that have been used so far to try make humanity moral have been thoroughly *immoral*. –

WHAT THE GERMANS LACK

I

Among Germans it is not enough to have spirit any more: you also need the courage of your spiritual convictions . . .

Perhaps I know the Germans, perhaps I can even tell them a thing or two. The new Germany represents a great quantum of competence, both inherited and instilled, so that it can even afford to squander this accumulated hoard of strength over a long period of time. This does *not* represent the ascendancy of a high culture, much less that of a delicate taste, a noble 'beauty' of the instincts; but instead the *most masculine* virtues that can be found anywhere in Europe. Plenty of zeal and self-respect, plenty of competence in communication and transaction, in reciprocity of duties, plenty of diligence, plenty of stamina – and a hereditary sense of moderation that needs to be goaded on rather than curbed. I should add that obedience still exists here without it being humiliating . . . And people do not look down on their opponents . . .

You can see that I want to be fair to the Germans: but I do not want to break faith with myself, – so I need to register my objections as well. It costs a lot to come to power: power makes people *stupid* . . . The Germans – they were once considered the people of thinkers: do they still think at all these days? – Germans have become bored with spirit, Germans have started to distrust spirit, politics absorbs all the seriousness from really spiritual matters – '*Deutschland, Deutschland über Alles*',[29] I am afraid that this was the end of German philosophy . . . 'Are there any German

---

[28] Pious fraud or holy lie.
[29] '*Germany, Germany above everything*', the first line of the German national anthem.

philosophers? Are there any German poets? Are there any *good* German books?' This is what I get asked by people abroad. I turn red, but with the courage that comes to me even in desperate situations I reply: 'Well, *Bismarck!*' – Should I also admit what people are reading these days? . . . Damned instinct of mediocrity! . . .

2

Is there anyone whose heart has not grown heavy when thinking about what the German spirit *could* be? But this is a people that has spent the better part of the last millennium wilfully making itself stupid: nowhere else have alcohol and Christianity – the two great European narcotics – been abused with greater depravity. And these have recently been joined by a third one that could kill off any refined or bold agility of the spirit all by itself: music, our constipated, constipating, German music. – How much sullen heaviness, dullness, humidity, pyjamas, how much *beer* there is in the German intellect! How is it even possible for young men who have dedicated their lives to the most spiritual goals to be so blind to the first instinct of spirituality, *the spirit's instinct of self-preservation* – that they drink beer? . . . Maybe the alcoholism of young scholars does not call their scholastic pretensions completely into question (you can be a great scholar even if you are completely devoid of spirit), but it is a problem in all other respects. – And is there anything that has *escaped* the mild degeneration that beer produces in spirit? I once put my finger on a case that is almost famous now – the degeneration of our first German free spirit, the *sensible* David Strauss, into a writer of beer-bench gospels and the 'new faith' . . . It wasn't for nothing that he set his pledge to the 'lovely brunette'[30] in verse – loyal to the very end . . .

3

I have been talking about German spirit: that it is getting coarser, that it is getting shallower. Is this enough? – In fact, I am worried about something else entirely: how German seriousness, German profundity, the German *passion* for spiritual things is going increasingly into decline. The *pathos* has changed, not just the intellect. – I occasionally come into contact with German universities: what an atmosphere you find among the scholars

[30] Beer.

there! How barren it is, how meek, how lukewarm the spirituality has become! It would be a profound misunderstanding if you were to cite German scholarship as a counter-example – and proof positive that you have not read a single word I have written. For the past seventeen years I have been tireless in exposing the *dispiriting* influence of our present-day research industry. The tremendous scope of scholarship condemns every individual to a severe helotism these days, which is the main reason why people with fuller, richer, *more profound* dispositions cannot find an appropriate education *or educator* any more. There is nothing our culture suffers from *more* than the surfeit of arrogant do-nothings and fragments of humanity. Entirely in *spite* of themselves, our universities are the real hothouses for this sort of atrophy of the spiritual instincts. And the whole of Europe is aware of this – nobody is fooled by power politics . . . Germany is increasingly viewed as the *lowlands* of Europe. – I am still *looking* for a German who *I* can be serious with in my own way, – and even more for one I can be cheerful with! *Twilight of the Idols*: oh, is there anyone these days who can understand *the sort of seriousness* a hermit is recovering from here! – Our cheerfulness is the most incomprehensible thing about us . . .

4

After even a cursory assessment it is obvious not only that German culture is in decline, but that there are plenty of good reasons why this is the case. Ultimately, nobody can give more than they have – this is true for individuals and this is true for peoples as well. If you invest all your energy in economics, world commerce, parliamentarianism, military engagements, power and power politics, – if you take the quantum of intelligence, seriousness, will, and self-overcoming that you embody and expend it all in this *one* direction, then there won't be any left for the other direction. Culture and the state – let us be honest with ourselves here – these are adversaries: '*Kultur-Staat*' is just a modern idea. The one lives off the other, the one flourishes at the expense of the other. All the great ages of culture have been ages of political decline: anything great in the cultural sense is apolitical, even *anti-political*. – Goethe's heart leapt up at the phenomenon of Napoleon, – it sank back *down* with the 'Wars of Liberation' . . . Just as Germany is emerging as a great power, France's significance is changing to that of a *cultural power*. Even today, much of what is new and serious, much of what is new and imbued with a sense of spiritual *passion* is migrating to Paris; the question of pessimism, for instance, the question of Wagner, almost all psychological and artistic questions get taken up there with incomparably greater finesse and care than in Germany, – the Germans are altogether *incapable* of this type of seriousness. – In the history of European culture, the rise of the '*Reich*' means one thing above all else: *a shift in emphasis*. Everyone already knows: in what matters most (which is still culture), the Germans have dropped out of the picture. People ask: do you Germans have a single spirit of European stature to show for yourselves these days? someone like your Goethe, your Hegel, your Heinrich Heine, your Schopenhauer? – The fact that there is not a single German philosopher any more is a never-ending source of amazement. –

5

The whole system of higher education in Germany has lost what matters most: the *goal* as well as the *means* to the goal. The fact that education, that *development* – and *not* 'the *Reich*' – is itself a goal, the fact that you need *educators* – and *not* schoolteachers or university scholars – to reach this goal, people have forgotten this . . . We need educators *who are themselves educated*, thoughtful, noble spirits, proven at every moment, proven by words and silences, the products of cultures that have grown ripe and sweet, – *not* the scholarly morons that schools and universities offer young people these days as 'higher wet nurses'. The *first* precondition of education is educators, and these are *lacking*, apart from exceptional exceptions: which is why German culture is in decline. – My distinguished friend Jakob Burckhardt in Basle is one of these rarest of exceptions: he is chiefly responsible for Basle's pre-eminence in humaneness. – German 'higher schooling' is in fact a brutal form of training that tries to process a horde of young men as quickly as possible for use – *and abuse* – in the civil service. 'Higher education' and *horde* – these are in contradiction from the outset. Any higher education is only for the exceptions: you have to be privileged to have the right to such a high privilege. Nothing great or beautiful could ever be common property: *pulchrum est paucorum hominum*.[31] – What are the *conditions* for the decline of German culture? That 'higher education' is not a *privilege* any more – the democratization

[31] Beauty is for the few.

of '*Bildung*',[32] the fact that it is becoming common and common*place* . . . And do not forget that military privileges practically compel people to pursue *too much* higher schooling, which leads to its downfall. – Nobody in contemporary Germany is free to give his children a noble education any more: our 'higher' schools are all geared to the most ambiguous sort of mediocrity with teachers, lesson plans, and curricular goals. And there is such an oppressive and indecent sense of hurry, as if something would be lost if a twenty-three-year-old is not 'finished' yet, does not have an answer to the 'ultimate question': 'what job? what calling?' – Higher types of humans, if I may say so, have no love of 'callings', for the very reason that that they know that they have been called . . . They have time, they take their time, they never think about being 'finished', – the way a high culture sees things, when you are thirty you are just a beginner, a child. – Our over-filled schools, our overworked, stupefied schoolteachers are a scandal: and to defend this situation, as the professors at Heidelberg have recently done – there might be is *cause* for this, – but there is no reason.

6

– In order to stay true to my type, which is *affirmative* and only reluctantly and parenthetically has anything to do with dispute or criticism, I will immediately put forward the three tasks that require an educator. People must learn to *see*, they must learn to *think*, they must learn to *speak* and to *write*: the goal in all three cases is a noble culture. – Learning to *see* – getting your eyes used to calm, to patience, to letting things come to you; postponing judgment, learning to encompass and take stock of an individual case from all sides. This is the *first* preliminary schooling for spirituality: *not* to react immediately to a stimulus, but instead to take control of the inhibiting, excluding instincts. Learning to *see*, as I understand it, is close to what an unphilosophical way of speaking calls a strong will: the essential thing here is precisely *not* 'to will', to be *able* to suspend the decision. Every characteristic absence of spirituality, every piece of common vulgarity, is due to an inability to resist a stimulus – you *have* to react, you follow every impulse. In many cases this sort of compulsion is already a pathology, a decline, a symptom of exhaustion, – almost everything that is crudely and unphilosophically designated a 'vice' is really

---

[32] *Bildung* means both education and culture as well as formation and development.

just this physiological inability *not* to react. – A practical application of having learned to see: your learning process *in general* becomes slow, mistrustful, reluctant. You let foreign things, *new* things of every type, come towards you while assuming an initial air of calm hostility, – you pull your hand away from them. To keep all your doors wide open, to lie on your stomach, prone and servile before every little fact, to be constantly poised and ready to put yourself into – *plunge* yourself into – other things, in short, to espouse the famous modern 'objectivity' – all this is in bad taste, it is *ignobility par excellence.* –

7

Learning to *think*: our schools do not have any idea what this means. Even in the universities, even among genuine philosophy scholars, logic is beginning to die out as a theory, a practice, a *craft*. Just look at German books: there is not even a dim recollection of the fact that thought requires a technique, a plan of study, a will to mastery, – that thinking wants to be learned like dancing, as a *type* of dancing . . . Has any German these days ever experienced the delicate shiver that a *light-footed* spirit sends streaming into every muscle! – The stiff clumsiness of a spiritual gesture, the hand with an *awkward* grasp – these are so paradigmatically German that people in other countries mistake them for the German character as such. The German does not have a *finger* for nuances . . . The fact that Germans have put up with their philosophers, and in particular with the most deformed concept-cripple ever to exist, the *great* Kant, is a pretty good indication of German grace and charm. – A *noble education* has to include *dancing* in every form, being able to dance with your feet, with concepts, with words; do I still have to say that you need to be able to do it with a pen too – that you need to learn to *write*? – But now I am becoming a complete mystery for German readers . . .

SKIRMISHES OF AN UNTIMELY MAN

I

My impossible ones. – *Seneca*: or the toreador of virtue. – *Rousseau*: or the return to nature *in impuris naturalibus*.[33] – *Schiller*: or the moral-trumpeter

---

[33] In natural dirtiness.

of Säckingen.[34] *Dante*: or the hyena who *writes poetry* in tombs. – *Kant*: or cant as intelligible character. – *Victor Hugo*: or the lighthouse on the sea of nonsense. – *Liszt*: or the school of fluency – with women. – *George Sand*: or *lactea ubertas*,[35] translated: the milk cow with 'a beautiful style'. – *Michelet*: or enthusiasm takes off its jacket . . . *Carlyle*: or pessimism as coughed-up lunch. – *John Stuart Mill*: or insulting clarity. – *Les frères de Goncourt*: or the two Ajaxes fighting with Homer. Music by Offenbach. – *Zola*: or 'the joy of stinking'. –

2

Renan. – Theology, or reason ruined by 'original sin' (Christianity). Witness Renan, who misses the mark with embarrassing regularity whenever he risks generalizing his yeses and nos. For instance, he would like to unite *la science* with *la noblesse*: but *la science* belongs with democracy, this is completely obvious. His desire to present an aristocratism of the spirit is no minor ambition: but at the same time, when faced with its counter-principle, the *évangile des humbles*,[36] he falls down on his knees and does not stop there . . . What good is all this free-thinking, modernity, cynicism, and turncoat flexibility if at some gut level you are still a Christian, a Catholic, and even a priest! Renan's inventiveness lies in seduction, just like a Jesuit and father confessor; his spirituality beams with a big, fat clerical smile, – like all priests, he only gets dangerous when he loves. Nobody can equal his life-threatening type of adoration . . . This spirit of Renan's, a spirit that *enervates*, is one more disaster for poor, sick, sick-willed France. –

3

Sainte-Beuve. – Nothing manly; full of a petty rage against any manly sort of spirit. Drifting around, refined, curious, bored, inquisitive – a woman at heart with a female vindictiveness and female sensuality. As a psychologist, a genius of *médisance*[37] and abuse; an inexhaustible wealth of means for carrying this out; nobody knows how to mix poison into praise better than he does. Plebeian in the lowest instincts and related to

---

[34] *The Trumpeter of Säckingen* (1854) was a humorous epic poem by Josef Viktor Scheffel.
[35] Milk in abundance.   [36] Gospel of the humble.   [37] Slander.

Rousseau's *ressentiment*: and *consequently* a romantic – since underneath all *romantisme* lies the hungering, howling, Rousseauian instinct for revenge. A revolutionary, but kept pretty much in check by fear. Lacking freedom in the face of anything strong (public opinion, the academy, the court, even Port-Royal[38]). Embittered by any greatness in humans or things, by anything that believes in itself. Poet and part female, enough to experience greatness as power; constantly squirming like that famous worm because he constantly feels stepped on. As a critic: lacking any standards, stability, backbone, with the tongue of a cosmopolitan *libertin* for many things, but without the courage to confess even to *libertinage*. As a historian: lacking philosophy, lacking the *power* of a philosophical vision, – as a result, turning down the task of judging in any matter of importance, holding up 'objectivity' as a mask. He acts differently wherever a refined, well-worn taste is the highest authority: there he really does have the courage to be himself and he takes pleasure in doing so, – there he is a *master*. – In some respects a preliminary version of Baudelaire. –

4

The *Imitatio Christi* is one of those books that I cannot pick up without a physiological feeling of repulsion: it exudes a scent of the eternal-feminine,[39] which is all right if you happen to be French – or Wagnerian . . . This saint talks about love in a way that makes even Parisian women wonder. – They say that this book was the source of inspiration for that *cleverest* of Jesuits, A. Comte, who wanted to lead his Frenchmen to Rome on the *round-about* path of science. I believe it: 'the religion of the heart' . . .

5

G. Eliot. – They have got rid of the Christian God, and now think that they have to hold on to Christian morality more than ever: that is an *English* form of consistency, and we do not want to blame the moral little females *à la* Eliot for it. In England, every time you take one small step towards emancipation from theology you have to reinvent yourself as a moral

---

[38] Port-Royal was the headquarters of Jansenism, a branch of Catholicism; it is also the title of a three-volume work by Sainte-Beuve on the Jansenist movement.
[39] A phrase from the last line of Goethe's *Faust*, Part II: 'The Eternal-Feminine / leads us on high.'

fanatic in the most awe-inspiring way. That is the *price* you pay there. – For the rest of us, things are different. When you give up Christian faith, you pull the rug out from under your right to Christian morality as well. This is *anything* but obvious: you have to keep driving this point home, English idiots to the contrary. Christianity is a system, a carefully considered, *integrated* view of things. If you break off a main tenet, the belief in God, you smash the whole system along with it: you lose your grip on anything necessary. Christianity presupposes that humans do not know, *cannot* know what is good for them or what is evil, they believe in God who has privileged knowledge of this. Christian morality is a command; it has a transcendent origin; it is beyond all criticism, all right to criticism; it has truth only if God is the truth, – it stands or falls along with belief in God. – When the English really believe that they 'intuitively' know all by themselves what is good and what is evil; and when, as a result, they think that they do not need Christianity to guarantee morality any more, this is itself just the *result* of the domination of the Christian value judgment and an expression of the *strength* and *depth* of this domination: so that the origin of English morality has been forgotten, so that no one can see how highly conditioned its right to exist really is. For the English, morality is not a problem yet . . .

6

George Sand. – I read the first *lettres d'un voyageur*:[40] false, contrived, bellows and exaggeration, like everything else that comes from Rousseau. I cannot stand this motley wallpaper style any more than I can stand the herd ambition to have generous feelings. Of course, the worst is the female coquetry with shades of manliness, with naughty-boy manners. – How cold she must have been with everything, this intolerable artist! She wound herself up like a watch – and wrote . . . Cold, like Hugo, like Balzac, like all romantics as soon as they composed! And how smug she must have been just lying there, this fertile writing-cow who had something German about her in the bad sense, just like Rousseau himself, her master, who, at any rate, became possible only when French taste went into decline! – But Renan adores her . . .

---

[40] *A Traveller's Letters*, published in 1837.

7

Moral for psychologists. – Psychology is not a form of back-street pamphleteering! Never observe *for the sake* of observing! This gives you a false optic, a squint, things become forced and exaggerated. Experiencing as *wanting*-to-experience – that does not work. You *cannot* look at yourself in the middle of an experience, your eye will turn into an 'evil eye'. A born psychologist instinctively guards against seeing for its own sake; the same is true for a born painter. He never works 'from nature', – he leaves it to his instinct, his *camera obscura*, to sift through and express the 'matter at hand', 'nature', the object of the 'experience' . . . Only the *general* case enters his consciousness, the conclusion, the result: he does not know how to abstract intentionally from an individual instance. – But what happens when people do things differently? Like the Parisian novelists, for instance, practising psychology everywhere as if it were a form of back-street pamphleteering and book-hawking? Reality gets ambushed, as it were, and every night you take home a handful of curiosities . . . And just look at what happens in the end – a collection of blots, a mosaic at best, at any rate something patched together and fidgety, a screaming clash of colours. The Goncourts make the worst job of it: they cannot put three sentences together without it hurting your eye, the *psychologist's* eye. – Artistically appraised, nature is no model. It exaggerates, it distorts, it leaves holes. Nature is *chance*. Studies 'from nature' seem to me to be a bad sign: they show subjugation, weakness, fatalism, – this practice of lying in the dirt in front of *petits faits*[41] is unworthy of an artist who is whole and complete. Seeing *what is* – that belongs to another species of spirit, an *anti-artistic*, factual one. You have to know *who* you are . . .

8

Towards a psychology of the artist. – One physiological precondition is indispensable for there to be art or any sort of aesthetic action or vision: *intoxication*. Without intoxication to intensify the excitability of the whole machine, there can be no art. There are many types of intoxication conditioned by a variety of factors, but they are all strong enough for the job. Above all, the intoxication of sexual excitement, the most ancient and

[41] Little facts.

original form of intoxication. There is also an intoxication that comes in the wake of all great desires, all strong affects; an intoxication of the festival, the contest, of the *bravura* performance, of victory, of all extreme movement; the intoxication of cruelty; intoxication in destruction; intoxication that occurs in certain meteorological conditions such as the intoxication of spring; or under the influence of narcotics; finally there is the intoxication of the will, the intoxication of a glutted and swollen will. – The essential thing about intoxication is the feeling of fullness and increasing strength. This feeling makes us release ourselves onto things, we *force* them to accept us, we violate them, – this process is called *idealizing*. We can get rid of a prejudice here: contrary to common belief, idealization does *not* consist in removing or weeding out things that are small and incidental. Much more decisive is an enormous drive to *force out* the main features so that everything else disappears in the process.

9

Someone in this state has enough fullness to enrich everything: everything he sees, everything he wants, he sees swollen, driven, robust, overloaded with strength. Someone in this state transforms things until they reflect his own power, – until they are the reflexes of his perfection. This *need* to make perfect is – art. He even finds inherent pleasure in things that he himself is not; in art, people enjoy themselves as perfection. – We could imagine the opposite condition, a specific anti-artistry of the instinct, – a way of being that impoverishes all things, dilutes them, makes them waste away. And in fact, history presents an abundance of anti-artists like this, the starvation victims of life who necessarily have to snatch things up, drain them dry, and make them *thinner*. This is the case with genuine Christians like Pascal: a Christian who is also an artist just *does not happen* . . . Don't try to be clever and throw Raphael or some other homoeopathic nineteenth-century Christian at me as a counter-example: Raphael said yes, Raphael *did* yes, which means that Raphael was no Christian . . .

10

The contrasting concepts of *Apollinian* and *Dionysian* that I introduced into aesthetics[42] – what do they mean, as types of intoxication? – Apollinian

---

[42] In *The Birth of Tragedy*.

intoxication stimulates the eye above all, so that it gets the power of vision. Painters, sculptors, epic poets are visionaries *par excellence*. In the Dionysian state, on the other hand, the entire system of affects is excited and intensified: so that it discharges all its modes of expression at once, releasing the force of presentation, imitation, transfiguration, transformation, and all types of mimicry and play acting, all at the same time. The essential thing is the ease of metamorphosis, the inability *not* to react (– similar to certain hysterics who can take on *any* role at the drop of a hat). It is impossible for a Dionysian to fail to understand any suggestion, he will not miss any affective signal, he has the most highly developed instinct for understanding and guessing, just as he possesses the art of communication to the highest degree. He enters into any skin, into any affect: he constantly transforms himself. – Music as we understand it today is also a total stimulation and discharge of the affects, but nonetheless it is only the remnant of a much fuller world of expressive affects, just a *residuum* of Dionysian histrionics. In order to make music possible as a distinct art form, a number of senses (and the muscular sense in particular) have been disabled (at least relatively, since rhythm always speaks to our muscles to some extent): so that people do not just immediately act out everything they feel. Nevertheless, *this* is the true Dionysian's normal (or at any rate, original) state; music is the gradual specialization of this state at the expense of the faculties most closely related to it.

11

Actors, mimes, dancers, musicians, and lyric poets are all related at a fundamental level and inherently united in terms of their instincts, but they have gradually specialized and separated off from each other – to the point where they have become opposites. Lyric poets were linked with musicians the longest, and actors with dancers. – *Architects* do not represent a Dionysian or an Apollinian state: for them it is the great act of will, the will that moves mountains, the intoxication of the great will that demands to be art. Architects have always been inspired by the most powerful people; architects have always been under the spell of power. Buildings are a visible manifestation of pride, the victory over gravity, the will to power; architecture is a way for power to achieve eloquence through form, sometimes persuading, even coaxing, at other times just commanding. The highest feelings of power and self-assurance achieve expression in a *great style*. Power that does not need to prove itself; that scorns to please; that does not answer lightly, that does not notice the presence of witnesses; that is unaware of any objections to itself; that rests fatalistically within *itself*, a law among laws: *this* is how the great style expresses itself. –

12

I finished reading the life of *Thomas Carlyle*, that unconscious and involuntary farce, that heroic-moral interpretation of dyspeptic states. – Carlyle, a man of strong words and attitudes, a rhetorician out of *necessity* who is constantly harassed by a yearning for a strong faith *and* the feeling that he is not up to the task (– which makes him a typical romantic!). A yearning for strong faith is *not* a proof of a strong faith, but rather its opposite. *If you have a strong faith* you can allow yourself the beautiful luxury of scepticism: you are certain enough, stable enough, committed enough for it. Carlyle anaesthetizes something in himself with both the *fortissimo* of his worship for people who have strong faith and his fury at people who are less naïve: he *needs* noise. A constant, ardent *dishonesty* towards himself – that is his *proprium*,[43] that is what makes and keeps him interesting. – In England, of course, it is his honesty that people admire . . . Well, that is English; and keeping in mind that the English are the people of perfect cant, it is not only comprehensible, it is even quite fair. Carlyle is basically an English atheist who stakes his honour on *not* being one.

13

Emerson. – Much more enlightened, eclectic, refined, much more given to wandering than Carlyle, above all happier . . . The sort of person who instinctively lives only on ambrosia and leaves behind anything indigestible. Compared to Carlyle, a man of taste. – Carlyle really loved Emerson but still said that 'he doesn't give *us* enough to chew on': which might in fact be true, but does not reflect badly on Emerson. – Emerson has the sort of kind and witty cheerfulness that discourages any seriousness; he just does not know how old he already is and how young he still will

---

[43] What is proper to him.

be, – he could apply Lope de Vega's saying to himself: '*yo me sucedo a mi mismo*'.[44] His spirit always finds reasons to be satisfied and even grateful; and every once in a while he touches on the cheerful transcendence of that honest man who came back from an amorous encounter *tamquam re bene gesta*.[45] '*Ut desint vires*', he said with gratitude, '*tamen est laudanda voluptas*'.[46] –

14

Anti-Darwin. – As far as the famous 'struggle for *existence*' is concerned, this seems to me to be more of an opinion than a proven fact at the moment. It takes place, but as an exception; the overall condition of life is *not* a state of need, a state of hunger, but rather abundance, opulence, even absurd squandering. Where there is a struggle, it is a struggle for *power* . . . You should not confuse Malthus with nature. – But assuming this struggle exists (and it does in fact happen), it is unfortunately the opposite of what Darwin's school would want, and perhaps what we might want too: namely to the disadvantage of the strong, the privileged, the fortunate exceptions. Species do *not* grow in perfection: the weak keep gaining dominance over the strong, – there are more of them, and besides, they are *cleverer* . . . Darwin forgot about spirit (– that is English!), *the weak have more spirit* . . . You have to need spirit in order to get it, – you lose it when you lose the need for it. Anyone with strength can do without spirit (– 'let it go!' people in Germany think these days – 'the *Reich* will still be ours' . . .[47]). You see that by spirit I mean caution, patience, cunning, disguise, great self-control, and everything involved in mimicry (which includes much of what is called virtue).

15

The casuistry of psychologists. – He knows human nature: but why does he study people in the first place? He wants to gain some small advantage over them, or even a big one, – he is a politician! . . . That other man over there knows human nature too: and you say that he is not in it for himself, that he is totally 'impersonal'. Look more closely! Perhaps he wants to gain

---

44 'I am my own successor.'   45 'As if the deed had been done well'.
46 'Though the power is lacking, the lust is praiseworthy.'
47 From the last lines of Luther's hymn 'A Mighty Fortress is our God.'

an even more *ignominious* advantage: to feel superior to people, to be able to look down on them, to stop thinking of himself as one of them. This 'impersonal' type *despises* people: and that first man is a more humane species, however it may seem. At least he puts himself on the same level, he puts himself *among* them . . .

16

The *psychological tact* of Germans seems to be called into question by a whole range of cases that I am too modest to list. I won't miss a great opportunity for defending my thesis in one case. I hold it against the Germans that they were wrong about *Kant* and his 'backdoor philosophy', as I call it, – this is *not* a sign of intellectual integrity. – There is also a notorious 'and' that I do not like hearing: the Germans say 'Goethe *and* Schiller', – I am afraid they even say 'Schiller and Goethe' . . . Don't people *know* this Schiller yet? – There are even worse cases of 'and'; I have heard with my own ears, although only from university professors, 'Schopenhauer *and* Hartmann' . . .

17

The most spiritual people (assuming they are the bravest) experience by far the most painful tragedies: but this is precisely why they honour life, because it provides them with their greatest adversities.

18

On the 'intellectual conscience'. – Nothing seems rarer to me these days than genuine hypocrisy. I really suspect that the gentle air of our culture is not good for this plant. Hypocrisy belongs to an age of strong faith: where people do not give up their faith even when they are *forced* into pretending to adopt another. People will just drop their own faith these days; or, more likely, they will take on an additional one, – in either case they stay *honest*. No doubt many more convictions are possible these days than in the past: possible means allowed, it means *harmless*. This is where tolerance of yourself comes from. – Tolerating yourself allows for multiple convictions: and these live together in harmony, – like everything else, they are careful not to compromise themselves. How do you compromise yourself these days? By having consistency. By walking in a straight line. By meaning fewer than five things at once. By being genuine . . . I am really afraid that there are a number of vices that modern people are just too comfortable for: and that these are almost extinct. Everything evil that is conditioned by a strong will – and perhaps there is nothing evil without a strong will – degenerates into a virtue in our mild air . . . The few hypocrites I have met are imitating hypocrisy: they are actors, like almost one in every ten people these days. –

19

Beautiful and ugly. – Nothing is more highly conditioned – let us say: *more limited* – than our feeling for beauty. Anyone trying to think about this feeling in abstraction from the pleasure human beings derive from humanity will immediately lose any sense of orientation. 'Beauty in itself' is an empty phrase, not even a concept. In beauty, human beings posit themselves as the measure of perfection; in select cases, they worship themselves in it. In this way, a species cannot help but say yes to itself and only itself. Its *lowest* instincts, those of self-preservation and self-propagation, shine through in sublimities like these. People think that the world itself is overflowing with beauty, – they *forget* that they are its cause. They themselves have given the world its beauty – but oh! only a very human, all too human beauty . . . Fundamentally, humanity is reflected in all things, people find beauty in everything that throws their image back at them: the judgment 'beautiful' is the *vanity of their species* . . . Of course a sceptic might hear a suspicious little whisper in his ear: does the world really become beautiful just because it is seen that way by human beings, of all creatures? People have *humanized* it: that is all. But nothing, absolutely nothing, guarantees that a *human being* is the standard of beauty. Who knows what a human being looks like in the eyes of a higher arbiter of taste? Daring, perhaps? Perhaps even funny? Perhaps a bit arbitrary? . . . 'O Dionysus, divine one, why do you pull on my ears?' Ariadne once asked her philosophical lover in one of those famous dialogues on Naxos. 'There is something amusing about your ears, Ariadne: why aren't they even longer?'[48]

---

[48] These allegedly famous dialogues were in fact written by Nietzsche himself, and were still unpublished in 1888, when he wrote *Twilight*.

20

Nothing is beautiful, only people are beautiful: all aesthetics is based on this naïveté, this is its *first* truth. Let us immediately add its second: the only thing ugly is a *degenerating* person, – this defines the realm of aesthetic judgment. – Physiologically, everything ugly weakens and depresses people. It reminds them of decay, danger, deadly stupors; it actually drains them of strength. The effect of ugliness can be measured with a dynamometer. Whenever someone is depressed, he is sensing the proximity of something 'ugly'. His feeling of power, his will to power, his courage, his pride – these sink with ugliness and rise with beauty . . . In both cases we are *drawing a conclusion*: the instincts are filled to the brink with accumulated premises. Ugliness is understood as a sign and symptom of degeneration: anything vaguely reminiscent of degeneracy causes us to judge the thing 'ugly'. Any sign of exhaustion, heaviness, age, fatigue, every time freedom is lacking, as with cramps, paralysis, and above all the smell, the colour, the form of disintegration, of putrefaction, even when it is rarified into a symbol – all of this prompts the same reaction, the value judgment 'ugly'. A *hatred* leaps up: what is it people hate when this happens? But there is no doubt: *the decline of their type*. They hate out of the deepest instinct of their species; this is a hatred full of shudders, caution, depth, far-sightedness, – it is the most profound hatred there is. Art is *profound* for the sake of this hatred . . .

21

Schopenhauer. – Schopenhauer, the last German who was worthy of consideration (– who was a *European* event like Goethe, like Hegel, like Heinrich Heine, and *not just* a local event, a 'national' one), is a first-rate case for a psychologist. Specifically, he is a viciously ingenious attempt to use the great self-affirmation of the 'will to live', the exuberant forms of life, in the service of their opposite, a nihilistic, total depreciation of the value of life. He interpreted *art*, heroism, genius, beauty, great sympathy, knowledge, the will to truth, and tragedy one after the other as consequences of 'negation' or some need to negate on the part of the 'will' – the greatest psychological counterfeit in history, Christianity excluded. On closer inspection, this just means that he is heir to the Christian interpretation: except that he also knew how to *approve* of what Christianity had rejected, the great cultural facts of humanity, although in a Christian, which is to say nihilistic manner (– namely as paths to 'redemption', as preliminary versions of 'redemption', as ways of stimulating the need for 'redemption' . . .)

22

I will take a single case. Schopenhauer talks about *beauty* with a melancholy passion, – why, in the final analysis? Because he sees it as a *bridge* you can cross to something further, or to develop the desire for something further . . . He sees it as a momentary redemption from the 'will' – it is an enticement to permanent redemption . . . He considers it particularly valuable as a redemption from the 'focal point of the will', from sexuality, – he thinks that the drive to procreate is *negated* by beauty . . . Bizarre saint! Someone is contradicting you, and I am afraid that it is nature. Why are the tones, colours, smells, and rhythmic movements of nature beautiful in the first place? What does beauty *bring out*? – Fortunately, a philosopher contradicts him too. No less an authority than the divine Plato (– as Schopenhauer himself calls him) asserts something else: that all beauty is a temptation to procreate, – that this is precisely the *proprium* of its effect, from the most sensual all the way up to the most spiritual . . .[49]

23

Plato goes even further. He says, with an innocence that only a Greek could have (and not a 'Christian'), that there could never have been a Platonic philosophy without such beautiful young men in Athens: the sight of them is what first puts the philosopher's soul in an erotic rapture and won't let it rest until it has sunk the seed of all high things into such beautiful soil.[50] Another bizarre saint! – You cannot believe your ears, even if you *can* believe Plato. At the very least, you have to think that people in Athens had a *different* way of philosophizing, especially in public. Nothing is less Greek than the hermit's conceptual cobweb-weaving, the *amor intellectualis dei*[51] *à la* Spinoza. Philosophy *à la* Plato is more accurately defined as an erotic contest, as the further development and internalization of the ancient agonistic gymnastics and its *presuppositions* . . . What ultimately grew out

---

[49] See Plato, *Symposium* 206b–207a.   [50] See *ibid.*, 208e–209c.   [51] Intellectual love of God.

of Plato's philosophical erotics? A new, artistic form of the Greek *agon*,[52] dialectics. – I still remember, *against* Schopenhauer and in Plato's honour, that the whole higher culture and literature of *classical* France also grew on the ground of sexual interest. You can search through it for gallantry, sensuousness, sexual competition, 'woman', – you will never look in vain.

24

L'art pour l'art.[53] – The struggle against purpose in art is always the struggle against the *moralizing* tendency in art, against its subordination to morality. *L'art pour l'art* means: 'morality can go to hell!' – but even this hostility reveals the overpowering force of prejudice. Once you exclude the purposes of sermonizing and improving people from art, it does not follow even remotely that art is totally purposeless, aimless, senseless, in short, *l'art pour l'art* – a worm swallowing its own tail. 'Better no purpose at all than a moral purpose!' – those are just words of passion. A psychologist, on the other hand, will ask: what does art do? Doesn't it praise? Doesn't it dignify? Doesn't it select? Doesn't it have preferences? All of this *strengthens* or *weakens* certain value judgments . . . Is this just incidental? accidental? completely unconnected to the artist's instinct? Or: isn't it the presupposition for an artist *to be able to . . .*? Is the artist's most basic instinct bound up with art, or is it bound up much more intimately with *life*, which is the meaning of art? Isn't it bound up with the *desirability of life*? – Art is the great stimulus to life: how could art be understood as purposeless, pointless, *l'art pour l'art*? – One question is left: art also presents a lot that is ugly, harsh, questionable in life, – doesn't this seem to spoil life for us? – And in fact, there have been philosophers who gave it this meaning: Schopenhauer taught that the overall aim of art was 'to free yourself from the will', and he admired the great utility of tragedy in 'teaching resignation'. – But this – I have already suggested – is a pessimist's optic, his 'evil eye' –: you need to ask artists themselves. *What is it about himself that the tragic artist communicates?* Doesn't he show his *fearlessness* in the face of the fearful and questionable? – This in itself is a highly desirable state; anyone who knows it will pay it the highest honours. He communicates it, he *has* to communicate it, provided he is an artist, a genius of communication. The courage and freedom of affect

[52] Contest.   [53] Art for art's sake.

in the face of a powerful enemy, in the face of a sublime hardship, in the face of a horrible problem, – this *victorious* state is what the tragic artist selects, what he glorifies. The martial aspects of our soul celebrate their saturnalia in the face of tragedy; anyone who is used to suffering, anyone who goes looking for suffering, the *heroic* man praises his existence through tragedy, – the tragedian raises the drink of sweetest cruelty to him alone. –

25

To accommodate people, to keep an open house with your heart, that is liberal, but that is no more than liberal. You recognize hearts that are capable of *noble* hospitality by the fact that many of their curtains are drawn and their shutters are closed: they keep their best rooms empty. But why? – Because they expect visitors one does *not* 'accommodate' . . .

26

We stop valuing ourselves enough when we communicate. Our true experiences are completely taciturn. They could not be communicated even if they wanted to be. This is because the right words for them do not exist. The things we have words for are also the things we have already left behind. There is a grain of contempt in all speech. Language, it seems, was invented only for average, mediocre, communicable things. People *vulgarize* themselves when they speak a language. – Excerpts from a morality for the deaf-mutes and other philosophers.

27

'This picture is bewitchingly beautiful!'[54] . . . The literary female, unsatisfied, flustered, with a barren heart and barren intestines, always listening with painful curiosity to the imperative that whispers from out of the depths of her organism '*aut liberi aut libri*':[55] the literary female, educated enough to understand the voice of nature even when it speaks Latin, and on the other hand vain and goose-like enough to speak French secretly to

---

[54] From Mozart's *The Magic Flute*, Act I, Scene 3.   [55] Either children or books.

herself, *'je me verrai, je me lirai, je m'extasierai et je dirai: Possible, que j'aie eu tant d'esprit?'*[56] . . .

28

The 'impersonal' ones have their say. – 'Nothing is easier for us than to be wise, patient, superior. We are dripping with the oil of leniency and sympathy, we are absurdly fair, we forgive everything. This is precisely why we should be somewhat stricter with ourselves; this is precisely why we should occasionally *cultivate* a little affect, a minor vice of an affect. It might be a bitter pill; and maybe we will laugh among ourselves at how we look when we swallow it. But what good is it? This is the only way we have left of overcoming ourselves: this is *our* asceticism, *our* penitence' . . . *To become personal* – the virtue of the 'impersonal' . . .

29

Excerpts from a doctoral exam. – 'What is the task of all higher schooling?' – To turn men into machines. – 'What method is used?' – They have to learn to be bored. – 'How is this done?' – Through the concept of duty. – 'Who is the model for this?' – The philologist: he teaches you how to grind away at your work. – 'Who is the perfect human?' – The civil servant. – 'What philosophy gives the highest formula for the civil servant?' – Kant's: the civil servant as thing-in-itself set to judge over the civil servant as phenomenon. –

30

The right to stupidity. – The tired worker with his slow breath and good-natured gaze, who lets things go as they will: a typical figure who, in this age of work (*and* the '*Reich*'! –), you come across in all walks of life; this worker lays claim to nothing less than *art* nowadays, including books, especially magazines – and, what is more, the beauties of nature, Italy . . . Faust's man of evening with 'dormant savage drives'[57] needs a summer holiday, a seaside resort, a glacier, a Bayreuth . . . During ages

---

[56] 'I shall look at myself, I shall read myself, I shall delight myself and I shall say: can I really have had so much wit?'
[57] Goethe, *Faust*, Part I, Scene 3.

like this, art has the right to *pure foolishness*, – as a type of holiday for the spirit, mind, and soul. Wagner understood this. *Pure foolishness* is therapeutic . . .[58]

31

Another problem of diet. – The way Julius Caesar guarded against sickliness and headaches: huge marches, the simplest regimen, staying outside for extended periods of time, constant strains and exertions – these are, basically, the general guidelines for protecting and maintaining the subtle, extremely vulnerable, most highly pressurized machine that is called genius. –

32

The immoralist speaks. – There is nothing a philosopher considers in *worse* taste than people *with desires* . . . If a philosopher just looks at what people are doing – even when he sees these bravest, most cunning, most enduring of animals stuck in some labyrinthine dilemma – how wonderful they look to him! He will still think well of them . . . But the philosopher despises people with desires, even 'desirable' people – and all desiderata in general, all human *ideals*. Philosophers would be nihilists if they could be, because as far as they are concerned there is nothing behind any human ideal. Or not even nothing – but unworthy, absurd, sick, cowardly, exhausted things, all the dregs from the *drained* cups of people's lives . . . People make such admirable realities, why do they lose all credibility when they desire? Do they have to compensate for being so good at reality? Do they have to make up for their actions, for straining their heads and wills whenever they act, by stretching their limbs into the imaginary and absurd? – The history of people's desiderata has always been the *partie honteuse*[59] of humanity: you should make sure that you do not read it for too long. People are justified by their reality, – it will justify them for ever. How much worthier is a real person compared to someone who was just wished for or dreamed up, a pack of lies? Compared to someone *ideal*? . . . And it is only the ideal person that a philosopher thinks in bad taste.

[58] Wagner describes his character Parsifal as a 'pure fool'.   [59] Shameful part.

33

The natural value of egoism. – Selfishness is worth only as much as the physiological value of the selfish person: it can be worth a lot or it can be worthless and despicable. Individuals can be seen as representing either the ascending or the descending line of life. This gives you a canon for deciding the value of their selfishness. If they represent the ascending line then they have a really extraordinary value, – and since the whole of life *advances* through them, the effort put into their maintenance, into establishing their optimal conditions, might even be extreme. Of course, 'individuals', as peoples and philosophers have understood them so far, are a mistake: individuals are nothing in themselves, they are not atoms, they are not 'links in the chain', they are not just legacies of a bygone era, – each individual is the entire single line of humanity up through himself . . . If he represents descending development, decay, chronic degeneration, disease (– illnesses are fundamentally consequences of decay, not its causes), then he is of little value and in all fairness he should be taking away as little as possible from those who have turned out well. He is really just a parasite on them . . .

34

Christian and anarchist. – Anarchists are mouthpieces of a *declining* stratum of society; when they work themselves into a state of righteous indignation demanding 'rights', 'justice', 'equal rights', they are just acting under the pressure of their own lack of culture, which has no way of grasping *why* they really suffer, – *what* they lack in life . . . A powerful causal impulse is at work in them: it has to be someone's fault that they are not doing very well . . . And even the righteous indignation does them good, all poor devils like to complain, – it gives them a little rush of power. Complaining and grumbling can even give life a charm that makes it bearable: there is a subtle dose of *revenge* in every complaint; people blame the fact that they are doing badly (and sometimes even their badness) on those who are different, as if that constituted a wrong, an *unauthorized* privilege. 'If I am just *canaille* then you should be too': out of this logic come revolutions. – Complaining never does any good: it comes from weakness. Whether you attribute your bad situation to other people or to *yourself* (socialists take the former strategy and Christians, for instance, take the latter), it does not really make any difference. What is common to both (we could also say what is *unworthy*) is that somebody is supposedly to *blame* for your suffering – basically, that sufferers are prescribing themselves the honey of revenge for their suffering. The objects of this need for revenge (as a need for *pleasure*) are occasional causes: sufferers find opportunities everywhere to quench their petty thirst for vengeance, – and to say it again: if they are Christians, they find these opportunities *in themselves* . . . The Christian and the anarchist – both are decadents. – But when Christians condemn, libel, and denigrate the '*world*', they are motivated by the same instinct that moves the socialist worker to condemn, libel, and denigrate *society*: even the 'Last Judgment' is the sweet consolation of revenge – the revolution that the socialist worker is waiting for, only a bit further off . . . Even the 'beyond' – what is a beyond for, if not to denigrate the here and now? . . .

35

Criticism of the morality of decadence. – An 'altruistic' morality, a morality in which selfishness *fades away* –, is always a bad sign. This is true for the individual, it is even more true for peoples. You are missing the best part when selfishness begins to fail. To choose instinctively what is harmful to *yourself*, to be *tempted* by 'disinterested' motives, this is practically the formula for decadence. 'Not to look for your own advantage' – that is just the moral fig leaf for an entirely different, namely physiological, state of affairs: 'I don't know how to *find* my own advantage any more' . . . Disintegration of the instincts! – People are done for when they become altruistic . . . – Instead of naïvely saying '*I* am not worth anything any more,' the moral lie in the decadent's mouth says 'nothing is worth anything, – *life* isn't worth anything' . . . At the end of the day, a judgment like this is very dangerous, it is infectious, – it quickly grows in society's morbid soil into a tropical vegetation of concepts, now as religion (Christianity), now as philosophy (Schopenhauerianism). Sometimes this sort of poisonous vegetation, which grows out of putrefaction, can poison *life* for millennia with its fumes . . .

36

Morality for doctors. – Sick people are parasites on society. It is indecent to keep living in a certain state. There should be profound social contempt for the practice of vegetating in cowardly dependence on doctors and practitioners after the meaning of life, the *right* to life, is gone. Doctors, for their part, would be the agents of this contempt, – not offering prescriptions, but instead a daily dose of *disgust* at their patients . . . To create a new sense of responsibility for doctors in all cases where the highest interests of life, of *ascending* life, demand that degenerate life be ruthlessly pushed down and thrown aside – the right to procreate, for instance, the right to be born, the right to live . . . Dying proudly when it is no longer feasible to live proudly. Death chosen freely, death at the right time, carried out with lucidity and cheerfulness, surrounded by children and witnesses: this makes it possible to have a real leave-taking where the leave-taker *is still there*, and a real assessment of everything that has been achieved or willed, a *summation* of life – all in contrast to the pathetic and horrible comedy that Christianity stages around the hour of death. Christianity should never be forgiven for perverting the dying person's weakness into a rape of the conscience, for perverting even the manner of death into a value judgment on people and the past! – More than anything, and in spite of all the cowardices of prejudice, this establishes the proper (which is to say physiological) appreciation of a so-called *natural* death: which, at the end of the day, is itself just an 'unnatural' death, a suicide. You are never destroyed by anyone except yourself. This is just a death under the most despicable conditions, an unfree death, a death at the *wrong* time, a coward's death. Out of love for *life* –, you should want death to be different, free, conscious, without chance, without surprises . . . Finally, a piece of advice for our dear friends the pessimists, and other decadents as well. We cannot help having been born: but we can make up for this mistake (because sometimes it is a mistake). When you *do away with* yourself you are doing the most admirable thing there is: it almost makes you deserve to live . . . Society – what am I saying! – *life* itself gets more of a benefit from this than from any sort of 'life' of renunciation, anaemia, or other virtues –, you liberate others from the sight of you, you liberate life from an *objection* . . . Pessimism, *pur, vert*,[60] is *first proven* by the self-refutation of our dear pessimists: you have to take one more step in its logic and not just negate life with 'will and representation' as Schopenhauer did –, first, you have to *negate Schopenhauer* . . . Incidentally, infectious as pessimism is, it does not increase the *amount* of overall sickliness in an age

---

[60] Pure and raw.

or a generation: it is an *expression* of the sickliness. You contract it as you contract cholera: you have to be sufficiently predisposed to morbidity. Pessimism itself does not create any more decadents; I remember figures showing no statistical difference in the total number of deaths during years of high cholera incidence as compared to other years.

37

Whether we have become more moral. – The whole *ferocious intensity* of moral stupidity that is known to pass for morality itself in Germany has, as expected, thrown itself into action against my notion of 'beyond good and evil': I could go on and on about this. Above all, I was told to consider the 'undeniable superiority' of our age when it comes to ethical judgment, our very real *progress* in this area: compared to *us*, a Cesare Borgia would never be positioned as a 'higher man', as a type of *overman* (which is what I do) . . . A Swiss editor of the *Bund*, while acknowledging the audacity of such a venture, went so far as to 'understand' my work to be proposing the abolition of all decent feelings. I am a*bund*antly grateful! – Let me respond by raising the question of *whether we have really become more moral.* The fact that everyone thinks so is already a mark against it . . . We modern men, very vulnerable, very sensitive, giving and taking hundreds of things into consideration, we actually imagine that the sensitive humanity we represent, the *achieved* unanimity in caring, in helpfulness, in mutual trust, is a sign of positive progress that puts us far ahead of men of the Renaissance. But this is what every age thinks, what it *has to* think. What is certain is that we cannot place ourselves in Renaissance conditions, not even in our imaginations: our nerves could not stand that reality, not to mention our muscles. But this inability does not prove that there has been any progress, only that things have changed in favour of a different and more mature sort of constitution, one that is weaker, more sensitive, and more vulnerable, and that will necessarily give rise to a *considerate* morality. If we were to abstract from our sensitivity and maturity, our physiological aging process, then our 'humanizing' morality would immediately lose its value too – morality never has an inherent value –: it would even inspire our contempt. On the other hand, we should be under no illusion that Cesare Borgia's contemporaries would not laugh themselves to death at the comic spectacle of us moderns, with our thickly padded humanity, going to any length to avoid bumping into a pebble. In fact, and without meaning to be, we are boundlessly funny with our modern 'virtues'... The loss of any hostile instincts that might arouse mistrust – and that is what our 'progress' really amounts to – represents just one of the consequences of a general loss of *vitality*: it takes a hundred times more care and caution for such a conditional and mature being to keep going. This is why people help each other, this is why everyone is sick to some extent, why everyone is a nurse. This is called 'virtue' –: with people who still knew a different sort of life – one that was fuller, more extravagant, more overflowing – it would have been called something else, maybe 'cowardice', 'misery', or 'old lady morality'... Our tenderized ethics is a consequence of decline (this is my claim, this is, if you will, my *innovation*); on the other hand, harsh and horrible ethics can be the consequence of a surplus of life: since a lot can risked, a lot can be challenged, a lot can also be *squandered*. What used to be the spice of life would be *poison* for us... To be indifferent, that is also a form of strength – and we are too old, too mature for this as well: our morality of sympathy (I was the first one to warn about it), which can be called *l'impressionisme morale*,[61] is one more expression of the physiological over-excitability that is characteristic of everything decadent. The movement that attempted to present itself scientifically in Schopenhauer's *morality of pity* – a very unfortunate attempt! – is the truly decadent movement in morality; as such, it is related to Christian morality at a very deep level. Strong ages, *noble* cultures see pity, 'neighbour love', and the lack of self and self-feeling as something contemptible. Ages should be measured by their *positive forces* – which makes the wasteful and disastrous Renaissance the last *great* age and us, we moderns with our anxious self-solicitude and our neighbour love, with our virtues of work, modesty, lawfulness, and science – accumulating, economic, machine-like – we are a *weak* age. Our virtues are conditioned and *prompted* by our weakness... 'Equality' (a certain factual increase in similarity that the theory of 'equal rights' only gives expression to) essentially belongs to decline: the rift between people, between classes, the myriad number of types, the will to be yourself, to stand out, what I call the *pathos of distance*,[62] is characteristic of every *strong* age. The tension, the expanse between the extremes is getting smaller and smaller these days – the extremes themselves are ultimately being blurred into similarity... All of our political theories *and* constitutions (very much including the '*Reich*') are

[61] Moral impressionism.   [62] Cf. *BGE* 257 and *GM* I.2.

consequences, necessary results of the decline; the unconscious effects of decadence have even come to dominate the ideals of some of the sciences. My objection to the whole discipline of sociology in England and France is that it has only experienced the *decaying forms* of society, and innocently uses its own instinct of decay as the *norm* for sociological value judgments. *Declining* life, the loss of all the forces of organization, which is to say separation, division, subordination, and domination, is formulated as an *ideal* in sociology today . . . Our socialists are decadents, but Mr Herbert Spencer is a decadent too, – he sees something desirable in the victory of altruism! . . .

38

My idea of freedom. – Sometimes the value of a thing is not what you get with it but what you pay for it, – what it *costs*. Here is an example. Liberal institutions stop being liberal as soon as they have been attained: after that, nothing damages freedom more terribly or more thoroughly than liberal institutions. Of course people know *what* these institutions do: they undermine the will to power, they set to work levelling mountains and valleys and call this morality, they make things small, cowardly, and enjoyable, – they represent the continual triumph of herd animals. Liberalism: *herd animalization*, in other words . . . As long as they are still being fought for, these same institutions have entirely different effects and are actually powerful promoters of freedom. On closer inspection, it is the war that produces these effects, the war *for* liberal institutions which, being a war, keeps *illiberal* institutions in place. And the war is what teaches people to be free. Because, what is freedom anyway? Having the will to be responsible for yourself. Maintaining the distance that divides us. Becoming indifferent to hardship, cruelty, deprivation, even to life. Being ready to sacrifice people for your cause, yourself included. Freedom means that the manly instincts which take pleasure in war and victory have gained control over the other instincts, over the instinct of 'happiness', for instance. People who have *become free* (not to mention *spirits* who have become free) wipe their shoes on the miserable type of well-being that grocers, Christians, cows, females, Englishmen, and other democrats dream about. A free human being is a *warrior*. – How is freedom measured in individuals and in peoples? It is measured by the resistance that needs to be overcome, by the effort that it costs to stay on *top*. Look for the highest type of free human beings where the highest resistance is constantly being overcome: five paces away from tyranny, right on the threshold, where servitude is a danger. This is true psychologically, if you understand 'tyrant' to mean the merciless and terrible instincts that provoke the maximal amount of authority and discipline against themselves – Julius Caesar, the most magnificent type –; this is true politically as well, just look at history. The peoples with any value at all *became* valuable, and not through liberal institutions: *great danger* made them into something deserving of respect, the danger that first made us know our resources, our virtues, our arms and weapons, our *spirit*, – the danger that *forces* us to be strong . . . *First* principle: you must need to be strong, or else you will never become it. – Those great hothouses for the strong, for the strongest type of people ever to exist, aristocratic communities in the style of Rome and Venice, understood freedom in precisely the sense I understand the word: as something that you have and do *not* have, that you *will*, that you *win* . . .

39

Critique of modernity. – Our institutions are no good any more: people are unanimous on this count. But this is *our* fault, not the fault of the institutions. After we lose all the instincts that give rise to institutions, we lose the institutions themselves because *we* are not suited to them any more. In every age, democratism has been the form in which the organizing force manifests its decline: In *Human, All Too Human* (I, 472) I already characterized modern democracy (together with its hybrid forms like the '*Reich*') as the *state's form of decline*. For there to be institutions, there needs to be a type of will, instinct, imperative that is anti-liberal to the point of malice: the will to tradition, to authority, to a responsibility that spans the centuries, to *solidarity* in the chain that links the generations, forwards and backwards *ad infinitum*. Where this will is present, you get something like the *imperium Romanum*: or like Russia, the *only* power that can wait, that can still make promises, whose body can endure, – Russia is the direct opposite of the miserable European provincialism and nervousness that has entered a critical phase with the establishment of the *Reich* . . . The West in its entirety has lost the sort of instincts that give rise to institutions, that give rise to a *future*: it might well be that nothing rubs its 'modern spirit' the wrong way more than this. People live for today, people live very fast, – people live very irresponsibly: and this is precisely what people call 'freedom'. The things that *make* an institution into an institution are despised, hated, rejected: people think that they are in danger of a new sort of slavery when the word 'authority' is so much as spoken out loud. The value-instincts of our politicians, our political parties, are so decadent that *they instinctively prefer* things that disintegrate, that accelerate the end . . . Witness *modern marriage*. It is clear that modern marriage is completely irrational: but this is an objection to modernity, not to marriage. The rationality of marriage lay in the fact that the husband had sole juridical responsibility: this gave marriage a centre of balance, while today it limps on both legs. The rationality of marriage lay in its principled indissolubility, which gave it an accent that knew *how to be heard* above the accidents of feeling, passion, and the distractions of the moment. The rationality also lay in the family's responsibility for choosing the spouse. With the growing indulgence of *love* matches, the whole basis of marriage has been eliminated, the very thing that *made* it an institution in the first place. You never, ever base an institution on an idiosyncrasy, and, as I have said, you do *not* base marriage on 'love', – you base it on sex drive; on the drive for property (woman and child as property); on the *drive to dominate* that keeps organizing the family (the smallest unit of domination), that *needs* children and heirs in order to maintain (even physiologically) the measure of power, influence, and wealth that has been achieved, in order to prepare for long tasks, for a solidarity of instincts between the centuries. Marriage as an institution already affirms the greatest, most enduring form of organization: when society cannot work as a whole to extend an affirmation to the most distant generations, marriage has stopped making sense. – Modern marriage has *lost* its meaning, – consequently, it is being abolished. –

40

The labour question. – What is stupid (basically, the degeneration of instinct that is the cause of *all* stupidity today) is that there is a labour question at all. Certain things *should not be called into question*: first imperative of the instinct. – I have no idea what people intend to do with European workers now that they have been called into question. The workers are doing far too well *not* to ask for more, little by little and with diminishing modesty. At the end of the day they have the great number in their favour. All hope is gone for developing a group of modest and self-sufficient types, Chinese types: and this would have been reasonable, this would have been nothing short of necessary. And what did we do? – We did everything possible to nip even the prerequisites for this move in the bud, – the instincts that let workers find their level, that let workers *be themselves*, have been smashed to the ground by the most irresponsible negligence. Workers were enlisted for the military, they were given the right to organize, the political right to vote: is it any wonder that workers today feel their existence to be desperate (expressed morally – to be an *injustice*)? But what do people *want*? We ask once more: what do they *will*? If you will an end, you have to will the means too: if you want slaves, then it is stupid to train them to be masters. –

41

'What I do *not* mean by freedom . . .'[63] – In times like these, giving in to your instincts is just one more disaster. The instincts contradict, disturb, destroy each other; I even define *modernity* as physiological self-contradiction. A rational education would have *paralysed* at least one of these instinct systems with iron pressure so that another could gain force, become strong, take control. Today the individual would first need to be made possible by being *cut down and pruned*: possible here means *complete* . . . And the opposite is what happens: the people who make the most passionate demands for independence, free development, and *laisser aller*[64] are the very ones for whom no reins *would be too firm* – this is true *in politicis*, this is true in art. But that is a symptom of *decadence*: our modern concept of 'freedom' is one more proof of the degeneration of the instincts. –

42

Where belief is necessary. – Nothing is more rare among moralists and saints than honesty; they might say the opposite, they might even *believe* it. Because if a belief is more useful, effective, convincing than *conscious* hypocrisy, hypocrisy will instinctively and immediately become *innocence*:

---

[63] A play on the first line of Max von Schenkendorf's poem 'Freedom' (1813), which reads 'the freedom I mean'.
[64] Letting go.

first principle for understanding great saints. Even with philosophers (another type of saint), their whole craft involves allowing only certain truths: namely the ones that their craft is publicly *sanctioned* to offer, – in Kantian terms, the truths of *practical* reason. They know what they *have to* prove; when it comes to this, they *are* practical, – they recognize each other by their agreement about 'truths'. – 'You should not lie' – this means: *beware*, my dear philosopher, of telling the truth . . .

43

A word in the conservative's ear. – What people did not use to know, what people these days do know, can know –, a *regressive development* or turnaround in any way, shape, or form is absolutely impossible. This is something that we physiologists, at least, do know. But all priests and moralists have believed that it was possible, – they *wanted* to set humanity back – *to cut humanity down* – to an *earlier* level of virtue. Morality was always a Procrustean bed. Even politicians have imitated the preachers of virtue on this point: there are parties even today that dream about a world of crabs, where everything *walks backwards*. But no one is free to be a crab. It is no use: we *have to* go forwards, and I mean *step by step further into decadence* (– this is *my* definition of modern 'progress' . . .). You can *inhibit* this development and even dam up the degeneration through inhibition, gather it together, make it more violent and *sudden*: but that is all you can do. –

44

My idea of genius. – Great human beings are like the dynamite of great ages, representing the accumulation of enormous force; they always presuppose, historically and physiologically, that extensive protection, collection, accumulation, and storage procedures have taken place on their behalf, – that an explosion has not taken place for a long time. If the tension has reached too high a level, the most accidental stimulus will be enough to bring a 'genius', a 'deed', a great destiny into the world. And the environment, the age, the '*Zeitgeist*', 'public opinion' – none of these matter! – Take the case of Napoleon. Revolutionary France (and pre-revolutionary France to an even greater extent) would have produced the opposite type of a Napoleon: in fact it *did*. And because Napoleon was *different*, the heir to a civilization that was stronger, longer, and older than what was dying off in France, he became master, he *was* the only master there. Great human beings are necessary, the age in which they appear is accidental: they almost always become masters of these ages, because they are stronger and older and represent a greater accumulation. The relation-ship between a genius and his age is like the relation between strong and weak or old and young: the age is always much younger, flimsier, and less self-assured, much more immature and childish. – The fact that people in present-day France think about this *much differently* (and in Germany too: but this does not matter), the fact that the theory of the *milieu*, a true neurotics' theory, has become sacrosanct and almost scientific, that it has even caught on with physiologists, all this 'smells bad', this is a bad train of thought. – People in England hold these theories too, but no one is going to get depressed about that. For the English, there are only two ways of putting up with geniuses and 'great human beings': either *democratically* like Buckle, or *religiously* like Carlyle. – Great human beings and ages are extraordinarily *dangerous*: sterility and every type of exhaustion follows in their wake. A great human being is an end; a great age, the Renaissance, for instance, is an end. Genius – in works, in deeds – is necessarily wasteful and extravagant: its greatness is in *giving itself away* . . . The instinct for self-preservation gets disconnected, as it were; the overwhelming pres-sure of the out-flowing forces does not allow for any sort of oversight or caution. This is called 'sacrifice'; people praise 'heroism' because of a hero's indifference to his own well-being, his devotion to an idea, a great cause, a fatherland: but this is all a misunderstanding . . . A hero pours out, pours over, consumes himself, does not spare himself, – fatalistically, disastrously, involuntarily, as a river is involuntary when it overflows its banks. But because people owe a lot to these sorts of explosions, they have given them a lot in return, for instance, a *higher type of morality* . . . That is, in fact, the way human gratitude works: it *misunderstands* its benefactors.

45

The criminal and what is related to him. – The criminal type, this is a strong type of person under unfavourable conditions, a strong person made ill. He needs a wilderness, a nature and form of existence that is somehow freer and more dangerous; this is where all the arms and armour of a strong person's instincts *rightfully* belong. His *virtues* are ostracized by society;

his liveliest drives quickly fuse with depressive affects, with suspicion, fear, dishonour. But this is almost the *recipe* for physiological degeneration. When somebody is forced into secrecy and suspense, forced to be cautious and sly for a long time just to do what he does best and likes to do most, he will become anaemic; and because he only ever experiences danger, persecution, and disaster from his instincts, even his feeling turns against these instincts – he feels them fatalistically. It is in society, our tame, mediocre, emasculated society, that a natural person from out of the mountains or the adventures of the sea necessarily degenerates into a criminal. Or almost necessarily: there are cases where a person like this proves stronger than society: the Corsican Napoleon is the most famous case. Dostoevsky's testimony is significant for the problem at hand – Dostoevsky, by the way, the only psychologist who had anything to teach me: he is one of the best strokes of luck in my life, even better than discovering Stendhal. This *profound* human being (who was right ten times over for giving little value to the superficial Germans) lived among Siberian convicts for a long time, completely hardened criminals with no chance of ever returning to society; and he found them very different from what he had expected – they were cut from the best, hardest, most valuable wood that grows out of any Russian soil. If we generalize from the case of the criminal: we can imagine beings who, for some reason, lack public approval, who know that they are not seen as beneficial or useful, – that Chandala[65] feeling that you are not seen as equal but as excluded, unworthy, polluted. All creatures like this have a subterranean hue to their thoughts and actions; everything about them is paler than in people whose beings are touched by daylight. But almost all forms of existence that we think well of today used to live in this half-funereal atmosphere: the scientific character, the artist, the genius, the free spirit, the actor, the merchant, the great discoverer . . . As long as *priests* are considered the highest type, *every* valuable type of person was devalued . . . The time will come – I promise – when the priest will be considered the *lowest* type, *our* Chandala, the most insincere, the most indecent type of person . . . Look how even today, under the mildest regimen of manners that has ever ruled the earth (or at least Europe), every deviation, every long, all too long *stay below*, every unusual or opaque form of existence, brings you closer to the type perfected in the criminal. All innovators of the spirit have at some

[65] Untouchable.

219

point had that pale and fatalistic sign of the Chandala on their foreheads: *not* because they were seen this way, but rather because they themselves felt a terrible gap separating them from everything conventional and honourable. Almost every genius has experienced the 'Catilinarian existence' as one aspect of his development: a hateful, vengeful, rebellious feeling against everything that already *is*, that has stopped *becoming* . . . Catiline – the pre-existing form of *every* Caesar. –

46

Here the view is free.[66] – It can be loftiness of the soul when a philosopher is silent; it can be love when he contradicts himself; it can be a courtesy of the knower to tell a lie. It took subtlety to say: *il est indigne des grand cœurs de répandre le trouble, qu'ils ressentent*[67]: only it must be added that it can also be greatness of soul not to be afraid in front of *what is most unworthy*. A woman who loves will sacrifice her honour; a knower who 'loves' may, perhaps, sacrifice his humanity; a god who loved became a Jew . . .

47

Beauty is no accident. – Even the beauty of a race or family, the grace and goodness in all its gestures, have been worked on: beauty, like genius, is the final result of the accumulated labour of generations. You need to have made considerable sacrifices for good taste; you need to have done many things, left many things undone for its sake (seventeenth-century France is admirable in both respects); good taste needs to have provided you with a principle of selection for company, location, clothing, sexual satisfaction; beauty needs to have been given preference over advantage, habit, opinion, inertia. The highest guiding principle: you cannot 'let yourself go', even in front of yourself. – Good things are inordinately expensive: and it is always the case that the one who *has* them is different from the one who *acquires* them. All good things are inherited: anything that is not inherited is imperfect, a beginning . . . Cicero registered his surprise at seeing how the men and boys of contemporary Athens were far and away more beautiful than the women: but look at how much work

---

[66] This line is taken from the final scene of Goethe, *Faust*, Part II.
[67] It is unworthy of great hearts to share the agitation that they feel.

and exertion in the service of beauty Athenian males had demanded of themselves for centuries! – Make no mistake about the method at work here: a simple discipline of feeling and thought amounts to practically nothing (– this is the great misunderstanding of German education, which is totally illusory): you first need to persuade the *body*. Strict adherence to significant and refined gestures and an obligation to live only with people who do not 'let themselves go' is more than enough to become significant and refined: two or three generations later and everything is already *internalized*. It is crucial for the fate of individuals as well as peoples that culture begin in the *right* place – *not* in the 'soul' (which was the disastrous superstition of priests and half-priests): the right place is the body, gestures, diet, physiology, *everything else* follows from this . . . This is why the Greeks are the *first cultural event* in history – they knew, they *did*, what needed to be done; Christianity, which despised the body, has been the greatest disaster for humanity so far. –

48

Progress, in my sense. – I talk about a 'return to nature' too, although it is not really a going-back as much as a *coming-towards* – towards a high, free, even terrible nature and naturalness, the sort of nature that plays, that *can* play, with great tasks . . . To speak *allegorically*: Napoleon was a piece of 'return to nature', as I understand it (*in rebus tacticis*,[68] for instance, or even better: *strategically*, as soldiers know). – But Rousseau – what did *he* really want to return to? Rousseau, this first modern person, idealist and rabble rolled into one; who needed moral 'dignity' in order to stand the sight of himself; sick from unrestrained vanity and unrestrained self-contempt. Even this deformity of a person who lay himself down on the threshold of a new age wanted to 'return to nature' – but once again: what did Rousseau want to return to? – I still hate Rousseau *in* the Revolution; it is the world-historical expression of this duality of idealist and rabble. I do not really care about the bloody farce played out in this Revolution, its 'immorality': what I hate is its Rousseauean *mortality* – the so-called 'truths' that give the Revolution its lasting effectiveness, attracting everything flat and mediocre. The doctrine of equality! . . . But no poison is more poisonous than this: because it *seems* as if justice itself

[68] In tactical matters.

is preaching here, while in fact it is the *end* of justice . . . 'Equality for the equal, inequality for the unequal' – that is what justice would *really* say: along with its corollary, 'never make the unequal equal'. – But the doctrine of equality was ushered in with such horror and bloodletting that this 'modern idea' *par excellence* acquired a type of glory and radiance, so that even the most noble spirits were seduced to the Revolution as a piece of *theatre*. But at the end of the day, this is no reason to keep treating it with respect. – I see only one person who perceived it correctly: with *disgust* – Goethe . . .

49

Goethe – not a German event but a European one: a magnificent attempt to overcome the eighteenth century by returning to nature, by coming *towards* the naturalness of the Renaissance, a type of self-overcoming on the part of that century. – He carried its strongest instincts within himself: sensibility, nature-idolatry, anti-historicism, idealism, as well as its unreality and revolutionary tendency (which, in the end, is only a form of unreality). He made use of history, science, antiquity, and Spinoza too, but above all he made use of practical activity; he adapted himself to resolutely closed horizons; he did not remove himself from life, he put himself squarely in the middle of it; he did not despair, and he took as much as he could on himself, to himself, in himself. What he wanted was *totality*; he fought against the separation of reason, sensibility, feeling, will (– preached in the most forbiddingly scholastic way by *Kant*, Goethe's antipode), he disciplined himself to wholeness, he *created* himself. . . In the middle of an age inclined to unreality, Goethe was a convinced realist: he said yes to everything related to him, – his greatest experience was of that *ens realissimum*[69] that went by the name of Napoleon. Goethe conceived of a strong, highly educated, self-respecting human being, skilled in all things physical and able to keep himself in check, who could dare to allow himself the entire expanse and wealth of naturalness, who is strong enough for this freedom; a person who is tolerant out of strength and not weakness because he knows how to take advantage of things that would destroy an average nature; a person lacking all prohibitions except for *weakness*, whether it is called a vice or a virtue . . . A spirit like this who

---

[69] The most real thing.

has *become free* stands in the middle of the world with a cheerful and trusting fatalism in the *belief* that only the individual is reprehensible, that everything is redeemed and affirmed in the whole – *he does not negate any more* . . . But a belief like this is the highest of all possible beliefs: I have christened it with the name *Dionysus*. –

50

You could say that in some ways Goethe and the nineteenth century shared the same aspirations: a universality in understanding, in approving, an attitude of letting everything come close to you, a bold realism, a respect for everything objective. How is it that the overall result of the nineteenth century was not a Goethe but a chaos, a nihilistic sigh, a loss of all bearings, an instinct of fatigue that *in praxi* keeps trying to *fall back into the eighteenth century*? (– as romanticism of feeling, for instance, as altruism and hyper-sentimentality, as feminism in taste, as socialism in politics.) Isn't the nineteenth century (and particularly as it is on its way out) just an intensified, *brutalized* eighteenth century, which is to say a *decadent* century? So that Goethe was just a passing interlude, lovely but to no avail, and not just for Germany but for all of Europe as well? – but you misunderstand great human beings if you look at them from the pathetic perspective of public utility. Perhaps *not* knowing how to make use of them is *just another aspect of greatness* . . .

51

Goethe is the last German I have any respect for; he would have felt three things that I feel, – and we are also in agreement about the 'cross' . . .[70] I am often asked why I bother writing in *German*: my worst readers are in my homeland. But who says that I even *want* to be read these days? – To create things that stand the test of time; striving for a little immortality in form, *in substance* – I have never been modest enough to demand less of myself. I am the first German to have mastered the aphorism; and aphorisms are the forms of 'eternity'; my ambition is to say in ten sentences what other people say in a book, – what other people do *not* say in a book . . .

I have given humanity the most profound book in its possession, my *Zarathustra*: soon I will give it its most independent. –

WHAT I OWE THE ANCIENTS

I

A word in closing about the world that I have tried to enter, a world that I have perhaps found a new way of entering – the ancient world. Even here, my taste (which may be the opposite of tolerant) is far from saying yes to everything it encounters: it does not like saying yes at all and would even prefer to say no, but would like most of all not to say anything at all . . . This is true for entire cultures, this is true for books, – it is also true for places and landscapes. There are really very few ancient books that made much of a difference in my life; they do not include the most famous ones. My sense of style, of epigrams as style, was roused almost immediately by contact with Sallust. I have not forgotten how surprised my admirable teacher Corssen was when he had to give his worst Latin student the very best grade –, I was finished at once. Concise, severe, with as much substance as possible at its base, a cold malice against 'beautiful words' as well as 'beautiful feelings' – this is where I found myself. You will notice a very serious ambition to adopt a *Roman* style, an '*aere perennius*'[71] of style in my works, even in my *Zarathustra*. – The same thing happened when I encountered Horace for the first time. To this day, no poet has given me the same sort of artistic delight that Horacian odes have done from the very start. Certain languages cannot even *want* what Horace is able to accomplish. This mosaic of words, where the force of every word flows out as a sound, a place, a concept, to the right and the left and all over the whole, a minimal range and minimal number of signs achieving a maximal semiotic energy – all this is Roman and, if you are inclined to believe me, *nobility par excellence*. All other poetry is a bit too popular in comparison, – just a prattle of feelings . . .

2

The Greeks have never given me impressions as strong as this; and to come right out and say it, the Greeks *cannot* be to us what the Romans are. You do not *learn* anything from the Greeks – their type is too foreign as well as too fluid to have an imperative, a 'classical' effect on us. Who could ever learn to write from a Greek! Who could ever have learned it *without* the

---

[71] More enduring than bronze.

Romans! . . . And please do not bring up Plato as a counter-example. I am a total sceptic when it comes to Plato and I have never been able to join in the conventional scholarly admiration of the *artist* Plato. In the end, I have the most refined ancient arbiters of taste on my side. It seems to me that Plato mixes up all the forms of style, which makes him a *first-rate* decadent of style: he has the same thing on his conscience as the Cynics who invented the *satura Menippea*.[72] The fact that the Platonic dialogue, this horribly smug, childlike type of dialectic, could strike anyone as charming – this could only happen to people who have never read any good French writers, – like Fontenelle, for instance. Plato is boring. – In the end, I have a deep distrust of Plato: I find him so much at odds with the basic Hellenic instincts, so moralistic, so proleptically Christian – he already has 'good' as the highest concept –, that I would just as soon refer to the whole Plato phenomenon in harsh terms like 'higher hoax' or, if you would prefer, 'idealism', than in any other way. We have paid a high price for the fact that this Athenian went to school with Egyptians (– or with Jews in Egypt? . . .). In the great disaster of Christianity, Plato represents that ambiguity and fascination (called an 'ideal') that made it possible for the nobler natures of antiquity to misunderstand themselves and step out onto the *bridge* that leads to the 'cross' . . . And how much Plato there still is in the concept of 'church', in the structure, system, and praxis of the church! – My vacation, my preference, my *cure* for all things Platonic has always been *Thucydides*. Thucydides, and perhaps Machiavelli's *Principe*,[73] are most closely related to me in terms of their unconditional will not to be fooled and to see reason in *reality*, – *not* in 'reason', and even less in 'morality' . . . Thucydides is the best cure for the 'classically educated' young man who has carried away a horrible, whitewashed image of the 'ideal' Greeks as the reward for his secondary-school training. You have to turn Thucydides over, line for line, and read his ulterior motives as clearly as his words: there are few thinkers with so many ulterior motives. He represents the most perfect expression of the *sophists' culture*, by which I mean the *realists' culture*; this invaluable movement right in the middle of the hoax of morals and ideals that was being perpetrated on all sides by the Socratic schools. Greek philosophy as the *decadence* of the

---

[72] A genre invented by Menippus the Cynic, in which philosophical views are expressed humorously, through a mixture of prose and verse.
[73] *The Prince.*

Greek instinct; Thucydides as the great summation, the final manifestation of that strong, severe, harsh objectivity that lay in the instincts of the more ancient Hellenes. In the end, what divides natures like Thucydides from natures like Plato is *courage* in the face of reality: Plato is a coward in the face of reality, – *consequently*, he escapes into the ideal; Thucydides has *self*-control, and consequently he has control over things as well . . .

3

To sense 'beautiful souls', 'golden means', or other perfections in the Greeks, admiring their ideal character, noble simplicity, repose in greatness – I was protected from this sort of 'noble simplicity' (which, in the final analysis, is a *niaiserie allemande*[74]) by my inner psychologist. I saw the Greeks' strongest instinct, the will to power, I saw them tremble in the face of the tremendous force of this drive, – I saw all their institutions grow out of the preventative measures they took to protect each other against their inner *explosives*. This tremendous inner tension vented itself outwardly in terrible and ruthless hostility: the city-states tore each other apart so that the citizens in each one were able to find peace from themselves. People needed to be strong: danger was close –, it was lurking everywhere. The magnificent, supple physicality, the bold realism and immoralism characteristic of the Hellenes was a *necessity*, not a 'nature'. It was only a consequence, it was not there from the beginning. And even in their festivals and arts they only wanted to feel that they were in a *position of strength*, to *show* that they were in a position of strength: these are ways of glorifying yourself and, at times, making yourself into an object of fear . . . Imagine judging the Greeks by their philosophers, as Germans do, using petty bourgeois Socraticism to try to learn what Hellenism was really all about! . . . Philosophers really are the decadents of the Greek world, the counter-movement to the ancient, noble taste (– to the *polis*, the agonistic instinct, the value of breeding, the authority of descent). Socratic virtues were preached *because* the Greeks did not have them: touchy, timid, fickle, each one a comedian, they had more than enough reasons for letting morality be preached to them. Not that it did any good: but big words and attitudes look so good on decadents . . .

---

[74] German foolishness.

4

I was the first one to take seriously that wonderful phenomenon that bears the name 'Dionysus' and use it to understand the older, still rich, and even overflowing Hellenic instinct: one that can only be explained as an *excess* of strength. Anyone investigating the Greeks (like Jakob Burckhardt in Basle, the most profound student of Hellenism alive today) immediately knows that something is going on here: Burckhardt added a special section on this phenomenon to his book *Greek Culture*. If you want a point of contrast, just look at the almost comic poverty of instinct among German philologists when they get near the Dionysian. The famous Lobeck in particular crawled into this world of mysterious states with all the venerable certainty of a worm that had dried up between books, and persuaded himself that it was scientific to be glib and childish to the point of nausea, – Lobeck spared no expense of scholarship in establishing that these curiosities really did not amount to anything. In fact, a few of the insights that the priests shared with the orgy participants might not have been entirely worthless, like the fact that wine stimulates desires, or that people can sometimes live on fruit, or that plants bloom in the spring and wilt in the fall. And the disconcerting wealth of rites, symbols, and myths of orgiastic origin that ran riot in the ancient world – all of this inspires Lobeck to new levels of brilliance. 'When the Greeks did not have anything else to do', he says (*Ablaophamus* I, 672), 'they laughed, jumped, and lounged about; and sometimes they sat down, cried, and complained, since occasionally people like doing this too. *Other* people then came along and looked for some sort of reason for this unusual behaviour; and so countless legends and myths arose to explain these customs. At the same time, people thought that the *funny doings* that happened to take place on the festival day were necessary parts of the celebration, and kept them on as a vital part of the religious service.' – This is detestable drivel; a Lobeck cannot be taken seriously for an instant. We get a very different impression when we examine the idea of 'Greece' developed by Winckelmann and Goethe and find that it is incompatible with the element at the root of Dionysian art – the orgiastic rite. As a matter of fact, I have no doubt that Goethe would have totally excluded anything of this kind from the possibilities of the Greek soul. *That is why Goethe did not understand the Greeks.* The *fundamental fact* of the Hellenic instinct – its 'will to life' – expresses itself only in the Dionysian mysteries, in the psychology of the

Dionysian state. What did the Hellenes guarantee for themselves with these mysteries? *Eternal* life, the eternal return of life; the future promised by the past and the past consecrated to the future; the triumphal yes to life over and above all death and change; the *true* life as the overall continuation of life through procreation, through the mysteries of sexuality. That is why the *sexual* symbol was inherently venerable for the Greeks, the truly profound element in the whole of ancient piety. All the details about the acts of procreation, pregnancy, and birth inspired the highest and most solemn feelings. In the doctrines of the mysteries, *pain* is pronounced holy: the 'woes of a woman in labour' sanctify pain in general, – all becoming and growth, everything that guarantees the future involves pain . . . There has to be an eternal 'agony of the woman in labour' so that there can be an eternal joy of creation, so that the will to life can eternally affirm itself. The word 'Dionysus' means all of this: I do not know any higher symbolism than this *Greek* symbolism of the Dionysian. It gives religious expression to the most profound instinct of life, directed towards the future of life, the eternity of life, – the pathway to life, procreation, as the *holy* path . . . It was Christianity with its fundamental *ressentiment against* life that first made sexuality into something unclean, it threw *filth* on the origin, the presupposition of our life . . .

5

The psychology of the orgiastic, as an overflowing feeling of life and strength where even pain acts as a stimulus, gave me the key to the concept of *tragic* feeling, a concept that had been misunderstood by Aristotle and even more by our pessimists. Tragedy is so far from proving anything about Hellenic pessimism in Schopenhauer's sense of the term that in fact it serves as the decisive refutation and *counter-example* to Schopenhauerian pessimism. Saying yes to life, even in its strangest and harshest problems; the will to life rejoicing in its own inexhaustibility through the *sacrifice* of its highest types – *that* is what I called Dionysian, *that* is the bridge I found to the psychology of the *tragic* poet. *Not* to escape horror and pity, not to cleanse yourself of a dangerous affect by violent discharge – as Aristotle thought –: but rather, over and above all horror and pity, so that *you yourself may be* the eternal joy in becoming, – the joy that includes even the eternal *joy in negating* . . . And with this I come back to the place that once served as my point of departure – the '*Birth of Tragedy*' was my first revaluation of all values: and now I am back on that soil where my wants, my *abilities* grow – I, the last disciple of the philosopher Dionysus, – I, the teacher of eternal return . . .

THE HAMMER SPEAKS

Thus Spoke Zarathustra[75]

'Why so hard!' – the kitchen coal once said to the diamond: 'aren't we close relations?'

Why so soft? O my brothers, I ask you as well: aren't you – my brothers?

Why so soft, so submissive and yielding? Why is there so much denial in your hearts? so little destiny in your gaze?

And don't you want to be destinies and merciless: how will you ever be able to join me in – triumph?

And if your hardness doesn't want to flash and cut and tear things apart: how will you ever be able to join me in – creating?

All creators are hard. And you will need to find it blissful to press your hand on millennia as if on wax, –

– Bliss, to write on the will of millennia as if on bronze, – harder than bronze, nobler than bronze. Only the noblest is completely hard.

Oh my brothers, I place this new tablet over you: become hard! – –

---

[75] From Part III, 'Of the Old and New Law-Tables', 29.

The Case of Wagner
A Musician's Problem

PREFACE

I will give myself a bit of a break. It is not just malice when I praise Bizet at Wagner's expense in this essay. I am joking about something that is no laughing matter. It was my fate to turn my back on Wagner; it was my triumph to take pleasure in anything ever again. Perhaps nobody had been more dangerously bound up with Wagnerianism. Nobody had resisted it more vigorously, nobody had been happier to get away from it. A long story! – Does anyone want a name for it? – If I were a moralist, who knows what I would call it! *Self-overcoming*, perhaps. – But a philosopher has no love for moralists . . . or for pretty phrases . . .

What does a philosopher demand of himself, first and last? To overcome his age, to become 'timeless'. So what gives him his greatest challenge? Whatever marks him as a child of his age. Well then! I am just as much a child of my age as Wagner, which is to say a *decadent*: it is just that I have understood this, I have resisted it. The philosopher in me has resisted it.

In fact the thing I have been most deeply occupied with is the problem of decadence, – I have had my reasons for this. 'Good and evil' is just a variant of this problem. Anyone who has kept an eye open for signs of decline understands morality as well, – understands what is hiding under its holiest names and value-formulas: *impoverished* life, the will to the end, the great exhaustion. Morality *negates* life . . . I needed a particular form of self-discipline for a task like this: – to take sides *against* everything sick in myself, including Wagner, including Schopenhauer, including the whole of modern 'humaneness'. – A profound alienation, a profoundly cold and sober attitude towards everything timely, time-bound: to want more than anything else an eye like *Zarathustra's*, an eye that looks out over the whole fact of humanity from a tremendous distance, – that looks *down* over it . . . Would any sacrifice be too much for a goal like this? Any 'self-overcoming'! Any 'self-denial'!

My greatest experience was a *recovery*. Wagner was just one of my sicknesses.

Not that I want to be ungrateful to this sickness. I argue here that Wagner is *harmful*, but I also argue that there *is* nevertheless someone who cannot do without him – the philosopher. Other people might be able to get along without Wagner: but a philosopher has no choice in the matter. He has to be the bad conscience of his age, – and that is why he needs to know it best. But where would he find a more knowledgeable guide, a more eloquent expert on the labyrinth of the modern soul, than in Wagner? Modernity speaks its most *intimate* language in Wagner: it does not hide its good or its evil, it has forgotten any sense of shame. And vice versa: if you are clear about good and evil in Wagner, you have just about summed up the *value* of modernity. – I understand perfectly when a contemporary musician says: 'I hate Wagner, but I can't stand any other kind of music.' But I would also understand a philosopher who explained: 'Wagner *sums up* modernity. It's no use, you need to start out as a Wagnerian . . .'

THE CASE OF WAGNER
Letter from Turin, May 1888

Ridendo dicere severum . . .[1]

I

Yesterday I heard *Bizet's* masterpiece for – would you believe it? – the twentieth time. Once again I waited with gentle devotion, once again I did not run away. I am surprised by this victory over my own impatience. The way a work like this makes you perfect! You become a 'masterpiece' yourself. – And every time I listen to *Carmen* I really seem to become more of a philosopher, a better philosopher than I thought I was before: I become so patient, so happy, so Indian, so *settled* . . . To sit for five hours: the first stage of holiness! – Can I add that Bizet's orchestral timbre is just about the only one I can still tolerate? That *other* orchestral timbre in vogue these days, the Wagnerian – brutal, artificial, and at the same time 'innocent', which lets it speak simultaneously to the three senses of the modern soul, – how harmful I find this Wagnerian timbre! I call it sirocco. I break out in a sullen sweat. *My* good weather is over.

This music seems perfect to me. It approaches lightly, supplely, politely. It is amiable, it does not *sweat*. 'All good things are light, everything divine runs along on delicate feet': first principle of my aesthetics. This music is evil, refined, fatalistic: it is nonetheless popular – it has the refinement of a race, not an individual. It is rich, it is precise. It builds, it organizes, it is finished: this makes it the opposite of that musical polyp,

---

[1] 'Say what is sombre through what is laughable' – a variant of Horace, *Satires* 1.24.

the 'infinity melody'. Have you ever heard more painful tragic accents on the stage? And how have they been achieved? Without grimaces! Without counterfeit! Without the *lie* of the grand style! – Finally: this music treats the listener as intelligent, even as a musician, – this is *also* the opposite of Wagner, who, whatever else, was in any event the most *impolite* genius in the world (Wagner treats us as if – –, he takes a single thing and repeats it until we are miserable, – until we start to believe it).

And once again: Bizet encourages me to be a better person. A better musician too, a better *listener*. Is it even possible to listen better? – I actually bury my ears *under* this music, I listen to its causes. It seems to me that I experience its origin – I tremble in the face of dangers that accompany some risk, I am charmed by strokes of luck that Bizet is innocent of. – Strange! I really do not think about it, or I do not *know* how much I think about it. Because completely different thoughts are running through my head the whole time . . . Has anyone noticed that music makes the spirit *free*? gives wings to thought? that you become more of a philosopher, the more of a musician you become? – The gray sky of abstraction illuminated in a flash as if by lightning; the light strong enough for the whole filigree of things; the great problems close enough to grasp; the world surveyed as if from a mountain. – I have just defined the *pathos* of philosophy. – And all of a sudden, *answers* fall into my lap, a small torrent of ice and wisdom, of *solved* problems . . . Where am I? – Bizet makes me fertile. Everything good makes me fertile. I do not know any other gratitude, and I do not have any other *proof* for what is good. –

2

This work also redeems; Wagner is not the only 'redeemer'. With it, you say goodbye to the *damp* North, to all the steam of the Wagnerian ideal. Even the plot redeems you from this. Mérimée gives it logic in passion, the shortest line, a *harsh* necessity; above all, it has what warm regions have, a dryness in the air, a *limpidezza* in the air. The climate here is different in every respect. A different sensuality is speaking here, a different sensibility, a different cheerfulness. This music is cheerful; but not with a French or German cheerfulness. Its cheerfulness is African; a fatefulness hangs over it, its happiness is short, sudden, without apology. I envy Bizet his courage for this sensibility, which until then had not found a language in the refined music of Europe, – the courage for this browner, more southern, scorched sensibility . . . How good this golden afternoon of its happiness is for us! We look out into the distance while listening to it: has the sea ever looked *smoother?* – And how the Moorish dance reassures us! How its lascivious melancholy is able to satisfy even our insatiability! – Finally, love, love that has been translated back into *nature!* Not the love of a 'higher virgin'! No Senta-sentimentality![2] But instead, love as fate, as *fatality*, cynical, innocent, cruel – and that is precisely what makes it *nature!* Love, whose method is war, whose basis is the *deadly hatred* between the sexes! – I do not know any other place where the tragic wit that is the essence of love expresses itself so strongly, is formulated with so much horror as in Don José's[3] last cry, which brings the work to an end:

> Yes! *I* have killed her,
> *I* – my beloved Carmen!

– This sort of perspective on love (the only one worthy of a philosopher –) is a rarity: it raises a work of art above thousands of others. Because, on average, artists are like everyone else, only worse – they *misunderstand* love. Wagner misunderstood it too. Everyone thinks that people in love are selfless because they want to advance the interests of another person, often at their own expense. But in return, they want to *possess* that other person . . . Even God is no exception here. He is far from thinking 'what difference does it make to you if I love you?'[4] – he becomes terrible if you do not love him in return. '*L'amour* [this saying holds true among both gods and men] *est de tous les sentiments le plus égoïste, et, par conséquent, lorsqu'il est blessé, le moins généreux*'[5] (B. Constant).

3

You already see how much this music *improves* me? – *Il faut méditerraniser la musique*:[6] I have reasons for this formula (*Beyond Good and Evil*, 255). The return to nature, health, cheerfulness, youth, *virtue!* – And I was even one of the most corrupted Wagnerians . . . I took Wagner seriously . . . Oh,

---

[2] Senta is the female protagonist of Wagner's *The Flying Dutchman*.
[3] Don José is the male protagonist of Bizet's *Carmen*.
[4] Goethe, *Wahrheit und Dichtung*, Book 14.
[5] Of all feelings, love is the most egoistic and, consequently, the least generous when it is wounded.
[6] It is necessary to Mediterraneanize music.

this old magician! How he had us all taken in! The first thing his art presents us with is a magnifying glass: you look through it and you do not believe your eyes – everything looks big, *even Wagner looks big* . . . What a clever rattlesnake! All his life he rattled on at us about 'sacrifice', 'loyalty', 'purity', he withdrew from the *corrupted* world with a praise to chastity! – And we believed him . . .

– But you do not hear me? You prefer even Wagner's *problem* to that of Bizet? I do not underestimate it either, it has its charms. The problem of redemption is certainly a venerable one. There is nothing Wagner has thought about more deeply than redemption: his operas are the operas of redemption. Someone or other is always being redeemed in them: a boy here, a girl there – this is *Wagner's* problem. – And how richly he varies his leitmotif! What rare, what profound evasions! Who if not Wagner has taught us that innocence loves to redeem interesting sinners? (which is the case with *Tannhäuser*). Or that even the wandering Jew gets redeemed, *settles down*, when he gets married? (the case with *The Flying Dutchman*). Or that dried-up old ladies would rather be redeemed by chaste young men? (the case with Kundry[7]). Or that beautiful girls prefer to be redeemed by a *Wagnerian* knight? (the case in *Meistersinger*). Or that even married women like being redeemed by a knight? (the case with Isolde[8]). Or that 'the old god', after being morally compromised in every respect, is finally redeemed by a free spirit and immoralist? (the case in the *Ring*). You should admire this last piece of profundity in particular! Do you understand it? I am careful – *not* to understand it . . . The fact that you can draw different lessons from these works is something I would rather demonstrate than deny. The fact that you can be driven to despair – *and* to virtue! – by a Wagnerian ballet (once again, the case in *Tannhäuser*). The fact that the worst consequences can follow from not going to bed on time (once again, the case in *Lohengrin*). The fact that you should never be too sure who you are really married to (the case in *Lohengrin*, for the third time) – Tristan and Isolde glorify the perfect spouse who, in a certain instance, has only one question: 'but why didn't you tell me that before? Nothing could be easier!' Answer:

> I cannot tell you that;
> and what you ask,
> you can never learn.

---

[7] In *Parsifal*.   [8] In *Tristan und Isolde*.

Lohengrin solemnly prohibits investigation and questioning. Wagner uses it to advocate the Christian idea 'you should and must *believe*'. Being scientific is a crime against everything highest and holiest . . . The *Flying Dutchman* preaches the sublime doctrine that a woman can take even the most restless spirit and fasten him down – in Wagnerian language, 'redeem' him. Now let us allow ourselves a question. Even if this were true, would it be desirable? – What happens to a 'wandering Jew' when some woman starts worshipping him and *fastens him down*? He just stops wandering;[9] he gets married and we stop caring about him. – Translated into reality: the danger to the artist, to the genius – and these are the real 'wandering Jews' – lies with women: adoring females are their ruin. Hardly anybody has enough character not to be ruined – 'redeemed', when he feels he is being treated like a god: – he immediately *condescends* to the level of a woman. – A man is a coward in the face of all eternal-feminine:[10] women know this. – In many cases of female love and perhaps in the most famous in particular, love is just a subtler *parasitism*, a nesting in a foreign soul, and occasionally even in foreign flesh – and oh! always at the expense of the 'host'! – –

You know what happened to Goethe in moralistic, old-maidish Germany. The Germans were always scandalized by him, his only real admirers were Jewish women. Schiller, the 'noble' Schiller who tossed big words into the Germans' ears, – *he* was a man after their heart. What did they blame Goethe for? The 'mount of Venus' and the fact that he wrote the *Venetian Epigrams*. Even Klopstock preached ethics at him; there was a time when Herder liked using the word 'Priapus' when talking about Goethe. Even *Wilhelm Meister* was supposedly only a symptom of decline, of 'going to the dogs' when it comes to morality. The 'menagerie of domestic animals', the 'worthlessness' of its hero, infuriated Niebuhr, for instance: who finally broke into a complaint that *Biterolf*[11] could have sung from beginning to end: 'Nothing is more painful than when a great spirit clips his own wings and tries his virtuosity in something far beneath him, *renouncing higher things*' . . . But above all, the superior brand of old maid was infuriated: all the petty courts, all types of 'Wartburgs'[12] in

---

[9] In German, the phrase 'the wandering Jew' translates as 'the eternal Jew'. Consequently, a precise translation of this sentence would read: 'He just stops being eternal . . .'

[10] A phrase from the last line of Goethe's *Faust*, Part II: 'The Eternal-Feminine / leads us on high.'

[11] Biterolf is a knight in Wagner's *Tannhäuser*.

[12] Wartburg is where Luther translated the Bible, and is said to have thrown an inkwell at the devil, who interrupted him there.

Germany crossed themselves against Goethe, against the 'unclean spirit' in Goethe. – *This* is the story Wagner set to music. He *redeemed* Goethe, that is clear; but in such a way that he cleverly sided with the superior old maids. Goethe is saved: – he is saved by a prayer, a superior old maid *led him on high . . .*[13]

– What would Goethe have thought of Wagner? – Goethe once asked himself what danger was suspended over all romantics: the fate awaiting romanticism. His answer: to suffocate on rehashed moral and religious absurdities. In short: *Parsifal* – – The philosopher has an epilogue to this. *Holiness* – perhaps the final thing that peoples and women get to see of higher values, the horizon of the ideal for everything myopic by nature. Among philosophers, though, like every horizon, a simple failure to understand, a type of shutting the door at the point where *their* world is just *beginning* – *their* danger, *their* ideal, what *they* desire . . . Put more politely: *la philosophie ne suffit pas au grand nombre. Il lui faut la sainteté.*[14] –

4

– I still need to tell the story of the *Ring*. This is the right place for it. It is a story of redemption too: only this time it is Wagner who gets redeemed. – For half of his life, Wagner believed in the *Revolution* as only a Frenchman could. He looked for it in the runic language of myth, he thought he had found the archetypal revolutionary in Siegfried. 'Where do all the world's problems come from?', Wagner asked himself. 'From old contracts', he answered, like any ideologue of the revolution. In plain language: from customs, laws, morals, institutions, from everything the old world, the old society, is based on. 'How do you get rid of all these problems? How do you abolish the old society?' Only by declaring war on 'contracts' (tradition, morality). *This is what Siegfried does.* He gets started early, very early: his origin already amounts to a declaration of war on morality – he comes into the world through adultery, through incest . . . This is *not* the saga – Wagner invented this radical streak; he *corrected* the saga on this point . . . Siegfried kept going the way he began: he always followed his first impulses, he overthrew all tradition, all respect,

[13] A play on the last line in Goethe's *Faust*, Part II, 'The Eternal-Feminine / leads us on high.'
[14] Philosophy is not good for the masses. What they need is holiness.

239

all *fear*. He strikes down whatever he does not like. He knocked down all the old deities without the least sign of respect. But his main project was *the emancipation of woman* – 'the redemption of Brünnhilde' . . . Siegfried *and* Brünnhilde; the sacrament of free love; the dawn of the golden age; the twilight of the gods, as far as the old morality is concerned – *wickedness has been abolished* . . . For a long time, Wagner's ship ran blithely along *this* course. There is no doubt that this is where Wagner looked for *his* highest goal. What happened? An accident. The ship hit a reef; Wagner was stranded. The reef was Schopenhauer's philosophy; Wagner was stranded on a *contrary* worldview. What had he set to music? Optimism. Wagner was ashamed of himself. Even worse, an optimism that Schopenhauer had coined a nasty epithet for – *reckless* optimism. He was ashamed of himself all over again. He thought long and hard, his situation seemed desperate . . . Finally, a solution dawned on him: the reef he had broken down on, what if he interpreted it as the *goal*, the secret aim, the true meaning of the journey? To break down right *here* – that was a goal too. *Bene navigavi, cum naufragium feci*[15] . . . And he translated the *Ring* into Schopenhauerian. Everything goes wrong, everything is a disaster, the new world is just as bad as the old one: – *Nothingness*, the Indian Circe beckons . . . Brünnhilde, who, according to the old conception, was to say goodbye with a song in honour of free love, leaving the world to the hope of a socialist utopia where 'all will be well', is now given something else to do. She has to study Schopenhauer first; she has to set the fourth book of the *World as Will and Representation* to verse. *Wagner was redeemed* . . . In all seriousness, this *was* a redemption. Wagner has a lot to thank Schopenhauer for. It took the *philosopher of decadence* to give the artist of decadence *himself* – –

5

The *artist of decadence* – that's the term for it. And this is where my seriousness begins. I am not going to look helplessly on while this decadent ruins our health – and our music at the same time! Is Wagner even a person? Isn't he really just a sickness? He makes everything he touches sick, – *he has made music sick* –

---

[15] When I am shipwrecked, I have navigated well.

A typical decadent, who has a sense of necessity in his corrupted taste, who uses it to lay claim to a higher taste, who knows how to enforce his corruption as a law, as progress, as fulfilment.

And people are not resisting this. Wagner's seductive power reaches monumental proportions, he is surrounded by smoke clouds of incense, misunderstandings about him are called 'gospel' – it is certainly not just the *poor of spirit* who have been persuaded by him!

I want to open the window a bit. Air! More air! – –

I am not surprised that people in Germany fooled themselves about Wagner. I would be surprised if they had not. The Germans made themselves a Wagner they could worship: they have never been psychologists, their gratitude takes the form of misunderstanding. But for people in *Paris* to fool themselves about Wagner! In Paris people are nothing *but* psychologists, for the most part. And in St Petersburg! Where people can guess at things that do not get guessed even in Paris! Wagner must be very closely related to the whole of European decadence for it not to perceive him as a decadent! He belongs to it: he is its protagonist, its biggest name . . . People honour themselves when they raise *him* to the sky. – Because the fact that people are not wary of him is itself a sign of decadence. The instinct is weakened. People are attracted to the things they should avoid. People raise the things to their lips that drive them faster into the abyss. – Do you want an example? But you only have to look at the regimen that people with anaemia or gout or diabetes prescribe for themselves. Definition of a vegetarian: a being that needs a strengthening diet. To experience harmful things as harmful, to be *able* to prohibit harmful things, is still a sign of youth, of vital energy. Exhausted people are *tempted* by harmful things: the vegetarian by vegetables. Sickness can itself be a stimulus of life: it is just that you have to be healthy enough for this stimulus! – Wagner propagates exhaustion: and *that* is why weak and exhausted people were attracted to him. Oh, the rattlesnake happiness of the old master when he saw that it was the 'little children' who were coming unto him! –

I put this viewpoint at the beginning: Wagner's art is sick. The problems he brings to the stage – purely hysterics' problems –, the convulsiveness of his affects, his over-charged sensibility, his taste that craves stronger and stronger spices, the instability that he disguises as a principle, and not least his choice of heroes and heroines, viewing these as physiological types (– a gallery of pathology! –): taken together, this presents a clinical picture that leaves no room for doubt. *Wagner est une névrose.*[16] Perhaps nothing is better known these days – at any rate nothing is studied more – than the protean character of degeneration that is pupating here as art and artist. Our doctors and physiologists have their most interesting case in Wagner, or at least a very complete case. Nothing is more modern than this total sickness, this maturity and over-excitement of the neurological mechanism, which is why Wagner is the *modern artist par excellence*, the Cagliostro of modernity. His art has the most seductive mixture of the things everyone needs most these days, – the three great stimuli of the exhausted: the *brutal*, the *artificial*, and the *innocent* (idiotic).

Wagner represents a great corruption of music. He realized how to use it to stimulate tired nerves, – in doing so he has made music sick. He has great inventive talent – in the art of getting the most exhausted people back on their feet and calling the half-dead back to life. He is the master of the hypnotic gesture, he throws the strongest people down like bulls. Wagner's *success* – his success with nerves and consequently with women – has made the whole world of ambitious musicians into disciples of his secret art. And not just ambitious musicians but also the *clever* ones . . . Only sick music makes money these days; our great theatres subsist on Wagner.

6

– I will allow myself another bit of fun. Suppose that Wagner's *success* were to materialize and assume the form of a philanthropic music scholar; and that it mingled with young artists in this disguise. What do you think it would say?

'My friends', it would say, 'let us have a few words between us. It is easier to write bad music than good music. What if it were more profitable too? more effective, persuasive, inspiring, reliable? more *Wagnerian*? . . . *Pulchrum est paucorum hominum.*[17] Bad enough! We know Latin, maybe we also know what is best for us. There are problems with beauty: we know that. So what is the point of beauty? Why not have greatness instead, or sublimity, or vastness, things that move the *masses*? – And once again, it is easier to be huge than to be beautiful; we know this . . .

---

[16] Wagner is a neurosis.   [17] The beautiful belongs to the few.

'We know the masses, we know theatre. The best people who go to the theatre, young German men, horned Siegfrieds and other Wagnerians, need the sublime, the profound, the overwhelming. This much we can do. And everyone else who goes, the educated cretins, the petty snobs, the eternal-feminine,[18] people with a happy digestive system, in short, the *people* – they also need the sublime, the profound, the overwhelming. They all use the same logic. "Anyone who knocks us over is strong; anyone who lifts us up is divine; anyone who gives us vague presentiments is profound." – Let us make up our minds, my fellow musicians: we want to knock them over, we want to lift them up, we want to give them vague presentiments. This much we can do.

'What it means to give people vague presentiments: our notion of "style" takes this as its point of departure. Above all, no thinking! Nothing is more compromising than a thought! Instead, the state *prior* to thinking, the throng of unborn thoughts, the promise of future thoughts, the world as it was before God's creation, – a recrudescence of chaos . . . Chaos gives rise to vague presentiments . . .

'To speak the language of the master:[19] infinity, but without melody.

'Second, as far as knocking people over is concerned, this is partly a matter for physiology. Let us pay particular attention to instruments. Some of them even persuade intestines (– they throw *open* the gates, as Handel says), others bewitch the spinal column. Tone colour is decisive here; what *makes* the tones is almost beside the point. Let us become more refined in *this* point! Why waste our energy with other things? Let our tones be distinctive to the point of idiocy! People will attribute it to our spirit if our tones keep them guessing! Let us irritate nerves, let us beat them dead, let us use thunder and lightning, – that knocks things over . . .

'But above all, *passions* knock things over. – Let us be clear about passions. Nothing comes cheaper than passion! You can forgo all the virtues of counterpoint, you do not need to learn anything, – you can always have passions! Beauty is tricky: let us be on guard against beauty! . . And particularly *melody*! Let us slander, my friends, let us slander, if we are taking this ideal at all seriously, let us slander melody! Nothing is more dangerous than a beautiful melody! Nothing is more sure to ruin the taste! We will be lost, my friends, if people start liking beautiful melodies again! . . .

---

[18] See nn. 10, 12 above.　　[19] Wagner was referred to as the master.

'*Principle*: melody is immoral. *Proof*: Palestrina. *Practical application*: *Parsifal*. The absence of melody even sanctifies . . .

'And this is the definition of passion. Passion – or the gymnastics of ugliness on the ropes of the enharmonic. – Let us dare to be ugly, my friends! Wagner dared! Let us not be afraid to roll out the mud of the most repulsive harmonies! Let us not spare our hands! This is the only way we can be *natural* . . .

'One final piece of advice! It might sum everything up. – *Let us be idealists!* – This is, if not the cleverest thing, then certainly the wisest thing we can do. In order to raise people up, we need to be elevated ourselves. Let us wander over the clouds, haranguing the infinite, surrounding ourselves with great symbols! *Sursum! Bumbum!* – there is no better piece of advice. The "heaving bosom" will be our argument, "beautiful feelings" are our advocate. Virtue has rights against even counterpoint. "How could anyone who improves us not be good himself?" This is how humanity has always reasoned. So let us improve humanity! – that will make us good (that will even make us "classicists": Schiller became a "classicist"). This search for lower forms of sense-stimulus, for so-called beauty, enervated the Italians: let us stay German! Even Mozart's relation to music was – as Wagner said to comfort *us* – basically frivolous . . . Let us never admit that music can be "relaxing"; that it can be "amusing"; that it can "cause pleasure". *Let us never cause pleasure!* – we will be lost if people start thinking hedonistically about art again . . . That is the bad old eighteenth century . . . As an aside, nothing could be more sensible against this than a dose of duplicity, *sit venia verbo*.²⁰ This is dignified. – And let us choose the hour when it is proper to cast black glances, to sigh in public, to sigh like Christians, to make a big show of Christian pity. "Humanity is corrupt: who will redeem it? *What will redeem it?*" – Let us not answer. Let us be cautious. Let us restrain our ambition to found religions. But nobody can doubt that *we* will redeem humanity, that *our* music is the only thing that redeems . . .' (Wagner's essay 'Religion and Art').

7

Enough! Enough! I am afraid that the ugly truth is only too obvious under my cheerful lines – a picture of decay in art, also of decay in artists. This

---

²⁰ Let this word be forgiven.

second, a character decay, might perhaps be provisionally expressed with the formula: the musician is now becoming an actor, his art is developing more and more into a talent for *lying*. I will have an opportunity (in a chapter of my major work entitled 'On the Physiology of Art'[21]), to go into detail about how this complete transformation of art into acting is an expression of physiological degeneration (a form of hysteria, to be precise), just like every single piece of corruption and infirmity in the art Wagner inaugurated: for instance, the uneasiness of the perspective that needs you to keep changing position. You completely fail to understand Wagner as long as you see him as just a game of nature, a piece of chance and temper, an accident. He was not an 'unfinished' genius, not 'unlucky', not 'contradictory', as people liked to say. Wagner was something *complete*, a typical decadent lacking any 'free will' whose every feature was a necessity. If there is anything interesting about Wagner, it is the logic with which a horrible physiological condition is advanced step by step, argument by argument, as a practice and procedure, as an innovation in principles, as a crisis in taste.

For the moment I am only going to look at the question of *style*. – What is the hallmark of all *literary* decadence? The fact that life does not reside in the totality any more. The word becomes sovereign and jumps out of the sentence, the sentence reaches out and blots out the meaning of the page, the page comes to life at the expense of the whole – the whole is not whole any more. But this is the image of every decadent style: there is always an anarchy of the atom, disintegration of the will, 'freedom of the individual', morally speaking, – or, expanded into a political theory, '*equal* rights for all'. Life, *equal* vitality, the vibration and exuberance of life pushed back into the smallest structures, all the rest *impoverished* of life. Paralysis everywhere, exhaustion, numbness *or* hostility and chaos: both becoming increasingly obvious the higher you climb in the forms of organization. The whole does not live at all any more: it is cobbled together, calculated, synthetic, an artifact. –

Wagner begins with a hallucination: not of tones but of gestures. Then he searches out a tonal semiotics for them. If you want to admire him, just watch him at work: how he separates, how he forges little unities, how he animates them, drives them out, makes them visible. But this drains him of strength: the rest is no good. His type of 'development' is

---

[21] Nietzsche never wrote this work.

so miserable, so awkward, so amateurish, his attempt to take things that have not grown *out of* each other and at least jumble them *in* with each other! The way he does this is reminiscent of the *frères de Goncourt*, who in any case are indispensable points of reference for Wagner's style: you feel a type of compassion for such a state of emergency. The fact that Wagner concealed his inability to create organic forms by making it into a principle, the fact that what he calls a 'dramatic style' is what we would call having no stylistic facility whatsoever – this is indicative of a daring, life-long habit of Wagner's: he posits a principle where a facility is lacking (– much different, by the way, from the old Kant, who preferred *another* form of daring: wherever he lacked a principle he postulated a 'faculty' for it in humanity . . .). To say it again: Wagner is admirable, amiable only in his inventiveness with the very small, in spinning out details, – it would be right to declare him a first-rate master in this regard, our greatest *miniaturist* in music, who can urge an infinity of meaning and sweetness into the smallest spaces. His richness in colours, in half-shadows, in the secrets of the dying light pampers you to the point where almost all other musicians seem too robust. – If you believe me, you will like Wagner for very different reasons than most people do these days. Wagner invented his musical devices to persuade the masses, and we balk at them as we would balk at a fresco that is much too bold and presumptuous. What do *we* care about the *agaante*[22] brutality of the *Tannhäuser* overture? Or the circus of the *Valkyries?* Everything about Wagner's music that has become popular, even outside the theatre, is in questionable taste and ruins the taste. The *Tannhäuser* march strikes me as suspiciously petty bourgeois; the overture to the *Flying Dutchman* is ado about nothing; the prelude to *Lohengrin* gives the first, overly insidious, overly successful example of how to hypnotize with music (– I do not like music whose only ambition is to persuade the nerves). But apart from Wagner the *magnétiseur*[23] and fresco-painter, there is another Wagner who lays small gems to the side: our greatest melancholic of music, full of glances, tenderness, and words of comfort that nobody had ever thought of before, the master in tones of melancholy and lethargic happiness . . . A lexicon of Wagner's most intimate words, short little things of five to fifteen bars, all of it music that *nobody knows* . . . Wagner had the virtue of decadents, pity – – –

[22] Irritating.   [23] Hypnotist.

8

– 'Very good! But how *can* you lose your taste to this decadent if you do not happen to be a musician, if you do not happen to be a decadent yourself?' – Quite the reverse! How can you *not*! Just give it a try! – You do not know who this Wagner is: an excellent actor! Is there a more profound, more *difficult* effect in theatre? Just look at these young men – paralysed, pale, breathless! These are Wagnerians: they do not know anything about music – Wagner gains complete control over them all the same . . . Wagner's art has the pressure of a hundred atmospheres: just keel right over, there is nothing else you can do . . . Wagner the actor is a tyrant, his affect throws every taste, every resistance right out of the window. – Who else has this persuasive power of gestures, who else sees gestures so distinctly, so immediately! This breath-holding of the Wagnerian affect, this sense of not wanting to break loose from extremes of feeling, this horrifying *duration* of states where even the moment threatens to strangle us – –

Was Wagner even a musician? In any case he was something *more*: an incomparable histrion, the greatest mime, the most astonishing genius of the theatre that Germany has ever seen, our *scenicist par excellence*. He belongs somewhere other than the history of music: he should not be mistaken for one of its genuine greats. Wagner *and* Beethoven – that is a blasphemy – and in the final analysis an injustice to Wagner too . . . He was as a musician what he was in general: he *became* a musician, he *became* a poet, because the tyrant in him, his actor's genius compelled him to. You will not begin to make sense of Wagner until you have made sense of his dominant instinct.

Wagner was *not* a musician by instinct. He proved this by abandoning all lawfulness and, more precisely, all musical style in order to make music into what he needed, a theatrical rhetoric, a means of expression, of intensifying gestures, of suggestion, of psychological picturesque. Accordingly, we can consider Wagner a first-rate inventor and innovator – *he vastly increased the linguistic capacity of music* –: he is the Victor Hugo of music as a language. All of which presupposes you agree that under certain conditions music is *allowed* not to be music, but instead language, instrument, *ancilla dramaturgica*.[24] Wagner's music, when it is not defended by theatrical taste, which is a very tolerant taste, is just plain bad music, perhaps

---

[24] Hand-maiden of the drama.

the worst ever written. When a musician cannot count to three any more he becomes 'dramatic', he becomes 'Wagnerian' . . .

Wagner almost discovered what magic is possible even with music that has been dissolved and made *elementary*, as it were. His awareness of this reached uncanny proportions, like his instinctive realization that he did not need any higher lawfulness, any *style*. The elementary is *enough* – tone, movement, colour, – in short, the sensuality of music. Wagner never works things out from some sort of musician's conscience as musicians do: he wants effects, nothing but effects. And he knows what he wants to have effects on! – He shows the same blithe lack of concern on this point that Schiller did, that every theatrical person does, and he has the same contempt for the world that he prostrates at his feet! . . . You are an actor by virtue of having one insight more than the rest of humanity: things do not need to *be* true in order to function *as if they were* true. Talma[25] formulated this claim: it contains the entire psychology of the actor, it contains – let us have no doubt about it! – its morality as well. Wagner's music is never true.

– But *it is taken to be true*: so everything is fine. –

As long as people are childish (and Wagnerian as well) they will even think of Wagner as rich, as the epitome of extravagance, as a big landowner in the realm of tones. People admire him for the same reason that young French people admired Victor Hugo, for his 'regal generosity'. Later, people admired them both for the opposite reason, seeing them as masters and models of economy, as *shrewd* hosts. Nobody comes close to them in officiating over a princely table at modest expense. – The Wagnerian, with his believer's stomach, actually fills up on the diet his master magically invokes. But the rest of us, who require *substance* above all in books as well as music, and who feel badly served by tables which are merely 'officiated over', are much worse off. In plain language: Wagner does not give us enough to chew on. His *recitativo* – very little meat, many more bones, and a lot of broth – I have christened '*alla genovese*': not that I have any intention of flattering the Genovese, but rather the *older recitativo*, the *recitativo secco*.[26] And as far as the Wagnerian 'leitmotif' is concerned, I have absolutely no culinary comprehension of it. If pressed, I might grant

[25] French actor.
[26] Dry recitative.

it the status of an ideal toothpick, an opportunity to get rid of the *remnants* of a meal. All that is left is Wagner's 'arias' – And now I won't say another word.

9

Above all, Wagner is an actor in the way he sketches out his plots. He begins by thinking of a scene that will have an absolutely certain effect, a real *actio** with an *haut-relief* of gestures, a scene that will *knock people over* – he thinks this through in depth, this is what he derives his characters from. Everything else follows from this, in keeping with a technical economy that has no reason to be subtle. It is *not* Corneille's public that Wagner needed to worry about: just the nineteenth century. Wagner would judge 'the one thing needed' just like any other actor today: a series of intense scenes, each one more intense than the last – and lots of very *clever* stupidity in between. He begins by trying to guarantee to himself that his work will be effective, he starts with the third act, he *proves* his work to himself through its final effect. With this sort of a theatrical understanding as a guide, there is no danger of inadvertently creating a drama. Drama requires *strict* logic: but what does logic matter to Wagner! To say it again: it is *not* Corneille's public he had to worry about, just Germans! We know the sort of technical problems that absorb all of a dramatist's energies, often making him sweat blood: how to give *necessity* to the knot and also to the resolution, so that there is only one possible outcome, while giving the impression of freedom (the principle of the least expenditure of energy). Now, this is the last thing Wagner would ever sweat blood over; he certainly expends the least energy over his knots and resolutions. Just look under the microscope at any of Wagner's 'knots' – you will get a good laugh, I promise you that. Nothing is funnier than the knot in *Tristan*, with the possible exception of the knot in *Meistersinger*. Wagner is no dramatist, don't be fooled for a minute. He loves the word 'drama': that is all – he always liked pretty words. The word 'drama' in his writings is

---

*[Nietzsche's] *Remark*. It has been a real misfortune for aesthetics that people always translate the word 'drama' as 'plot'. Wagner is not the only one to make this mistake; everyone does it; even philologists who should know better. Classical drama had *scenes of great pathos* in mind – it specifically excluded the plot (which it placed *before* the beginning or *behind* the scenes). The word 'drama' is of Doric origin: and following Doric linguistic usage it means the 'event', 'story', both words in the hieratic sense. The most ancient drama presented the local legends, the 'sacred story' that the grounding of the cult was based on (– which is to say not a 'doing' but rather a 'happening': in Doric, *dran* has absolutely no connotations of 'doing').

nevertheless just a misunderstanding (*and* a piece of cleverness: Wagner always put on airs with the term 'opera' –); in about the same way that the word 'spirit' in the New Testament is just a misunderstanding. – He was not enough of a psychologist for drama; he instinctively evaded psychological motivation – how? By replacing it with idiosyncrasies . . . Very modern, right? very Parisian! very decadent! . . . By the way, the *knots* that Wagner could in fact solve with dramatic inventions are something else entirely. I will give an example. Take a case where Wagner needs a female voice. A whole act *without* a female voice – that just won't do! But none of the 'heroines' happens to be free at the moment. What does Wagner do? He emancipates the oldest woman in the world, Erda:[27] 'get up, grandma! You have to go sing!' Erda sings. Wagner's purpose is served. He immediately gets rid of the old lady again. 'Why did you come at all? Get out of here! Go back to sleep, will you!' – *In summa*: a scene full of mythological tremors that gives the Wagnerian *vague presentiments* . . .

– 'But the *content* of Wagnerian texts! Their mythical content, their eternal content!' – Question: how do you test this content, this eternal content? – The chemist answers: translate Wagner into reality, into modernity, – let us be even more cruel! into the bourgeoisie! What would happen to Wagner then? – Just between us, I have tried it. There is nothing funnier, nothing I would recommend more highly than to retell Wagner in *youthful* proportions while taking a stroll: for instance, with Parsifal as a theology candidate with a good secondary-school education (– this last being indispensable for *pure stupidity*). What a surprise you will get! Would you believe that as soon as you strip them of her heroic skin, every single Wagnerian heroine becomes pretty much indistinguishable from Madame Bovary! – which lets you see that Flaubert *could* have translated his heroine into Scandinavian or Carthaginian and, properly mythologized, offered her to Wagner as a libretto. Yes, Wagner is only interested the same problems that interest the little Parisian decadents these days, just writ large. Always five steps away from the hospital! Entirely modern, entirely *metropolitan* problems! Don't doubt it! . . . Have you noticed (it belongs to this association of ideas) that Wagnerian heroines do not have any children? – They are not *able* to . . . The desperation with which Wagner attacked the problem of getting Siegfried born shows just *how* modern his feelings were at this point. – Siegfried 'emancipated women' – but

---

[27] Goddess of wisdom in Wagner's *Ring* cycle. (*Erde* is German for 'earth'.)

without any hope for descendants. – Finally, a fact that leaves us speech-less: Parsifal is Lohengrin's father! How did he manage that? – Should we be reminding ourselves here that 'chastity works *miracles*'? . . . *Wagner dixit princeps in castitate auctoritas.*[28]

10

Just to add another word about Wagner's writings: they are, among other things, a lesson in *cleverness*. Wagner uses a system of procedures that can be applied to hundreds of other cases, – let anyone with ears hear. I might have some claim to public appreciation if I formulate precisely the three most valuable procedures:

Anything that Wagner *cannot* do is reprehensible.

Wagner could do many more things: but he does not want to, – out of a principled sense of rigour.

Anything that Wagner *can* do cannot be imitated by anyone else, nobody has done it before him, nobody *will* do it after him . . . Wagner is divine . . .

These three claims are the essence of Wagner's literature; everything else is – 'literature'.

– Not all music has needed literature before now: it would be good to look for a sufficient reason for this. Is it that Wagner's music is too hard to understand? Or is he afraid of the opposite, that it is too easy, – that people do not find him *difficult enough*? – In fact, he repeated a single claim throughout his life: that his music was not just music! That it was more meaningful than just music – infinitely more meaningful! . . . '*Not just music*' – no musician talks this way. To say it again, Wagner could not create from a totality, he had no choice at all, he had to work piecemeal, with 'motives', gestures, formulas, doublings and multiplyings a hundred times over, as a musician he is still a rhetorician – that is why he fundamentally *needs* to bring the 'it means' into the foreground. 'Music is only ever a tool!': that was his theory, that was above all the only *practice* possible for him. But no musician thinks this way. – Wagner needed literature to persuade the world to take his music seriously, to consider it profound, 'because it has infinite *meaning*'; all his life he was the commentator on

---

[28] Said by Wagner, principal authority on chastity.

the 'Idea'. – What does Elsa mean?[29] But have no doubt: Elsa is the 'unconscious *spirit of the people*' (– 'with this realization I unavoidably became a complete revolutionary' –).

Let us remember that Wagner was young at the time when Hegel and Schelling were seducing people's minds; that he achieved, that he grasped in his hands, something only Germans took seriously – 'the Idea', by which I mean something dark, uncertain, and full of vague presentiments; with Germans, clarity is an objection, logic is a refutation. Schopenhauer harshly accused Hegel and Schelling's epoch of lacking integrity – harshly but also unfairly: that old pessimistic counterfeiter – he did not have any more 'integrity' than his famous contemporaries did. Let us keep morality out of this: Hegel is a *taste* . . . And not just a German taste but a European one! – a taste that Wagner understood! – that he felt equal to! that he immortalized! – He just applied it to music – he invented a style that 'meant the infinite', – he became *Hegel's heir* . . . Music as 'Idea' – –

And how well people understood Wagner! – The same type of people who enthused over Hegel get enthusiastic about Wagner these days; in Wagner's school, people even *write* in Hegelian! – German young men understood him better than anyone else did. The two words 'infinite' and 'meaning' were enough: they filled these young men with feelings of supreme well-being. It was not *music* that Wagner conquered them with, it was the 'Idea': – the fact that his art is full of riddles, the way it plays hide-and-seek under a hundred symbols, its polychromatic ideal – this is what led and lured these young men to Wagner; it is Wagner's genius in building clouds, his gripping, dipping, slipping through the air, his everywhere and nowhere, exactly the same techniques that Hegel once used to tempt and seduce them! – In the middle of Wagner's multiplicity, fullness, and caprice they feel they have justified – 'redeemed' – themselves in their own eyes. They tremble as they hear the *great symbols* becoming audible from out of a shadowy distance and resonating in his art with muted thunder; they are not bothered when things occasionally turn gray, gruesome, and cold. After all, they are *related* to bad weather, to German weather, just as Wagner is himself! Wotan is their god, but Wotan is the god of bad weather . . . They are right, these German young men, given what they are like: how *could* they miss what we miss in Wagner, we who are

---

[29] Female protagonist of Wagner's *Lohengrin*.

different, *we halcyon ones – la gaya scienza*; light feet; wit, fire, grace; the great logic; the dance of the stars; over-exuberant spirituality; the shiver of southern light; *smooth* seas – perfection . . .

I I

– I have explained where Wagner belongs –*not* to the history of music. What significance does he have for this history nonetheless? *The appearance of the actor in music*: a capital event that gives us pause to think and perhaps also to fear. In a formula: 'Wagner and Liszt'. – The integrity of musicians, their 'genuineness', has never been put so dangerously to the test. It is almost tangible: the great success, success with the masses, is not the prerogative of the genuine any more, – you have to be an actor to be successful! – Victor Hugo and Richard Wagner – they signify the very same thing: in declining cultures, wherever the masses are given the final word, genuineness becomes superfluous, detrimental, a liability. Only actors arouse a *lot* of enthusiasm. – This ushers in the *golden age* for actors – for actors and for everything related to their type. Wagner marches (amid the sound of drums and whistles) at the head of all performing artists, all presenters, all virtuosos; he began by convincing the music directors, machinists, and stage singers. And do not forget the orchestral musicians: – he 'redeemed' them from boredom . . . The movement Wagner created extends even into the realm of knowledge: disciplines related to the movement are slowly emerging out of centuries-old scholasticism. As an example, I would single out *Riemann's* distinguished work on rhythm: he was the first to apply the concept of punctuation to music (unfortunately using an ugly term: he called it 'phrasing'). – These are the best of Wagner's admirers, I am grateful to say; they are the ones who deserve the most respect – they are right to admire Wagner. They are united by the same instinct, they see their highest type in him; he ignited them with his own embers, and since then they have felt transformed into a power, a great power even. Here, if anywhere, Wagner has had a really *beneficial* influence. Never before have these disciplines seen so much thinking, willing, working. Wagner gave all these artists a new conscience: now they are demanding of themselves – and *achieving* – things they had never demanded before their involvement with Wagner – they had been too modest. A new spirit has prevailed in the theatre ever since Wagner's spirit has prevailed: people are making the most rigorous demands, there is a lot of tough criticism and not much praise, – the good, the excellent, has become the rule. Taste is not essential any more; not even voices are essential. Wagner is sung only with ruined voices: that has 'dramatic' effects. Even talent is ruled out. *Espressivo* at any price (which is what the Wagnerian ideal, the decadence ideal, demands) does not sit well with talent. *Espressivo* only needs *virtue* – by which I mean rote training, automatism, 'self-denial'. Not taste, not voices, not talent: the Wagnerian stage needs only one thing – *Teutons*! . . . Definition of a Teuton: obedience and long legs . . . It is of profound significance that Wagner emerged at the same time as the *Reich*: both facts prove the same thing – obedience and long legs. – There has never been more obedience – or better orders. Wagnerian music directors in particular are worthy of an age that posterity will one day refer to, with a sort of timid respect, as *the classical age of war*. Wagner knew how to command; he was the great teacher of this as well. He commanded as the inexorable will to himself, as lifelong discipline-in-itself: Wagner might be the greatest example of self-violation in the history of art (– he is even worse than Alfieri,[30] his next of kin in other respects. Remark of a Turinese.).

12

The insight that our actors are more admirable than ever does not mean that they are any less dangerous . . . But who could still doubt what I want, – what three *demands* have led me, in my anger, my concern, my love of art, to open my mouth?

That theatre not gain control over art.
That actors not seduce what is genuine.
That music not become an art of lying.   FRIEDRICH NIETZSCHE

Postscript

– The seriousness of these last words will allow me to pass along a few sentences from an unpublished treatise; at the very least, this will leave no doubts about how serious I am when it comes to this subject. The treatise is called: *What Wagner is Costing Us*.

---

[30] Italian dramatist.

You pay a big price for being a follower of Wagner. People are still vaguely aware of this fact. Even Wagner's success, his *victory*, has not completely dispelled this awareness. At one point, though – for almost three-quarters of Wagner's life – this awareness was strong and terrible, like a feeling of bleak hatred. The resistance Wagner met among us Germans cannot be prized or honoured highly enough. People defended themselves against him as if he were a disease, – *not* using reasons – you do not refute a disease –, but instead with scruples, mistrust, disaffection, disgust, with an ominous seriousness, as if a great danger were creeping around in him. Our honoured aestheticians from three schools of German philosophy made fools of themselves by waging an absurd war against Wagnerian principles with their *if*s and *because*s – Wagner could not care less about principles, even his own! – The Germans had enough intelligence in their instincts to forbid themselves from using these *if*s and *because*s. An instinct becomes weaker if it rationalizes itself: because the very *act* of rationalization represents a weakness. And this *muted* resistance to Wagner might not be the least of the signs that the German character still retains a degree of health, the trace of an instinct for harm and danger, in spite of the totalizing character of European decadence. This is a credit to us, it even gives us hope: France would not have this much health at its disposal any more. The Germans, historically the *procrastinators par excellence*, are the most backward of all civilized peoples in Europe these days: this has its advantages, – it means that they are the *youngest*.

You pay a big price for being a follower of Wagner. Germans have only recently forgotten one way of being scared of him, – the wish *to get rid of him* that they felt whenever they could.[*] – Do you remember a strange event where at long last that old feeling re-emerged out of nowhere? It was at Wagner's funeral when the first German Wagner society, the one from Munich, laid a wreath on his grave; its *inscription* immediately became famous. It read: 'Redemption for the Redeemer'[31]! Everyone marvelled at

*[Nietzsche's] *Remark.* – Was Wagner even German? There are reasons for asking this. It is hard to find any German traits in him. Being the great pupil that he was, he learned to imitate a lot of Germanisms – that is all. His character even *contradicts* what had so far been seen as German: not to mention German musicians! – His father was an actor named Geyer. A *Geyer* [vulture] is almost an *Adler* [eagle] . . . What has circulated so far as 'The Life of Wagner' is *fable convenue* [a convenient story] if not worse. I admit that I have misgivings about any claim whose only evidence comes from Wagner himself. He did not have enough pride to be truthful about himself. Nobody had less pride; just like Victor Hugo, he remained faithful to himself even when it came to biography, – he was always an actor.

31 These are the last words of *Parsifal*.

the stroke of inspiration behind this inscription, as well as the good taste that seemed so characteristic of Wagner's followers; but many people also (strangely enough!) made the same small correction: Redemption *from* the Redeemer!' – People breathed freely again. –

You pay a big price for being a follower of Wagner. Let us measure this through its effect on culture. Who has this movement really brought into the foreground? What has it bred more and more of? – Most of all, the arrogance of the laymen, of the art-idiots. This is what organizes societies these days, it is what wants to get its 'taste' accepted, it is what wants to be the judge even *in rebus musicis et musicantibus*.[32] Second: a growing indifference towards that strict, noble, conscientious schooling in the service of art; what is put in its place is a faith in genius or, to speak frankly: brazen dilettantism (– whose formula is found in *Meistersinger*). Third, and worst of all: the *theatrocracy* –, the sheer idiocy of believing in the *priority* of the theatre, that theatre has the right to *dominate* over the arts, over art . . . But Wagnerians need to be told a hundred times to their faces just *what* theatre is: that it is *below* art, that it will always just be something secondary, cruder, bent into shape, lied into shape for the masses! Wagner did not change anything about this either: Bayreuth[33] is grand opera – and not even *good* opera . . . Theatre is a form of demonolatry in matters of taste, theatre is a rebellion of the masses, a plebiscite *against* good taste . . . *This is precisely what the case of Wagner proves*: he won over the crowds, – he ruined taste, he ruined our taste even for opera! –

You pay a big price for being a follower of Wagner. What does it do to your spirit? *Does Wagner liberate the spirit?* – He has an affinity for everything equivocal, every ambiguity, everything that in general persuades the uncertain without letting them know *what* they are being persuaded of. Wagner is a seducer in the grand style. There is nothing tired, enervated, life-threatening, or world-denying in matters of spirit that his art fails to defend secretly – he shrouds the blackest obscurantism inside the light of the ideal. He flatters every nihilistic (– Buddhistic) instinct and disguises it in music, he flatters every aspect of Christianity, every form in which religion expresses decadence. Just open your ears: everything that has ever grown on the soil of *impoverished* life, the whole counterfeit of

---

[32] Of music and musicians.
[33] Wagner built the *Festspielhaus* in Bayreuth for the performance of his music dramas. It opened in 1876.

transcendence and the beyond, has its most sublime advocate in Wagner's art – *not* through formulas: Wagner is too clever for formulas – but by persuading sensuality – and sensuality makes the spirit brittle and tired. Music as Circe . . . His final work is his greatest masterpiece in this respect. *Parsifal* will always keep its status in the art of seduction as *a stroke of seductive genius* . . . I admire this work, I would like to have written it myself; failing this, *I understand it* . . . Wagner was never more inspired than at the end. He allies beauty and disease with such finesse that the work casts a shadow, as it were, over his earlier art: – the early works seem too bright, too healthy. Do you understand this? Health and brightness having the effect of a shadow? Almost of an *objection*? . . . This is how close we are to being *pure fools* . . . There was never a greater master in dull, hieratic fragrances, – nobody had ever known this much about every *little* infinity, everything trembling and exuberant, all the feminisms from out of the idioticon of happiness! – Just drink the philtres of this art, my friends! You will never find a more pleasant way of enervating your spirit, of forgetting your masculinity under a rosebush . . . Oh, this old magician! This Klingsor[34] of all Klingsors! How he wages war on *us*, us free spirits! How his magic-maiden tones pander to every type of cowardice in the modern soul! – There was never such a *deadly hatred* of knowledge! – You need to be a cynic to stop being seduced here, you need to be able to bite in order to stop worshipping here. Well then, you old seducer! The cynic is warning you – *cave canem*[35] . . .

You pay a big price for being a follower of Wagner. I see young men who have been exposed to his infection for a long time. The first, relatively innocent, effect is the corruption of taste. Wagner has the same effect as constant use of alcohol. He dampens things, he coats the stomach. Specific effect: degeneration of the rhythmic feeling. In the end, what the Wagnerian calls rhythmic is what I myself (following a Greek saying) call 'moving the swamp'. Much more dangerous is the corruption of concepts. The young man turns into a mooncalf, – an 'idealist'. He transcends rational inquiry; this raises him to the level of the master. And he plays the part of philosopher; he writes *Bayreuther Blätter*;[36] he solves all problems in the name of the father, the son, and the holy master. Of course, the corruption of the nerves is the most uncanny thing of all. Just

---

[34] Evil magician in Wagner's *Parsifal*.   [35] Beware of the dog.
[36] The monthly bulletin of the Wagner Societies, to which Wagner himself contributed.

wander through a big city at night: all around you, you hear the sound of instruments being violated with a sort of solemn fury – mixed with a wild howling sound. What is going on? – Young men are worshipping Wagner . . . Bayreuth rhymes with coldwater sanatorium.[37] – Typical telegram from Bayreuth: *bereits bereut*.[38] – Wagner is bad for young men; he is disastrous for women. What is a female Wagnerian, medically speaking? – It seems to me that a doctor cannot be too serious in how he presents young women with this alternative of conscience: one *or* the other. – But they have chosen already. You cannot serve two masters if one of them is named Wagner. Wagner redeemed women; and in return, women built Bayreuth for him. Complete devotion, complete sacrifice: there is nothing you would not give to him. The female impoverishes herself for the sake of the master, she becomes touching, she stands naked in front of him. – The female Wagnerian – the most charming ambiguity there is today: she *embodies* the cause of Wagner, – his cause *triumphs* in her sign . . . Oh, this old robber! He robs us of our young men, he even steals our women and drags them into his cave . . . Oh, this old Minotaur! What he has cost us already! Every year a train of the most beautiful young men and women are led into his labyrinth for him to devour, – every year all of Europe intones 'off to Crete! Off to Crete!' . . .

Second postscript

– It seems that my letter is open to misunderstanding. Certain faces show furrows of gratitude; I even hear modest rejoicing. Here as in many places, I would prefer to be understood. – But ever since a new animal has come to live in the vineyards of the German spirit, the *Reichs*-worm, the famous *Rhinoxera*,[39] nobody understands a single thing I say. Even the *Kreuzzeitung*[40] testifies to this, not to mention the literary *Centralblatt*.[41] – I have given the Germans the most profound books in their possession – reason enough why they do not understand a word of them . . . If *this* piece wages war against Wagner – and against a German 'taste' as well –, if I have harsh words for the Bayreuth cretinism, the last thing I want to do is celebrate any *other* musician. When it comes to Wagner, *other* musicians do not even come into the picture. Things are bad everywhere.

---

[37] *Bayreuth* and *Kaltwasserheilanstalt*. These do not in fact rhyme in German.
[38] Regrets already.   [39] Nietzsche's coinage.
[40] A contemporary newspaper.   [41] A survey of scholarly publications.

Decline is universal. The disease runs deep. If Wagner is the name for the *downfall of music*, as Bernini is for the downfall of sculpture, he is not the cause. He just accelerated the tempo, – although, of course, the way he did this caused people to stand horrified in the face of this sudden downward, abyss-ward plunge. He had the naïveté of decadence: this was his advantage. He believed in it, he was not held back by any twists in the logic of decadence. Other people *hesitated* – that set them apart. But that is all! . . . What Wagner had in common with 'the others' – I will give a list: the decline in organizing energy; the abuse of traditional methods without any ability to *justify* this abuse, without any 'for the sake of which'; counterfeit in duplicating great forms – forms that nobody is strong, proud, self-assured, *healthy* enough for these days; too much liveliness in the smallest parts; affect at any price; refinement as the expression of *impoverished* life; nerves increasingly taking the place of flesh. – I only know of one musician these days who could create an overture as *a unified whole*: and nobody knows him . . . The music that is famous these days is not 'better' music in comparison with Wagner, just more indecisive, just more indifferent: – more indifferent, because the half is dismissed *when the whole is present*. But Wagner was whole, Wagner was wholly corrupted; Wagner was courage, will, *conviction* in corruption – does anyone still care about Johannes Brahms? . . . His fortune was a German misunderstanding: he was taken to be Wagner's antagonist, – an antagonist was *needed*! – This does not make for *necessary* music, it generally makes for too much music! – When you are not rich, you should have enough pride to be poor! . . . It is undeniable that Brahms occasionally aroused people's sympathy, apart from any partisan interests or partisan misunderstandings, a fact I could not understand for a long time: until finally, almost accidentally, I realized that he produces effects on a particular type of person. He has the melancholy of inability; he does *not* create out of fullness, he has a *thirst* for fullness. If you disregard his imitations, what he borrows from grand old styles or exotic-modern ones – he is master of the copy –, his own distinctive input is his *longing* . . . All types of unsatisfied people, people who are filled with longing, can sense this. He is not enough of a person, not enough of a focal point . . . The 'impersonal' types, people who are peripheral, can understand this, – they love him for it. In particular, he is the musician for a type of unsatisfied woman. Fifty steps further on: and you have the female Wagnerian – just as you find Wagner fifty steps beyond Brahms –, the female Wagnerian, a more distinctive, more interesting, and above all *more graceful* type. Brahms is affecting as long as he is left to his secret enthusiasms or to mourn over himself – he is 'modern' to this extent–; he grows cold, we stop caring about him as soon as he becomes the *heir* to the classics . . . People like saying that Brahms is the *heir* to Beethoven: this is the most cautious euphemism I know. – Any music today that claims to be in the 'grand style' is *either* false to us *or* false to itself. This alternative is thought-provoking enough: it suggests a casuistry about the value of the two cases. 'False to *us*': most people instinctively protest against this – they do not want to be lied to –; personally, I would always prefer this type to the other ('false to *itself*'). That is *my* taste. To put it more simply, for sake of the 'poor in spirit', Brahms – *or* Wagner . . . Brahms is *no* actor. – You can subsume a large number of *other* musicians under the concept of Brahms. – I won't say anything about Wagner's clever apes, Goldmark, for instance: the 'Queen of Sheba' puts you in the zoo, – you are on display. – Only small things can be done well, done masterfully these days. This is the only area where integrity is still possible. – But nothing can cure music *in* what matters, *from* what matters, from its fate of being an expression of physiological contradiction, – of being *modern*. The best instruction, the most conscientious schooling, the most fundamental intimacy, even isolation in the company of the old masters – these are only palliative measures or, strictly speaking, *illusory* ones, because people do not have the right physiological presuppositions any more: whether we are talking about the strong race of a Handel or the overflowing animal vitality of a Rossini. – Not everyone has the *right* to every teacher: the same goes for whole historical epochs. – It is in theory possible that somewhere in Europe there might still be *remnants* of stronger generations, untimely types of people: this might prove to be a source of *belated* beauty and perfection, even in music. But the best we could experience would be exceptions. The *rule* is that corruption is in control, corruption is fatal, and no god will save music from this. –

Epilogue

– Every question about the value of a *person* condemns the spirit to a narrow little world; but let us escape this world for a moment so we can breathe freely again. A philosopher will have to wash his hands after dealing with 'the case of Wagner' for so long. – I will give my thoughts on what is *modern*. – Every age has a measure of force that is also a measure of which virtues it is allowed to have or not have. Either it has the virtues of *ascending* life: in which case it finds the virtues of declining life repugnant at the most basic level. Or it is itself a life in decline, – in which case it also needs the values of decline, and it hates everything that justifies itself out of fullness, solely out of the superabundance of forces. Aesthetics is inextricably linked to these biological presuppositions: there is an aesthetic of decadence, there is a *classical* aesthetic, – 'beauty-in-itself' is a fantasy, like all of idealism. – In the narrower sphere of so-called moral values you will not find a greater contrast than between *master-morality* and the morality of *Christian* value concepts: this last having grown on soil that is morbid through and through (– the Gospels present exactly the same physiological types that you find described in Dostoevsky's novels); on the other hand, master morality ('Roman', 'heroic', 'classical', 'Renaissance') is the sign language of a sound constitution, of *ascending* life, of the will to power as the principle of life. Master morality *affirms* just as instinctively as Christian morality *negates* ('God', 'beyond', 'self-lessness' are pure negations). The former shares its fullness with things – it transfigures and enhances the world and makes it *rational* –, the later impoverishes the value of things and makes them pale and ugly, it *negates* the world. 'World' is a Christian insult. – *Both* of these opposing forms in the optics of value are necessary: they are ways of seeing that cannot be approached with reasons and refutations. You do not refute Christianity, you do not refute an eye disease. It was the climax of scholarly idiocy to fight pessimism as if it were a philosophy. The concepts 'true' and 'not true' do not seem to me to have any meaning for optics. – The only thing people have to watch out for is falseness, the instinctive duplicity that positively wills *not* to see these oppositions as oppositions: this was the case with Wagner, for example, whose will had considerable expertise in falseness like this. To glance surreptitiously towards master morality, *noble* morality (– the Icelandic sagas are really the most important document of this morality) while mouthing the opposite doctrine, the 'gospel of the lowly', the *need* for redemption! . . . By the way, I admire the modesty of the Christians who go to Bayreuth. There are certain words that I personally would not tolerate coming from the mouth of a Wagner. There are ideas that do *not* belong in Bayreuth . . . What? A Christianity tidied up for female Wagnerians, perhaps *by* female Wagnerians? Because in his later days Wagner was utterly *feminini generis* –? Once again, I think that

Christians are too modest these days . . . If Wagner was a Christian, well then maybe Liszt was a Church Father! – The need for *redemption*, the embodiment of all Christian needs, has nothing to do with clowns like this: it is the most honest expression of decadence, it affirms decadence in the most convinced, most painful way, in sublime symbols and practices. The Christian wants to *escape* from himself. *Le moi est toujours haïssable.*[42] – On the other hand, noble morality, master morality, is rooted in a triumphant *self*-directed yes, – it is self-affirmation, self-glorification of life, it needs sublime symbols and practices too, but only because 'its heart is too full'. All *beautiful*, all *great* art, belongs here: the essence of both is gratitude. On the other hand it is inextricably linked with an instinctive aversion to decadents, a scorn, even a horror of their symbolism: this is almost proof of it. The noble Romans viewed Christianity as *foeda superstitio*:[43] just remember how the last German with a noble taste, how Goethe viewed the cross. You will not find more valuable, more *necessary* opposites . . .[*]

– But falseness of the sort seen in Bayreuth is not an exception these days. We are all familiar with the unaesthetic ideals of the Christian *Junkers*. This *innocence* among opposites, this 'good conscience' in lying, is really *modern par excellence*, it is almost definitive of modernity. Biologically, modern people represent a *contradiction of values*, they fall between two stools, they say yes and no in the same breath. Is it any wonder that falseness has become flesh and even genius in precisely our age? That *Wagner* 'dwelled among us'? I have good reasons for calling Wagner the Cagliostro of modernity . . . But against our knowledge and against our wills, our bodies all have values, words, formulas, and morals with *contrary* derivations, – physiologically considered, we are *false* . . . A *diagnosis of the modern soul* – where would it begin? With a resolute incision into this contradictoriness of instincts, by separating out its opposing values, by performing a vivisection on its most *instructive* case. – The case of Wagner is a *lucky case* for the philosopher, – you can hear that this essay is inspired by gratitude . . .

---

[42] The 'I' is always hateful.
[43] Vile superstition.
[*][Nietzsche's] *Remark.* My *Genealogy of Morality* was the first book to demonstrate the opposition between '*noble* morality' and 'Christian morality': perhaps there has never been a more decisive turn in the history of religious and moral knowledge. This book, my touchstone for what belongs to me, has the good luck of being accessible to only the highest and most rigorous minds: nobody *else* has the ears for it. You need to have passion for things that nobody else has passion for these days . . .

Nietzsche contra Wagner
From the Files of a Psychologist

FOREWORD

The following chapters have all been selected from my earlier writings, and not without some caution – several of them date from 1877 –; I have made some clarifications, and above all abbreviations. Read one after the other, they will leave no doubt about either Richard Wagner or me: we are antipodes. You will realize other things as well: for example, that this is an essay for psychologists but *not* for Germans . . . I have my readers everywhere, in Vienna, in St Petersburg, in Copenhagen and Stockholm, in Paris, in New York – I do *not* have any in Europe's flatlands, Germany . . . And I might drop a word into the ears of my dear Italians, who I *love* as much as I love myself . . . *Quousque tandem, Crispi*[1] . . . Triple alliance: an intelligent people can only enter into a *mésalliance* with the '*Reich*' . . .

Friedrich Nietzsche
Turin, Christmas 1888

WHERE I ADMIRE[2]

I believe that artists often do not know what they can do best because they are too vain and have set their minds on something prouder than these small plants seem to be that are new, strange, and beautiful and really capable of growing to perfection on their soil. That which in the last instance is good in their own garden and vineyard is not fully appreciated by them, and their love and insight are not of the same order. Here is a musician who, more than any other musician, is a master at finding the tones from the realm of suffering, dejected, tormented souls and at giving speech even to mute misery. Nobody equals him at the colours of late autumn, at the indescribably moving happiness of a last, very last, very briefest enjoyment; he knows a tone for those secret, uncanny midnights of the soul, where cause and effect seem to have gone awry and something can come to be 'from nothing' at any moment; more happily than anyone else, he draws from the very bottom of human happiness and so to speak from its drained cup, where the most bitter and repulsive drops have merged, for better or for worse, with the sweetest ones; he knows how the soul wearily drags itself along when it can no longer leap and fly, or even

---

[1] 'How far, for heaven's sake, Crispi'; Francesco Crispi (1818–1901), Italian prime minister (1887–91; 1893–6).
[2] Adapted from *GS* 87.

walk; he has the shy glance of concealed pain, of understanding without solace, of taking farewell without confession; yes, as the Orpheus[3] of all secret misery he is greater than anyone, and he has incorporated into art some things that seemed inexpressible and even unworthy of art – for instance, the cynical rebellion achieved only by those who have suffered the most, as well as some very small and microscopic features of the soul, the scales of its amphibious nature, as it were –, yes, he is a *master* at the very small. But he doesn't *want* to be! His *character* likes great walls and bold frescos much better! . . . It escapes him that his *spirit* has a different taste and disposition – the opposite perspective – and likes best of all to sit quietly in the corners of collapsed houses – there, hidden, hidden from himself, he paints his real masterpieces, which are all very short, often only a bar long – only there does he become wholly good, great, and perfect; perhaps only there. – Wagner is someone who has suffered deeply – his *superiority* to other musicians. – I admire Wagner wherever he has set *himself* to music. –

WHERE I OFFER OBJECTIONS[4]

This is not to say that I consider this music to be healthy, and least of all precisely where it concerns Wagner. My objections to Wagner's music are physiological objections: why disguise them with aesthetic formulas? After all, aesthetics is nothing but applied physiology. – My 'fact', my '*petit fait vrai*',[5] is that I stop breathing easily once this music starts affecting me; that my *foot* immediately gets angry at it and revolts – it has a need for tempo, dance, march – not even the young German emperor could march to Wagner's *Kaisermarsch* –, it demands chiefly from music the raptures found in *good* walking, striding, leaping, and dancing – but doesn't my stomach protest, too? My heart? My circulation? Aren't my intestines saddened? Do I not suddenly grow hoarse as I listen . . . To listen to Wagner, I need *pastilles Gérandel*[6] . . . And so I ask myself: what does my whole body actually *want* from music? Because there is no soul . . . Its own *relief*, I believe, as if all animal functions should be quickened by easy, bold, exuberant, self-assured rhythms; as if iron, leaden life should

---

[3] The legendary Orpheus was supposed to be able to do extraordinary things, such as bringing his wife back from the dead, through the power of his music.
[4] Adapted from *GS* 368.   [5] Little true fact.
[6] Probably a reference to Geraudel's pastilles, a French cough drop.

be gilded by golden, tender, oil-smooth melodies. My melancholy wants to rest in the hiding-places and abysses *of* perfection: that's what I need music for. But Wagner has a sickening effect. – What is the theatre to *me*? The cramps of its moral ecstasies that satisfy the 'people' – and who isn't 'the people'! The whole hocus-pocus of gestures of the actor! – You will guess that I am essentially anti-theatrical, that I regard the theatre, this art of the masses *par excellence*, with the same deep contempt from the bottom of my soul that every artist today will feel. *Success* in the theatre – with that one sinks in my esteem for ever; *lack* of success – then I prick up my ears and start to feel some respect . . . – But Wagner, apart from the Wagner who created the loneliest music in existence, was, conversely, essentially a man of the theatre and an actor, perhaps the most enthusiastic mimomaniac that ever existed, *even as a musician*. And, incidentally, if it was Wagner's theory that 'the drama is the end; the music is always merely its means'–,[7] his *practice* was always, from beginning to end, 'the attitude is the end; the drama, and music, too, is always merely *its* means'. Music as a means of clarification, strengthening, internalization of the dramatic gesture and the actor's appeal to the senses; and the Wagnerian drama a mere occasion for many dramatic attitudes! – Beside all other instincts, he had the *commanding* instinct of a great actor in absolutely everything: and, as I said, even as a musician. – I once made this clear to a Wagnerian *pur sang*,[8] with some trouble – clarity and a Wagnerian! Need I say more? And I had reasons to add: 'Do be a bit more honest with yourself – after all, we're not in Bayreuth![9] In Bayreuth, one is honest only as a mass; as an individual one lies, lies to oneself. One leaves oneself at home when one goes to Bayreuth; one relinquishes the right to one's own tongue and choice, to one's taste, even to one's courage as one has it and exercises it within one's own four walls against God and world. No one brings the finest senses of his art to the theatre; very least the artist who works for the theatre, – there is no solitude, nothing perfect can bear to have witnesses . . . In the theatre, one is people, herd, female, pharisee, voting cattle, patron, idiot – *Wagnerian*: there, even the most personal conscience is vanquished by the levelling magic of the great number, there, the 'neighbour' reigns; there, one *becomes* a neighbour . . .'

---

[7] Wagner, *Opera and Drama* (1850–1), Introduction.   [8] Of pure blood.
[9] Wagner built the *Festspielhaus* in Bayreuth for the performance of his music dramas. It opened in 1876.

INTERMEZZO[10]

– I will say another word for the choicest of ears: what *I* really want from music. That it be cheerful and profound, like an afternoon in October. That it be distinctive, exuberant, and tender, a sweet little female, full of grace and dirty tricks . . . I will never admit that a German *could* know what music is. The people called 'German musicians', the greatest above all, are *foreigners*, Slavs, Croats, Italians, Dutch – or Jews; or else Germans of a strong race, *extinct* Germans like Heinrich Schütz, Bach, and Handel. I myself am still enough of a Pole to give up all other music for the sake of Chopin: there are three reasons why I will make an exception for Wagner's *Siegfried Idyll*, perhaps also for Liszt, who excels all other musicians when it comes to the noble accents of his orchestration; finally everything that has grown up beyond the Alps – *on this side* . . . I wouldn't know how to do without Rossini, or even less without my southernness in music, the music of my Venetian maestro, Pietro Gasti.[11] And when I say 'beyond the Alps', I really am only saying Venice. When I look for another word for music, I always only find the word 'Venice'. I cannot tell any difference between tears and music, I know the happiness of not being able to think of the *South* without a shudder of apprehension.

I lately stood on the bridge
in the dark of the night.
A song came from out of the distance:
pouring away in golden drops
over the trembling space.
Gondolas, lights, music –
it swam drunkenly away into the twilight . . .

My soul, a stringed instrument,
secretly sang a barcarole,
moved by invisible forces
trembling with bright bliss.
– Did anyone hear? . . .

---

[10] Adapted from *EH*, 'Clever', 7.
[11] Heinrich Köselitz, a composer and friend of Nietzsche's whom Nietzsche called Peter Gast. One of Köselitz's works is entitled 'The Lion of Venice'.

WAGNER AS A DANGER

1 [12]

The objective pursued by modern music in what is now, in a strong but nonetheless obscure phrase, designated 'endless melody' can be made clear by imagining that one is going into the sea, gradually relinquishing a firm tread on the bottom and finally surrendering unconditionally to the watery element: one is supposed to *swim*. Earlier music constrained one – with a delicate or solemn or fiery movement back and forth, faster and slower – to do something quite different, to *dance:* in pursuit of which the needful preservation of orderly measure compelled the soul of the listener to a continual *self-possession:* the charm of all *good* music rested upon the reflection of the cooler air produced by this self-possession and warm breath of musical enthusiasm. – Richard Wagner desired a different type of movement, – he overthrew the physiological presupposition of previous music. Swimming, floating – no longer walking, dancing . . . Perhaps this is the decisive thing. The 'endless melody' – *wants* to break up all evenness of tempo and force and sometimes even to mock it; and it is abundantly inventive in what, to the ear of earlier times, sounds like rhythmic paradoxes and blasphemies. Imitating, mastering a taste like this would involve music in the greatest danger conceivable – the complete degeneration of the feeling for rhythm, *chaos* in place of rhythm . . . This danger is especially great when such music leans more and more on a wholly naturalistic art of acting and language of gesture uninfluenced and uncontrolled by any rule of plastic art, and wants nothing other than *effects* . . . *Espressivo* at any price and music in the service of, enslaved to, gesture – *that is the end* . . .

2 [13]

What? Would it be the supreme virtue of a performance, as our present-day musical performers really seem to believe, to achieve an unsurpassable *haut relief* [14] under all circumstances? Is this, when applied, for instance, to Mozart, not simply a sin against the spirit, against the cheerful,

---

[12] Adapted from *HAH*, Vol. II, 'Assorted Opinions and Maxims', 134.
[13] Adapted from *The Wanderer and his Shadow*, 165.   [14] High relief.

enthusiastic, tender, frivolous spirit of Mozart, who was happily not a German and whose seriousness is a good-natured, golden seriousness and *not* the seriousness of a good little German bourgeois . . . not to mention the seriousness of the 'Stone Guest'[15] . . . Or do you think that *all* music is the music of the 'Stone Guest', – *all* music needs to leap out of the wall and rattle the intestines of the audience? . . . You think that this is when music starts having some *effect*! – But *who* does it affect? People who a *noble* artist never should affect, – the masses! the immature! the conceited! the sickly! the idiots! the *Wagnerians*! . . .

A MUSIC WITHOUT A FUTURE[16]

Of all the arts that grow up on a particular cultural soil under particular social and political conditions, music is the sort of plant that appears *last*, perhaps because it is the most interior and, consequently, the latest to arrive, – in the autumn and deliquescence of the culture to which it belongs. It was only in the art of the Dutch musicians that the soul of the Christian Middle Ages found its full resonance, – their tonal architecture is the posthumous but genuine and equal sister of the Gothic. It was only in the music of Handel that there sounded the best that the soul of Luther and his like contained, the Jewish-heroic impulse that gave the Reformation the character of greatness – the old Testament made into music, *not* the New. It was only Mozart who gave forth the age of Louis XIV and the art of Racine and Claude Lorraine[17] in *ringing* gold. It was only in the music of Beethoven and Rossini that the eighteenth century sang itself out: the century of enthusiasm, of shattered ideals and of *fleeting* happiness. All true, all original music is swan-song. – Perhaps our latest music too, dominant and thirsting for dominance though it is, only has a limited lifespan ahead of it: for it arose from a culture that is going speedily downhill, a *sunken* culture; it presupposes a certain *catholicity of feeling* together with a joy in all old, indigenous 'nationalisms', monstrous and otherwise. Wagner's appropriation of the old sagas and songs, which learned prejudice had held up as something Germanic *par excellence* – today we can laugh about it –, the reanimation of these Scandinavian monsters with a thirst for ecstatic sensuality and asceticism – this entire

[15] Character in *Don Giovanni*.
[16] Adapted from *HAH*, Vol. ii, 'Assorted Opinions and Maxims', 171.
[17] Claude Lorraine; adoptive name of Claude Gellée (1600–82): French landscape painter.

Wagnerian giving and taking in regard to material, shapes, passions, and nerves also clearly expresses the *spirit of his music*, given that it, like all music, does not know how to speak unambiguously of itself: because music is a *woman* . . . One must not allow oneself to be misled as to this state of affairs by the fact that we are at the moment living in a reaction *within* a reaction. The age of national wars, of ultramontane martyrdom,[18] this whole *entr'acte* character that colours the state of affairs in Europe these days, might in fact raise a certain art, like that of Wagner, to a sudden glory without guaranteeing it a *future*. The Germans themselves have no future . . .

WE ANTIPODES[19]

Perhaps it may be recalled, at least among my friends, that initially I approached the modern world with a few crude errors and over-estimations and, in any case, with *hope*. I understood – on the basis of who knows what personal experiences? – the philosophical pessimism of the nineteenth century as a symptom of a higher force of thought, of a more victorious *fullness* of life than had been expressed in the philosophies of Hume, Kant, and Hegel, – this *tragic* insight struck me as the most beautiful luxury of our culture, its most precious, noblest, and most dangerous type of squandering; but still, in view of its over-richness, as its *permitted* luxury. Similarly, I explained Wagner's music to myself as the expression of a Dionysian might of the soul: I believed that I heard in it the earthquake through which some pent-up primordial force is finally released – indifferent about whether it sets everything else which is called culture atremble. You see what I misjudged, you also see what I *gave* to Wagner and Schopenhauer – myself . . . Every art, every philosophy can be considered a cure and aid in the service of growing or declining life: it always presupposes suffering and sufferers. But there are two types of sufferers: first, those who suffer from a *superabundance* of life – they want a Dionysian art as well as a tragic outlook and insight into life – then, those who suffer from an *impoverishment* of life and demand quiet, stillness, calm seas *or else* intoxication, paroxysm, stupor from art

---

[18] Ultramontane martyrdom: ultramontanism was a term used to refer to the Catholic movements that upheld papal supremacy in France, Germany, and the Netherlands in the seventeenth and eighteenth centuries.

[19] Adapted from *GS* 370.

and philosophy. Revenge against life itself – the most voluptuous type of intoxication for people who are impoverished in this way! . . . Wagner as well as Schopenhauer responds to the dual need of the latter type – they negate life, they slander it, and this makes them my antipodes. – He who is richest in fullness of life, the Dionysian god and man, can allow himself not only the sight of what is terrible and questionable but also the terrible deed and every luxury of destruction, decomposition, negation; in his case, what is evil, nonsensical, and ugly seems allowable, as it seems allowable in nature, because of an overflow in procreating, fertilizing forces capable of turning any desert into bountiful farmland. Conversely, he who suffers most and is poorest in life would need mainly mildness, peacefulness, goodness in thought and in deed – what is called humaneness these days – and, if possible, also a god who truly would be a god for the sick, a *saviour*; as well as logic, the conceptual comprehensibility of existence even for idiots – the typical 'free spirits', like the 'idealists and 'beautiful souls', are all decadents – in short, a certain warm, fear-repelling narrowness and confinement to optimistic horizons which allows for a *dumbing down* . . . Thus I gradually came to understand Epicurus, the antithesis of a Dionysian Greek, and equally the 'Christian', who really is simply a kind of Epicurean who follows the principle of hedonism *as far as possible* with his 'faith makes *blessed'* – over and above every principle of intellectual integrity . . . If I have any advantage over other psychologists, it is that my vision is keener for that most difficult and insidious form of *backward inference* with which the most mistakes are made – the inference from the work to the maker, from the deed to the doer, from the ideal to the one who *needs it*, from every manner of thinking and valuing to the commanding *need* behind it. – Nowadays I avail myself of this primary distinction concerning artists of every type: is it *hatred* of life or *superabundance* of life that has become creative here? In Goethe, for instance, superabundance has become creative, in Flaubert it is hatred: Flaubert, a new edition of Pascal, but as an artist, based on the instinctive judgment: 'Flaubert est toujours *haïssable*, l'homme n'est rien, *l'œuvre est tout*'[20] . . . He tortured himself when he wrote, just as Pascal tortured himself when he thought – they both felt unegoistic . . . 'Selflessness' – that principle of decadence, the will to the end in art as in morality. –

[20] 'Flaubert is always hateful, man is nothing, the work is everything.'

WHERE WAGNER BELONGS[21]

France is still the seat of the most spiritual and sophisticated culture in Europe today, and the *pre-eminent* school of taste: but you have to know how to find this 'France of taste'. The *Norddeutsche Zeitung*,[22] for instance, or people whose mouthpiece it is, see the French as 'barbarians', – personally, I look for the 'dark continent', the place where 'the slaves' should be freed, in the vicinity of north Germans . . . People belonging to the *first* France keep themselves well hidden: there might be only a small number of people in which it loves and lives, people who might not have the sturdiest legs to stand on, some of them fatalists, sombre and ill, some of them pampered and over the top, people who have the *ambition* to be artificial, – but they possess everything left in the world of superiority and gentleness. Perhaps Schopenhauer is more at home and settled now in this France of the spirit (which is also a France of pessimism) than he ever was in Germany; his major works have been translated twice already, the second translation is so good that I now prefer to read Schopenhauer in French (– he was an accident among Germans, as I am – the Germans cannot get a grip on us, they cannot get a grip on anything at all because they only have paws to grip with). Not to mention Heinrich Heine, – *l'adorable Heine*, they say in Paris –, who has been in the flesh and blood of the subtler and more promising lyric poets of Paris for a while now. What do German oxen know of the *délicatesses* of a nature like this! – Finally, as far as Wagner goes, it is so obvious, you could touch with your hand, although perhaps not with your fist, that Paris is the true soil for Wagner: the more French music learns to develop according to the needs of the *âme moderne*,[23] the more 'Wagnerianized' it becomes, – as if it were not already Wagnerized enough. – We should not let Wagner himself lead us astray on this point – it was really bad of Wagner in 1871 to deride Paris in his agony . . . In Germany, Wagner is nonetheless just a misunderstanding: who would be less able to understand anything about Wagner than, for instance, the young emperor? – Nonetheless, the fact remains certain for anyone familiar with movements in European culture that French romanticism and Richard Wagner belong most closely and intimately together. They were all dominated by literature, up to their eyes and ears – the first European artists with an education in *world*

---

[21] Adapted from *BGE* 254, 256.   [22] A northern German newspaper.   [23] Modern soul.

literature – for the most part, they were themselves writers, poets, go-betweens and mixers of the arts and the senses, all of them fanatics of *expression*, great discoverers in the realm of the sublime as well as the repugnant and repulsive, even greater discoverers in effects, in showmanship, in the art of window displays, all of them talents far above their genius –, *virtuosos* through and through, with uncanny access to everything tempting, seductive, compelling, and subversive, born enemies of logic and straight lines, longing for the foreign, the exotic, the monstrous, all opiates of the senses and of the understanding. On the whole, an adventurously daring, splendidly violent, high-flying, high-ascending type of artist, who first taught *their* century – and it is the century of the *masses* – the concept 'artist'. But *sick* . . .

WAGNER AS APOSTLE OF CHASTITY

1[24]

– Is this still German?
It's from a German heart, this murky howling?
From German flesh this self-aimed disembowelling?
It's German, then, this type of priestly feel,
This incense-scented sensuous appeal?
This broken, falling, swaggered swaying?
This unassured singsong-saying?
This nun-eyed *Ave*-chiming leavening,
This falsely raptured heaven-overheavening? . . .

– Is this still German?
Just think! You're standing there, the doorway's near . . .
It's Rome! Rome's faith without the text, you hear.

2[25]

There is not necessarily an antithesis between chastity and sensuality; every good marriage, every real affair of the heart, transcends this antithesis. But even in a case where there really is an antithesis, there is fortunately no need for it to be a tragic antithesis. This ought to be true, at least for

---

[24] Adapted from *BGE* 256.   [25] Adapted from *GM* III. 2.

all healthy, cheerful mortals who are far from seeing their precarious balancing act between 'animal and angel' as necessarily one of the arguments against existence, – the best and the brightest amongst them, like Goethe, like Hafiz,[26] actually found in it one *more* of life's charms . . . Such 'contradictions' are what make existence so seductive . . . On the other hand, it is only too clear that if Circe's unfortunate animals are made to praise chastity, they will only see in it and *praise* the opposite of themselves – and oh! we can only imagine the tragic grunting and excitement! – that embarrassing and superfluous antithesis which Richard Wagner undeniably wanted to set to music and stage at the end of his life. *But why?* it is fair to inquire.

3[27]

While we are here, we cannot avoid asking what concern that manly (oh-so-unmanly) 'country bumpkin', that poor devil and child of nature, Parsifal,[28] was to Wagner, who ended up using such suspect means to turn him into a Catholic – and what? Was this Parsifal meant to be taken *seriously?* Because I (like Gottfried Keller) am in no position to dispute that he has been *laughed* at . . . We might wish, – that Wagner's *Parsifal* was meant to be funny, like an epilogue and satyr play with which the tragedian Wagner wanted to take leave of us, of himself, and above all of *tragedy* in a manner fitting and worthy of himself, namely by indulging in an excessive bout of the most extreme and deliberate parody of the tragic itself, of the whole, hideous, earthly seriousness and earthly misery from the past, of the finally defeated, *crudest form* of perversion, of the ascetic ideal. After all, *Parsifal* is operetta material *par excellence* . . . Is Wagner's *Parsifal* his secret, superior laugh at himself, his triumph at attaining the final, supreme freedom of the artist, his artistic transcendence? – Wagner knowing how to *laugh* at himself? . . . As I said, it would be nice to think so: because what would an *intentionally serious Parsifal* be like? Do we really need to see in it 'the spawn of an insane hatred of knowledge, mind, and sensuality' (as someone once argued against me)? A curse on the senses and the mind in a single breath and hatred? An apostasy and return to sickly Christian and obscurantist ideals? And finally an

---

[26] Persian lyric poet of the fourteenth century; especially well known in Germany because of Goethe's great partiality for his poetry.
[27] Adapted from *GM* III. 3.   [28] *Parsifal* was Wagner's final music drama.

actual self-denial, self-annulment on the part of an artist who had hitherto wanted the opposite with all the force of his will, namely for his art to be the *highest intellectualization and sensualization*? And not just his art: his life too. Recall how enthusiastically Wagner followed in the footsteps of the philosopher Feuerbach in his day: Feuerbach's dictum of 'healthy sensuality'[29] – that sounded like the pronouncement of salvation to the Wagner of the 1830s and 1840s, as to so many Germans (– they called themselves the '*Young* Germans'). Did he finally *learn something different*? Because it at least seems that at the end, he had the will to *teach something different*... Did *hatred of life* gain control over him, as with Flaubert? ... Because *Parsifal* is a work of malice, of vindictiveness, a secret poisoning of the presuppositions of life, a *bad* work. – The preaching of chastity remains an incitement to perversion: I despise anyone who does not regard *Parsifal* as an attempt to assassinate ethics. –

HOW I BROKE AWAY FROM WAGNER

1[30]

In the summer of 1876, right in the middle of the first *Festspiel*, I took leave of Wagner. I cannot stand ambiguities: since coming to Germany, Wagner had acceded step by step to everything that I hate – even to anti-Semitism ... At that time it was indeed high time *to take my leave*: and I immediately received a confirmation of the fact. Richard Wagner, seemingly the all-conquering, actually a decaying, despairing decadent, suddenly sank down helpless and shattered before the Christian cross...[31] Was there no German with eyes in his head, empathy in his conscience, for this dreadful spectacle? Was I the only one who – *suffered* from it? – Enough, this unexpected event illumined for me like a flash of lightning the place I had left - and likewise gave me those subsequent horrors that he feels who he has passed through a terrible peril unawares. As I went on alone, I trembled; not long afterwards I was sick, more than sick, I was *weary*, weary of the unending disappointment with everything we modern men have left to inspire us, of the energy, labour, hope, youth, love

---

[29] Feuerbach's *Principle of the Philosophy of the Future* appeared in 1843. See esp. §§31ff. of that work.
[30] Adapted from *HAH*, Vol. II, 'Assorted Opinions and Maxims', Preface, 3.
[31] 'Richard Wagner ... Christian cross': alludes to Wagner's last work, *Parsifal* (produced at Bayreuth in 1882).

everywhere *squandered*; weary with disgust at the whole idealist pack of lies and softening of conscience that had here once again carried off the victory over one of the bravest; weary, last but not least, with the bitterness of a suspicion – that, after this disappointment, I was condemned to mistrust more profoundly, despise more profoundly, to be more profoundly *alone* than ever before. Because I had had nobody except Richard Wagner . . . I have always been condemned to Germans . . .

2[32]

Henceforth alone and sorely mistrustful of myself, I thus, and not without a sullen wrathfulness, took sides *against* myself and *for* everything painful and difficult precisely for *me*: – thus I again found my way to that courageous pessimism that is the antithesis of all idealistic mendacity, and also, as it seems to me today, the way to *myself*, – to *my* task. That concealed and imperious something for which we for long have no name until it finally proves to be our task – this tyrant in us takes a terrible retribution for every attempt we make to avoid or elude it, for every premature decision, for every association on equal terms with those with whom we do not belong, for every activity, however respectable, if it distracts us from our chief undertaking, – even indeed for every virtue that would like to shield us from the severity of our own most personal responsibility. Illness is the answer every time we begin to doubt our right to *our* task, every time we begin to make things easier for ourselves. Strange and at the same time terrible! It is our *alleviations* for which we have to atone the most! And if we afterwards want to return to health, we have no choice: we have to burden ourselves *more heavily* than we have ever been burdened before . . .

THE PSYCHOLOGIST HAS A WORD

1[33]

The more a psychologist – a born, inevitable psychologist and unriddler of souls – turns to exceptional cases and people, the greater the danger that he will be choked with pity: he *needs* hardness and cheerfulness more

---

[32] Adapted from *HAH*, Vol. II, 'Assorted Opinions and Maxims', Preface, 4.
[33] Adapted from *BGE* 269.

than anyone else. The ruin, the destruction of higher people, of strangely constituted souls, is the rule: it is horrible always to have a rule like this in front of your eyes. The manifold torment of the psychologist who discovered this destruction, who first discovered and then kept rediscovering (in *almost* every case) the whole inner 'hopelessness' of the higher person, the eternal 'too late!' in every sense, throughout the entirety of history, – this torment might become the cause of his own *destruction* one day . . . In almost every psychologist, you find a telling inclination and preference for dealing with normal, well-ordered people. This reveals that the psychologist is in constant need of a cure, of a type of forgetting and escape from the things that make his insight and incisiveness, that make his *craft* weigh heavily on his conscience. It is characteristic of him to be afraid of his memory. He is easily silenced by other people's judgments: he listens with an unmoved face to how they honour, admire, love, and transfigure what he has *seen*, – or he keeps his silence hidden by expressly agreeing with some foreground opinion. Perhaps the paradox of his condition becomes so horrible that the 'educated' develop a profound admiration for the very things he has learned to regard with *profound pity and contempt* . . . And who knows if this is not just what has happened in all great cases so far: people worshipped a god, – and that 'god' was only a poor sacrificial animal . . . *Success* has always been the greatest liar – and the *work*, the *deed*, is a success too. The great statesman, the conqueror, the discoverer – each one is disguised by his creations to the point of being unrecognizable. The work of the artist, of the philosopher, is what invents whoever has created it, whoever was *supposed* to have created it . . . 'Great men', as they are honoured, are minor pieces of bad literature, invented after the fact, – in the world of historical values, counterfeit *rules* . . .

2[34]

– These great authors, for example, this Byron, Musset, Poe, Leopardi, Kleist, Gogol, – I do not dare name greater names, but I mean them – they are, and perhaps have to be, men of the moment, sensual, absurd, and fivefold, thoughtless and sudden in trust and mistrust; with souls that generally hide some sort of crack; often taking revenge in their work for

[34] Adapted from *BGE* 269.

some inner corruption, often flying off in search of forgetfulness for an all too faithful memory, idealists from the vicinity of the *swamp* – what torture these great artists and higher people in general are for the first ones to guess what they really are . . . We are all advocates of the mediocre . . . We can imagine that *these* men will be subject to those eruptions of boundless pity, particularly from females (who are clairvoyant in the world of suffering and whose desires to help and save far exceed their ability actually to do so) – pity that the masses, the *adoring* masses, above all, will overload with nosy and smug interpretations . . . This pitying is continually deceived as to its own strength; females would like to believe that love makes *all things* possible, – this is their true *superstition*. Oh, those who know hearts can guess how impoverished, helpless, presumptuous, and mistaken even the best and deepest love really is – how much more likely it is to *destroy* than to rescue . . .

3[35]

– The spiritual arrogance and disgust of anyone who has suffered deeply (order of rank is almost determined by just *how* deeply people can suffer), the trembling certainty that saturates and colours him entirely, a certainty that his sufferings have given him a *greater knowledge* than the cleverest and wisest can have, that he knows his way around and was once at home in many distant and terrifying worlds that '*you* don't know anything about!' . . . this spiritual, silent arrogance of the sufferer, this pride of knowledge's chosen one, its 'initiate', almost its martyr, needs all kinds of disguises to protect itself from the touch of intrusive and pitying hands, and in general from everyone who is not its equal in pain. Profound suffering makes you noble; it separates. – One of the most refined forms of disguise is Epicureanism, and a certain showy courage of taste that accepts suffering without a second thought and resists everything sad and profound. There are 'cheerful people' who use cheerfulness because it lets them be misunderstood: – they *want* to be misunderstood. There are 'scientific people' who use science because it gives a cheerful appearance, and because being scientific implies that a person is superficial: – they *want* to encourage this false inference . . . There are free, impudent spirits who would like to hide and deny that they are basically shattered,

---

[35] Adapted from *BGE* 270.

incurable hearts – this is the case with Hamlet: and then even stupidity can be the mask for an ill-fated, all too certain certainty. –

EPILOGUE

1[36]

I have often asked myself whether I am not more deeply indebted to the hardest years of my life than to all the rest. What my innermost nature tells me is that everything necessary, seen from above and in the sense of a *great* economy, is also useful in itself, – it should not just be tolerated, it should be *loved* . . . *Amor fati:*[37] that is my innermost nature. – And as far as my long infirmity is concerned, isn't it the case that I am unspeakably more indebted to it than I am to my health? I owe a higher health to it, a health that becomes stronger from everything that does not kill it off! *I owe my philosophy to it as well* . . . Only great pain is the final liberator of the spirit, as the teacher of the *great suspicion* that turns every U into an X,[38] a real, proper X, which is to say the *penultimate* letter before the final one . . . Only great pain, that long, slow pain that takes its time and in which we are burned, as it were, over green wood –, forces us philosophers to descend into our ultimate depths and put aside all trust, everything good-natured, everything that veils, or is mild or average – things in which formerly we may have found our humanity. I doubt that such pain makes us 'better': but I know that it makes us *deeper*. Whether we learn to pit our pride, our scorn, our willpower against it, like the American Indian who, however badly tormented, repays his tormentor with the malice of his tongue; or whether we withdraw before pain into nothingness, into mute, rigid, deaf self-surrender, self-forgetting, self-extinction: one emerges from such dangerous exercises in self-mastery as a different person, with a few more question marks, – above all with the *will* henceforth to question further, more deeply, severely, harshly, evilly, and quietly than anyone on earth had ever questioned before . . . The trust in life is gone: life itself has become a *problem*. – Yet one should not jump to the conclusion that this necessarily makes one gloomy, a barn

---

[36] Adapted from *GS*, Preface, 3.   [37] Love of fate.
[38] 'To make a U out to be an X' is a standard German expression for trying to pretend that a thing is something completely different from what it is.

owl! Even love of life is still possible, – only one loves *differently* . . . It is like the love for a woman who gives us doubts . . .

2^{39}

One thing is strangest of all: after all this, one will have a different taste – a *second* taste. From such abysses, also from the abyss of *severe suspicion*, one returns newborn, having shed one's skin, more ticklish and malicious, with a more delicate taste for joy, with a more tender tongue for all good things, with merrier senses, with a more dangerous second innocence in joy, more childlike, and at the same time a hundred times subtler than one had ever been before. Moral: one pays the price for being the most profound spirit of all millennia, – one gets *rewarded* as well . . . I will provide an example right away.

Oh, how repulsive enjoyment is to us now, that crude, muggy, brown enjoyment as understood by those who enjoy it, our 'educated', our rich, and our rulers! How maliciously we nowadays listen to the great fairground boom-boom with which the 'educated person' and urbanite today allows art, books and music – aided by spirituous beverages – to violate him for 'forms of spiritual enjoyment'! How the theatrical cry of passion now hurts our ears; that whole romantic uproar and tumult of the senses that is loved by the educated mob together with its aspirations towards the sublime, the elevated, the distorted, how foreign it has become to our taste! No, if we convalescents still need art, it is *another kind* of art – a mocking, light, fleeting, divinely untroubled, divinely artificial art that, like a bright flame, blazes into an unclouded sky! Above all: an art for artists, *only for artists!* In addition we will know better afterwards what is first and foremost needed *for that*: cheerfulness – *any* cheerfulness, my friends! . . . There are some things we now know too well, we knowing ones: oh, how we nowadays learn as artists to forget well, to be good at *not* knowing! . . . And as for our future: one will hardly find us again on the paths of those Egyptian youths who make temples unsafe at night, embrace statues, and want by all means to unveil, uncover, and put into a bright light whatever is kept concealed for good reasons.[40] No, we have

---

[39] Adapted from *GS*, Preface, 4.
[40] Plutarch reports that in a temple in the Egyptian city of Sais, there was a veiled statue of the goddess Isis with the inscription: 'I am everything that is, that was, and that will be, and no mortal has <ever> raised my veil.' In his *Critique of Judgment* (1790, §49) Kant says that this inscription

grown sick of this bad taste, this will to truth, to 'truth at any price', this youthful madness in the love of truth: we are too experienced, too serious, too jovial, too burned, too *deep* for that . . . We no longer believe that truth remains truth when one pulls off the *veil*; – we have lived too much to believe this . . . Today we consider it a matter of decency not to wish to see everything naked, to be present everywhere, to understand and 'know' everything. Tout *comprendre – c'est tout mépriser*[41] . . . 'Is it true that God is everywhere?', a little girl asked her mother: 'I think that's indecent!' – a hint for philosophers! . . . One should have more respect for the *shame* with which nature has hidden behind riddles and iridescent uncertainties Perhaps truth is a woman who has grounds *for not letting her grounds be seen?* . . . Perhaps her name is – to speak Greek – *Baubo?*[42] . . . Oh, those Greeks! They knew how to *live*: what is needed for that is to stop bravely at the surface, the fold, the skin; to worship appearance, to believe in shapes, tones, words, in the whole *Olympus of appearance*! Those Greeks were superficial – *out of profundity* . . . And isn't this precisely what we are coming back to, we daredevils of the spirit who have climbed the highest and most dangerous peak of current thought and looked around from up there, looked *down* from up there? Are we not just in this respect – Greeks? Worshippers of shapes, tones, words? And therefore – *artists?* . . .

is 'perhaps the most sublime thing ever said'. In a short historical essay 'Die Sendung Moses' the German poet and dramatist Friedrich Schiller (1759–1805) speculates on a possible influence of this cult on Moses and thus on the origin of monotheism. Schiller also wrote a poem entitled 'Das Verschleierte Bild zu Sais' which told of an Egyptian youth who was especially eager to know The Truth. One night he broke into the temple and violated the prohibition by lifting the veil, but when found the next morning, he could not report what he had seen and died an 'early death'. The romantic poet Novalis (1772–1801) gives two further variants (1798–9). In the first the youth left the young woman he loved, Rosenblütchen, to go in search of wisdom, truth, etc. When he arrived at the temple he fell asleep and dreamed that when he lifted the veil of the statue 'Rosenblütchen sank into his arms.' In the second variant, when he lifted the veil, he saw himself.

[41] To understand *all* is to despise all.

[42] When the goddess Demeter was grieving over the abduction of her daughter by Hades, god of the underworld, the witch Baubo made her laugh again for the first time by lifting her skirts and exposing herself.

Glossary of names

Adonis, Greek mythological figure
Alexander the Great (356–323 BC), king of Macedonia
Alfieri, Vittorio, Count (1749–1803), Italian dramatist
Amphitryon, Greek mythological figure
Aphrodite, Greek mythological figure
Ariadne, Greek mythological figure
Aristotle (384–322 BC), Greek philosopher
Asclepius, Greek god of medicine
Augustine of Hippo (354–430), Church Father

Baader, Franz Xaver von (1765–1841), German philosopher
Bach, Johann Sebastian (1685–1750), German composer
Bacon, Francis (1561–1626), English philosopher
Balzac, Honoré de (1799–1850), French novelist
Baudelaire, Charles (1821–67), French poet
Bauer, Bruno (1809–82), German theologian
Beethoven, Ludwig van (1770–1827), German composer
Berlioz, Hector (1803–69), French composer
Bernini, Gianlorenzo (1598–1680), Italian sculptor
Bismarck, Otto von (1815–98), German statesman
Bizet, Georges (1838–75), French composer
Boccaccio, Giovanni (1313–75), Italian novelist
Borgia, Cesare (1476–1507), Florentine nobleman
Bourget, Paul (1852–1935), French novelist and writer
Brahms, Johannes (1833–97), German composer
Brandes, Georg (1842–1927), Danish art critic and scholar

Brendel, Karl Franz (1811–68), German editor and writer
Brochard, Victor (1848–1907), French philosopher
Buckle, Henry Thomas (1821–62), English historian
Bülow, Hans von (1830–94), German pianist and conductor
Burckhardt, Jakob (1818–97), German historian
Byron, George Gordon, Lord (1788–1824), English poet

Caesar, Gaius Julius (100–44 BC), Roman statesman and general
Cagliostro, Alessandro di (1743–95), Italian charlatan
Carlyle, Thomas (1795–1881), Scottish philosopher and
    historian
Catilina, Lucius Sergius (c. 108–62 BC), Roman nobleman and
    conspirator
Chopin, Frédéric (1810–49), Polish composer
Cicero, Marcus Tullius (106–43 BC), Roman orator, statesman and
    philosopher
Circe, Greek mythological figure
Comte, Auguste (1798–1857), French philosopher
Confucius (c. 551–479 BC), Chinese sage
Constant, Benjamin (1767–1830), French novelist
Cornaro, Luigi (1475–1566), Italian writer
Corneille, Pierre (1606–84), French dramatist
Crispi, Francesco (1818–1901), Italian prime minister 1887–91 and
    1893–6

Dante Alighieri (1265–1321), Italian poet
Darwin, Charles (1809–82), English biologist
Delacroix, Ferdinand (1798–1863), French painter
Descartes, René (1596–1650), French philosopher
Dionysus, Greek god
Dostoevsky, Fyodor (1821–81), Russian novelist
Dühring, Karl Eugen (1833–1921), German philosopher

Eliot, George (Evans, Mary Ann) (1819–90), English novelist
Emerson, Ralph Waldo (1803–82), American philosopher
Epicurus (341–270 BC), Greek philosopher
Ewald, Heinrich (1803–75), German theologian

Feuerbach, Ludwig (1804–72), German philosopher
Fichte, Johann Gottlieb (1762–1814), German philosopher
Flaubert, Gustave (1821–80), French novelist
Fontenelle, Bernard le Bovier de (1657–1757), French writer
France, Anatole (Thibault, Jacques Anatole) (1844–1924), French writer
Francis of Assisi (c. 1181–1226), Christian saint

Goethe, Johann Wolfgang von (1749–1832), German poet, novelist, and
    statesman
Gogol, Nikolai Vasilevich (1809–52), Russian novelist
Goldmark, Karl (1830–1915) Hungarian-Austrian composer
Goncourt, Edmond de (1822–96), French novelist and writer
Goncourt, Jules de (1830–70), French novelist and writer
Gyp (Mirabeau, Sybille Gabrielle de) (1850–1932), French writer

Hafiz (fourteenth century), Persian lyric poet
Handel, George Frideric (1685–1759), German composer
Hartmann, Eduard von (1842–1906), German philosopher
Hegel, Georg Wilhelm Friedrich (1770–1831), German philosopher
Heine, Heinrich (1797–1856), German poet
Heraclitus (c. 540–475 BC), Presocratic philosopher
Herder, Johann Gottfried von (1744–1803), German poet and writer
Hillebrand, Karl (1829–84), German scholar
Horace (Quintus Horatius Flaccus) (65–8 BC), Roman poet
Hugo, Victor (1802–85), French novelist
Hume, David (1711–76), Scottish philosopher

Ibsen, Henrik (1828–1906), Norwegian dramatist

Kant, Immanuel (1724–1804), German philosopher
Keller, Gottfried (1819–90), Swiss-German poet and novelist
Kleist, Heinrich von (1777–1811), German dramatist and novelist
Klopstock, Friedrich Gottlieb (1724–1803), German poet

La Rochefoucauld, François (1613–80), French writer
Lao-tse (c. 604–531 BC), Chinese sage, founder of Taoism
Leibniz, Gottfried Wilhelm (1646–1716), German philosopher

Lemaître, François Elie Jules (1853–1914), French critic and dramatist
Leopardi, Giacomo (1789–1837), Italian poet
Liszt, Franz (1811–86), Hungarian composer
Lobeck, Christian August (1781–1860), German philologist
Lorraine, Claude (1600–82), French painter
Loti, Pierre (Viaud, Loius Marie Julien) (1850–1923), French novelist
Lucretius (Titus Lucretius Carus) (c. 99–55 BC), Roman poet and
  philosopher
Luther, Martin (1483–1546), German theologian and leader of
  Protestant Reformation

Machiavelli, Niccolò (1469–1527), Italian politician and theorist
Malthus, Thomas (1766–1834), English economist
Maupassant, Guy de (1850–93), French poet and novelist
Meilhac, Henri (1831–97), French dramatist
Menippus the Cynic (third century BC), Greek philosopher
Mérimée, Prosper (1803–70), French dramatist and writer
Michelet, Jules (1798–1874), French historian
Mill, John Stuart (1806–73), English philosopher
Mithras, Indo-Iranian sun-god
Mohammed (570–633), prophet of Islam
Molière (Poquelin, Jean-Baptiste) (1622–73), French dramatist
Moloch, deity of idolatrous Israelites
Montaigne, Michel de (1531–92), French essayist and philosopher
Mozart, Wolfgang Amadeus (1756–91), Austrian-German composer
Musset, Alfred de (1810–57), French writer

Napoleon Bonaparte (1769–1821), French emperor
Niebuhr, Barthold Georg (1776–1831), German statesman and historian
Nohl, Karl Friedrich Ludwig (1831–85), German musician and writer

Offenbach, Jacques (1819–90), French composer
Osiris, Egyptian god

Palestrina, Giovanni Pierluigi da (c. 1525–94), Italian composer
Parmenides (fifth century BC), Presocratic philosopher
Pascal, Blaise (1623–62), French philosopher
Paul, Saint (3–65), early Church Father

Petronius (d. 66), Roman writer
Pindar (522–443 BC), Greek poet
Plato (c. 427–347 BC), Greek philosopher
Poe, Edgar Allen (1809–49), American poet and short-story writer
Pohl, Richard (1826–96), German editor

Racine, Jean (1639–99), French dramatist
Ranke, Leopold von (1795–1886), German historian
Raphael (Raffaello Santi or Sanzio) (1483–1520), Italian painter
Rée, Paul (1849–1901), German philosopher
Renan, Ernest (1823–92), French historian
Riemann, Karl Wilhelm (1849–1919), German music theorist
Robespierre, Maximilien (1758–94), French revolutionary
Rossini, Gioacchino (1792–1868), Italian composer
Rousseau, Jean-Jacques (1712–78), French philosopher and novelist

Saint-Simon, Henri de (1760–1825), French religious and social thinker
Sainte-Beuve, Charles-Augustin de (1804–69), French critic and
    historian
Sallust (Gaius Sallustius Crispus) (86–34 BC), Roman historian
Salomé, Lou von (1861–1937), Russian writer
Sand, George (Dupin, Amandine, Baronne Dudevant) (1804–76),
    French novelist
Savonarola, Girolamo (1452–98), Italian religious reformer
Scheffel, Josef Viktor (1826–86), German poet
Schelling, Friedrich Wilhelm Joseph (1775–1854), German philosopher
Schenkendorf, Max von (1783–1817), German poet
Schiller, Friedrich (1759–1805), German dramatist, poet, and historian
Schleiermacher, Friedrich (1768–1834), German philosopher and
    theologian
Schopenhauer, Arthur (1788–1860), German philosopher
Schumann, Robert (1810–56), German composer
Schütz, Heinrich (1585–1672), German composer
Seneca, Lucius Annaeus (c. 4 BC–AD 65), Roman writer
Shakespeare, William (1564–1616), English poet and dramatist
Socrates (469–399 BC), Greek philosopher
Spencer, Herbert (1820–1903), English philosopher
Spinoza, Baruch (1632–77), Dutch philosopher

Spitteler, Carl (1845–1924), German writer
Stein, Heinrich von (1857–1887), German philosopher and poet
Stendhal (Beyle, Henri) (1783–1842), French novelist
Strauss, David (1808–74), German theologian and writer

Taine, Hippolyte (1828–93), French historian and art historian
Talma, François Joseph (1763–1826), French actor
Thucydides (c. 460–400 BC), Athenian historian
Tolstoy, Leo, Count (1828–1910), Russian novelist
Treitschke, Heinrich von (1834–96), German historian

Vega, Lope de (1562–1635), Spanish dramatist and poet
Vischer, Friedrich Theodor (1807–87), German philosopher and novelist
Voltaire (Arouet, François-Marie) (1694–1778), French novelist and
    philosopher

Wagner, Cosima (1837–1930), daughter of Franz Liszt and wife of
    Richard Wagner
Wagner, Richard (1813–83), German composer
Widmann, Josef Viktor (1842–1911), German poet and writer
Winckelmann, Johann Joachim (1717–68), German archaeologist

Zola, Emile (1840–1902), French novelist

Index

Index

Index

Index

Index

Index

CAMBRIDGE TEXTS IN THE HISTORY OF PHILOSOPHY

Titles published in the series thus far

Aquinas *Disputed Questions on the Virtues* (edited by E. M. Atkins and Thomas Williams)
Aristotle *Nicomachean Ethics* (edited by Roger Crisp)
Arnauld and Nicole *Logic or the Art of Thinking* (edited by Jill Vance Buroker)
Augustine *On the Trinity* (edited by Gareth Matthews)
Bacon *The New Organon* (edited by Lisa Jardine and Michael Silverthorne)
Boyle *A Free Enquiry into the Vulgarly Received Notion of Nature* (edited by Edward B. Davis and Michael Hunter)
Bruno *Cause, Principle and Unity* and *Essays on Magic* (edited by Richard Blackwell and Robert de Lucca with an introduction by Alfonso Ingegno)
Cavendish *Observations upon Experimental Philosophy* (edited by Eileen O'Neill)
Cicero *On Moral Ends* (edited by Julia Annas, translated by Raphael Woolf)
Clarke *A Demonstration of the Being and Attributes of God and Other Writings* (edited by Ezio Vailati)
Classic and Romantic German Aesthetics (edited by J. M. Bernstein)
Condillac *Essay on the Origin of Human Knowledge* (edited by Hans Aarsleff)
Conway *The Principles of the Most Ancient and Modern Philosophy* (edited by Allison P. Coudert and Taylor Corse)
Cudworth *A Treatise Concerning Eternal and Immutable Morality* with *A Treatise of Freewill* (edited by Sarah Hutton)
Descartes *Meditations on First Philosophy*, with selections from the *Objections and Replies* (edited by John Cottingham)
Descartes *The World and Other Writings* (edited by Stephen Gaukroger)
Fichte *Foundations of Natural Right* (edited by Frederick Neuhouser, translated by Michael Baur)
Herder *Philosophical Writings* (edited by Michael Forster)
Hobbes and Bramhall on Liberty and Necessity (edited by Vere Chappell)
Humboldt *On Language* (edited by Michael Losonsky, translated by Peter Heath)
Kant *Critique of Practical Reason* (edited by Mary Gregor with an introduction by Andrews Reath)
Kant *Groundwork of the Metaphysics of Morals* (edited by Mary Gregor with an introduction by Christine M. Korsgaard)
Kant *The Metaphysics of Morals* (edited by Mary Gregor with an introduction by Roger Sullivan)
Kant *Prolegomena to any Future Metaphysics* (edited by Gary Hatfield)
Kant *Religion within the Boundaries of Mere Reason and Other Writings* (edited by Allen Wood and George di Giovanni with an introduction by Robert Merrihew Adams)
La Mettrie *Machine Man and Other Writings* (edited by Ann Thomson)
Leibniz *New Essays on Human Understanding* (edited by Peter Remnant and Jonathan Bennett)
Lessing *Philosophical and Theological Writings* (edited by H. B. Nisbet)

Malebranche *Dialogues on Metaphysics and on Religion* (edited by Nicholas Jolley and David Scott)
Malebranche *The Search after Truth* (edited by Thomas M. Lennon and Paul J. Olscamp)
Medieval Islamic Philosophy (edited by Muhammad Ali Khalidi)
Melanchthon *Orations on Philosophy and Education* (edited by Sachiko Kusukawa, translated by Christine Salazar)
Mendelssohn *Philosophical Writings* (edited by Daniel O. Dahlstrom)
Newton *Philosophical Writings* (edited by Andrew Janiak)
Nietzsche *The Anti-Christ, Ecce Homo, Twilight of the Idols, and Other Writings* (edited by Aaron Ridley and Judith Norman)
Nietzsche *Beyond Good and Evil* (edited by Rolf-Peter Horstmann and Judith Norman)
Nietzsche *The Birth of Tragedy and Other Writings* (edited by Raymond Geuss and Ronald Speirs)
Nietzsche *Daybreak* (edited by Maudemarie Clark and Brian Leiter, translated by R. J. Hollingdale)
Nietzsche *The Gay Science* (edited by Bernard Williams, translated by Josefine Nauckhoff)
Nietzsche *Human, All Too Human* (translated by R. J. Hollingdale with an introduction by Richard Schacht)
Nietzsche *Untimely Meditations* (edited by Daniel Breazeale, translated by R. J. Hollingdale)
Nietzsche *Writings from the Late Notebooks* (edited by Rüdiger Bittner, translated by Kate Sturge)
Novalis *Fichte Studies* (edited by Jane Kneller)
Schleiermacher *Hermeneutics and Criticism* (edited by Andrew Bowie)
Schleiermacher *Lectures on Philosophical Ethics* (edited by Robert Louden, translated by Louise Adey Huish)
Schleiermacher *On Religion: Speeches to its Cultured Despisers* (edited by Richard Crouter)
Schopenhauer *Prize Essay on the Freedom of the Will* (edited by Günter Zöller)
Sextus Empiricus *Against the Logicians* (edited by Richard Bett)
Sextus Empiricus *Outlines of Scepticism* (edited by Julia Annas and Jonathan Barnes)
Shaftesbury *Characteristics of Men, Manners, Opinions, Times* (edited by Lawrence Klein)
Adam Smith *The Theory of Moral Sentiments* (edited by Knud Haakonssen)
Voltaire *Treatise on Tolerance and Other Writings* (edited by Simon Harvey)